Physical Education and Sport Studies

ooks are to ... ned on or before
w

Advanced Level Student Revision Guide
2nd Edition

Dr. Dennis Roscoe Editor

Former Head of School of Maths and Sciences, Knowsley Community College.
Former Biomechanics consultant, Assistant Examiner, Team Leader and Question Setter with AEB A Level Physical Education.
National Event Coach then National Potential Coach with UK Athletics.
Author, 'Physical Education and the Study of Sport', A Level PE Text, and many others.
Publisher and Editor with Jan Roscoe Publications.

Jan Roscoe B.Ed. (Hons), M.Sc.

Former Lecturer in Physical Education at Leicester and Trent Polytechnics.
Former Teacher of A level Physical Education and Human Biology at Widnes Sixth Form College.
Former Anatomy and Physiology consultant and Question Setter with AEB A Level Physical Education.
Author, 'Physical Education and the Study of Sport', A Level PE Text, and many others.
Publisher and Anatomy and Physiology Consultant with Jan Roscoe Publications.

John Honeybourne B.Ed, Adv.Dip.Ed., M.A.(Ed).

Head of Sixth Form and Senior Teacher at Baverstock School in Birmingham.
Formerly Director of Physical Education at City of Stoke on Trent Sixth Form College.
Chair of Examiners (A Level and A/S level PE) for EDEXCEL and Question Setter for OCR.
Formerly Chief Examiner and Reviser for AEB 'A' level Physical Education and Principal Examiner for OCR.
Joint Author of 'Advanced PE and Sport 2nd Ed. (A Level PE text); Advanced PE and Sport (A/S level PE text); PE for You (GCSE PE text); Advanced PE and Sport Resource Pack. Editor of CD ROMS in Sports Psychology and Skill Acquisition. He is also currently an HMI Additional Inspector for post-16 Education.

Dr. Bob Davis

Former Principal Lecturer in Physical Education, Madeley College of Higher Education
Former Lecturer in Physical Education, Worcester College of Higher Education;
Former Chief Examiner, Question Setter for Contemporary Issues, History of Sport and Comparative Studies in PE, Reviser and Practical Moderator with AEB A Level Physical Education;
Principal Examiner for OCR A Level Physical Education, OCR Revisor and Senior Moderator;
Author, 'Physical Education and the Study of Sport', A Level PE Text, Teachers' Guides, and many others.

Dr Frank Galligan

Former Lecturer in Physical Education Worcester College of Higher Education.
Former member of MEG Regional GCSE Physical Education Subject Group, and Examiner with AEB A Level Physical Education,.
Research associate for De Montfort University at the International Centre for Sports History and Culture.
Former examiner for OCR A Level Physical Education, question reviser for Edexcel A2 / AS level Physical Education.
Executive member of British Society of Sports History, Editor of Philathletic Newsletter.
Author, 'Advanced PE for Edexcel', and Teachers' Guides.

Jan Roscoe Publications

First published as 1 901 424 20 0 in 1998 by Jan Roscoe Publications
Holyrood 23 Stockswell Road
Widnes
Cheshire
WA8 4PJ
United Kingdom

0151 420 4446
0151 495 2622 fax
jroscoe@rapid.co.uk e-mail

A Catalogue record for this book is available from the British Library

Reprint January 1999
Reprint January 2000
Second edition January 2001

ISBN   1 901424 32 4

Cover photograph by Jan Roscoe

Published via QuarkXpress 4.0
and CorelDraw 4.0

Printed and bound by Poplar Services
Poplar House
Jackson Street
St Helens
WA9 3AP

01744 23363
01744 451242 fax

INTRODUCTION

Examination courses in Physical Education and Sport Studies have now become established within the post-16 curriculum and are a very popular and successful part of school, college or higher education.

This new edition has been written to address the change in content and style of AS / A2 Physical Education and Sport Studies programmes which commenced in September 2000.

Physical Education and Sport Studies courses are multidisciplinary in nature, covering anatomy and physiology, exercise physiology, biomechanics, skill acquisition, sports psychology, contemporary studies, comparative studies, global issues and historical studies. These subject areas have generated a substantial quantity of specialist literature each with its own specific language. At times you may be overwhelmed by the amount of material covered in a one or two year examination course. 'Physical Education and Sport Studies Advanced Level Student Revision Guide' addresses the problem of dealing with copious notes by providing ten short chapters each containing summary pages that describe and illustrate key concepts, followed by exam-style questions and comprehensive answers for the nine subject areas listed above. The tenth chapter looks at the latest style of question which links together different parts or modules within a course. Different styles of 'synoptic' question are favoured by different exam syllabuses, so we give examples of each style of question (and answer) in this last chapter of the book.

Modern terminology, nomenclature and units have been used wherever possible. At the end of the book there is a comprehensive index available for easy reference.

Although this revision book is directly aimed at students preparing for Advanced Level (AS or A2) Physical Education and Sport Studies, it should also provide an invaluable resource for BTEC / GNVQ Sport Studies / Science courses.

HOW TO USE THIS REVISION GUIDE

The ideal use of this Revision Guide would be to purchase it at the start of the course and relate each of the summary pages to the specific areas of the syllabus as an aide memoire. The inclusion of specific questions and full answers, which relate to the summary pages, provide a means of self-testing. Don't be tempted to find out the answers before attempting a question.

In reality, whole examination questions contain a much broader content than those given in this guide. Examiners will attempt to examine more than one area of the syllabus within the context of one full question and therefore it is important that you revise all aspects of your syllabus.

The main use of the Revision Guide should be during the final revision period leading up to your examinations, as it should help you to understand and apply concepts i.e. link summary content with examination question.

The aim of this Student Guide is to provide an aid that enhances syllabus analysis, and to raise your level of success in examinations. In using this book, you must be aware of your syllabus requirements and therefore carefully select appropriate topics which are specific to your syllabus needs.

THE QUALITY OF AUTHORS

In order to create for the student a product of high quality, we have brought together an expert team of writers, who have considerable experience in teaching 'A' Level Physical Education, who have written past and current examination syllabuses, who have set and marked examination questions within this subject area and taught at revision workshops throughout the UK. Much of the material within this book has been thoroughly student tested.

We hope that this Revision Guide will prove useful to staff and students. Jan Roscoe Publications will welcome any comments you would wish to make about the book's utility or layout. Thank you for using our work.

Dennis Roscoe
Jan Roscoe.

ACKNOWLEDGMENTS

We would like to thank the authors for their cooperation and adherence to our demanding deadlines, Poplar Services for their patience in allowing us to experiment with new software and linking our work to their computers, and the JRP staff, Linda Underwood, Jane Carter, Ian Lowthian and Susan Street for working hard in the background while I put this book together.

Dennis Roscoe
Editor.

Contents

Chapter 1 - Applied Anatomy and Physiology
Jan Roscoe

Chapter 2 - Exercise Physiology
Jan Roscoe

THE SKELETON

ANATOMY and PHYSIOLOGY

APPENDICULAR   &   AXIAL
- Shoulder girdle   - Skull
- Hip girdle   - Vertebral column
- Leg and arm bones   - Ribs & sternum

- Names of major bones.

SKELETAL FUNCTIONS
- Lever system.
- Surface area for attachment of muscle
  tendons and ligaments.
- Shape.
- Support.
- Red / white blood cell manufacture.
- Stores fats and minerals.

TYPES OF BONES & PRINCIPAL FUNCTIONS
- Long :   e.g. femur : lever.
- Short :   e.g. carpals : strength and lightness.
- Flat :   e.g. pelvis : surface area for muscle & tendon
  attachments, cranium : skull protection.
- Irregular :   e.g. vertebrae : protection of spinal cord,
  patella (sesamoid) increases mechanical
  advantage of quadriceps tendon.

BONY FEATURES
- Protrusions   For example, tibial tuberosity / iliac spine.
- Depressions   For example, bicipital groove.
- Function of these features is to increase surface area for
  attachment of ligaments and muscle tendons.

BONE TISSUE - structure and function of :

CARTILAGE
- Hyaline : smooth, solid matrix (forms joints).
- White fibro : tough and slightly flexible (between
  vertebrae).
- Yellow elastic : soft and elastic (ear lobe).

PERIOSTEUM
- The periosteum is an outer protective covering.
- Which provides attachment for muscle tendons and ligaments.
- Deeper layers are responsible for growth in bone width.

Haversian system [101]
basic structure of
compact & spongy bone
←— 0.5 mm —→

LS of long bone [102]
hyaline cartilage
compact bone
periosteum
spongy bone

JOINTS

ARTICULATION
- A place where two or more bones meet to form a joint.
JOINT TYPES
- FIBROUS or immovable : for example, between bones of the cranium.
- CARTILAGINOUS or slightly moveable : for example, vertebral discs.
- SYNOVIAL or freely moveable :

F/E	= Flexion/Extension
Ab/Ad	= Abduction/Adduction
R	= Rotation
C	= Circumduction

JOINT TYPE	MOVEMENT RANGE	eg. BODY PLACE : ARTICULATING BONES
Ball & socket	3 axes F/E Ab/Ad R C	Hip : femur, acetabulum of pelvis. Shoulder : scapula, humerus.
Hinge	1 axis F/E	Knee : femur, patella, tibia. Elbow : humerus, radius, ulna.
Pivot	1 axis R	Spine : Atlas : odontoid process of axis (turns head side to side). Elbow : proximal ends of radius and ulna.
Condyloid	2 axes F/E Ab/Ad = C	Knuckles joint of fingers : metacarpals, phalanges. Wrist : radius, carpals.
Saddle	2 axes F/E Ab/Ad = C	Joint at base of thumb : carpal, metacarpal.
Gliding	a little movement in all directions	Centre of chest : clavicle, sternum. Spine : articulating surfaces. Wrist : carpals. Ankle : tarsals.

STRUCTURE & FUNCTION OF A TYPICAL SYNOVIAL JOINT

- Synovial fluid (S) (lubricates joint, maintains joint stability).
- Synovial membrane (M) (secretes synovial fluid).
- Capsular ligament (C) (joins bones of the joint).
- Articular or hyaline cartilage (A) (prevents friction between bones).
- Bursae (prevent friction and wear between a bone and a ligament
  or tendon which glide against each other).
- Pads of fat (cushions joint, acts as shock absorbers).
- Menisci (help bones fit together better to stabilise the joint).

[103]
S
M
C
A

MAJOR ACTIVE MUSCLES INVOLVED IN SPORTS TECHNIQUES

body part / joint	movement pattern	active muscles
SHOULDER GIRDLE	elevation	upper fibres of trapezius, levator scapulae.
	depression	lower fibres of trapezius, pectoralis minor.
	rotation / adduction	serratus anterior, rhomboids.
SHOULDER JOINT	adduction	pectoralis major, anterior deltoid, corocobrachialis, latissimus dorsi.
	abduction	posterior deltoid, supraspinatus.
	flexion	anterior deltoid, pectoralis major, corocobrachialis.
	extension	latissimus dorsi, posterior deltoid, teres major.
	medial rotation	subscapularis, pectoralis major, latissimus dorsi.
	lateral rotation	teres minor, infraspinatus.
UPPER ARM / ELBOW	flexion	biceps brachii, brachialis, brachioradialis.
	extension	triceps brachii, anconeus.
RADIO-ULNA PIVOT	supination	supinator, biceps brachii.
	pronation	pronator teres, pronator quadratus.
WRIST	extension	extensor carpi ulnaris, carpi radialis brevis, extensor digitorum
	flexion	flexor carpi radialis, flexi carpi ulnaris.
	adduction	extensor carpi ulnaris.
	abduction	extensor carpi radialis, longus, brevis.
TRUNK / SPINE	flexion	rectus abdominus.
	extension / hyperextension	erector spinae (sacrospinalis).
	internal flexion	internal obliques, external obliques, quadratus lumborum.
HIP JOINT	flexion	iliopsoas, quadriceps, pectineus, sartorius, tensor fascia latae.
	extension	hamstrings, gluteus maximus.
	adduction	adductor longus / magnus / brevis, pectineus, gracilis.
	abduction	gluteus maximus / medius / minimus, sartorius, tensor fascia latae.
	medial rotation	gluteus minimus, tensor fascia latae.
	lateral rotation	gluteus maximus, psoas major, sartorius.
KNEE JOINT	flexion	hamstrings - biceps femoris, semimembranosus, semitendinosus, sartorius.
	extension	quadriceps - rectus femoris, vastus medialis, vastus intermedius, vastus lateralis.
ANKLE	plantar - flexion	gastrocnemius, soleus, tibialis posterior
	dorsi - flexion	tibialis anterior, peroneus brevis.

RELATIONSHIP of MUSCULAR SYSTEM to SKELETAL SYSTEM
- Names of major muscles in relation to joint action.
- Attachments :
  - Tendons attach muscle to bone to transmit muscle force.
  - Ligaments attach bone to bone.
  - Periosteum provides attachment for muscle tendons and ligaments.

FUNCTION OF MUSCLES
- Antagonistic muscle action :
  - Agonist is the muscle that actually contracts to move the joint.
  - Antagonist is the muscle that relaxes in opposition to the agonist.
  - Fixator holds joint in position which stabilises the origin of the prime mover.
  - Synergist holds body position so that the agonist can operate.

- Movement Analysis, example : curling a bar:
  Agonist = biceps, antagonist = triceps, fixator = deltoid, synergist = trapezius.

POSTURE
- Common Postural defects :
  Kyphosis, Lordosis and Scoliosis.

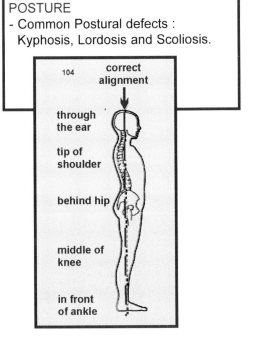

104   correct alignment

through the ear

tip of shoulder

behind hip

middle of knee

in front of ankle

BODY PLANES AND AXES

BODY PLANES & AXES

Plane — an imaginary flat surface running through the body.

Axis of rotation — an imaginary line about which the body rotates or spins, at right angles to the plane.

PLANES :

Frontal — divides body into front and back sections : abduction, adduction, lateral flexion.
— whole body movements include cartwheel.

Sagittal — divides the body into left and right sections : flexion, extension, dorsiflexion plantarflexion.
— whole body movements include somersaults, pole vault take off, sprinting.

Transverse — divides the body into upper and lower sections : medial / lateral rotation, supination, pronation whole body movements - twisting / turning, spinning skater / discus / hammer / ski turns.

As a student you will have to identify the major planes and axes in physical activity.

MUSCLE

FIBRE TYPES

Major differences — speed of contraction
— muscle fibre force
— muscle endurance.
- These are genetically determined.
- Could account for specialisms of individuals.

SLOW TWITCH type 1 (red)
- High in triglycerides, myoglobin, capillaries, mitochondria.
- Sustains low intensity exercise.
FAST TWITCH type 11: FOG type 11a (white)
- Adaptive training response resists fatigue.
- Characteristics are midway between ST and FTG11b.
FAST TWITCH type 11: FTG type 11b (white)
- High in PC, glycogen, myosin ATPase activity.
- Intensity high, duration short, contractile / relaxation time fast.

Responses to Training
- Endurance training results in type 11b being converted to type11a.
- Could explain why long steady work can result in loss of speed.
- High intensity anaerobic training causes increase in size and number of FT fibres (hypertrophy, hyperplasia respectively).
- Lack of training causes atrophy.

Recruitment
- Based on intensity of exercise.

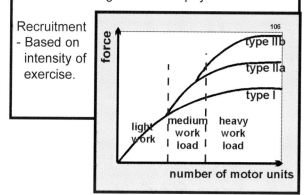

TYPES OF MUSCLE CONTRACTION (mc)

ISOMETRIC mc
- This is the muscular contraction where the tension developed occurs with no change in length.
- Otherwise known as a static contraction or position.
- Improves muscle strength at fixed joint angle.
- Does not develop aerobic fitness.
- Can be done anywhere.
- Examples : rugby scrum, tug of war, chins - holding bent arm position.

ISOKINETIC mc
- This type of muscle contraction acts at a constant speed over the full range of motion, therefore the tension developed by the muscle is over the full range of motion.
- Needs special hydraulic weights machine = expense.
- Develops aerobic and anaerobic fitness.
- Strength is developed over the full range of motion but movement at a constant velocity may not assist strength development at the speed of motor recruitment required for a specific sports activity.

ISOTONIC mc
- Here muscles contract at a speed controlled by performer.
- Motor unit recruitment is at the speed required for the specific sports activity.
- Develops aerobic and anaerobic fitness.
- Most physical activities are isotonic.

Isokinetic and isotonic muscle contraction can be :

CONCENTRIC mc
- This is muscle action involving the shortening of muscle fibres whilst developing tension, as origin and insertion of active muscle move towards each other.
- Example : Chins - use of biceps brachii in upward phase

ECCENTRIC mc
- This is muscle action involving the lengthening of muscle fibres whilst developing tension as origin and insertion move away from each other.
- Example : Chins - use of biceps in downward phase.
- Can result in DOMS (delayed onset muscle soreness), possibly due to structural damage to muscle membranes.

PLYOMETRIC
- Work occurs during for example bounding exercises in which maximum effort is achieved during eccentric mc.

SKELETAL MUSCLE

Fasciculus
- is a bundle containing muscle fibres.

Muscle fibre
- is a muscle cell containing myofibrils.

Long myofibril
- consists of a chain of contractile protein filaments - actin and myosin.

Sarcomere
- is the functional unit of the muscle fibre Voluntary or Neurogenic muscle.

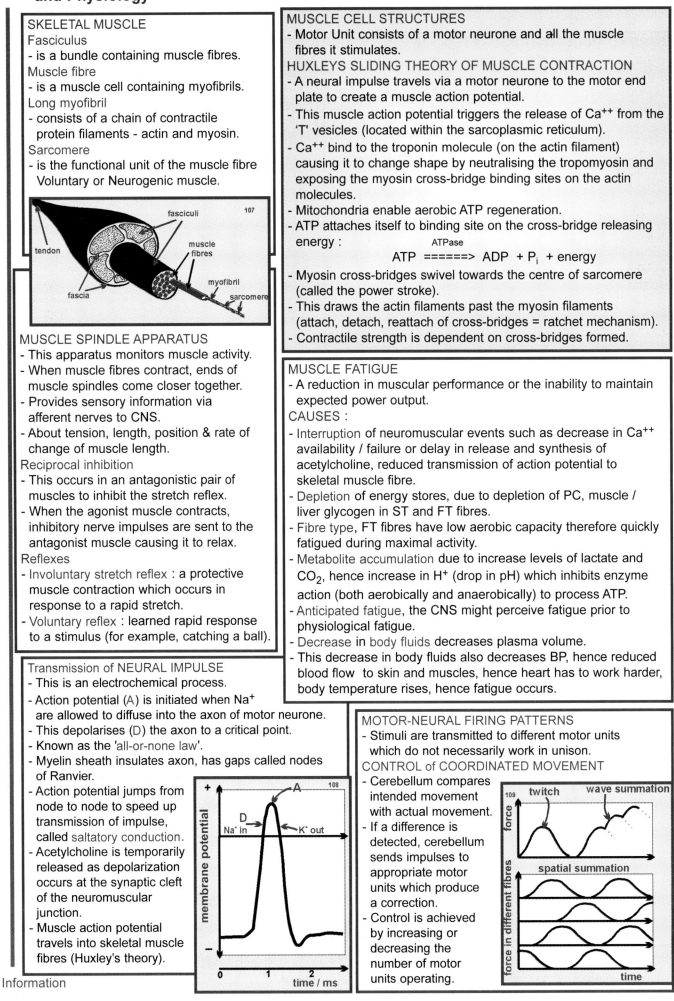

MUSCLE SPINDLE APPARATUS
- This apparatus monitors muscle activity.
- When muscle fibres contract, ends of muscle spindles come closer together.
- Provides sensory information via afferent nerves to CNS.
- About tension, length, position & rate of change of muscle length.

Reciprocal inhibition
- This occurs in an antagonistic pair of muscles to inhibit the stretch reflex.
- When the agonist muscle contracts, inhibitory nerve impulses are sent to the antagonist muscle causing it to relax.

Reflexes
- Involuntary stretch reflex : a protective muscle contraction which occurs in response to a rapid stretch.
- Voluntary reflex : learned rapid response to a stimulus (for example, catching a ball).

Transmission of NEURAL IMPULSE
- This is an electrochemical process.
- Action potential (A) is initiated when Na^+ are allowed to diffuse into the axon of motor neurone.
- This depolarises (D) the axon to a critical point.
- Known as the 'all-or-none law'.
- Myelin sheath insulates axon, has gaps called nodes of Ranvier.
- Action potential jumps from node to node to speed up transmission of impulse, called saltatory conduction.
- Acetylcholine is temporarily released as depolarization occurs at the synaptic cleft of the neuromuscular junction.
- Muscle action potential travels into skeletal muscle fibres (Huxley's theory).

MUSCLE CELL STRUCTURES
- Motor Unit consists of a motor neurone and all the muscle fibres it stimulates.

HUXLEYS SLIDING THEORY OF MUSCLE CONTRACTION
- A neural impulse travels via a motor neurone to the motor end plate to create a muscle action potential.
- This muscle action potential triggers the release of Ca^{++} from the 'T' vesicles (located within the sarcoplasmic reticulum).
- Ca^{++} bind to the troponin molecule (on the actin filament) causing it to change shape by neutralising the tropomyosin and exposing the myosin cross-bridge binding sites on the actin molecules.
- Mitochondria enable aerobic ATP regeneration.
- ATP attaches itself to binding site on the cross-bridge releasing energy :

$$ATP \xrightarrow{ATPase} ADP + P_i + energy$$

- Myosin cross-bridges swivel towards the centre of sarcomere (called the power stroke).
- This draws the actin filaments past the myosin filaments (attach, detach, reattach of cross-bridges = ratchet mechanism).
- Contractile strength is dependent on cross-bridges formed.

MUSCLE FATIGUE
- A reduction in muscular performance or the inability to maintain expected power output.

CAUSES :
- Interruption of neuromuscular events such as decrease in Ca^{++} availability / failure or delay in release and synthesis of acetylcholine, reduced transmission of action potential to skeletal muscle fibre.
- Depletion of energy stores, due to depletion of PC, muscle / liver glycogen in ST and FT fibres.
- Fibre type, FT fibres have low aerobic capacity therefore quickly fatigued during maximal activity.
- Metabolite accumulation due to increase levels of lactate and CO_2, hence increase in H^+ (drop in pH) which inhibits enzyme action (both aerobically and anaerobically) to process ATP.
- Anticipated fatigue, the CNS might perceive fatigue prior to physiological fatigue.
- Decrease in body fluids decreases plasma volume.
- This decrease in body fluids also decreases BP, hence reduced blood flow to skin and muscles, hence heart has to work harder, body temperature rises, hence fatigue occurs.

MOTOR-NEURAL FIRING PATTERNS
- Stimuli are transmitted to different motor units which do not necessarily work in unison.

CONTROL of COORDINATED MOVEMENT
- Cerebellum compares intended movement with actual movement.
- If a difference is detected, cerebellum sends impulses to appropriate motor units which produce a correction.
- Control is achieved by increasing or decreasing the number of motor units operating.

THE HEART

CARDIAC ANATOMY - GROSS STRUCTURE
- The heart consists of three layers :
Pericardium
- Double layer bag surrounding the heart, reduces friction.
Myocardium
- This is striped cardiac muscle tissue consisting of united
  fibres joined by intercalated discs.
- Activated by 'all-or-none law' and myogenic in nature.
Endocardium
- The endocardium is an inner glistening membrane,
  prevents friction between heart muscle & flowing blood.
CHAMBERS :
Top
- The right and left atria have thin walls.
Bottom
- Right and left ventricles have thicker walls.
- The left ventricle wall is the thickest.
- Since this ventricle pumps blood to the main body mass.
Septum
- Consists of myocardial tissue (muscle) and divides the
  heart into a dual action pump.
VALVES :
Cuspid
- Mitral / bicuspid sited between left atria and left ventricle.
- Tricuspid sited between right atria and right ventricle.
Semi lunar
- Semi lunar valves guard the pulmonary artery and aorta.
- And control direction of blood flow.
BLOOD VESSELS attached to the heart :
Right side   - vena cavae, pulmonary artery.
Left side   - pulmonary vein, aorta.
Coronary BLOOD SUPPLY :
Arteries   - supply glucose and O_2 to myocardial
                   tissue.
Coronary veins - transport CO_2 and other wastes from
                   heart muscle.

CARDIAC DYNAMICS
Cardiac impulse
- Is an electrical impulse which originates from
  the pacemaker in the sinoatrial (SA) node.
- It initiates contractions of the cardiac muscle.
CARDIAC CYCLE
Diastole (0.5 s)
- Relaxed heart muscle fills with blood.
- Cuspid valves open, semi lunar valves close.
Systole (contracting heart muscle) 0.3 s
- Atrial systole, the SA node impulse causes a
  wave-like contraction over the atria forcing
  blood past cuspid valves into ventricles.
- Ventricular systole, the impulse reaches the AV
  node, cuspid values close, ventricular pressure
  rises as ventricles contract, semi-lunar valves
  open, blood is pushed out into pulmonary artery
  (lungs) and aorta
  (around body).

PULSE
- A wave of
  pressure produced
  by the contraction
  of the left ventricle.

110 **The CARDIAC IMPULSE**
myogenic   bundle of HIS   Purkinje fibres
SA node
AV node

HEART RATE
(HR)
- HR is the number of beats per minute (bpm).
- Average resting HR
        - males 70 bpm, females 72 bpm.
- HR trained   = 60 bpm (less = bradycardia).
- HR untrained = 70-90 bpm.
- HR max   = 220 - age.
Stroke volume **(SV)**
- SV is the volume of blood pumped by the left
  ventricle of the heart per beat.
- SV trained   = 110 ml.
- SV untrained = 70 ml.

Cardiac output **($\dot{Q}$)**
- This is the volume of blood pumped by
  the left ventricle of the heart in one minute.
- The product of stroke volume and heart rate :
- $\dot{Q}$ = SV x HR
untrained person at rest :
- $\dot{Q}$ = 80 x 70 = 5.60 l/min (or dm^3 min^{-1}).
untrained person during maximal exercise :
- $\dot{Q}$ = 110 x 190 = 19.81 l/min (or dm^3 min^{-1}).
endurance athlete at rest :
- $\dot{Q}$ = 110 x 51 = 5.61 l/min.
endurance athlete during maximal exercise :
- $\dot{Q}$ = 190 x 200 = 38 l/min.

Electrical activity of the heart measured using an
electrocardiogram (ECG):

111
R
lub = closure
    of cuspid valves
dub = closure of
    semilunar valves
T wave
P wave
Q   S
a = diastole
b = systole

atria	a	b	a
ventricles	a		b	a

0.0   0.2   0.4   0.6   0.8   time / s

- P wave represents the
  excitation of the atria (known
  as atrial depolarisation).
- QRS complex represents excitation of both ventricles (known as ventricular depolarisation).
- T wave indicates the repolarisation of both ventricles as they relax.

Information

HEART RATE RESPONSE TO EXERCISE

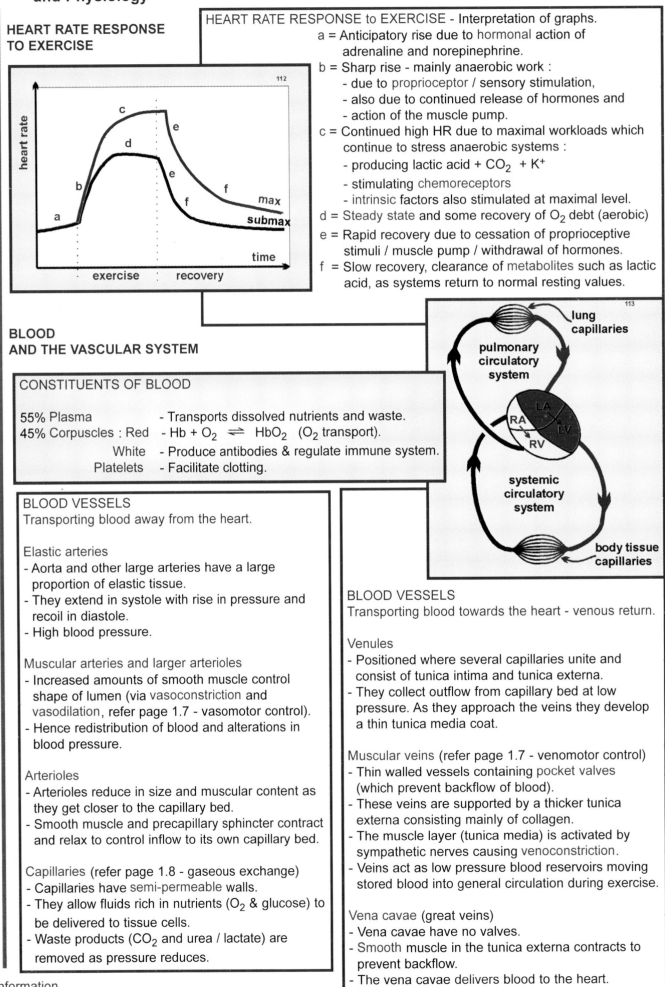

HEART RATE RESPONSE to EXERCISE - Interpretation of graphs.

a = Anticipatory rise due to hormonal action of adrenaline and norepinephrine.

b = Sharp rise - mainly anaerobic work :
- due to proprioceptor / sensory stimulation,
- also due to continued release of hormones and
- action of the muscle pump.

c = Continued high HR due to maximal workloads which continue to stress anaerobic systems :
- producing lactic acid + CO_2 + K^+
- stimulating chemoreceptors
- intrinsic factors also stimulated at maximal level.

d = Steady state and some recovery of O_2 debt (aerobic)

e = Rapid recovery due to cessation of proprioceptive stimuli / muscle pump / withdrawal of hormones.

f = Slow recovery, clearance of metabolites such as lactic acid, as systems return to normal resting values.

BLOOD AND THE VASCULAR SYSTEM

CONSTITUENTS OF BLOOD

55% Plasma	- Transports dissolved nutrients and waste.
45% Corpuscles : Red	- Hb + O_2 $\rightleftharpoons$ HbO_2 (O_2 transport).
White	- Produce antibodies & regulate immune system.
Platelets	- Facilitate clotting.

BLOOD VESSELS
Transporting blood away from the heart.

Elastic arteries
- Aorta and other large arteries have a large proportion of elastic tissue.
- They extend in systole with rise in pressure and recoil in diastole.
- High blood pressure.

Muscular arteries and larger arterioles
- Increased amounts of smooth muscle control shape of lumen (via vasoconstriction and vasodilation, refer page 1.7 - vasomotor control).
- Hence redistribution of blood and alterations in blood pressure.

Arterioles
- Arterioles reduce in size and muscular content as they get closer to the capillary bed.
- Smooth muscle and precapillary sphincter contract and relax to control inflow to its own capillary bed.

Capillaries (refer page 1.8 - gaseous exchange)
- Capillaries have semi-permeable walls.
- They allow fluids rich in nutrients (O_2 & glucose) to be delivered to tissue cells.
- Waste products (CO_2 and urea / lactate) are removed as pressure reduces.

BLOOD VESSELS
Transporting blood towards the heart - venous return.

Venules
- Positioned where several capillaries unite and consist of tunica intima and tunica externa.
- They collect outflow from capillary bed at low pressure. As they approach the veins they develop a thin tunica media coat.

Muscular veins (refer page 1.7 - venomotor control)
- Thin walled vessels containing pocket valves (which prevent backflow of blood).
- These veins are supported by a thicker tunica externa consisting mainly of collagen.
- The muscle layer (tunica media) is activated by sympathetic nerves causing venoconstriction.
- Veins act as low pressure blood reservoirs moving stored blood into general circulation during exercise.

Vena cavae (great veins)
- Vena cavae have no valves.
- Smooth muscle in the tunica externa contracts to prevent backflow.
- The vena cavae delivers blood to the heart.

THE VASCULAR SYSTEM (continued)

BLOOD PRESSURE
= BLOOD FLOW X PERIPHERAL RESISTANCE
- sphygmomanometer (measures BP)

	rest	dynamic exercise	static exercise	
systolic	120	170	200	mmHg
diastolic	80	88	120	

- The bigger the cross sectional area (CSA) the slower the flow.
- CSA affects peripheral resistance.
- During exercise, systolic blood pressure (SBP) increases as a result of increased Q .
- Due to increased venous return and actions of respiratory and muscle pumps.
- Very little change in diastolic blood pressure (DBP)
- Except during static exercise - see example values above.
- Increased blood velocity due to decreased CSA helps drive blood quickly through the venal system.

The relationships between cross sectional area, pressure and velocity of blood are shown in the graph above.

VASOMOTOR CONTROL

- This is concerned with the ability of muscular arteries and arterioles to change their shape.
- During exercise sympathetic nerves carry impulses to smooth muscle walls of arteries and arterioles supplying non-active tissues.
- This causes vasoconstriction.
- In contrast, sympathetic stimulation in arteries and arterioles supplying blood to active skeletal muscle is reduced.
- Therefore these vessels dilate, vasodilation.
- And additional blood flows into active muscles.
- As a result of vasomotor control, blood flow is diverted to skeletal muscle where it is needed.
- Otherwise known as blood shunting or the vascular shunt.

VENOMOTOR CONTROL

- Regulation of blood flow by changes in shape in veins is limited due to thin tunica media.
- SNS (sympathetic nervous system) can alter lumen a little to affect changes in blood velocity.
- Called venoconstriction.

VENOUS RETURN MECHANISM depends on :

- Gravity, the actions of muscle, respiratory and cardiac pumps (Starling's law of the heart).
- The action of valves in the lower limb prevents backflow.
- Venoconstriction.

GASEOUS TRANSPORT

MECHANICS OF BREATHING
- Concerned with changes in lung volumes and associated changes in pulmonary air pressure.

Inspiration at rest
- External intercostal muscles and diaphragm contract, internal intercostals relax.
- Effect : volume of thoracic cavity increases, pleural and pulmonary pressures less than atmospheric pressure, so air rushes in.

Inspiration during exercise
- Additionally, scalenes, sternocleidomastoid, pectoralis minor muscles contract to create bigger volume, therefore more air rushes in.

Expiration at rest
- External intercostals and diaphragm relax.
- Effect : decrease in lung volume, increase in pleural and pulmonary pressure, therefore air is forced out.

Expiration during exercise
- Internal intercostal and abdominal muscles contract, air is forced out more rapidly.

The Vascular Shunt

WARM-UP
- Prepares the vascular system for action as described above.

COOL-DOWN
- helps return the vascular system to pre-exercise state.
- As illustrated in the vascular shunt.

Information

GASEOUS TRANSPORT (continued)

LUNG STRUCTURE

Trachea
- This consists of an incomplete ring of cartilage which keeps airway open and allows swallowing.
- Ciliated lining and mucous glands in nose, pharynx, larynx, trachea and bronchi provide a cleaning mechanism.

Pulmonary pleura
- This secretes pleural fluid which reduces friction between lung tissue and ribs, aids inspiration as pleural pressure reduces, and expiration as pleural pressure increases.

Lung tissue - alveolar structure
- Elastic, moist, permeable single layered epithelium surrounded by network of capillaries, adapted for gaseous exchange.

GASEOUS EXCHANGE

GASEOUS EXCHANGE
- This depends on partial pressure of each gas, gas solubility and temperature.
- Partial pressure (p) : the pressure a gas exerts within a mixture of gases.
- Gases diffuse from high to low pressure.

In the alveoli :
- Maximum possible haemoglobin pO_2 = 13.3kPa, (as in alveolar air).
- In venous blood (arriving from tissues) pO_2 = 5.3kPa.
- Thus haemoglobin is forced to be saturated at 98% O_2.
- i.e. Hb + O_2 ==> HbO_2 (at 98%).
- pCO_2 in venous blood is higher in alveoli.
- Therefore CO_2 diffuses across alveolar membrane (from blood to air in lung) and is expired.

At tissue cell site :
- Arriving (arterial) blood pO_2 is greater than tissue pO_2.
- Myoglobin has a greater affinity for O_2 than Hb.
- Therefore O_2 is released into tissue cells.
- This O_2 is transported by myoglobin to the mitochondria.
- Where aerobic tissue cell respiration takes place.
- CO_2 diffuses across in opposite direction (from tissue to departing blood).

CO_2 transported in venous blood as :
- Carbonic acid (73%).
- Carbaminohaemoglobin (23%).
- Dissolved in plasma (7%).
- This CO_2 is excreted from the lungs during expiration.

AIR PATHWAY Air route
- nasal cavity
  => pharynx
    => larynx
      => trachea
        => bronchi
          => bronchioles
            =>respiratory bronchioles
            =>alveolar ducts
            =>alveoli.

ASTHMA
- Recurrent attacks making breathing difficult, particularly during exhalation.
- Caused by increased constriction of smooth muscle of bronchioles to a variety of stimuli.
- And / or by increased mucous secretions and swelling of mucous membrane lining respiratory bronchioles.
- Exercise-induced asthma (EAI) :
  - Bronchioles dilate during exercise (for example during running).
  - And constrict at end of exercise making breathing difficult.

- Treatment : steroid-based inhalers, which need to be registered for competitions.

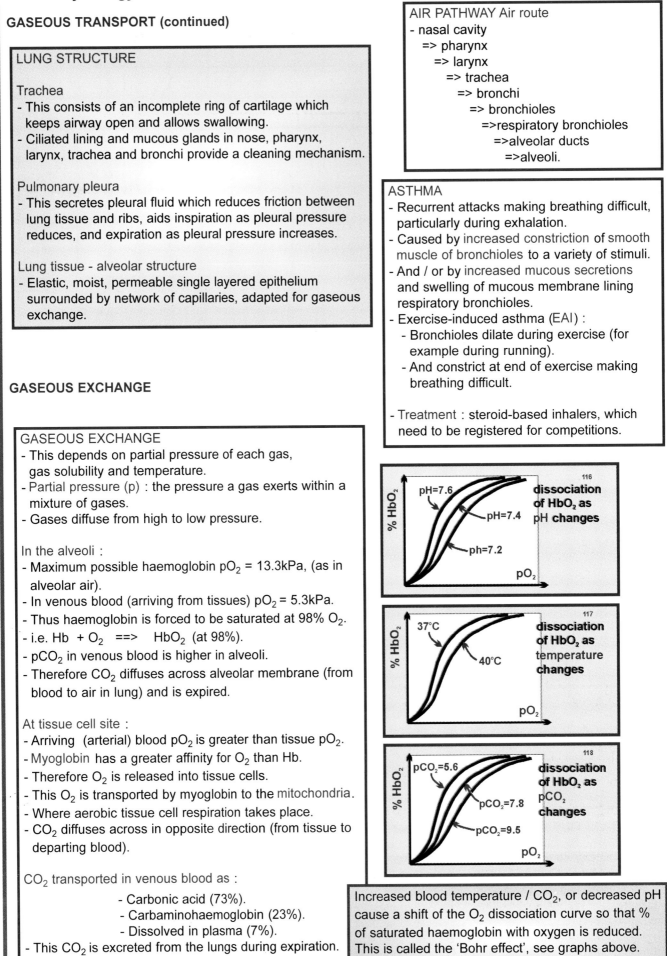

Increased blood temperature / CO_2, or decreased pH cause a shift of the O_2 dissociation curve so that % of saturated haemoglobin with oxygen is reduced. This is called the 'Bohr effect', see graphs above. More O_2 is then available to active tissue.

RESPIRATION

EFFICIENCY OF GAS PROCESS

The efficiency of the gas process is due to :
- A thin alveolar membrane and :
- Short distance between alveolar membrane and capillary network (less than 0.5μm) (the distance across which gas molecules have to travel is very small).
- A large surface area inside the alveoli (the surface across which molecules must be exchanged is very large).
- A moist lining which enables rapid solution of gas molecules.
- A constant blood supply into which gas can diffuse.
- Large amounts of red blood corpuscles (in blood), and myoglobin (in muscle cells).

PULMONARY RESPIRATION
- The process of supplying fresh air to alveoli.

TISSUE RESPIRATION
- The process by which cells use oxygen in order to release energy.

O_2 and CO_2 differences between inhaled and exhaled air

	inhaled(%)	exhaled (rest)(%)	exhaled (exercise)(%)
O_2	21	17	15
CO_2	0.003	3	6

LUNG VOLUMES and CAPACITIES

LUNG VOLUMES
- Of untrained and trained subjects at rest (see graph on right).

Lung capacities are made up of combinations of lung volumes :
- Inspiratory capacity   = TV + IRV   (3600 ml).
- Expiratory capacity   = TV + ERV (1700 ml).
- Vital capacity (VC)   = TV + IRV + ERV (4800 ml).
- Functional residual capacity = RV + ERV (2400 ml).
- Total lung capacity   = VC + RV   (6000 ml).

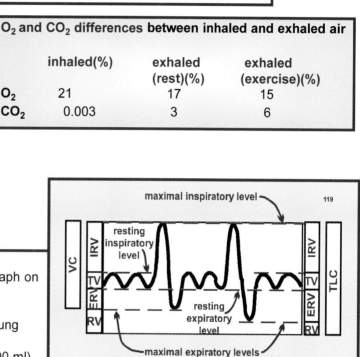

CHANGES in MINUTE VENTILATION with EXERCISE

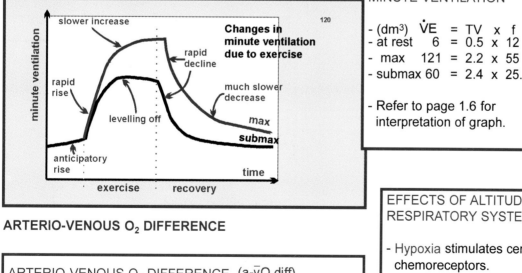

Changes in minute ventilation due to exercise

MINUTE VENTILATION

- (dm^3) $\dot{V}E$ = TV x f
- at rest   6 = 0.5 x 12
- max   121 = 2.2 x 55
- submax 60 = 2.4 x 25.

- Refer to page 1.6 for interpretation of graph.

ARTERIO-VENOUS O_2 DIFFERENCE

ARTERIO-VENOUS O_2 DIFFERENCE (a-$\bar{v}O_2$diff)
- This is the difference between the amount of O_2 leaving and returning to the heart.
- Examples :

at rest :   a-$\bar{v}O_2$diff = 5 ml O_2 per 100 ml blood.
during exercise :   a-$\bar{v}O_2$diff = 15 ml O_2 per 100 ml blood.

EFFECTS OF ALTITUDE ON THE RESPIRATORY SYSTEM

- Hypoxia stimulates central and peripheral chemoreceptors.
- Which cause increases in f and TV during the first week of residence.
- Decreased CO_2 makes urine more alkaline.

THE MECHANISMS OF REGULATION ON BODY SYSTEMS

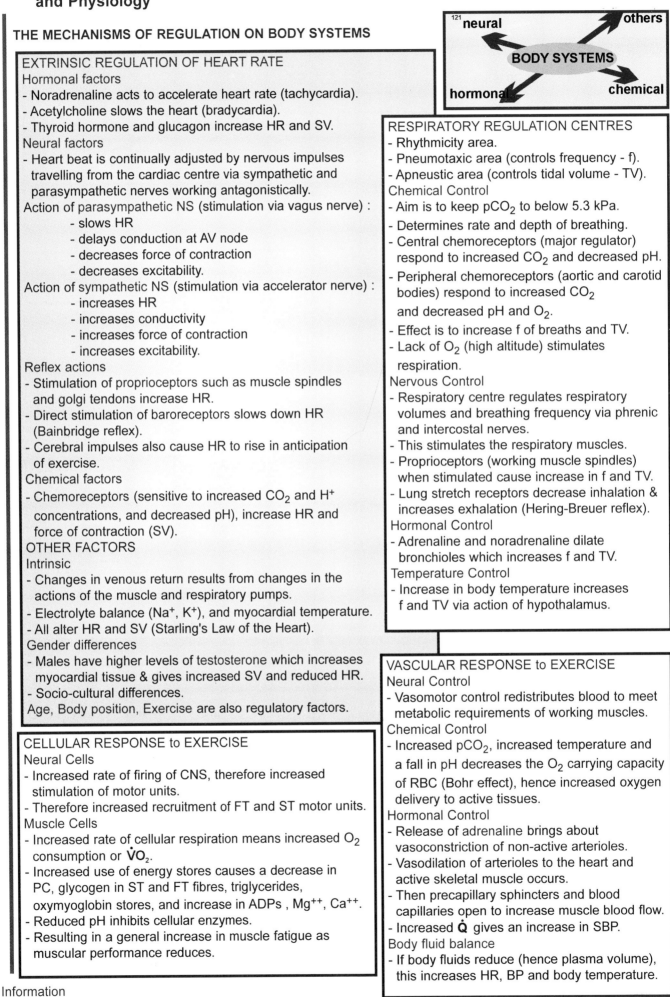

EXTRINSIC REGULATION OF HEART RATE

Hormonal factors
- Noradrenaline acts to accelerate heart rate (tachycardia).
- Acetylcholine slows the heart (bradycardia).
- Thyroid hormone and glucagon increase HR and SV.

Neural factors
- Heart beat is continually adjusted by nervous impulses travelling from the cardiac centre via sympathetic and parasympathetic nerves working antagonistically.

Action of parasympathetic NS (stimulation via vagus nerve) :
- slows HR
- delays conduction at AV node
- decreases force of contraction
- decreases excitability.

Action of sympathetic NS (stimulation via accelerator nerve) :
- increases HR
- increases conductivity
- increases force of contraction
- increases excitability.

Reflex actions
- Stimulation of proprioceptors such as muscle spindles and golgi tendons increase HR.
- Direct stimulation of baroreceptors slows down HR (Bainbridge reflex).
- Cerebral impulses also cause HR to rise in anticipation of exercise.

Chemical factors
- Chemoreceptors (sensitive to increased CO_2 and H^+ concentrations, and decreased pH), increase HR and force of contraction (SV).

OTHER FACTORS

Intrinsic
- Changes in venous return results from changes in the actions of the muscle and respiratory pumps.
- Electrolyte balance (Na^+, K^+), and myocardial temperature.
- All alter HR and SV (Starling's Law of the Heart).

Gender differences
- Males have higher levels of testosterone which increases myocardial tissue & gives increased SV and reduced HR.
- Socio-cultural differences.

Age, Body position, Exercise are also regulatory factors.

RESPIRATORY REGULATION CENTRES
- Rhythmicity area.
- Pneumotaxic area (controls frequency - f).
- Apneustic area (controls tidal volume - TV).

Chemical Control
- Aim is to keep pCO_2 to below 5.3 kPa.
- Determines rate and depth of breathing.
- Central chemoreceptors (major regulator) respond to increased CO_2 and decreased pH.
- Peripheral chemoreceptors (aortic and carotid bodies) respond to increased CO_2 and decreased pH and O_2.
- Effect is to increase f of breaths and TV.
- Lack of O_2 (high altitude) stimulates respiration.

Nervous Control
- Respiratory centre regulates respiratory volumes and breathing frequency via phrenic and intercostal nerves.
- This stimulates the respiratory muscles.
- Proprioceptors (working muscle spindles) when stimulated cause increase in f and TV.
- Lung stretch receptors decrease inhalation & increases exhalation (Hering-Breuer reflex).

Hormonal Control
- Adrenaline and noradrenaline dilate bronchioles which increases f and TV.

Temperature Control
- Increase in body temperature increases f and TV via action of hypothalamus.

CELLULAR RESPONSE to EXERCISE

Neural Cells
- Increased rate of firing of CNS, therefore increased stimulation of motor units.
- Therefore increased recruitment of FT and ST motor units.

Muscle Cells
- Increased rate of cellular respiration means increased O_2 consumption or $\dot{V}O_2$.
- Increased use of energy stores causes a decrease in PC, glycogen in ST and FT fibres, triglycerides, oxymyoglobin stores, and increase in ADPs , Mg^{++}, Ca^{++}.
- Reduced pH inhibits cellular enzymes.
- Resulting in a general increase in muscle fatigue as muscular performance reduces.

VASCULAR RESPONSE to EXERCISE

Neural Control
- Vasomotor control redistributes blood to meet metabolic requirements of working muscles.

Chemical Control
- Increased pCO_2, increased temperature and a fall in pH decreases the O_2 carrying capacity of RBC (Bohr effect), hence increased oxygen delivery to active tissues.

Hormonal Control
- Release of adrenaline brings about vasoconstriction of non-active arterioles.
- Vasodilation of arterioles to the heart and active skeletal muscle occurs.
- Then precapillary sphincters and blood capillaries open to increase muscle blood flow.
- Increased $\dot{Q}$ gives an increase in SBP.

Body fluid balance
- If body fluids reduce (hence plasma volume), this increases HR, BP and body temperature.

Information

QUESTIONS

JOINTS and MUSCLES

1) a) The knee joint plays an important role in many sporting activities.
  i) Draw a diagram to show the location of the following structures within a knee joint : menisci; cruciate ligaments; hyaline (articular cartilage).
  (4 marks)
  ii) Give a brief description of the structure and function of two of these components. (4 marks)
b) The athlete in the diagram on the right is using the hang technique during the flight phase of a long jump. Identify one agonist muscle acting on each of the following joints as the athlete moves into the hang position : spine, hip, knee. (3 marks)
c) Explain with the aid of pin-man diagrams how the centre of mass of the athlete changes from the take-off position to the flight phase shown in the diagram on the right. (cross reference Biomechanics p 3.5) (3 marks)
d) Why is it important to warm-up muscle tissue prior to long jumping? (2 marks)

MUSCLES and MOVEMENT ANALYSIS

2) The swimmer on the right is practising a block start. The table below is a joint and muscle analysis of this start position.

a) Name the joints labelled as **X**, **Y** and **Z**. (3 marks)
b) Provide the missing information for letters **A, B, C, D, E** and identify the muscle function and type of muscle contraction being performed by B and E. (7 marks)

Joint	Joint type	Articulating bones	Movement produced	Active muscle
X	A	humerus and scapula	extension	B
Y	ball and socket	femur and pelvis	C	iliopsoas
Z	hinge	D	dorsiflexion	E

3) a) The diagram on the right shows movements of the arms, legs, hands and feet of a student during a flat-out sprint.
  i) Identify the movement patterns occurring at three of the joints numbered 1 to 5. (3 marks)
  ii) Identify, for each case, the prime mover / agonist which brings about movement at joints 1, 2 and 3. (3 marks)
  iii) Suggest two factors which affect the range of movement at the hip joint. (2 marks)
b) Sketch a diagram to show the type of lever operating at the ankle joint during the rear leg extension phase of the sprinting action. Label the effort, fulcrum and load on your diagram. (cross reference Biomechanics p 3.6) (4 marks)

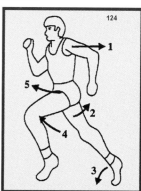

Characteristic	Slow twitch type	Fast twitch type
contractile time / ms	110	40
mitochondrial density	high	low
glycogen stores	low	high
phosphocreatine stores	low	high
capillary density	high	low
sarcoplasmic reticulum	poorly developed	well developed
oxidative enzyme activity	high	low

c) Skeletal muscle contains both slow and fast twitch fibres but the proportion of each depends upon the function of a muscle as a whole. The table lists some of the differences between slow and fast twitch muscle fibres of a sprinter.

  i) Suggest why the muscles concerned in maintaining the trunk posture of the body of the sprinter might be expected to have a larger percentage of slow twitch muscle fibres. (2 marks)
  ii) Using the table explain why fast twitch fibres may build up an oxygen debt. (2 marks)
  iii) Account for the difference in the speed of contraction of the two types of fibre. (2 marks)
  iv) Sketch graphs to illustrate the tensions generated for both slow and fast twitch muscle fibres against time. (2 marks)

MUSCLES and MOVEMENT ANALYSIS continued

4) a) The tissue of the major superficial muscles is categorised as 'skeletal'.

   i) Identify the other two categories of muscle tissue.   (2 marks)

   ii) In what major way does the control of skeletal muscle differ from that of the other two categories?   (2 marks)

b) The diagram on the right represents a high jumper during the take-off phase of the movement.

   i) Identify the 18 muscles indicated in the diagram.   (9 marks)

   ii) Identify the muscles that are mainly responsible for the powerful flexion of the knee joint. (3 marks)

   iii) From the muscles identified in **b) i)** give an example of a fusiform muscle type.   (1 mark)

   iv) How does the arrangement of pennate muscle fibres assist in the powerful flexion of the hip joint?   (2 marks)

(Diagram after Wirhed, Athletic Ability and the Anatomy of Motion, 2nd edition 1997, page 156)

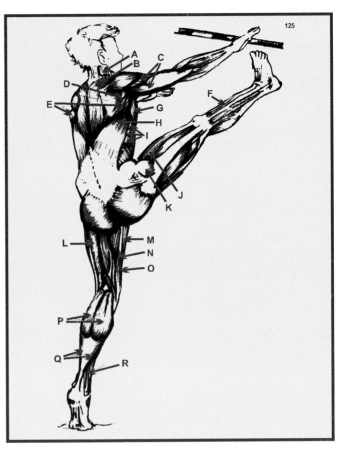

5) The diagram on the left shows a shot putter during the delivery phase of the technique .

a) List the bones that articulate in the shoulder and knee joints.   (4 marks)

b) Briefly explain the movement sequence of the right arm during the delivery phase of the shot put.   (3 marks)

c) With reference to the diagrams, name the main contracting muscles involved in the extension of the right elbow, knee and hip joints.   (6 marks)

d) Using an example from the diagram explain what is meant by a fixator muscle.   (3 marks)

e) Explain the upward movement of the shot with reference to Newton's 1st and 3rd laws of Motion. (cross reference Biomechanics p 3.3)   (4 marks)

f) What feature of the ankle joint and its associated calf muscles enables it to be more efficient in exerting force on the body than almost any other joint in the body?   (2 marks)

BODY PLANES and AXES

6) a) Identify the planes shown in the diagram on the right.   (3 marks)

b) Name and describe the position of the three major axes about which rotation may take place, and give a sporting example for each axis identified.   (6 marks)

c) Identify the major planes and axes involved in the following movements :

   i) Back somersault.

   ii) Cartwheel.   (4 marks)

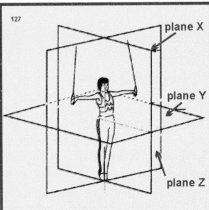

TYPES of MUSCLE CONTRACTION

7) Differentiate and give examples of concentric, static and eccentric work.   (6 marks)

STRUCTURE of SKELETAL MUSCLE

8) The diagrams on the right show a single unit (sarcomere) of a muscle fibre in the relaxed and contracted state. The diagrams marked with a **C** are simplified as compared to those marked with a **B**. All the diagrams are not necessarily drawn to scale.

a) Which of the diagrams marked with a **C** matches the banding patterns of those marked with an **B**? (1 mark)

b) Which regions (zones or bands) in **B1** and **B2** are composed of:
   i) actin only
   ii) myosin only
   iii) actin and myosin? (3 marks)

c) Describe what happens to the following regions during normal (isotonic) contraction :
   i) the Z lines
   ii) the I bands
   iii) the A bands
   iv) the H zones. (4 marks)

d) Explain your answers to part **c)** in terms of the sliding filament mechanism. (4 marks)

e) Explain, in terms of the sliding filament mechanism, why a fully extended muscle cannot exert its maximum force. (4 marks)

f) Explain why muscles can only contract actively and how a contracted muscle is subsequently re-stretched when relaxed. (4 marks)

NEUROMUSCULAR STRUCTURES and CONTROL

9) Identify the different regions of a motor neurone and next to each part identified list its function. (6 marks)

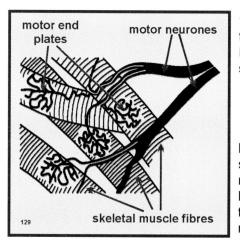

motor end plates
motor neurones
skeletal muscle fibres
129

10) a) Diagram 129 on the left has been created from a slide of skeletal tissue as seen with a light microscope at a magnification of 800 times. It shows part of two motor units. Use evidence from the drawing to suggest :
   i) A meaning of the term motor unit. (2 marks)
   ii) Why all the muscle fibres shown will not necessarily contract at the same time. (3 marks)

b) Briefly describe the sequence of events at the motor end-plate which leads to an action potential passing along the muscle fibre. 4 marks)

c) Describe some of the factors which determine muscle speed and tension characteristics. (4 marks)

d) Explain the role of motor units in controlling the strength of muscular contractions in sports movements. (10 marks)

CARDIAC DYNAMICS

11) a) Describe the flow of blood through the heart, identifying the major structures, including blood vessels, and their related functions. (8 marks)

b) Graph 130 on the right shows the relationship between pressure, volume and heart sounds during the cardiac cycle.
Using your knowledge of the cardiac cycle explain the significance of these changes from systole to diastole. (4 marks)

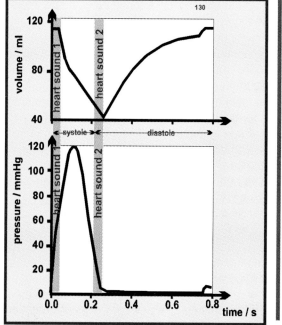

CARDIAC STRUCTURE AND DYNAMICS - QUESTIONS (continued)

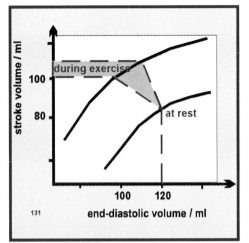

131

11) c) Graph 131 on the right shows the usual response of stroke volume before and during exercise.

i) Define stroke volume and end-diastolic volume.   (2 marks)
ii) Stroke volume can be computed by using a simple equation :
Stroke volume = end-diastolic volume - end-systolic volume
Using the information from the graph, work out the end-systolic volume before exercise has commenced.   (2 marks)
iii) How is the Frank Starling's 'Law of the Heart Mechanism' involved in increasing stroke volume during exercise?   (3 marks)
iv) Identify the hormonal agent responsible for changes in stroke volume from the pre-exercise level to an increased volume during the exercise period. How does this agent affect myocardial tissue?   (2 marks)
    v) What is the usual response of heart rate during the same bout of exercise?   (1 mark)
d) Endurance training results in aerobic physiological adaptations, some of which are illustrated in table below..

	Elite endurance-trained athlete	Untrained subject
Resting heart rate (bpm)	50	70
Maximum heart rate (bpm)	210	190
Resting stroke volume of left ventricle (ml)	110	70
Maximum stroke volume of left ventricle (ml)	190	100

i) Compare and contrast the heart of the elite endurance-trained athlete with the untrained subject. Give reasons for the differences in stroke volume at rest.   (6 marks)
ii) Calculate the maximum cardiac output for the elite endurance-trained athlete. Show your calculation.   (2 marks)

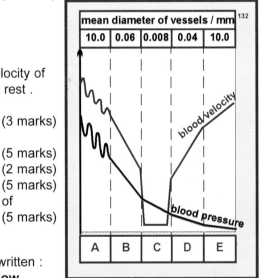

132

STRUCTURE AND FUNCTION OF THE VASCULAR SYSTEM

12) The diagram on the right shows the variations in pressure and velocity of blood as it passes through the circulatory system while the body is at rest .
a) What types of blood vessels are represented by A B C D and E?   (3 marks)
b) Explain the variations in velocity and pressure in vessel type A.   (5 marks)
c) Why is the velocity of the blood low in vessel type C?   (2 marks)
d) What is the physiological significance of this?   (5 marks)
e) What changes in the diagram would you expect during some form of rhythmic exercise? Explain your answer.   (5 marks)

13) A simple calculation for the calculation of blood pressure can be written :
    Blood Pressure = Cardiac Output x Resistance to blood flow
a) Identify two factors which cause resistance to the flow of blood through blood vessels.   (2 marks)
b) Blood pressure is quoted as two numbers. An example would be : 120/80 mmHg. Explain what each of these numbers refer to.   (2 marks)
c) The right ventricle of the heart is less muscular then the left ventricle.
    i) Explain the effect that this has on blood going to the lungs.   (2 marks)
    ii) What is the advantage of this effect?   (2 marks)
d) With regard to the supply of substances to, and the removal from working muscles, explain why it is necessary for the blood to be under relatively high pressure.   (4 marks)
e) In the veins, blood pressure is relatively low. As a result, there is not enough pressure to return the blood in the veins quickly enough to fill the heart. Describe three factors which help speed the return of blood in the veins to the heart during exercise.   (3 marks)
f) With reference to blood pressure within the capillary bed supplying working muscles, identify and briefly explain what happens during rhythmic aerobic exercise of several minutes duration, and a single weight-lift held for the required three seconds.   (5 marks)

STRUCTURE AND FUNCTION OF THE VASCULAR SYSTEM - QUESTIONS (continued)

14) The table shows the rate of blood flow (in cm³ per minute) to different parts of the body in a trained male athlete, at rest and while exercising at maximum effort on a cycle ergometer.
Study the data carefully before answering the following questions.

Organ or system	Estimated blood flow in cm³ min⁻¹	
	At rest	During max effort
Skeletal muscle	1000	26400
Coronary vessels	250	1200
Skin	500	750
Kidneys	1000	300
Liver & Gut	1250	375
Other organs	1000	975

a) The rate of blood flow to the 'entire body' increases significantly during exercise. Explain briefly how the heart achieves this.   (3 marks)

b) What percentage of the total blood flow is directed to the skeletal muscle (show your calculations):
   i) at rest
   ii) during maximum effort?   (2 marks)

c) List the physiological changes that occur in the blood and working muscles during exercise. Explain how these changes act as stimuli to increase the rate of blood flow.   (6 marks)
d) Comment on the blood flow to the kidneys and to the liver and gut, both at rest and during exercise.(3 marks)
e) Why should food not be consumed within three hours of starting participation in a vigorous sport?   (3 marks)
f) Does strenuous activity have an effect on the rate of blood flow to the brain? Briefly explain your answer.
(3 marks)

CARDIO-RESPIRATORY DYNAMICS

15) a) The diagram below shows the responses of respiration and heart rate to exercise that might occur in running a 3000 metres track race. Using the information in this diagram, explain why both heart rate and ventilation follow similar trends.   (10 marks)

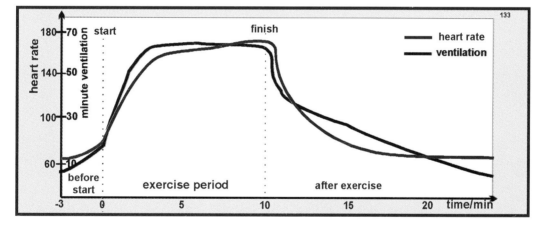

b) Discuss how the sympathetic and parasympathetic nervous systems affect heart and ventilation rates.
(4 marks)

STRUCTURE and FUNCTION of the RESPIRATORY SYSTEM

16) a) Starting with the trachea, name all the structures a molecule of air would encounter on its way to the alveoli.   (3 marks)
b) Describe the pleura of the lungs. What is their function?   (3 marks)
c) Describe the mechanism of inspiration during physical activity.   (6 marks)
d) Identify the chemical stimuli that control the rate and depth of breathing.   (3 marks)
e) How do they control respiration during exercise?   (6 marks)

OXYGEN DISSOCIATION

17) a) Exercise displaces the oxygen dissociation curve to the right as blood pH falls due to increased carbon dioxide pressure (concentration), and temperature increases.

i) Using the data provided in the table, plot both sets of data in the same way as the oxygen dissociation curve. On the y axis plot % saturation of haemoglobin with oxygen, and oxygen partial pressure on the x axis. **(4 marks)**

ii) Draw a vertical line at a spot on the x axis where the oxygen partial pressure is at 5 kPa and follow the line up through the curves. What do you notice about the saturation of haemoglobin with oxygen for the two curves? **(3 marks)**

% saturation of Haemoglobin with Oxygen		
Partial Pressure of O$_2$ (kPa)	for pCO$_2$ 5.3 kPa	for pCO$_2$ 9.3 kPa
1.3	7	4
2.6	27	15
3.9	53	35
5.3	70	58
6.6	79	71
7.9	85	82
9.3	90	88
10.5	95	94
11.8	98	98
13.0	100	100

iii) What does the effect of increased carbon dioxide partial pressure in venous blood as it passes through muscle tissue have on the release of oxygen from haemoglobin into muscle cell tissue? Explain your answer.
(Note that pO$_2$ is about 5 kPa in venous haemoglobin) **(5 marks)**

iv) In terms of the release of oxygen to the working muscle fibres during exercise, what is the significance of the steep part of the oxygen dissociation curve? **(2 marks)**

b) **i)** What factors encourage the dissociation of oxyhaemoglobin and the release of oxygen to the working muscle fibre during exercise? **(3 marks)**

ii) State the type of muscle fibre for which these considerations of oxygen release have the greatest effect and briefly explain your choice. **(3 marks)**

LUNG VOLUMES and CAPACITIES

18) a) The diagram on the right represents the lung volume changes based on a number of spirometer readings during various breathing actions. With reference to the trace, briefly explain the following terms :

i) Resting tidal volume (TV).
ii) Expiratory reserve volume (ERV).
iii) Vital capacity (VC).
iv) Residual volume (RV). **(4 marks)**

b) Why does tidal volume increase only slightly during exercise? **(3 marks)**

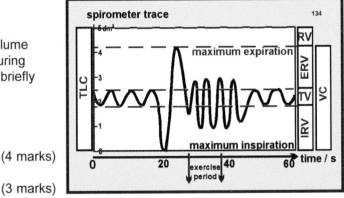

c) Define minute ventilation? Calculate its value at rest for this subject, showing your calculations. **(3 marks)**

d) Explain why the lungs cannot be completely emptied? **(2 marks)**

e) What is meant by anatomical dead space of the respiratory system? **(2 marks)**

f) Explain why it is not possible to identify elite endurance performers from their spirometer traces. **(2 marks)**

ANSWERS

The answer for each mark awarded is notated by the ❐ symbol - where there are more ❐ symbols than there are marks available, marks would be given for any choice up to the maximum available. Usually, the precise wording specified in an answer would not be required - answers with the same meaning would be acceptable. In Science areas, sometimes the precise words used in terminology would be required.

JOINTS and MUSCLES

1) a) i)
   See diagram on right, marks awarded for :
❐ General shapes of bones.
   Position on diagram and labelling of :
❐ Hyaline cartilage.   ❐ Menisci.   ❐ Cruciate ligaments.

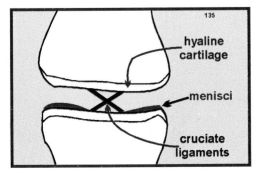

JOINTS AND MUSCLES - ANSWERS QUESTION 1 (continued)

1) a) ii)

A maximum of 2 marks for each structure from :

Menisci :

☐ Extra layers of fibro cartilage / disc-shaped flattened at edges / tough, slightly flexible mass of fibres.

☐ Evens out irregularities between knee joint bones.

☐ Deepens knee joint socket to give greater stability.

Cruciate ligaments :

☐ Consist of bundles of white fibrous tissue that cross over within the knee joint to secure tibia and femur during knee movements.

Hyaline cartilage :

☐ Consists of smooth bluish-white solid yet resilient matrix which prevents bones from rubbing together, allows freedom at joint ends, absorbs impact.

1) b)

Spine - one mark from :	Hip - one mark from :	Knee - one mark from :
☐ Erector spinae.	☐ Gluteus maximus.	☐ Biceps femoris.
☐ Trapezius.	☐ Biceps femoris.	☐ Semitendinosus.
	☐ Semitendinosus.	☐ Semimembranosus.
	☐ Semimembranosus.	☐ Sartorius.

1) c)

Explain with the aid of diagrams how the centre of mass of the athlete changes from the take-off position to the flight phase shown.

☐ Three marks for 3 diagrams showing the approximate position of the centre of mass - see diagram 136.

☐ The idea that this red dot represents the position of the overall mass of the body.

1) d)

Why is it important to warm-up muscle tissue prior to long jumping?

2 marks for two from :

☐ Raises muscle temperature.

☐ To increase glycolytic enzyme action

☐ And ATP conversion.

☐ And reduce muscle response time.

☐ Stretching enables musculature to operate over its full range.

MUSCLES AND MOVEMENT ANALYSIS

2) a)

Name the joints labelled as X, Y and Z.

3 marks for :

☐ X = shoulder joint.

☐ Y = hip joint.

☐ Z = ankle joint.

2) b)

Joint and muscle analysis of swim block start position. Provide the missing information for letters A, B, C, D, and E.

1 mark for each letter :

☐ A = ball and socket.   ☐ B = posterior deltoid or teres major or latissimus dorsi.   ☐ C = flexion.

☐ D = tibia and talus.   ☐ E = tibialis anterior or peroneus brevis.

Identify the muscle function and type of muscle contraction being performed by B and E.

2 marks for :

☐ Muscle function B and E : agonist muscle or prime mover.

☐ Type of muscle contraction at B and E : isometric muscle contraction.

3) a) i)

3 marks for three from :

☐ 1 = extension.   ☐ 2 = extension.   ☐ 3 = plantar flexion.   ☐ 4 = flexion.   ☐ 5 = flexion.

▎**MUSCLES AND MOVEMENT ANALYSIS - ANSWERS QUESTION 3 (continued)**

3) a) ii)

The prime movers / agonists in the respective joints are :

❑ Joint number 1 - (posterior) deltoid / latissimus dorsi.

❑ Joint number 2 - gluteus maximus / semitendinosus / semimembranosus / biceps femoris.

❑ Joint number 3 - gastrocnemius / soleus / tibialis anterior.

3) a) iii)

Factors which affect the range of movement at the hip joint :

　　2 marks for two from :

❑ Shape of ball and socket joint / shape of bones.

❑ Extensibility of attached muscles / muscle tendons.

❑ Elasticity of attached ligaments.

❑ Length of muscle / bulk of muscle.

3) b)

The type of lever operating at the ankle joint during the rear leg extension phase of the sprinting action. Label the effort, fulcrum and load on your diagram.

　　4 marks for :

❑ Diagram as diagram 137.

❑ Position and direction of effort **E**.

❑ Position and direction of load **L**.

❑ Position of fulcrum.

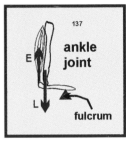

3) c) i)

Postural muscles in the trunk would have more slow twitch fibres because.

　　2 marks for two from :

❑ They maintain posture for long periods of time.

❑ It would be important not to get fatigued easily.

❑ No need for fast / powerful contraction.

3) c) ii)

Fast twitch fibres may build up an Oxygen debt because they have :

❑ Poor blood supply.

❑ Low capillary density.

❑ Few mitochondria.

❑ Therefore less O_2 supplied because fewer oxidative enzymes.

3) c) iii)

The two types of fibre contract at different speeds because of :

❑ High glycogen content of fast twitch fibres, (low in slow twitch fibres).

❑ High levels of phosphocreatine (PC) stores in fast twitch fibres, (low levels in slow twitch fibres).

❑ Fast twitch fibres have well developed sarcoplasmic reticulum, which means more Ca^{++} available and improved transportation system for nutrients (e.g. glucose) compared to slow twitch fibres.

❑ Fast twitch fibres are attached to large motor neurones with fast conductive velocity (small contractile time), compared to smaller motor neurones for slow twitch fibres.

3) c) iv)

　　See two diagrams on the right. Marks awarded for :

❑ Far diagram, fast twitch - short duration, high force.

❑ Near diagram, slow twitch - long duration, low force.

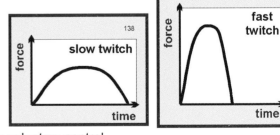

4) a) i)

❑ Striped cardiac / heart (muscle).

❑ Smooth / visceral (muscle).

4) a) ii)

❑ Skeletal muscle is the only category of muscle that is under voluntary control.

❑ Whereas cardiac and smooth muscle types are involuntary.

4) b) i)

　　The muscles indicated in the diagram are : (1 mark given for two muscles identified) :

❑ A = sternocleidomastoid.

❑ B = trapezius.

❑ C = triceps brachii.

❑ D = teres minor.

❑ E = teres major.

❑ F = tibialis anterior.

❑ G = pectoralis major.

❑ H = latissimus dorsi.

❑ I = serratus anterior.

❑ J = rectus femoris.

❑ K = tensor fascia latae.

❑ L = biceps femoris.

❑ M = adductor longus.

❑ N = gracilis.

❑ O = sartorius.

❑ P = gastrocnemius.

❑ Q = soleus.

❑ R = tibialis posterior.

MUSCLES AND MOVEMENT ANALYSIS - ANSWERS Question 4 (continued)

4) b) ii)

The muscles responsible for the powerful flexion of the knee joint are (3 marks for three from) :

❐ Biceps femoris.   ❐ Semitendinosus.   ❐ Semimembranosus.
❐ Gastrocnemius.   ❐ Sartorius.   ❐ Tensor fascia latae.

4) b) iii)

A fusiform muscle type is spindle shaped with an expanded belly, examples are :

❐ Triceps.   ❐ Tibialis anterior.

4) b) iv)

The arrangement of pennate muscle fibres assist in hip flexion because :

❐ Flat muscle fibres are arranged around a central tendon, example biceps femoris.
❐ This provides a strong, powerful action but with limited movement range.

5) a)

Bones which articulate at :

Shoulder :   Knee (2 marks for two from) :

❐ Scapula.   ❐ Humerus.   ❐ Femur.   ❐ Tibia.   ❐ Patella.

5) b)

❐ From diagram **A** :   Shoulder extended and abducted, elbow flexed, wrist pronated and hyper-extended.
❐ From diagram **B** :   Shoulder flexed and elevated, elbow extended,.
❐ Wrist pronated and extended, and phalanges extended.

5) c)

From the diagrams, the agonist muscles acting on the respective joints are :

2 marks for two from : right elbow :

❐ Triceps brachii.   ❐   Anconeus.

2 marks for two from : knee :

❐ Rectus femoris.   ❐ Vastus lateralis.   ❐ Vastus medialis.   ❐ Vastus intermedius.

2 marks for two from : hip :

❐ Gluteus maximus.   ❐ Biceps femoris.   ❐ Adductor magnus.   ❐ Semimembranosus.
❐ Semitendinosus.

5) d)

2 marks for two from :

❐ Fixator muscles hold joints in position.
❐ Which stabilises the origin of the prime mover.
❐ So that the prime mover can act more efficiently.

1 mark for example :

❐ For example, trapezius fixes the scapula in position so that the origin of deltoid can act on the shoulder joint.

5) e)

Explain the upward movement of the shot with reference to Newton's 1st and 3rd laws of Motion.

Newton's 1st law - 2 marks for two from :

❐ This law applies to objects at rest or moving at constant velocity.
❐ Apart from a short period during the middle of the throw, the shot will be accelerating - so this law will not apply.
❐ If the shot were moving at constant velocity, all the forces would cancel out - zero resultant (net) force.

Newton's 3rd law - 2 marks for two from :

❐ This law applies when a person pushes on an object - in this case the shot.
❐ The force exerted on the shot by the thrower is equal in size but opposite in direction to the force exerted on the thrower by the shot.
❐ So as the thrower pushes on the shot - the shot pushes back on the thrower.
❐ Throwers can use this to stop them falling out of the front of the circle, they use the force from the shot backwards on them for this.

5) f)

What feature of the ankle joint and its associated calf muscles enables it to be more efficient.

2 marks for two from :

❐ It is a class 2 lever.
❐ In which the effort (force in the muscle) is smaller than the load.
❐ Hence large forces can be exerted on the ground by using a relatively small force in a muscle.

BODY PLANES and AXES

6) a)

❐ Z is in the frontal plane.   ❐ Y is in the transverse plane.   ❐ X is in the sagittal plane.

6) b)

Identify, describe and give a sporting example for each of the three major axes of the body.

❐ The transverse axis is horizontal - side to side - between opposite hip bones.

❐ Examples - sit ups, high jump Fosbury Flop movement.

❐ The frontal axis is horizontal - front to back - between belly button and lumbar spine.

❐ Example - bowling action in cricket.

❐ The vertical axis - top to bottom - between top of head and point between feet.

❐ Examples - spinning skater, hammer throw.

6) c) i)

    Back somersault :

❐ Sagittal plane.   ❐ Transverse axis.

6) c) ii)

    Cartwheel :

❐ Frontal plane.   ❐ Frontal axis.

TYPES of MUSCLE CONTRACTION

7)

❐ Concentric work : muscle shortens whilst developing tension.

❐ Example biceps muscle during an arm flexion movement. Known as a positive contraction.

❐ Static work (isometric contraction) : develops muscle tension without changing length.

❐ Example rugby scrum.

❐ Eccentric work : muscle lengthen whilst developing tension.

❐ Example, biceps muscle during arm extension movement. Known as a negative contraction.

STRUCTURE OF SKELETAL MUSCLE

8) a)

❐ **C1** matches **B1** and **C2** matches **B2**.

8) b) i)

❐ Actin = **I** band.

8) b) ii)

❐ Myosin = **H** zone.

8) b) iii)

❐ Actin and myosin = **A** band.

8) c) i)

❐ **Z** lines move closer together.

8) c) ii)

❐ **I** bands narrow / shorten.

8) c) iii)

❐ **A** bands remain the same width.

8) c) iv)

❐ **H** zone disappears.

8) d)

The sliding filament mechanism explains the diagrams as follows :

❐ The **Z** lines move closer together as the actin filaments slide together between the myosin filaments.

❐ **I** bands get narrower as the **Z** lines move in closer to the A bands.

❐ **A** bands do not change because the myosin filaments do not change during the contraction.

❐ The **H** zones disappear because the actin filaments meet in the centre between the myosin filaments.

8) e)

A fully extended muscle cannot exert its maximum force because :

❐ When a muscle is fully extended there is not much overlap between the actin and myosin filaments.

❐ Therefore not many cross-bridges can form between them.

❐ Therefore maximum force cannot be generated.

❐ Because it is the cross-bridges that supply the force to slide the filaments in the contraction.

STRUCTURE OF SKELETAL MUSCLE - ANSWERS QUESTION 8 (continued)

8) f)
The reasons muscles can only contract actively, and why a muscle can be restretched when relaxed are :
- ❏ The cross-bridges between the myosin and actin can only move actively in one direction.
- ❏ Which is towards the centre of the sarcomere.
- ❏ When relaxed, they are stretched by the contraction of another muscle (known as an agonist).
- ❏ As muscles work in pairs to produce antagonistic muscle action.

NEUROMUSCULAR STRUCTURES and CONTROL

9)
The different regions of a motor neurone and their functions are :
  6 marks for six from (3 marks could be given for labelled diagram) :
- ❏ Cell body contains the nucleus and therefore the genetic material for protein synthesis.
- ❏ Dendrites are branched outgrowths from the cell body.
- ❏ Which receive signals from other neurones via cell body to the axon.
- ❏ Axon (nerve fibre) consists of a single long extension from the cell body.
- ❏ The axon may be covered in segments by a myelin sheath.
- ❏ The gaps between myelin sheath segments are called nodes of Ranvier.
- ❏ The effect of the nodes of Ranvier is to speed up impulse transmission.
- ❏ The axon transmits impulses away from the cell body.
- ❏ Towards other neurones or effector cells such as muscle fibres.

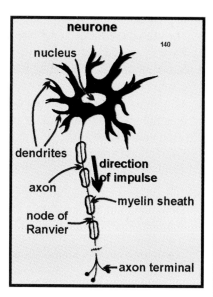

10) a) i)
- ❏ A motor unit consists of a motor neurone which connects to a group of muscle fibres.
- ❏ The connection is made by specialised structures called motor end-plates.

10) a) ii)
Muscle fibres which are part of two motor units will not necessarily contract at the same time because :
- ❏ Motor nerve fibres have different lengths, hence the impulse takes less time down a shorter one, which will cause its muscle fibre to contract earlier (than others connected to longer nerve fibres).
- ❏ It is not necessary for both motor units to be stimulated at the same time = spatial summation.
- ❏ Hence if the shorter of the two motor units is stimulated all the muscle fibres connected to that motor unit will contract - this is the 'all-or-none law'.
- ❏ But at the same time the longer of the two motor units could be resting and so those muscle fibres connected to that motor neurone would be in a state of relaxation.

10) b)
The sequence of events leading to an action potential passing along a muscle fibre is :
  4 marks for four from (items in sequence) :
- ❏ A nerve impulse arrives at motor end plate Ca^{++} triggers the release of acetylcholine from synaptic end bulb.
- ❏ Acetylcholine diffuses across the synaptic cleft to post synaptic receptors on muscle sarcolemma.
- ❏ This increases permeability of the post synaptic membrane to sodium and potassium.
- ❏ Which causes the membrane to become depolarised.
- ❏ Thus the nerve action potential is followed by muscle action potential.
- ❏ Hence the impulse begins to spread over muscle tissue.

10) c)
Factors which determine muscle speed and tension are :
  4 marks for four from :
- ❏ Strength and frequency of stimulus :
- ❏ The greater strength and frequency of stimulus, the greater the muscle tension and speed of contraction.
- ❏ Recruitment of motor units (spatial summation) :
- ❏ While some motor units are active, others are relaxed, producing smooth movements rather than jerky movements.
- ❏ The use of proprioceptors which provide sensory information which can be used to regulate speed and tension.
- ❏ Percentage type of motor units ie fast twitch / slow twitch motor units - a greater percentage of ST motor units means decreased muscle tension and speed of movement.
- ❏ Larger diameter motor neurones and myelinated axons conduct action potentials faster therefore giving increased muscle speed.
- ❏ Length of muscle fibres.
- ❏ Type of muscular contraction : isometric, isotonic and isokinetic.
- ❏ Simple reflex responses - pain (hand withdraws from a hot handle).

NEUROMUSCULAR STRUCTURES AND CONTROL - ANSWERS QUESTION 10 (continued)

10) d)
Motor units control the strength of muscular contractions via :
   10 marks for ten from :
   ❏ The 'all-or-none-law' for muscle contraction means that all fibres in that motor unit will contract maximally at the same time.
   ❏ A muscle twitch : Created by a single stimulus.
   ❏ Wave summation : A rapid repetition of firing of impulses means that muscle fibres belonging to the motor unit (in which impulses occur) do not have time to relax.
   ❏ Therefore force exerted by the muscle fibres connected with that single motor unit increases.
   ❏ Gradation of contraction : Stimulation of many motor units increases strength of contraction.
   ❏ Effect is to produce the graded strengths required in sports movements.
   ❏ Spatial summation : Different motor units which contain different groups of muscle fibres spread across a muscle as a whole, are successively stimulated.
   ❏ This results in contractions across the whole muscle.
   ❏ Because different groups of muscle fibres are successively stimulated, any particular fibre will have a short period of inactivity between contractions, thereby reducing fatigue so the muscle as a whole can work longer.
   ❏ Long periods of sustained contraction produces isometric contraction.
   ❏ Fibre type of motor units : In addition there is a degree of specialisation among the units, a particular unit will control mainly one of the two main fibre types.
   ❏ The fast twitch motor units have large motor neurones, high motor neurone recruitment threshold and fast nerve conduction velocity.
   ❏ Therefore the tension in the whole muscle is large (since it is possible for a greater rate of motor unit firing for mainly fast twitch units) when compared with :
   ❏ Slow twitch motor units that have smaller motor neurones, low recruitment and slow impulse velocity.
   ❏ From a practical perspective the fast twitch motor units will be responsible for large forces that can be generated quickly.
   ❏ Whereas the slow twitch motor units are used in activities requiring endurance (less force but lasting longer).

CARDIAC STRUCTURE AND DYNAMICS

11) a)
Describe the flow of blood through the heart, identifying the major structures, including blood vessels, and their related functions.
   8 marks for eight from :
   ❏ The heart consists of myocardium, four chambers (atria and ventricles) and valves.
   ❏ The septum is myocardial tissue and divides the heart into a dual-action pump.
   ❏ Deoxygenated blood from the head and lower extremities of the body returns to the right atrium via the superior and inferior vena cavae respectively.
   ❏ At the same time, oxygenated blood is returning to the left atrium from the lungs via the pulmonary veins.
   ❏ The atria are thin-walled since they only have to pump blood into the bottom chambers.
   ❏ Blood passes through the tricuspid valve (on the right side) and mitral (bicuspid) valve on the left side into the ventricles.
   ❏ The ventricles are much longer and larger vessels because they have to be strong enough to pump blood into the two circulatory systems.
   ❏ When the right ventricle contracts (during ventricular systole) the tricuspid valve closes, preventing back flow of blood into the right atrium.
   ❏ And forcing the pulmonary valve open.
   ❏ Causing blood to be ejected via the pulmonary arteries towards the lungs.
   ❏ Where blood is oxygenated.
   ❏ At the same time, the thicker muscular wall of the left ventricle contracts
   ❏ And the mitral (bicuspid) valve closes.
   ❏ As blood is directed passed the aortic valve and into the systemic circulatory system.

CARDIAC STRUCTURE AND DYNAMICS - ANSWERS QUESTION 11 (continued)

11) b)
Explain the significance of the changes in pressure, volume and heart sounds from systole to diastole.
    4 marks for four from :
- Just prior to systole, ventricular volume is high and pressure is low (at the end of ventricular diastole).
- Next ventricular myocardium is stimulated (ventricular depolarisation).
- Followed by ventricles contracting (systole) and associated sharp rise in pressure.
- And decrease in volume.
- As cuspid valves close to prevent back flow of blood into the atria.
- Creating the first of the heart sounds 'lub'.
- When ventricular pressure exceeds the pressure of the pulmonary artery and aorta, the semi-lunar valves open.
- To eject blood into the pulmonary artery and aorta.
- Followed by the start of ventricular diastole, when pressure and volume are at their lowest points.
- Once the pressure inside the aorta and pulmonary arteries is greater than ventricular pressure.
- The semi-lunar vales close (2nd heart sound of 'dub') at the start of ventricular diastole.
- Where pressure remains very low and volume increases to pre-systolic values.

11) c) i)
Define stroke volume and end-diastolic volume.
    2 marks for :
- Stroke volume is the volume of blood pumped by the left ventricle of the heart per beat.
- End-diastolic volume is the amount of blood that remains in the left ventricle at the very end of diastole.

11) c) ii)
Using the information from the graph, work out the end-systolic volume before exercise has commenced.
    2 marks for :
-                  80   = 120   -   end-systolic volume before exercise.
- Therefore, end-systolic volume before exercise   = 40 ml

11) c) iii)
How is the Frank Starling's 'Law of the Heart Mechanism' involved in increasing stroke volume during exercise?
    3 marks for :
- During exercise venous return increases.
- Causing myocardial tissue to be stretched further than a rest.
- Resulting in myocardium to contract with greater force.

11) c) iv)
Identify the hormonal agent responsible for changes in stroke volume from the pre-exercise level to an increased volume during the exercise period. How does this agent affect myocardial tissue?
    3 marks for :
- Noradrenaline.
- Sympathetic nerve endings release noradrenaline.
- Which targets pacemaker (SA node) to increase force of contraction.

11) c) v)
What is the usual response of heart rate during the same bout of exercise?
- Heart rate rises proportionally to workload.

11) d) i)
Compare and contrast the heart of the elite endurance-trained athlete with the untrained subject. Give reasons for the differences in stroke volume at rest.
    2 marks for :
- The trained heart has an increased stroke volume at rest of 40 ml and during maximum exercise of 90ml.
- Lower resting heart by 20 beats and higher maximum heart rate by 30 beats when compared with the untrained person.
    4 marks for reasons :
- Enlargement of heart muscle (hypertrophy of heart muscle = bradycardia).
- Allowing the heart to contract with more force.
- Therefore ejecting more blood per beat (SV).
- And improved capillarisation of myocardial tissue to produce a more efficient pump.
- Therefore at rest the elite endurance-trained athlete has to pump less times to move the same volume of blood as an untrained heart.
- Thus resulting in a lower resting heart rate.

CARDIAC STRUCTURE AND DYNAMICS - ANSWERS QUESTION 11 (continued)

11) d) ii)
Calculate the maximum cardiac output for the endurance-trained athlete. Show your calculation.
  2 marks for two from :
☐ $\dot{Q}$ = SV   x   HR
☐ $\dot{Q}$ = 170   x   210
☐   = 35700 ml
☐ Or 35.7 l/min or 35.7 lmin^{-1}.

STRUCTURE AND FUNCTION OF THE VASCULAR SYSTEM

12) a)
  1 mark given for two correct choices, 2 marks for four correct choices, 3 marks for all correct :
☐ A - Arteries.   ☐ B - Arterioles.   ☐ C - Capillaries.   ☐ D - Venules.   ☐ E - Veins.

12) b)
Variations of velocity and pressure in vessel type A are caused by :
  5 marks for five from :
☐ As the ventricles contract (systole), blood is forced out of the heart into the arteries.
☐ This blood is under high pressure and flows at high velocity.
☐ Arteries are stretched by cardiac output (high blood pressure) during ventricular systole.
☐ As ventricles relax (diastole), blood is no longer forced out into the arteries.
☐ Artery walls recoil (contract inwards) during diastole.
☐ This is because blood is under lower pressure and at a slower velocity.

12) c)
The reasons for low blood velocity in vessel type C :
  2 marks for two from :
☐ Each capillary has a very small diameter, and therefore a small cross sectional area. But there are a very large number of capillaries into which the blood must flow.
☐ The total cross sectional area of capillaries is many times bigger than the arteries (and arterioles) from which the blood flows.
☐ Therefore the blood spreads out into all this space (in the capillary bed) and hence slows down substantially.

12) d)
The physiological significance of low blood velocity in vessel type C :
☐ Low velocity of blood allows time for physiological changes between blood in capillaries and tissues namely :
☐ Dissociation of oxyhaemoglobin to release oxygen.
☐ Diffusion of oxygen from blood to tissues.
☐ Carbon Dioxide from tissues to blood.
☐ Nutrients from blood to tissues.
☐ Waste products such as urea from tissues to blood.

12) e)
Changes produced during exercise would be :
  5 marks for five from :
☐ Refer to graph in diagram on right - changes labelled (narrow lines).
☐ Systolic blood pressure increases as work intensity increases.
☐ This results from increased cardiac output due to larger venous return.
☐ And increased muscle massage (muscle pump) and breathing movements (respiratory pump).
☐ Diastolic blood pressure hardly changes since this pressure reflects the pressure in the arteries when the heart is at rest (during diastole).
☐ Blood velocity rises to help drive blood quickly through the vasculature. (Hence via an increased heart rate and stroke volume, up to five times the volume of blood is driven through tissue per second than at rest).

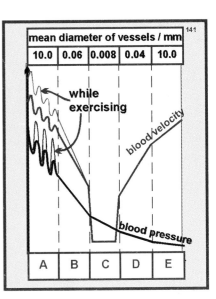

STRUCTURE AND FUNCTION OF THE VASCULAR SYSTEM

13) a)
Factors which cause resistance to blood flow through blood vessels are :
2 marks for two from :
❐ Friction between moving blood and the walls of blood vessels.
❐ Length of blood vessels.
❐ Diameter / lumen width of blood vessels.
❐ Viscosity of blood.

13) b)
❐ The first number (120 mmHg) refers to systolic blood pressure or blood pressure when heart (ventricles) is (are) contracting.
❐ The second number (80 mmHg) refers to diastolic blood pressure or blood pressure when heart (ventricles) is (are) relaxing.

13) c) i)
The right ventricle being less muscular has the effect :
❐ That the right ventricle has less powerful contractions than the left.
❐ Therefore lower blood pressure in pulmonary circulation to the lungs.

13) c) ii)
❐ The advantage is that the lungs do not fill with tissue fluid.
❐ Which would interfere with O_2 uptake by the lungs.
❐ High pressure would rupture capillary walls.

13) d)
It is necessary for there to be relatively high blood pressure to working muscle because :
❐ High blood pressure is needed to force tissue fluid (blood plasma).
❐ Out of capillaries into muscle tissue to surround active muscle tissues which are not in direct contact with the blood.
❐ This tissue fluid supplies oxygen and other nutrients (such as glucose) to tissue cells.
❐ And removes waste products (such as lactic acid and urea).

13) e)
Factors which help venous return are :
3 marks for three from :
❐ Action of muscle pump - rhythmic contractions of skeletal muscles squeezes veins to increase venous return.
❐ Action of one-way valves (pocket valves) ensure one way flow of venous blood back towards the heart.
❐ Action of the respiratory pump - downwards movements of the diaphragm associated with strong breathing action.
❐ This increases abdominal pressure on veins, pushing blood towards the thorax.
❐ And decreases thoracic pressure : sucking blood in veins towards the heart.
❐ Venomotor control - smooth muscles in thin wall of veins constrict reducing slightly size of lumen (venoconstriction), thereby increasing blood velocity.
❐ Starling's Law of the heart - atria (during emptying, after atrial systole) have lower pressure than the large veins causing a pressure gradient that aids venous return.

13) f)
5 marks for five from :
❐ Rhythmic aerobic exercise lowers blood pressure.
❐ As smooth muscle in smaller arterioles relaxes.
❐ And precapillary sphincters periodically relax causing capillary beds to open.
❐ Weight lifting raises both systolic and diastolic blood pressures to force blood into the capillary bed.
❐ Because this isometric position reduces the actions of the muscle and respiratory pumps.
❐ Which in turn reduces venous return, cardiac output, blood pressure and capillary blood flow.
❐ Therefore both systolic and diastolic pressures increase to force more blood through the capillaries of working muscles.

14) a)
Cardiac output increases during exercise because of :
❐ Increased heart rate.
❐ Increased stroke volume.
❐ Therefore increased cardiac output.

STRUCTURE AND FUNCTION OF THE VASCULAR SYSTEM - ANSWERS QUESTION 14 (continued)

14 b) i)
The percentage of total blood flow directed to skeletal muscle at rest is :
❑ $\dfrac{1000 \times 100}{5000} = 20\%$.

14) b) ii)
The percentage of total blood flow directed to skeletal muscle at rest is :
❑ $\dfrac{264000 \times 100}{30000} = 88\%$.

14) c)
Onset of exercise causes the following changes :
   3 marks for three from :
❑ Increase in concentration of adrenaline.
❑ Drop in oxygen levels.
❑ Rise in carbon dioxide levels.
❑ Decrease in pH levels / increase in acidity.
❑ Increase in temperature.
❑ Increase in concentration of ADP.
❑ Increase in concentration of potassium and / or magnesium ions.
   Specific explanation : linked to causes identified above, 3 marks for three from :
❑ Increased concentration of adrenaline acts directly on the heart.
❑ And increased concentration of potassium and / or magnesium also act directly on the heart to increase heart rate / blood flow as 'preparation for action' / response.
❑ A significant drop in oxygen concentration stimulates increase in heart rate in order to increase oxygenation of blood via respiration processes.
❑ Increase in carbon dioxide concentration stimulates increase in heart rate in order to increase rate of excretion of carbon dioxide via respiration processes.
❑ Increase in blood temperature stimulates heart rate / blood flow in order to move blood to the surface areas for cooling purposes.
❑ Increase in acidity (decrease in pH level) stimulates increase in blood flow in order to increase elimination of carbon dioxide via respiration .
❑ Rise in ADP stimulates enzyme activity to convert ADP back to ATP, but this process also requires oxygen and hence contributes to the reduction on oxygen concentration levels in the blood.
❑ High levels of potassium and magnesium are largely dealt with by the kidneys, but because of the 'blood shunt' mechanism, this occurs mainly after the exercise period.
   Or general explanation :
❑ These changes reflect disturbances to homeostatic equilibrium caused by high levels of exercise.
❑ Appropriate receptors in various parts of the body pick up the kinds identified above.
❑ Which in turn stimulate the heart to beat faster and hence increase blood flow in order to deal with the changes and / or attempt to return the body's systems to equilibrium / homeostasis.

14) d)
On the blood flow to the kidneys, liver and gut :
❑ These organs are the only ones to show a decrease in blood flow during exercise.
❑ They have a high blood flow at rest as they are involved in the processing of blood.
❑ The processing of blood function is delegated to secondary importance while exercise is taking place.

14) e)
Food should not be consumed within 3 hours of vigorous sport because :
❑ Digestion and absorption of food takes time and also requires adequate blood supply.
❑ The reduced blood flow during exercise prevents normal gut functioning and can cause stomach cramps.
❑ If the gut is full, then there will be some denial of blood shunt to the working muscles which could result in a degree of impaired performance.

14) f)
The effect of blood flow to the brain during exercise :
   3 marks for three from :
❑ Blood supply to the brain is not affected.
❑ Or there is a very slight decrease during exercise (particularly during maximal exercise - this is why fainting can occur in this case).
❑ It is necessary for the brain to function normally during exercise.
❑ Therefore normal blood supply must be maintained.

CARDIO-RESPIRATORY DYNAMICS

15) a)

Increases in heart rate and ventilation go hand in hand because :
Just prior to exercise :
   1 mark for one from :
- ❏ Heart rate and ventilation increase by small amounts (anticipatory rise).
- ❏ This is due to psychological factors which cause the release of hormones such as adrenaline.

During the first minute of the exercise period :
   3 marks for three from :
- ❏ Heart rate and ventilation increase rapidly due to a period of anaerobic energy production.
- ❏ During which time there are inadequate supply of oxygen to working muscles (thus producing an oxygen deficit).
- ❏ And increased proprioceptive stimulation (nervous reflexes in working joints and muscles).
- ❏ And hormonal release.

As the heart muscle gets warmer, due to increased workloads :
   3 marks for three from :
- ❏ Venous return increases.
- ❏ HR will continue to rise (intrinsic factor).
- ❏ The production of waste products (such as lactic acid - chemical), from anaerobic respiration, will accumulate in the muscle and blood.
- ❏ And further stimulate a more gradual increases in heart rate until the completion of the exercise.
- ❏ Indicating an increased reliance on anaerobic metabolism.
- ❏ As muscle pH decreases even further (chemical).
- ❏ Whilst ventilation reaches a steady state showing that O_2 uptake and O_2 consumption are reaching a steady state (chemical).

During the recovery :
   3 marks for three from :
- ❏ Heart rate and ventilation rapidly decline during the first two minutes.
- ❏ This is due to the cessation of the muscle pump and proprioceptive stimulation and adrenaline (intrinsic, neural and hormonal factors), and phosphagen restoration.
- ❏ Followed by a much slower recovery period during which metabolites such as carbon dioxide and lactic acid are cleared (chemical), and excess heat removed.
- ❏ And body systems return to resting values.

15) b)

The sympathetic and parasympathetic nervous systems affect :
   Heart rates (2 marks for two from) :
- ❏ Prior to and during the exercise period heart rate increases. This is due to the effects of sympathetic nervous stimulation.
- ❏ Which transmits impulses from the cardiac centre to the pacemaker or SA node.
- ❏ This is followed by the action of parasympathetic nervous stimulation.
- ❏ Which responds to circulatory messages received from the sensory receptors by sending out impulses via the vagus or parasympathetic nerve to the pacemaker to slow down heart rate during the recovery period.
   Ventilation Rates (2 marks for two from) :
- ❏ The rhythmicity centre controls basic rate of breathing.
- ❏ Via two nerve circuits which work antagonistically.
- ❏ To bring about inspiration and expiration.

STRUCTURE and FUNCTION of the RESPIRATORY SYSTEM

16) a)

Molecule of air travels from the trachea to alveoli via :
   (1mark for two, 2 marks for four, 3 marks for all) :
- ❏ Trachea.
- ❏ Larynx.
- ❏ Bronchi.
- ❏ Bronchioles.
- ❏ Respiratory bronchioles.
- ❏ Alveolar ducts.

STRUCTURE and FUNCTION of the RESPIRATORY SYSTEM

16) b)
The Pleura of the lungs is a :
   1 mark for one from :
- ❒ Double skinned bag containing pleural fluid.
- ❒ Inner surface is attached to the lungs (visceral pleura).
- ❒ Outer surface (parietal pleura) is attached to the thoracic wall and diaphragm.

The function of the pleura :
   2 marks for two from :
- ❒ The pleural fluid reduces friction between the two membranes to allow them to move easily on one other during breathing.
- ❒ During inspiration, as the outer pleura expands (the inspiratory musculature contracts - external intercostals and accessories - see 16) c) below - ribcage moves outwards), the pressure between the pleura gets smaller.
- ❒ This reduced pressure drags the inner pleura outwards.
- ❒ The greater air pressure inside the lungs forces the inner lung surface outwards increasing lung volume.
- ❒ Conversely, during expiration, lung volume decreases, producing an increase in pleural pressure causing the lungs to contract and expel air (expiration).

16) c)
The mechanism of inspiration during physical activity :
   6 marks for six from :
- ❒ Phrenic and intercostal nerves send impulses to respiratory muscles.
- ❒ This causes the external intercostal muscles to contract.
- ❒ And also causes accessory muscles (sternocleidomastoids, scalenes, and pectoral minor) to contract.
- ❒ And causes an increase in the size of the thorax.
- ❒ Thus decreasing the intrapleural and alveolar pressures.
- ❒ So that air moves along a pressure gradient from the atmosphere into the lungs.
- ❒ The larger atmospheric air pressure forces air through the bronchus into the lower pressure lung space.

16) d)
The chemical stimuli controlling rate and depth of breathing :
- ❒ pCO_2 (is the major regulator of respiration).   ❒ pO_2.   ❒ pH.

16) e)
The chemical stimuli control rate and depth of breathing by :
- ❒ Effect of exercise is to increase the production of CO_2, and H^+, and decrease O_2 and pH.
- ❒ An increase in pCO_2 or a decrease in pH stimulates the peripheral and central chemoreceptors.
- ❒ Which send nerve impulses into the inspiratory control centre in the medulla.
- ❒ Then out via the phrenic and intercostal nerves to the respiratory muscles.
- ❒ Which contract more forcefully (increased TV) and more frequently (increased f).
- ❒ The response is to decrease pCO_2, and increase pH and pO_2.

OXYGEN DISSOCIATION

17 a) i)
   See graph in diagram on the right. Marks awarded for :
- ❒ Correctly labelled and scaled axes.
- ❒ Correctly plotted points for pCO_2 = 5.3 kPa.
- ❒ Correctly plotted points for pCO_2 = 9.3 kPa.
- ❒ Appropriate lines drawn.

17) a) ii)
   From the graph :
- ❒ At 5.3 kPa saturation of Hb is 67%.
- ❒ At 9.3 kPa saturation of Hb is 53% - a difference of 14%. (approximately)
- ❒ These curves show how increasing levels of CO_2 affect the dissociation of oxyhaemoglobin.

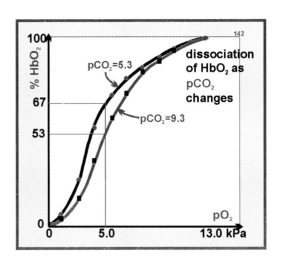

OXYGEN DISSOCIATION - ANSWERS Question 17) a) continued

17) a) iii)
The effect of increased pCO_2 in venous blood as it passes through muscle tissue :
   5 marks for five from :
- Oxygen is given up readily to muscle cells.
- Most of the carbon dioxide produced is converted to carbonic acid in the red blood cell.
- During this reaction the hydrogen ions released react with oxyhaemoglobin to produce haemoglobinic acid.
- This reaction thus releases further oxygen from the haemoglobin into the muscle cell tissue.
- Active muscle releases a lot more carbon dioxide as the muscle switches to anaerobic respiration thus further lowering blood pH.
- The lactic acid produced in the lactic anaerobic respiration process also tends to lower blood pH.
- This causes even more oxygen to be released.

17) a) iv)
The steep part of the O_2 dissociation curve means :
- A small decrease in pO_2 within the range relevant to the steep part of the curve.
- Results in the release of relatively large amounts of oxygen.

17) b) i)
The factors encouraging dissociation of HbO_2 are :
   Consult graphs on this topic on page 1.9 of this book, 3 marks for three from :
- Increased concentration gradient due to low pO_2 in tissues.
- Increase in temperature.
- Decrease in pH value.
- Increase in CO_2 concentrations.

17) b) ii)
The type of muscle fibre most able to utilise HbO_2 dissociation :
- Slow twitch (ST) fibre / type 1 because they have the greater blood supply.
- ST have more myoglobin.
- ST have a greater oxidative potential / greater capacity for aerobic respiration.

LUNG VOLUMES and CAPACITIES

18) a) i)
   Definitions :
- Resting tidal volume is that volume of air that is breathed in or out during one breath at rest.

18) a) ii)
- Expiratory reserve volume is that volume of air that can be forcibly expired over & above resting tidal volume.

18) a) iii)
- Vital capacity is the maximal volume of air that can be forcibly expired after maximal inspiration in one breath.

18) a) iv)
- Residual volume is that volume of air remaining in the lungs after maximal expiration.

18) b)
The effects of exercise on Tidal Volume :
- During exercise there are increased levels of pCO_2.
- Stimulate breathing muscles to increase rate of breathing.
- Which limits the amount of air that can move in and out of the lungs in one breath.

18) c)
- Minute ventilation is the total volume of air inspired or expired in one minute.
- Minute ventilation is calculated as a product of resting tidal volume and breathing rate per minute.
- Therefore $\dot{V}E$ = 500 x 12 = 6000cm^3 or 6 litres or 6dm^3.

18) d)
- If completely emptied, the lungs would collapse.
- Due to surface tension the lungs would be unable to be re-inflated (opposite surfaces of the lungs would stick together, the surfaces would adhere to one another).

18) e)
Anatomical dead space is :
   2 marks for two from :
- Those parts of the respiratory system not well supplied with capillaries.
- Which are therefore incapable of being involved in gaseous exchange.
- Example parts : pharynx, larynx, trachea, bronchi, bronchioles.

LUNG VOLUMES and CAPACITIES - ANSWERS Question 18 continued

18) f)
Elite endurance performers cannot be identified from their spirometer trace because :
2 marks for two from :
❏ Because spirometers measure lung volumes / capacities they are poor predictors of athletic performance.
❏ Because there is no definite scientific and provable link between lung capacity (of an untrained individual) and athletic potential.
❏ On the other hand, individuals with larger lung capacities could well (when trained) have substantial aerobic potential.

Jan Roscoe

SELECTED BIBLIOGRAPHY

ADAM   1999   Interactive Physiology - multipack CDROMS.   Benjamin / Cummings.

Bastian, G.F.   1993   An Illustrated Review of Anatomy and Physiology - Series.   Addison Longman.
- The Skeletal and Muscular Systems.
- The Nervous System.
- The Respiratory System.
- The Cardiovascular System.

Beashel, P.   1996   Advanced Studies in Physical Education and Sport.   Thomas Nelson.

Blakey, P.   1992   The Muscle Book.   Bibliotek Books.

Boulton & Hawker.   1988   Functional Anatomy - Sports Science Video.   University of Western Australia.

Clegg, C.   1995   Exercise Physiology.   Feltham Press.

Davis, R.J. et.al.   2000   Physical Education and the Study of Sport 4e.   Mosby.

EAI   1999   CDROM, The Dynamic Human - version 2.0.   McGraw-Hill.

Foss, M.L.   1998   Fox's Physiological basis for Exercise and Sport.   McGraw-Hill.

Honeybourne, J. et al.
2000   Advanced Level Physical Education and Sport 2e.   Nelson Thornes.
2000   Advanced Level Physical Education and Sport for AS level.   Nelson Thornes.
2001   Teacher's Resource Pack   Nelson Thornes.

Galligan, F. et al.   2000   Advanced PE for Edexcel.   Heinemann.

Kingston, B.   1996   Understanding Muscles, A Practical Guide to Muscle Function. Chapman & Hall.

McArdle, W.D.   2000   Essentials of Exercise Physiology 2e.   Lippincott, Williams and Wilkins.

Powers, S.K.   2000   Exercise Physiology, Theory and Applications 4e. McGraw-Hill.

Roscoe, J.V.   2000   Teacher's Guide to Physical Education and the Study of Sport 4e
Anatomy &Physiology.   Jan Roscoe Publications.

Thompson, C.W.   1998   Manual of Structural Kinesiology 13e.   WC Brown / McGraw-Hill.

Wesson, K. et.al.   2000   PE and Sport a Complete A level Guide 2e.   Hodder and Stoughton.

Wilmore, J.H.   1999   Physiology of Sport and Exercise 2e.   Human Kinetics.

Wirhed, R.   1997   Athletic Ability and the Anatomy of Motion 2e.   Mosby.

ENERGY CONCEPTS

EXERCISE PHYSIOLOGY

ENERGY
- Is the capacity to do work (measured in joules)
- Work = force x distance moved
- POWER = $\dfrac{\text{Energy (joules)}}{\text{time (sec)}}$ = ?   Watts

CHEMICAL ENERGY
- Is energy that is produced by a complex series of chemical reactions.
- Which can then be made available as mechanical energy.

KINETIC ENERGY
- Is energy due to movement which can be caused by muscular contraction.

POTENTIAL ENERGY
- Is stored energy due to gravity.

ATP
- Adenosine triphosphate

EXOTHERMIC REACTIONS
- Give out energy (via enzyme ATPase).
- ATP is the energy currency of the body.

$$ATP \xrightarrow{\text{ATPase}} ADP + P_i + Energy$$

- This reaction releases energy which causes muscle to contract (and all other bodily functions).
- Only 2 secs supply during maximum work.
- Then ATP is created via the energy systems depending on intensity and duration of the exercise period.

ENDOTHERMIC REACTIONS
- Take in energy (i.e. restoration of ATP from ADP).

ATP/ PC (PHOSPHOCREATINE) SYSTEM
- Alactic anaerobic energy system.
- High intensity maximum work.
- Duration short (dominant system from 3-10 sec.).
- After 10 seconds of flat out work all the PC is used up.
- No oxygen needed therefore ANAEROBIC metabolism.
- Takes place in muscle sarcoplasm.

THE COUPLED REACTION
- Is the two stage process by which PC is used to recreate ATP once it has broken down into ADP + P_i

- Stage 1 $PC \xrightarrow{\text{creatine kinase}} P_i + C + energy$
- Stage 2 $energy + ADP + P_i ===> ATP$
- Net effect $PC + ADP ===> ATP + C$

TRAINING ADAPTATIONS
- Increase in ATP/ PC stores.
- Delayed alactic / lactic threshold.

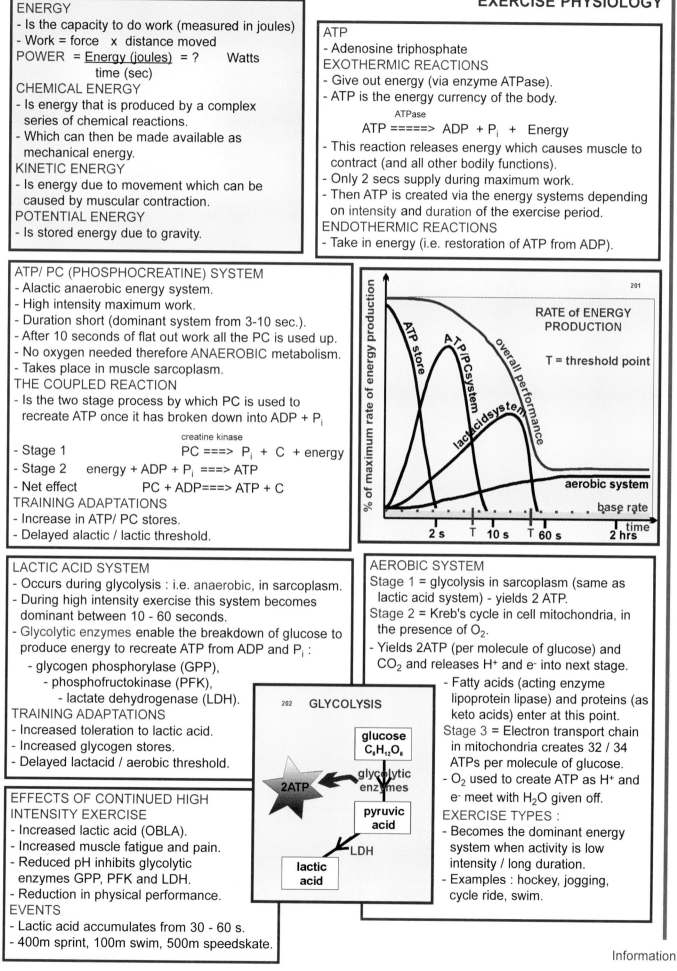

201

RATE of ENERGY PRODUCTION

T = threshold point

% of maximum rate of energy production

ATP store

ATP/PCsystem

lactacidsystem

overall performance

aerobic system

base rate

2 s   T   10 s   T   60 s   time 2 hrs

LACTIC ACID SYSTEM
- Occurs during glycolysis : i.e. anaerobic, in sarcoplasm.
- During high intensity exercise this system becomes dominant between 10 - 60 seconds.
- Glycolytic enzymes enable the breakdown of glucose to produce energy to recreate ATP from ADP and P_i :
    - glycogen phosphorylase (GPP),
    - phosphofructokinase (PFK),
    - lactate dehydrogenase (LDH).

TRAINING ADAPTATIONS
- Increased toleration to lactic acid.
- Increased glycogen stores.
- Delayed lactacid / aerobic threshold.

EFFECTS OF CONTINUED HIGH INTENSITY EXERCISE
- Increased lactic acid (OBLA).
- Increased muscle fatigue and pain.
- Reduced pH inhibits glycolytic enzymes GPP, PFK and LDH.
- Reduction in physical performance.

EVENTS
- Lactic acid accumulates from 30 - 60 s.
- 400m sprint, 100m swim, 500m speedskate.

202   **GLYCOLYSIS**

glucose $C_6H_{12}O_6$

glycolytic enzymes

2ATP

pyruvic acid

LDH

lactic acid

AEROBIC SYSTEM
Stage 1 = glycolysis in sarcoplasm (same as lactic acid system) - yields 2 ATP.
Stage 2 = Kreb's cycle in cell mitochondria, in the presence of O_2.
- Yields 2ATP (per molecule of glucose) and CO_2 and releases H^+ and e^- into next stage.
- Fatty acids (acting enzyme lipoprotein lipase) and proteins (as keto acids) enter at this point.
Stage 3 = Electron transport chain in mitochondria creates 32 / 34 ATPs per molecule of glucose.
- O_2 used to create ATP as H^+ and e^- meet with H_2O given off.

EXERCISE TYPES :
- Becomes the dominant energy system when activity is low intensity / long duration.
- Examples : hockey, jogging, cycle ride, swim.

MITOCHONDRIA

MITOCHONDRIA
- Located immediately beneath sarcolemma to provide energy for transport of ions and metabolites across sarcolemma.
- Located deep within muscle fibres to provide energy for muscle contraction (via ATP).
- Act as power plants of the cell
- Where O_2 is consumed via the Electron Transport Chain in the creation of ATP.
- Slow twitch fibres have large numbers.

EFFICIENCY OF RESPIRATION
- Depends on food fuel biomechanical pathway :

Anaerobic route :
- 2 ATP from each mol. of glucose
- Rapid fuel breakdown.

Aerobic route :
- 36-38 ATP from each mole. of glucose = 18-19 times efficient than anaerobic route.

ENERGY CONTINUUM

ENERGY CONTINUUM
- This term prescribes the dominance of energy systems in relation to intensity and duration of workload.
- Factors affecting energy continuum :
  - Level of fitness : including training adaptations,
  - Diet : high CHO diet helps replenish glycogen stores, dietary supplements such as creatine and glutamine enhance anaerobic work.
  - Availability of O_2, for example reduced pO_2 at altitude.

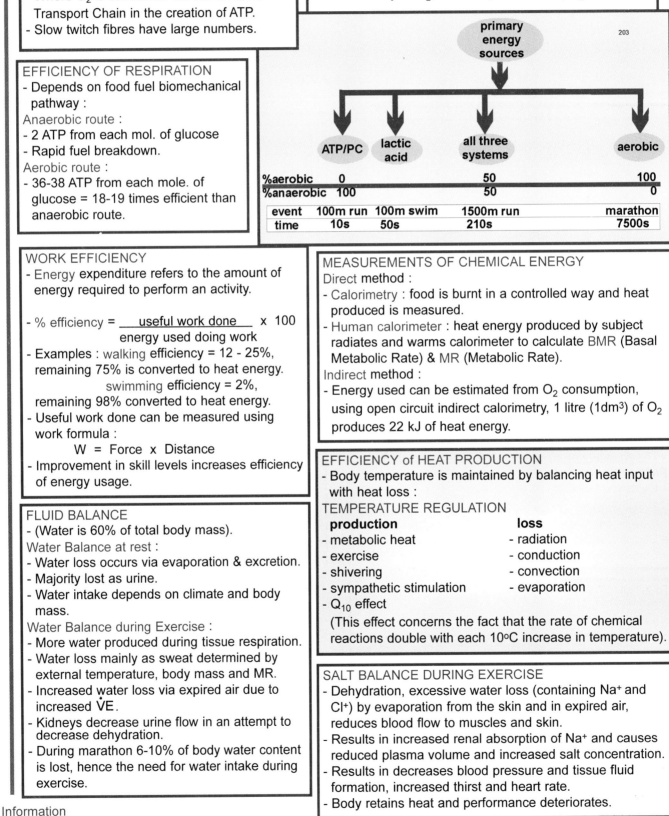

event	100m run	100m swim	1500m run	marathon
time	10s	50s	210s	7500s

WORK EFFICIENCY
- Energy expenditure refers to the amount of energy required to perform an activity.

- % efficiency = $\dfrac{\text{useful work done}}{\text{energy used doing work}} \times 100$
- Examples : walking efficiency = 12 - 25%, remaining 75% is converted to heat energy.
  swimming efficiency = 2%, remaining 98% converted to heat energy.
- Useful work done can be measured using work formula :
  $$W = \text{Force} \times \text{Distance}$$
- Improvement in skill levels increases efficiency of energy usage.

MEASUREMENTS OF CHEMICAL ENERGY
Direct method :
- Calorimetry : food is burnt in a controlled way and heat produced is measured.
- Human calorimeter : heat energy produced by subject radiates and warms calorimeter to calculate BMR (Basal Metabolic Rate) & MR (Metabolic Rate).
Indirect method :
- Energy used can be estimated from O_2 consumption, using open circuit indirect calorimetry, 1 litre ($1dm^3$) of O_2 produces 22 kJ of heat energy.

EFFICIENCY of HEAT PRODUCTION
- Body temperature is maintained by balancing heat input with heat loss :

TEMPERATURE REGULATION

production	loss
- metabolic heat	- radiation
- exercise	- conduction
- shivering	- convection
- sympathetic stimulation	- evaporation

- Q_{10} effect
(This effect concerns the fact that the rate of chemical reactions double with each 10°C increase in temperature).

FLUID BALANCE
- (Water is 60% of total body mass).
Water Balance at rest :
- Water loss occurs via evaporation & excretion.
- Majority lost as urine.
- Water intake depends on climate and body mass.
Water Balance during Exercise :
- More water produced during tissue respiration.
- Water loss mainly as sweat determined by external temperature, body mass and MR.
- Increased water loss via expired air due to increased $\dot{V}E$.
- Kidneys decrease urine flow in an attempt to decrease dehydration.
- During marathon 6-10% of body water content is lost, hence the need for water intake during exercise.

SALT BALANCE DURING EXERCISE
- Dehydration, excessive water loss (containing Na^+ and Cl^+) by evaporation from the skin and in expired air, reduces blood flow to muscles and skin.
- Results in increased renal absorption of Na^+ and causes reduced plasma volume and increased salt concentration.
- Results in decreases blood pressure and tissue fluid formation, increased thirst and heart rate.
- Body retains heat and performance deteriorates.

THE RECOVERY PROCESS

OXYGEN DEFICIT
- The difference between the O_2 required during exercise and the O_2 actually consumed during the activity.

EXCESS POST EXERCISE OXYGEN CONSUMPTION (EPOC) or O_2 DEBT
- Oxygen consumed after exercise is finished will replace ATP & glycogen stores as soon as possible.
- EPOC is the excess O_2 consumed following exercise which is needed to replace ATP (which has been converted to ADP during activity period).
- And remove lactic acid created during previous exercise.
- 2 components : ALACTACID, and LACTACID.

RESPIRATORY EXCHANGE RATIO

RESPIRATORY EXCHANGE RATIO (RER) or RQ
- Determined by measurement of respiratory gases.

$$RER = \frac{\text{amount of } CO_2 \text{ produced}}{\text{amount of } O_2 \text{ used}}$$

- Used to estimate energy expenditure per litre of O_2 consumed.
- Used to estimate proportion of fats and CHO being oxidised.
- RER = 0.85, means that equal mixture of fats and CHO (carbohydrate) are being burnt.
- RER for : fats = 0.70, protein = 0.80, and CHO = 1.0
- When RER value exceeds 1.00, anaerobic respiration occurs, since more CO_2 is produced than O_2 consumed.

Oxygen consumption during exercise and recovery 204

ALACTACID COMPONENT
- Involves conversion of ADP back to PC & ATP.
- Known as restoration of muscle phosphagen.
- A very rapid process (120s for full restoration).
- Size 2 to 3.5 litres (of O_2).

ACHIEVED VIA THREE MECHANISMS
- Aerobic conversion of CHO into CO_2 & H_2O to manufacture ATP from ADP + P_i.
- Some of the ATP is immediately utilised to create PC using the 'coupled reaction'.
- Small amount of ATP is remanufactured via glycogen producing small amounts of lactic acid.

LACTACID COMPONENT
- High intensity exercise up to 60 seconds creates lactic acid.
- Relatively large amounts of lactic acid (15 to 20 times the resting value of 1 to 2 mmol/ litre) are produced during high intensity exercise.
- O_2 is needed to remove this lactic acid.
- Which begins to restore muscle and liver glycogen.
- The recovery process is relatively slow i.e. up to 1 hr.

FATE OF LACTIC ACID
- Oxidation into CO_2 + H_2O 65%
- Conversion into glycogen then stored in   20%
  muscle and liver (Cori Cycle)
- Conversion into protein   10%
- Conversion into glucose   5%

EFFECTS of TRAINING on the ALACTACID COMPONENT
- Increase ATP and PC stores in muscle cells.
- Improved ability to provide O_2.
- Therefore increase in possible size of alactacid component.

IMPLICATIONS for INTERVAL TRAINING
- If there is only a short interval between bouts of exercise.
- Level of phosphagen stores gradually reduces.

RESTORATION OF MUSCLE GLYCOGEN STORES
- Short duration high intensity exercise, restoration takes up to 2 hours.
- Prolonged low intensity aerobic exercise, restoration can take days.
- High carbohydrate diet speeds up this process.
- Therefore there is a need for athlete to enable full restoration to take place as soon as possible after the activity.
- Sportspeople should take high CHO loaded drinks immediately following exercise.

INCREASED BODY TEMPERATURE and HORMONAL RELEASE increase EPOC.

RESTORATION of MYOGLOBIN
- Myoglobin is reoxygenated within 2 minutes.

IMPLICATIONS for INTERVAL TRAINING
- Recovery between bouts of exercise is dependent on heart rate values (as HR falls during recovery, its value is a measure of the state of lactacid recovery).
- Active recovery / cool-down speeds up removal of lactic acid.
- Variance in sessions doesn't always stress lactic acid system.

EXERCISE AND NUTRITION

METABOLISM
- Is the sum total of all the chemical reactions that take place in the human body to sustain life.

BASAL METABOLIC RATE (BMR)
- Is the least rate of energy usage needed to carry out basic body functions.
- Measured lying down after 8 hours sleep and 12 hours fasting.

TOTAL METABOLIC RATE
- Is the sum of BMR + energy requirements for ALL daily activities.

FUEL FOR EXERCISE
- A balanced diet contains the correct proportions of CHO, fats, proteins minerals, vitamins, water and roughage needed to maintain good health.
- The liver acts as the food fuel exchange organ.

CHO (CARBOHYDRATE) (60% of balanced diet)
- Is the principal energy giver.
- Absorbed as glucose (monosaccharides) in small intestine.
- Circulates as blood glucose and acts as an immediate fuel food for high intensity anaerobic exercise.
- Excess stored as muscle and liver glycogen.
- Then excess converted to fat.
- 1 gm of CHO yields 17kJ of energy.

CARBO / GLYCOGEN LOADING
- For endurance events.
- Principles :
  depletion / repletion.

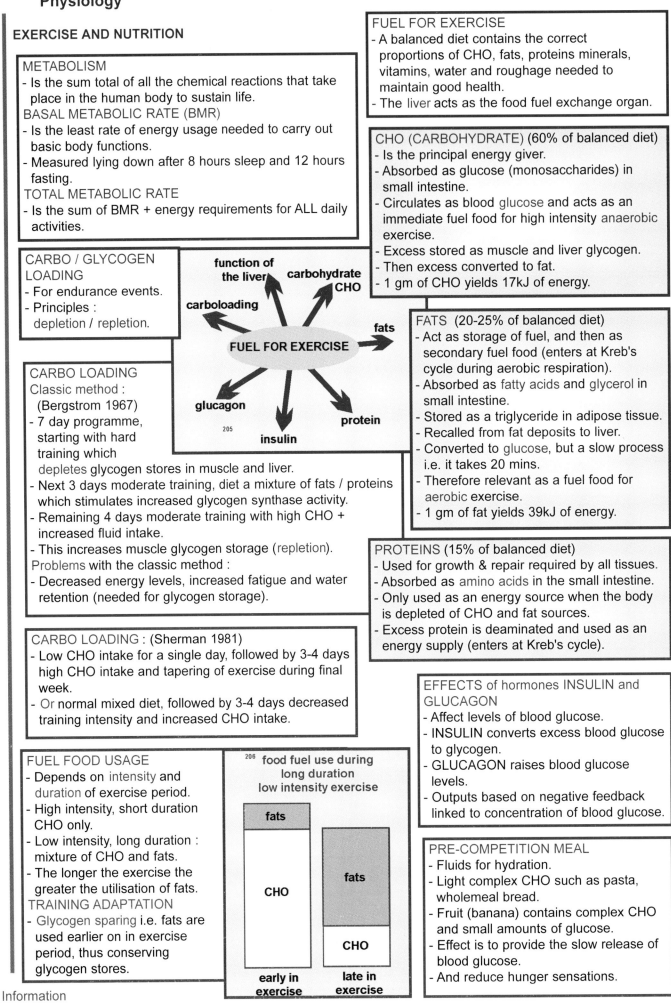

FATS (20-25% of balanced diet)
- Act as storage of fuel, and then as secondary fuel food (enters at Kreb's cycle during aerobic respiration).
- Absorbed as fatty acids and glycerol in small intestine.
- Stored as a triglyceride in adipose tissue.
- Recalled from fat deposits to liver.
- Converted to glucose, but a slow process i.e. it takes 20 mins.
- Therefore relevant as a fuel food for aerobic exercise.
- 1 gm of fat yields 39kJ of energy.

CARBO LOADING
Classic method :
  (Bergstrom 1967)
- 7 day programme, starting with hard training which depletes glycogen stores in muscle and liver.
- Next 3 days moderate training, diet a mixture of fats / proteins which stimulates increased glycogen synthase activity.
- Remaining 4 days moderate training with high CHO + increased fluid intake.
- This increases muscle glycogen storage (repletion).
Problems with the classic method :
- Decreased energy levels, increased fatigue and water retention (needed for glycogen storage).

PROTEINS (15% of balanced diet)
- Used for growth & repair required by all tissues.
- Absorbed as amino acids in the small intestine.
- Only used as an energy source when the body is depleted of CHO and fat sources.
- Excess protein is deaminated and used as an energy supply (enters at Kreb's cycle).

CARBO LOADING : (Sherman 1981)
- Low CHO intake for a single day, followed by 3-4 days high CHO intake and tapering of exercise during final week.
- Or normal mixed diet, followed by 3-4 days decreased training intensity and increased CHO intake.

EFFECTS of hormones INSULIN and GLUCAGON
- Affect levels of blood glucose.
- INSULIN converts excess blood glucose to glycogen.
- GLUCAGON raises blood glucose levels.
- Outputs based on negative feedback linked to concentration of blood glucose.

FUEL FOOD USAGE
- Depends on intensity and duration of exercise period.
- High intensity, short duration CHO only.
- Low intensity, long duration : mixture of CHO and fats.
- The longer the exercise the greater the utilisation of fats.

TRAINING ADAPTATION
- Glycogen sparing i.e. fats are used earlier on in exercise period, thus conserving glycogen stores.

PRE-COMPETITION MEAL
- Fluids for hydration.
- Light complex CHO such as pasta, wholemeal bread.
- Fruit (banana) contains complex CHO and small amounts of glucose.
- Effect is to provide the slow release of blood glucose.
- And reduce hunger sensations.

FITNESS

PHYSICAL FITNESS
- This is the capability to meet physical and physiological demands made by a sporting activity.

HEALTH RELATED FITNESS
- This concept represents aspects of physical fitness such as flexibility, endurance and body composition, which are associated with improving general health.

MOTOR FITNESS
- This is the capability to perform successfully at a particular game.

PHYSICAL FITNESS (207)
- cardiovascular respiratory endurance — bleep test
- speed — 30m sprint
- strength — 1RM
- local muscle endurance — Abdominal curl bleep test
- flexibility — sit & reach test
- endurance — Cooper's 12min run
- strength endurance — Wingate 30s test
- body composition — skinfolds

MOTOR FITNESS (208)
- speed — 30m sprint
- power — Sergeant jump
- agility — Illinois run
- reaction time — stick drop test
- static balance — beam balance
- coordination — juggling
- dynamic balance — cartwheel

AEROBIC CAPACITY
- The ability to do work which is dependent on the aerobic mechanism of energy supply.
- Expressed as O_2 uptake.

$\dot{V}O_{2max}$

- Maximum amount of O_2 that a person can consume per minute during a progressive exercise test to exhaustion.
- Stresses Slow Twitch fibres.
- Relevant to activities / games lasting longer than a few minutes.

FACTORS AFFECTING $\dot{V}O_{2max}$
- Ability of the muscular cellular tissue system to extract O_2 (peripheral factors).
- Combined ability of cardiovascular / respiratory systems to transport O_2 (central factors).

USEFULNESS of $\dot{V}O_{2max}$ TESTING
- Gives maximal physiological capacity.
- Identifies weaknesses.
- Repeated tests give comparative profiles.

TRAINING EFFECTS ON $\dot{V}O_{2max}$
- Large increases of $\dot{V}O_{2max}$ due to :
  - aerobic adaptation of heart & lungs (refer to page 2.8)
  - increased capillary density surrounding muscle tissue
  - increased enzyme activity within mitochondria
  - therefore increased $a\text{-}\bar{v}O_2$diff means more O_2 is available for tissue cell respiration.

SPORTS SPECIFIC TESTS
- Recognise specificity of event.
- Example sprinting on a non-motorised treadmill.
- Use of flume pools for swimmers, paddle ergometers for canoeists, ski walking and rowing machines.

RELIABILITY of TESTS
- A test that gives consistent tests following retesting.

VALIDITY of TESTS
- A test measures what is claims to measure.

LIMITATIONS of TESTING
- Some tests are less reliable because there are so many variables which can vary between individuals taking a test.
- Examples would include the motivation of the individual to complete a test, or the skill level or technique of the subject.

AEROBIC TESTS

$\dot{V}O_{2max}$ by DIRECT MEASUREMENT
- Exhaled gas is passed through a GAS ANALYSER.
- Estimates CO_2 exhaled (per minute).
- Computer calculates $\dot{V}O_2$.
- For example, treadmill test / cycle ergometry.

PREDICTED $\dot{V}O_{2max}$ by INDIRECT MEASUREMENT
- Based on linear relationships between $\dot{V}O_2$ and heart rate.
- Measure HR, predict $\dot{V}O_{2max}$ from tables linking HR with $\dot{V}O_{2max}$.
- Examples, Queen's College Step Test, Harvard or Fitech Step Test, PWC170 Test.
- Or based on the relationship between distance run and $\dot{V}O_{2max}$.
- Examples, NCF Multistage Shuttle Run Test (bleep test), Cooper's 12 min Running Test.

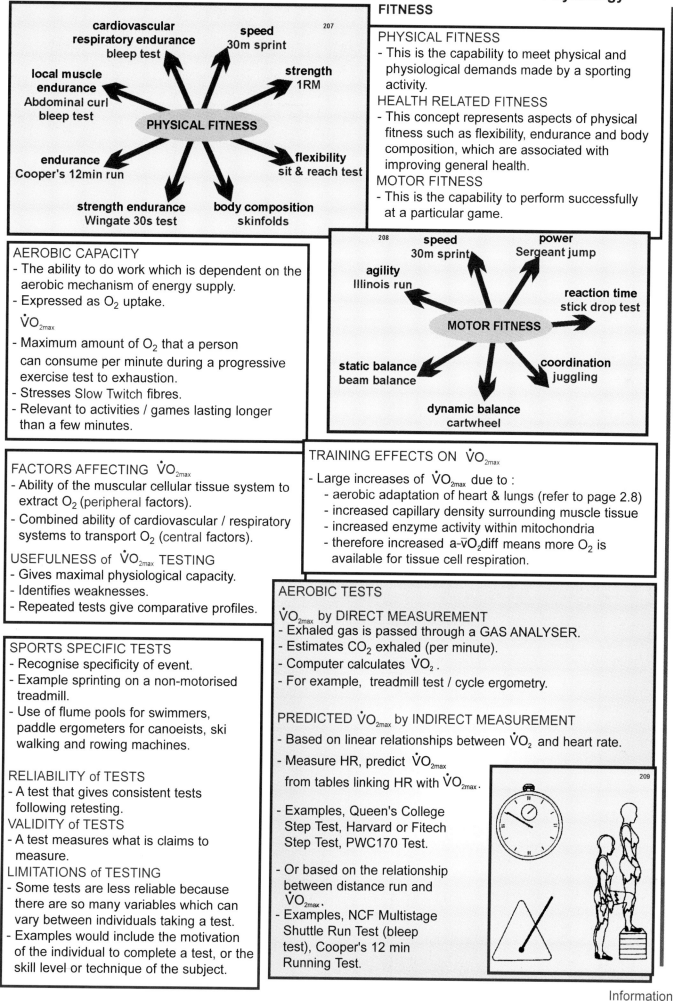

(209)

2.6 Exercise Physiology

ANAEROBIC CAPACITY AND TESTS

ANAEROBIC CAPACITY
- This is the maximum amount of energy that can be created by anaerobic glycolysis.
- Measured by high intensity tests lasting up to 60s.
- Highest power output is represented as peak power (this is the alactacid capacity, produced by ATP-PC system).
- Lower output represented by lactacid capacity (lactic acid system).
- Stresses FTG (Fast Twitch Glycolytic) fibres.
- Relevant to high intensity sports such as sprints.
- The Wingate 30 s cycling test has high reliability for mean and peak power, although alactacid and lactacid capacities cannot be clearly separated.

TRAINING APPLICATION
- Anaerobic Power only increased when training loads exceed 85 % of 1RM, low repetitions and sets (refer to page 2.7).

ANAEROBIC POWER TESTS
- Anaerobic Power is the maximum rate at which energy can be produced by the ATP/PC system.
- Sargeant (Vertical) Jump : high reliability, does not take into account length of levers.
- Standing long jump : less reliable because it is a more difficult skill.
- Margaria-Kalaman staircase climb estimates peak power:

$$P = \frac{m \times 9.8 \times D}{t}$$

high reliability, biased towards subject's body mass (m in kg).
- Isokinetic lido testing gives a high correlation between lean body mass and strength of knee extensors.

TRAINING PRINCIPLES AND PRACTICES

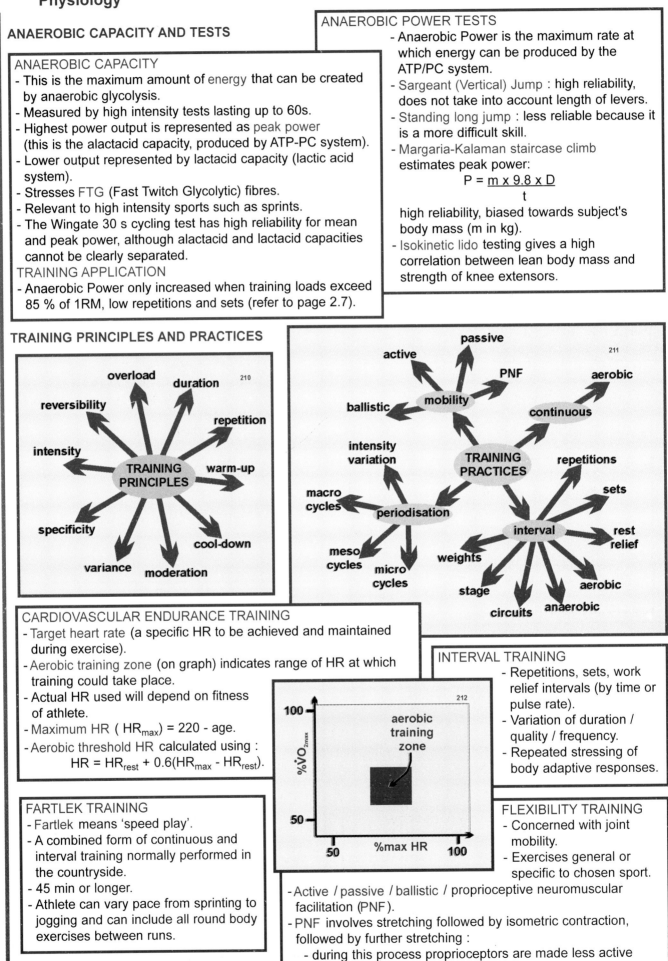

CARDIOVASCULAR ENDURANCE TRAINING
- Target heart rate (a specific HR to be achieved and maintained during exercise).
- Aerobic training zone (on graph) indicates range of HR at which training could take place.
- Actual HR used will depend on fitness of athlete.
- Maximum HR (HR_{max}) = 220 - age.
- Aerobic threshold HR calculated using :
$$HR = HR_{rest} + 0.6(HR_{max} - HR_{rest}).$$

INTERVAL TRAINING
- Repetitions, sets, work relief intervals (by time or pulse rate).
- Variation of duration / quality / frequency.
- Repeated stressing of body adaptive responses.

FARTLEK TRAINING
- Fartlek means 'speed play'.
- A combined form of continuous and interval training normally performed in the countryside.
- 45 min or longer.
- Athlete can vary pace from sprinting to jogging and can include all round body exercises between runs.

FLEXIBILITY TRAINING
- Concerned with joint mobility.
- Exercises general or specific to chosen sport.

- Active / passive / ballistic / proprioceptive neuromuscular facilitation (PNF).
- PNF involves stretching followed by isometric contraction, followed by further stretching :
  - during this process proprioceptors are made less active
  - hence allowing further stretching.

STRENGTH TRAINING

STRENGTH TRAINING
- Dynamic strength
    - Maximum strength (1RM = 1 Repetition Maximum).
        - Strength Endurance.
            - Plyometrics.
- Static strength
    - Isometric training
Training for :
- Maximum Strength = low repetitions (<4) / high loading (>85% of 1 RM).
- Dynamic Strength = fast movements (near sport demand) / 4 - 10 repetitions / moderate to high loading (70-80%).
- Strength Endurance = high repetitions (>15) / low loading (<60%).
- % loading based on 100%= 1RM.
Plyometrics
- Uses Stretch Reflex to increase muscle force.
- Eccentric contraction requires bigger force.

LONG-TERM ANAEROBIC ADAPTIVE RESPONSES TO TRAINING

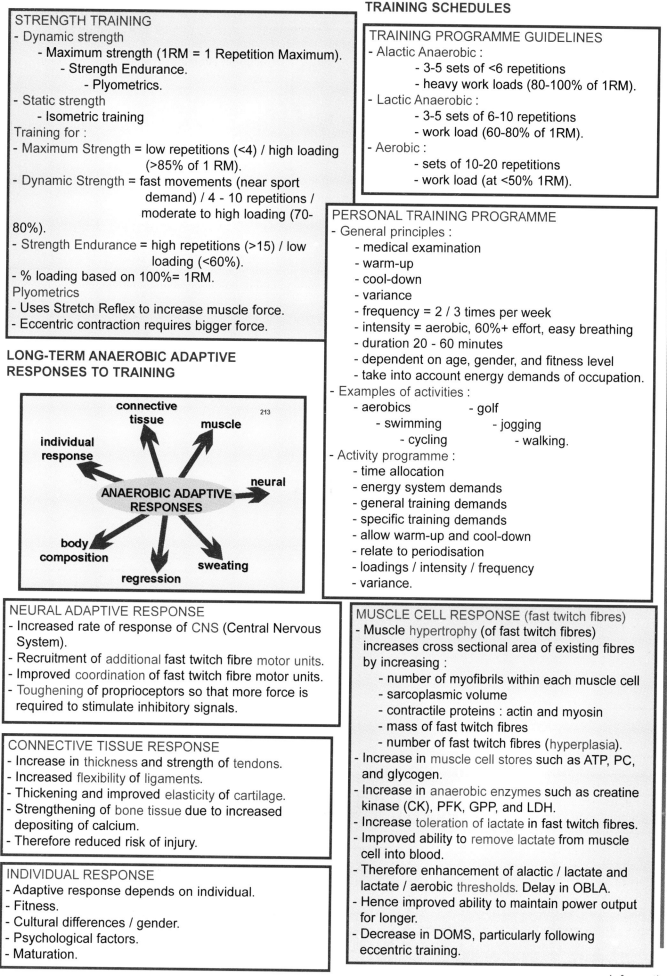

connective tissue — muscle — individual response — neural — body composition — ANAEROBIC ADAPTIVE RESPONSES — regression — sweating

213

TRAINING SCHEDULES

TRAINING PROGRAMME GUIDELINES
- Alactic Anaerobic :
    - 3-5 sets of <6 repetitions
    - heavy work loads (80-100% of 1RM).
- Lactic Anaerobic :
    - 3-5 sets of 6-10 repetitions
    - work load (60-80% of 1RM).
- Aerobic :
    - sets of 10-20 repetitions
    - work load (at <50% 1RM).

PERSONAL TRAINING PROGRAMME
- General principles :
    - medical examination
    - warm-up
    - cool-down
    - variance
    - frequency = 2 / 3 times per week
    - intensity = aerobic, 60%+ effort, easy breathing
    - duration 20 - 60 minutes
    - dependent on age, gender, and fitness level
    - take into account energy demands of occupation.
- Examples of activities :
    - aerobics   - golf
        - swimming   - jogging
            - cycling   - walking.
- Activity programme :
    - time allocation
    - energy system demands
    - general training demands
    - specific training demands
    - allow warm-up and cool-down
    - relate to periodisation
    - loadings / intensity / frequency
    - variance.

NEURAL ADAPTIVE RESPONSE
- Increased rate of response of CNS (Central Nervous System).
- Recruitment of additional fast twitch fibre motor units.
- Improved coordination of fast twitch fibre motor units.
- Toughening of proprioceptors so that more force is required to stimulate inhibitory signals.

CONNECTIVE TISSUE RESPONSE
- Increase in thickness and strength of tendons.
- Increased flexibility of ligaments.
- Thickening and improved elasticity of cartilage.
- Strengthening of bone tissue due to increased depositing of calcium.
- Therefore reduced risk of injury.

INDIVIDUAL RESPONSE
- Adaptive response depends on individual.
- Fitness.
- Cultural differences / gender.
- Psychological factors.
- Maturation.

MUSCLE CELL RESPONSE (fast twitch fibres)
- Muscle hypertrophy (of fast twitch fibres) increases cross sectional area of existing fibres by increasing :
    - number of myofibrils within each muscle cell
    - sarcoplasmic volume
    - contractile proteins : actin and myosin
    - mass of fast twitch fibres
    - number of fast twitch fibres (hyperplasia).
- Increase in muscle cell stores such as ATP, PC, and glycogen.
- Increase in anaerobic enzymes such as creatine kinase (CK), PFK, GPP, and LDH.
- Increase toleration of lactate in fast twitch fibres.
- Improved ability to remove lactate from muscle cell into blood.
- Therefore enhancement of alactic / lactate and lactate / aerobic thresholds. Delay in OBLA.
- Hence improved ability to maintain power output for longer.
- Decrease in DOMS, particularly following eccentric training.

LONG-TERM AEROBIC ADAPTIVE RESPONSES TO TRAINING

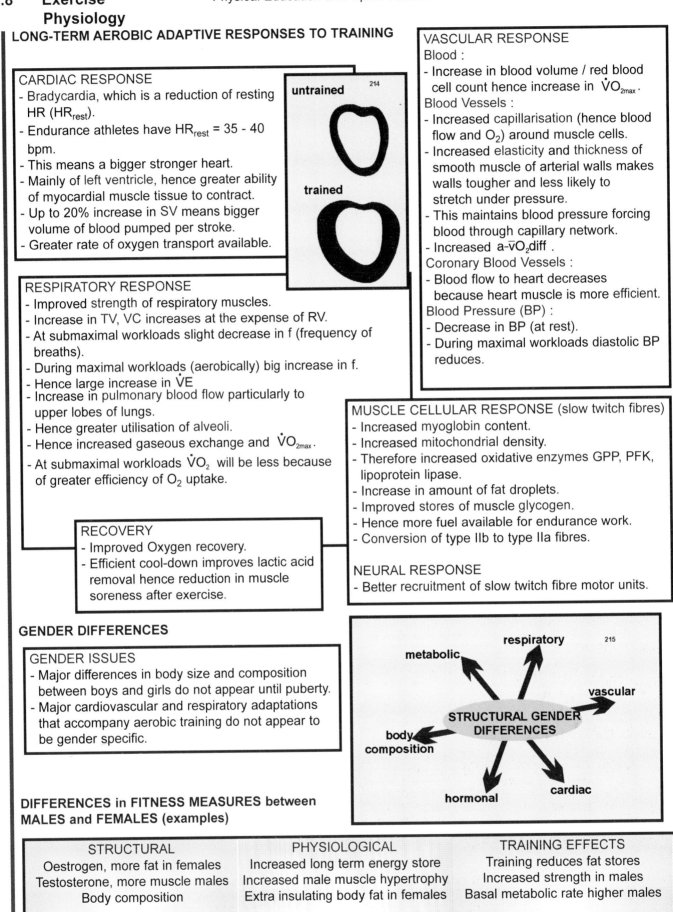

CARDIAC RESPONSE
- Bradycardia, which is a reduction of resting HR (HR_{rest}).
- Endurance athletes have HR_{rest} = 35 - 40 bpm.
- This means a bigger stronger heart.
- Mainly of left ventricle, hence greater ability of myocardial muscle tissue to contract.
- Up to 20% increase in SV means bigger volume of blood pumped per stroke.
- Greater rate of oxygen transport available.

untrained   214
trained

VASCULAR RESPONSE
Blood :
- Increase in blood volume / red blood cell count hence increase in $\dot{V}O_{2max}$.

Blood Vessels :
- Increased capillarisation (hence blood flow and O_2) around muscle cells.
- Increased elasticity and thickness of smooth muscle of arterial walls makes walls tougher and less likely to stretch under pressure.
- This maintains blood pressure forcing blood through capillary network.
- Increased a-$\bar{v}O_2$diff .

Coronary Blood Vessels :
- Blood flow to heart decreases because heart muscle is more efficient.

Blood Pressure (BP) :
- Decrease in BP (at rest).
- During maximal workloads diastolic BP reduces.

RESPIRATORY RESPONSE
- Improved strength of respiratory muscles.
- Increase in TV, VC increases at the expense of RV.
- At submaximal workloads slight decrease in f (frequency of breaths).
- During maximal workloads (aerobically) big increase in f.
- Hence large increase in $\dot{V}E$
- Increase in pulmonary blood flow particularly to upper lobes of lungs.
- Hence greater utilisation of alveoli.
- Hence increased gaseous exchange and $\dot{V}O_{2max}$.
- At submaximal workloads $\dot{V}O_2$ will be less because of greater efficiency of O_2 uptake.

MUSCLE CELLULAR RESPONSE (slow twitch fibres)
- Increased myoglobin content.
- Increased mitochondrial density.
- Therefore increased oxidative enzymes GPP, PFK, lipoprotein lipase.
- Increase in amount of fat droplets.
- Improved stores of muscle glycogen.
- Hence more fuel available for endurance work.
- Conversion of type IIb to type IIa fibres.

NEURAL RESPONSE
- Better recruitment of slow twitch fibre motor units.

RECOVERY
- Improved Oxygen recovery.
- Efficient cool-down improves lactic acid removal hence reduction in muscle soreness after exercise.

GENDER DIFFERENCES

GENDER ISSUES
- Major differences in body size and composition between boys and girls do not appear until puberty.
- Major cardiovascular and respiratory adaptations that accompany aerobic training do not appear to be gender specific.

respiratory   215
metabolic
vascular
STRUCTURAL GENDER DIFFERENCES
body composition
hormonal
cardiac

DIFFERENCES in FITNESS MEASURES between MALES and FEMALES (examples)

STRUCTURAL	PHYSIOLOGICAL	TRAINING EFFECTS
Oestrogen, more fat in females	Increased long term energy store	Training reduces fat stores
Testosterone, more muscle males	Increased male muscle hypertrophy	Increased strength in males
Body composition	Extra insulating body fat in females	Basal metabolic rate higher males
Respiratory volumes - body size	Smaller people have smaller $\dot{V}E$	No gender differences (size only)
Smaller hearts in females	Smaller SV, faster HR_{rest} in females	Bradycardia similar M and F
Smaller blood volume in females	Smaller $\dot{V}O_{2max}$ in females	Aerobic capacity similar M and F

ERGOGENIC AIDS

ERGOGENIC AID
- Any means of improving the efficiency and enhancing the quality of sporting performance.

MECHANICAL AIDS
- Nasal strip enables easier breathing.
- Specialist equipment such as carbon fibre bike frames are lighter and more aerodynamically efficient.
- Lycra sports clothing reduces drag.

LEGAL PHYSIOLOGICAL ERGOGENIC AIDS
ALTITUDE TRAINING.
- A predominantly endurance-based exercise programme consisting of 2 visits of at least two weeks duration per visit, to altitude (normally between 1800-3000 metres).
- Second visit just prior to major competition.
- Benefits : reversible physiological adaptations (increased Hb concentration, increases in myoglobin, mitochondria and oxidative enzymes.
- On return to sea level are increased $\dot{V}O_{2max}$ and tissue cell respiration leading to enhanced aerobic performance.
- Risks : hypoxia, altitude sickness.

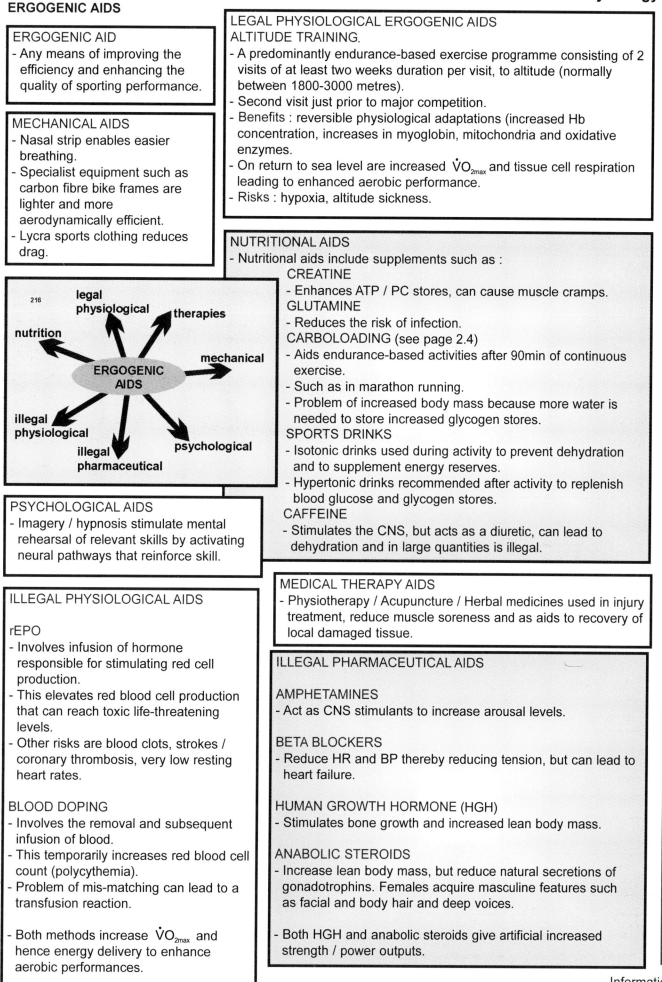

216

legal physiological

nutrition

therapies

ERGOGENIC AIDS

mechanical

illegal physiological

illegal pharmaceutical

psychological

NUTRITIONAL AIDS
- Nutritional aids include supplements such as :
CREATINE
- Enhances ATP / PC stores, can cause muscle cramps.
GLUTAMINE
- Reduces the risk of infection.
CARBOLOADING (see page 2.4)
- Aids endurance-based activities after 90min of continuous exercise.
- Such as in marathon running.
- Problem of increased body mass because more water is needed to store increased glycogen stores.
SPORTS DRINKS
- Isotonic drinks used during activity to prevent dehydration and to supplement energy reserves.
- Hypertonic drinks recommended after activity to replenish blood glucose and glycogen stores.
CAFFEINE
- Stimulates the CNS, but acts as a diuretic, can lead to dehydration and in large quantities is illegal.

PSYCHOLOGICAL AIDS
- Imagery / hypnosis stimulate mental rehearsal of relevant skills by activating neural pathways that reinforce skill.

MEDICAL THERAPY AIDS
- Physiotherapy / Acupuncture / Herbal medicines used in injury treatment, reduce muscle soreness and as aids to recovery of local damaged tissue.

ILLEGAL PHYSIOLOGICAL AIDS

rEPO
- Involves infusion of hormone responsible for stimulating red cell production.
- This elevates red blood cell production that can reach toxic life-threatening levels.
- Other risks are blood clots, strokes / coronary thrombosis, very low resting heart rates.

BLOOD DOPING
- Involves the removal and subsequent infusion of blood.
- This temporarily increases red blood cell count (polycythemia).
- Problem of mis-matching can lead to a transfusion reaction.

- Both methods increase $\dot{V}O_{2max}$ and hence energy delivery to enhance aerobic performances.

ILLEGAL PHARMACEUTICAL AIDS

AMPHETAMINES
- Act as CNS stimulants to increase arousal levels.

BETA BLOCKERS
- Reduce HR and BP thereby reducing tension, but can lead to heart failure.

HUMAN GROWTH HORMONE (HGH)
- Stimulates bone growth and increased lean body mass.

ANABOLIC STEROIDS
- Increase lean body mass, but reduce natural secretions of gonadotrophins. Females acquire masculine features such as facial and body hair and deep voices.

- Both HGH and anabolic steroids give artificial increased strength / power outputs.

HYPOKINETIC DISORDERS | AGING AND EXERCISE

HYPOKINETIC DISORDERS

- Definition : diseases that develop partly due to insufficient exercise.

OSTEOPOROSIS
- This is an age-related condition in which reduction of bone mass takes place.
- This is due to reabsorption of minerals that form part of bone structure.
- Making bones porous, brittle and liable to break.

INACTIVITY
- This leads to poor flexibility as muscles, tendons and ligaments become shorter and tighter.
- Often resulting in back pain.

OSTEOARTHRITIS
- This is a condition where joints thicken with fluid-filled pockets, restricting joint flexibility.

OBESITY
- Overweight condition of the body.
- Exceeding 25% in males and 35% in females.
- Often caused by positive energy balance.
- Problem of heat dissipation due to fat insulation.
- Cardiovascular system has to work harder.
- Therefore obesity is often associated with CHD, hypertension, atherosclerosis and mechanical injury such as weakened joints.

CARDIOVASCULAR DISEASES
- Atherosclerosis, the furring up of arteries caused by irregular lipid deposits.
- Can lead to hypertension.
- Angina produces severe chest pains resulting from reduced oxygen supply to myocardial tissue.

THROMBOSIS
- Otherwise known as blood clot.
- This condition can cut blood supply to heart (coronary thrombosis) or brain (stroke).
- Blockage of any artery or vein with a thrombosis is a life threatening condition which prevents any exercise.
- Break up of a clot, pieces of which could migrate to the heart or brain, would cause heart attack or stroke

AGEING
- Includes all the changes that occur in the body.
- Restricted joint flexibility, (osteoarthritis).
- Increased body fat.
- Osteoporosis, decreased bone mineral (oestrogen deficiency and lack of physical activity in females).
- Muscle atrophy and cardiovascular and respiratory.

AEROBIC DECLINE
Cardiovascular
- Decline in HR_{max} (HR_{max} = 220 - age).
- Increase in resting pulse rate due to decreased SV.
- Artery hardening increases resting systolic BP.
- Recovery takes longer after exercise.

Respiratory
- $\dot{V}O_{2max}$ declines about 10% per decade due to reduction in SV & HR_{max} & lack of aerobic exercise.
- VC & forced expiratory volume decreases with age.
- RV larger hence less air exchanged per breath.
- Less elasticity of alveoli walls & reduced strength of respiratory muscles decreases $\dot{V}O_{2max}$.
- Lower a-$\bar{v}O_2$diff since less O_2 extracted by muscles.

ANAEROBIC DECLINE
- Muscle and strength atrophy, shift towards ST fibres.
- Thinner myelinated sheath lengthens reaction times.
- Loss of neurones affects short term memory and coordination.

TRAINING PROGRAMME
- Refer page 2.7 above.

TRAINING EFFECTS
Cardiovascular
- Exercise slows down degenerative diseases (CHD).
- Exercise increases High Density Lipoproteins HDL, and decreases Low Density Lipoproteins LDL (LDL are responsible for depositing cholesterol and narrowing lumen of artery), hence BP stable.
- Thus preventing hypertension.

Respiratory
- Exercise slows down decline in $\dot{V}O_{2max}$.

Body Composition
- Exercise reduces obesity by burning off excess fat during and after activity when MR remains elevated.
- Cardiac workload less with lower body mass.
- Exercise relieves symptoms of osteoarthritis.
- Exercise prevents osteoporosis.

Neuromuscular
- Exercise sustains strength and coordination levels.
- Exercise enhances tensile strength & flexibility of tendons and ligaments.
- Thus allowing for a fuller range of joint movement.

Psychological
- Immediately following activity a person experiences a feeling of well being, reduction in anxiety.
- Long term increase in work performance, hence a more positive attitude to work.
- Improved self-esteem and self-efficacy.
- Benefits of social interaction.

QUESTIONS

ENERGY CONCEPTS and ATP RESYNTHESIS

1) a) i) Define energy, and briefly describe how energy
is   released from food in the body?   (5 marks)
   ii) A student was interested in calculating the
   energy output of a subject bench stepping.
   The weight of the subject was 700N. The bench
   height was 0.4 m and the subject stepped at a
   rate of 30 steps per minute for 10 minutes.
   Using the following formulae calculate the work
   done for the total exercise period (show your
   working).

Work = bodyweight x vertical distance per min x 10 min.
                                    (2 marks)
b) The figure on the right summarises the process of
cellular respiration in humans. Key words have been
omitted from the rectangular boxes labelled **A** and **B**.
   i) Identify the appropriate substances formed
   from the pyruvic acid.   (2 marks)
   ii) State under what conditions **A** would be
   formed, and state where and in what conditions
   substance **B** is commonly found in relatively
   large amounts.   (3 marks)
   iii) List two ways in which the substance **B** is
   disposed of in the body.   (2 marks)
   iv) Using the information in the figure describe
   how ATP is created aerobically.   (6 marks)
   v) Compare the relative efficiency of ATP
   production via the aerobic and anaerobic
   routes. Explain your answer.   (3 marks)

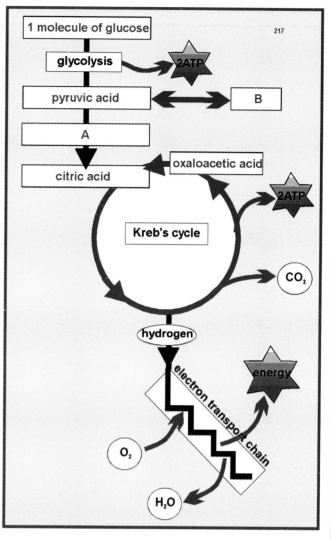

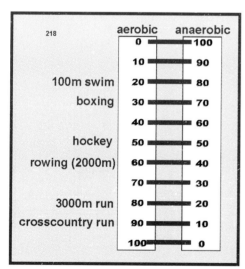

ENERGY CONTINUUM

2) The diagram on the left is an energy continuum in relation to a
variety of sports activities.
a) Explain the concept 'the energy continuum'.   (2 marks)
b) At each end of the continuum examples of sporting activities have
been omitted. Give one example of a sporting activity that is
predominantly anaerobic and one example of a sporting activity that is
predominantly aerobic.   (2 marks)
c) Suggest two factors that need to be considered in evaluating sports
activities on the basis of their relative position on the energy
continuum.   (2 marks)
d) Explain, using specific examples, why a game of hockey has aerobic
and anaerobic components.   (4 marks)

LACTIC ACID SYSTEM / EPOC

3) A student performs a flat-out 50 metre freestyle swim in 50 seconds.
a)   **i)** Describe how most of the ATP is regenerated during the swim.   (4 marks)
         ii) Sketch a graph which shows the use of the appropriate energy systems against time during the swim.
                                    (3 marks)

LACTIC ACID SYSTEM / EPOC - QUESTION 3 continued

Blood lactate mmol l⁻¹	Rate of working watts
1.0	100
1.2	200
1.5	400
2.2	600
4.5	800
6.5	900
8.5	1000

3) b)

i) The data in the table on the right illustrate the relationship between the concentration of blood lactate and rate of working. Using the data in this table plot a graph to illustrate the relationship between blood lactate concentration and rate of working (watts).

(3 marks)

ii) Using the data, explain how you would deduce that, around 200 watts, most of the work is done aerobically, and at around 900 watts, most of the work is done anaerobically. Identify the approximate point at which the lactate threshold or onset of blood lactate accumulation (OBLA) occurs on your graph. (3 marks)

iii) What processes are involved in excess post-exercise oxygen consumption (EPOC)? (5 marks)

iv) Part of the recovery process after anaerobic exercise involves myoglobin. Explain the function of myoglobin during the recovery process. (2 marks)

v) There are several ways by which lactic acid can be removed from active muscles. Identify the major pathway for the removal of lactic acid and the organs and tissues involved. (4 marks)

c) How does light exercise influence lactate removal? (3 marks)

MUSCLE FATIGUE

4) a) What is muscle fatigue? (2 marks)

b) Describe the possible causes of fatigue during :

i) Maximal exercise lasting 2 to 10 seconds. (3 marks)

ii) Submaximal exercise lasting between 2 to 4 hours. (3 marks)

iii) How could information on oxygen debt recovery be of use to an athlete and coach in the design of training sessions? (6 marks)

RESPIRATORY EXCHANGE RATIO

5) a) Define respiratory exchange ratio (RER or RQ). (1 mark)

b) Show how the data in the following equation can be used to calculate the RER and identify the fuel food that is being oxidised :

$$C_{17}H_{35}COOH + 26O_2 \longrightarrow 18CO_2 + 18H_2O + energy$$

(3 marks)

c) State two advantages of fats over carbohydrates as energy storage molecules. (2 marks)

METABOLISM / NUTRITION

6) a) i) Explain the term metabolism. (2 marks)

ii) A student has been asked to estimate the energy costs when playing a game of hockey, lasting one hour and 10 minutes. His body weight at the start of the game is 69 kilograms. The energy expenditure needed for the hockey game is 0.8 kJ/kg/min above his basal metabolic rate. Calculate his energy requirements during the hockey game. Show your workings. (2 marks)

b) i) Describe food fuel usage during the hockey game. (2 marks)

ii) Briefly describe the metabolic role of the liver during the hockey game. (2 marks)

iii) How can a high carbohydrate diet influence metabolism after the hockey game? (2 marks)

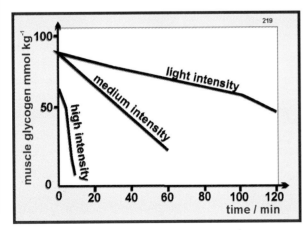

EXERCISE and NUTRITION

7) a) A student performs light, medium and high intensity workloads on a cycle ergometer. The rate of glycogen depletion in the quadriceps femoris muscle during the three exercise periods is illustrated in the graph on the left.

i) Describe the pattern of glycogen depletion at the three workloads. (3 marks)

ii) What would the fuel food usage be at high intensity workloads and low intensity workloads? (3 marks)

iii) Recommend a method of optimizing glycogen repletion following hard physical activity. (3 marks)

EXERCISE and NUTRITION - QUESTION 7 continued

7) b) i) Prescribe a prudent recommendation for approximate percentages of protein, lipid and carbohydrate intake for an average 17 year old student who wishes to maintain a physically active lifestyle. (3 marks)
ii) Suggest some general dietary guidelines you would give to a gymnast who is preparing for a major competition. (3 marks)

8) a) Discuss how a balanced diet could be manipulated to increase an athlete's glucose reserves prior to a marathon race. (6 marks)
b) Describe how an athlete is able to control his / her body temperature during a marathon race. (4 marks)

OXYGEN CONSUMPTION / FITNESS MEASURES

9) The table on the right shows the increase in maximal oxygen uptake ($\dot{V}O_{2max}$) in males and females at different relative training intensities.

Relative Training Intensity	Increase in $\dot{V}O_{2max}$ Males	Females
1.2	0.14	0.33
1.4	0.25	0.39
1.6	0.37	0.45
1.8	0.48	0.51

a) **i)** Define the term $\dot{V}O_{2max}$ and identify its units of measurement which would allow you to compare the fitness of two individual runners. (2 marks)
ii) Using the data in the table, plot a graph to show the relationship between relative training intensity and increase in $\dot{V}O_{2max}$ in both males and females. (4 marks)
b) What relationship is shown between the relative training intensity and :
i) The $\dot{V}O_{2max}$ in both males and females over the whole range.
ii) The $\dot{V}O_{2max}$ in both males and females at the same relative intensity. (4 marks)
c) State three physiological differences between males and females that would influence their relative powers of endurance. (3 marks)
d) **i)** What is meant by the term 'relative training intensity' and in what ways could relative training intensity be measured. (3 marks)
e) What other factors contribute to the effectiveness of a training programme for an individual sports man or woman? (4 marks)

FITNESS TESTING

10) a) With reference to fitness testing, explain what is meant by the following terms :
i) Reliability and validity. (2 marks)
ii) Maximal and sub-maximal. (3 marks)
b) What are the disadvantages of :
i) Maximal tests. (2 marks)
ii) Sub-maximal tests. (2 marks)
c) **i)** The step test is a simple fitness test. Explain why its use in determining $\dot{V}O_{2max}$ could be criticised. (5 marks)
ii) During the step tests, the oxygen uptake of a subject was measured. Sketch a graph to illustrate oxygen uptake against time and use your graph to explain the concept of steady state. (5 marks)
iii) The cycle ergometer can also be used in simple fitness testing. Explain why its use in determining predicted $\dot{V}O_{2max}$ is generally considered to be more accurate than that of the step test. (2 marks)
d) Explain why fitness tests specific to particular sports are considered more useful than non-specific tests. (4 marks)

STRENGTH TRAINING / FITNESS COMPONENTS

11) a) What is meant by the term 1 repetition maximum (1RM) and how would you assess an athlete's strength? (3 marks)
b) You have been asked to devise a strength training programme for a fit 18 year old sprinter.
i) Identify and explain the use of four important training principles that need to be considered when planning this athlete's training programme. (4 marks)
ii) Describe the activities within one strength training session for this athlete. (4 marks)
iii) How is ATP regenerated during maximal strength work? (3 marks)

STRENGTH TRAINING / FITNESS COMPONENTS - QUESTION 11 continued

11) c) Identify some of the causes of muscle soreness after intense training and suggest how it can be prevented?   (4 marks)
d) Explain the physiological advantages of a strength training programme for a practising athlete.   (6 marks)
e) In addition to strength work, most physical activities involve the fitness components coordination, flexibility and endurance. Give an example of the types of training and adaptive response of the muscle to each of these fitness components.   (6 marks)

INTERVAL TRAINING

12) Study the table on the right which outlines some interval training regimes for the training of different fitness components in a track athlete.

Component	Training regime
Alactic anaerobic	3 x (10 x 50 m)
Lactic anaerobic	2 x (3 x 400m)
Aerobic	1 x (3 x 1000m)

a) Briefly explain the meaning and purpose of the term 'set' in interval training.   (4 marks)
b) What important information is missing from these outline interval training regimes.   (3 marks)
c) Select two of the regimes in the table and briefly explain how their particular fitness components respond to such training.   (8 marks)
d) Discuss the relative importance of these three energy systems for performance in a 'game' type activity such as football.   (5 marks)

PRINCIPLES OF TRAINING : REVERSIBILITY, WARM-UP, COOL-DOWN

13) a) Briefly explain :
     i) How an organised fitness programme results in training effects.   (2 marks)
     ii) What is meant by the reversibility of training effects.   (2 marks)
b)   i) When an appropriate training programme stops, what happens to the cardiovascular system which helps to explain the reversibility of endurance training effects.   (7 marks)
     ii) Fast ball games require players to make quick decisions to cues and respond immediately with powerful movements. When training stops, what happens to the muscles and the nervous system which helps to explain the reversibility of these aspects of fitness?   (5 marks)
c) Compared with the effects of a continuous training programme, explain why it is possible to improve sports performance when training is resumed after a rest due to injury, despite the reversibility of training effects which will have occurred during the rest period.   (4 marks)
d) From a physiological standpoint, explain why warm-up and cool-down are important within an exercise regime.
                                                                                   (8 marks)

PERIODISATION

14) a) Discuss the concept of periodisation and outline its particular application to a strength-training programme for your particular sport.   (10 marks)
b) Why is it important to vary the loading patterns for each of the periods you have identified?   (5 marks)

ERGOGENIC AIDS AND PHYSICAL PERFORMANCE

15) a)   i) Explain the meaning of the word 'acclimatisation' and describe the physiological processes by which an elite athlete adapts to altitude.   (10 marks)
          ii) How is aerobic training affected by altitude and by a subsequent return to sea level?   (6 marks)

b) What is an ergogenic aid? Briefly provide a summary of the role that nutritional supplements play in improving performance.   (8 marks)

c)   i) Describe the method of blood doping and its potential for improving endurance performance.
                                                                                   (4 marks)
          ii) Erythropoietin (EPO) is a hormone produced by the kidneys, which stimulates the production of red blood cells under conditions of hypoxia and anaemia. Human EPO can now be produced outside the human body with a recombinant DNA technique and is identified as rEPO. Discuss the health issues that are associated with the use of rEPO in sport.   (4 marks)

EXERCISE and HEALTH

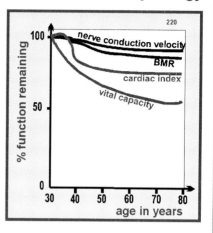

16) a) The graph on the right shows the physiological changes associated with ageing. Some of the changes which occur with age can be explained in terms of changes in our tissues. Briefly explain the decline in function of the body systems shown in this graph. (4 marks)
b) In ageing the mass of the skeleton declines with loss of mineral content of our bones. Why are skeletal changes more pronounced in women? (3 marks)

c)   **i)** Identify two causes of the 'middle-aged spread'.   (2 marks)
         ii) Identify two health risk hazards that are associated with 'middle-aged spread'.   (2 marks)

d) Regular exercise can positively influence several health risks.
         i) Briefly describe an outline for a week's exercise programme that would be suitable for an overweight and ageing adult. In your answer identify major fitness component(s) to be stressed.   (8 marks)
         ii) When older people are physically active, most of the changes associated with ageing are lessened. Describe the effects of aerobic and anaerobic exercise on bodily systems.   (6 marks)

ANSWERS

The answer for each mark awarded is notated by the ❐ symbol - where there are more ❐ symbols than there are marks available, marks would be given for any choice up to the maximum available. Usually, the precise wording specified in an answer would not be required - answers with the same meaning would be acceptable. In Science areas, sometimes the precise words used in terminology would be required.

ENERGY CONCEPTS and ATP RESYNTHESIS

1) a) i)
❐   Definition : energy is the capacity or ability to perform work.
Brief overview of how energy is released from food in the body:
   4 marks for four from :
❐   Fuel foods are fuel stored in the body, the first is carbohydrate CHO (digested to glucose).
❐   The second type of fuel food consists of fats (digested to fatty acids & glycerol).
❐   These are used to create chemical energy in the form of adenosine triphosphate (ATP).
❐   This is an endothermic reaction (it takes in energy from the food and creates the ATP).
❐   This process is both aerobic and anaerobic, within all living tissue.
❐   ATP is an immediate usable form of chemical energy for all body processes.
❐   Including that used by skeletal muscle to perform mechanical work.
❐   The usage of ATP to create energy is an exothermic reaction.
1) a) ii)
❐   Work done = 700 x 0.4 x 30 x 10.
❐   = 84000 Joules or 840kJ.
1) b) i)
❐   **B** is lactic acid.
❐   **A** is acetyl CoA, conditions for **A** are aerobic.
1) b) ii)
❐   Conditions for **A** are aerobic.
❐   Conditions for **B** are anaerobic.
❐   Lactic acid is found in (muscle cell) sarcoplasm
1) b) iii)
   2 marks for two from :
❐   Substance **B** (lactic acid) is oxidised into carbon dioxide and water.
❐   And converted to glycogen.
❐   And converted to protein.
❐   And converted to glucose.

ENERGY CONCEPTS AND ATP RESYNTHESIS - ANSWERS QUESTION 1) b) (continued)

1) b) iv)
How ATP is created aerobically :
   3 marks for three from :
❐ In the presence of oxygen.
❐ In the cell mitochondria.
❐ Oxaloacetic acid and acetyl CoA combine to form citric acid.
❐ To enter Kreb's cycle where pairs of hydrogen atoms are released.
❐ CO_2 is formed.
❐ 2ATP are produced.
   3 marks for three from :
❐ Co-enzymes transport hydrogen atoms (ions and electrons) into the electron transport chain.
❐ Hydrogen ions and electrons are charged with potential energy.
❐ Which is released in a step by step manner.
❐ As O_2 is delivered to react with the hydrogen ions and electrons.
❐ To create a large energy yield per mole of glucose (32 / 34 ATP) and water.

1) b) v)
   1 mark for :
❐ Aerobic route is 18-19 times more efficient than anaerobic route / or 36-38 ATP produced aerobically
    compared with 2 ATP, produced anaerobically for one molecule of glucose.
   2 marks for two from (explanation) :
❐ Anaerobic production of ATP is the incomplete breakdown of one molecule of glucose (glycolysis), therefore
    very limited ATP production.
❐ Whereas the aerobic production of ATP completely breaks down the glucose molecule.
❐ To release all potential energy (energy stored in the molecules).
❐ Hence a much higher energy yield.

ENERGY CONTINUUM

2) a)
   2 marks for two from :
❐ The energy continuum is a concept used to describe the type(s) of respiration.
❐ And describes the shares of anaerobic and aerobic types of respiration.
❐ Demanded by different types of physical activities (games or sports).

2) b)
❐ Anaerobic : 100m sprint, javelin throw, long jump, weight lift.
❐ Aerobic : marathon, jogging, long distance swimming, long distance cycling.

2) c)
Two factors required to evaluate the place of an activity in the energy continuum :
   2 marks for two from :
❐ The total amount of ATP required during that activity.
❐ Or power or rate at which ATP is required during the performance.
❐ Intensity and duration of the exercise period.

2) d)
The energy demands of hockey :
   4 marks for four from :
❐ Skills in the game are largely anaerobic.
❐ Example, short fast dribble stresses ATP / PC system.
❐ Repetition back to back sprints stresses lactic acid system.
❐ Playing duration normally exceeds 1 hour giving time for recovery for player in off the ball situations.
❐ Production of ATP via the aerobic system.

LACTIC ACID SYSTEM / EPOC

3) a) i)
How is ATP regenerated during a flat out 50m swim (50s)?
  4 marks for four from :
❑ Lactic Acid System
❑ Process called glycolysis or the incomplete breakdown of sugar.
❑ Glycolytic enzymes (for example, phosphofructokinase - PFK) assist breakdown of glucose.
❑ Without oxygen being present.
❑ Takes place in the muscle cell sarcoplasm.
❑ Molecule of glucose is broken down to release 2ATP.
❑ Pyruvic acid which is converted to lactic acid.
❑ By enzyme lactate dehydrogenase.

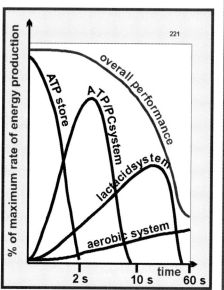

3) a) ii)
  Sketch graph upper right, 3 marks given for three from :
❑ ATP store used up after 2 seconds or less.
❑ ATP / PC system building to a peak at 3 seconds (between 2 and 4 seconds), dropping to zero after 9 seconds (7 to 10 seconds).
❑ Lactacid system peaking at around 20 seconds (15 - 25 seconds), dropping to zero at around 50 seconds.
❑ Aerobic system building gradually from zero, always less than other system contributions.
  No marks given for relative size of the contributions except that the aerobic system is less than the others.

3) b) i)
  See graph below, marks given for :

❑ Layout of x, y axes.
❑ Correct plotting of points.
❑ Correct curve or line.

3) b) ii)
How would you deduce that at 200W most of the work is done aerobically, and at 900W most work is done anaerobically?
  2 marks for two from :
❑ At 200 watts workload is low intensity.
❑ And regeneration of ATP is predominantly oxidative.
❑ And so blood lactate level is very low therefore aerobic (lactate is not produced if plenty of O_2 is present).
❑ Whereas at 900 watts there is a sharp rise in blood lactate level (lactate is produced when not enough O_2 is present).
❑ This big increase in lactate is associated with the 9 fold increase in work rate.
  1 mark for :
❑ Identifying OBLA point on graph (between 2 and 4 mmol l^{-1}).

3) b) iii)
What processes are involved in EPOC?
  1 mark for :
❑ The use of O_2 during recovery to replenish ATP stores.
  2 marks for : Rapid components :
❑ Replacement of ATP-PC stores (Alactacid component).
❑ Replenishment of O_2 stores in blood and tissues, for example, myoglobin with oxygen.
  2 marks for two from : Slower components :
❑ Removal of lactate (mainly oxidised - lactacid component).
❑ Replacement of glycogen stores.
❑ Restoration of heart and respiratory muscles to resting values.
❑ Tissue repair.

3) b) iv)
  2 marks for two from : function of myoglobin :
❑ This iron protein molecule (located within skeletal muscle).
❑ Transports O_2 from HbO_2 (in blood) to the mitochondria.
❑ And finally saturates itself to recover as a temporary storage site for O_2.

Answers

LACTIC ACID SYSTEM / EPOC - ANSWERS QUESTION 3) b) (continued)

3) b) v)
 2 marks for major pathway :
- ❐ Lactic acid is converted back to pyruvic acid.
- ❐ And the majority of lactate is oxidised within cell mitochondria.

Organs and tissues which are involved in the removal of lactic acid :
 2 marks for two from :
- ❐ Oxidation occurs in slow twitch muscle fibres (once sufficient O_2 is available).
- ❐ Blood transports lactic acid (for oxidation) to other organs which have not been operating under anaerobic conditions.
- ❐ Such as liver, kidneys, brain, heart.

3) c)
How does light exercise influence lactate removal?
 3 marks for three from :
- ❐ Keeps blood capillaries dilated.
- ❐ Avoids blood pooling.
- ❐ Flushing oxygenated blood through the muscle.
- ❐ Increasing the oxidation of lactic acid and removing lactate from the muscle cells.

MUSCLE FATIGUE

4) a)
 2 marks for two from : muscle fatigue is :
- ❐ The inability of a muscle to maintain its strength of contraction or tension.
- ❐ So that the strength of contraction becomes progressively weaker.
- ❐ Until the muscle no longer responds.

4) b) i)
What are the causes of fatigue during the first 2 - 10 seconds of maximal exercise?
- ❐ Depletion of PC stores.
- ❐ Lack of O_2.
- ❐ Neural fatigue or decrease in neural activity.

4) b) ii)
What are the causes of fatigue during 2 - 4 hours of submaximal exercise?
 3 marks for three from :
- ❐ Depletion of muscle and liver glycogen stores.
- ❐ Gradual build up of lactic acid.
- ❐ Blood acidosis or a fall in muscle pH / inhibits enzyme action.
- ❐ Build up of H^+ ions / increases in ADP affecting ionic balance of cell membrane wall.
- ❐ All this inhibits the contractile processes.
- ❐ Neural fatigue, such as failure to stimulated an action potential to cross from the motor neurone to muscle fibre.
- ❐ Muscle sheath / fibre damage due to repetitive trauma.
- ❐ Psychological fatigue.

4) b) iii)
How could information on O_2 debt recovery be of use to an athlete and coach in the design of training sessions?
 2 marks for two from :
- ❐ Recovery of the phosphagens stores (PC) are very rapid (i.e. within a couple of minutes).
- ❐ Therefore athlete is able to perform many repetitions of high quality, short duration (i.e. up to between 8-10 seconds worth of maximal exercise) bouts of exercise.
- ❐ A major problem facing the athlete performing within the lactic acid system is the inhibiting effect on performance when there is a build up of lactic acid.
 4 marks for four from : the implications :
- ❐ Adequate rest relief between repetitions.
- ❐ Use of active recovery to facilitate removal of lactate.
- ❐ Variation of workload from one session to the next.
- ❐ For example, one high intensity session where the lactic acid system is stressed.
- ❐ Followed by a moderate intensity aerobic or anaerobic session (stressing the ATP-PC system).

RESPIRATORY EXCHANGE RATIO

5) a)
❏ The respiratory exchange ratio (RER) is the ratio of CO_2 expired to O_2 consumed in the lungs.

5) b)
❏ 1 mark given for extracting the information that there are 18 CO_2 to 26 O_2 in this process.
❏ Therefore RER = $\dfrac{18\ CO_2}{26\ O_2}$ = 0.69.

❏ Fuel food for this process is fats.

5) c)
Two advantages of fats over carbohydrates as energy storage :
    2 marks for two from :
❏ Fats provide twice the energy yield of carbohydrates.
❏ During physical activity fats provide an unlimited supply of potential energy.
❏ Whereas CHO (stored as glycogen) is limited to around 1 hour 30 minutes.

METABOLISM / NUTRITION

6) a) i)
Metabolism is :
❏ Sum total of all chemical and energy reactions.
❏ Which take place within the human body.

6) a) ii)
The energy costs of a game of hockey are :
❏ Energy = energy expenditure per minute per kg of body mass x body mass x time taken = 0.8 x 69 x 70.
❏ Energy = 3864 kJ.

6) b) i)
Food fuel usage during the game of hockey is :
❏ Initially carbohydrate metabolism (use of liver and muscle glycogen stores and blood glucose).
❏ Later on in the game a mixture of carbohydrate and fat metabolism (20 mins onwards).

6) b) ii)
The metabolic role of the liver is :
    2 marks for two from :
❏ Converts liver and muscle glycogen to glucose (glycogenolysis).
❏ Recalls fatty acids, and breaks them down into acetyl co-enzyme A (acetyl Co A).
❏ And glycerol to liver, converts to glucose (gluconeogenesis).

6) b) iii)
A high carbohydrate diet after the hockey game can influence metabolism by :
    2 marks for two from :
❏ High CHO diet increases the rate of refuelling of glycogen levels.
❏ High CHO diet increases glycogen levels (concept of supercharging).
❏ Stored as glycogen in the liver and muscle.

EXERCISE and NUTRITION

7) a) i)
The pattern of glycogen depletion after intense, medium, and light exercise is :
    3 marks for three from :
❏ High intensity - rapid depletion.
❏ 13 mmol kg^{-1} left in under 10 mins.
❏ Medium intensity - steady decline.
❏ 20 mmol kg^{-1} left after 60 mins.
❏ Low intensity - much slower decline.
❏ 50 mmol kg^{-1} left after 120 mins.

7) a) ii)
The food fuel usage at high intensity and low intensity exercise would be :
❏ High intensity work CHO metabolism.
❏ Low intensity work shift towards fat metabolism (glycogen sparing).
❏ Some CHO.

EXERCISE AND NUTRITION - ANSWERS QUESTION 7) a) (continued)

7) a) iii)
A method of optimizing glycogen repletion after hard physical activity would be :
   3 marks for three from :
- ❑ Active cool-down / Cori cycle / conversion of lactic acid into glycogen.
- ❑ High CHO diet as soon as possible after activity to enhance glycogen refuelling.
- ❑ Scheduled rest days when little glycogen is used.
- ❑ Variations in training loads i.e. hard, medium to easy so that glycogen stores are not heavily taxed all the time.

7) b) i)
The approximate percentages of protein, lipid and carbohydrate in a diet for an active 17 year old would be :
   3 marks for :
- ❑ CHO 50% - 60%.
- ❑ Fat 25% - 35%.
- ❑ Protein 10% - 15%.

7) b) ii)
Dietary guidelines for a gymnast preparing for a major competition :
   3 marks for three from :
- ❑ Regular weighing.
- ❑ Limit fat intake.
- ❑ Increase liquid intake (rehydration).
- ❑ Maintain a balanced diet that stresses high CHO content.
- ❑ Use of food supplements such as creatine, glutamine, iron tablets and vitamin C.

8) a)
Manipulation of a balanced diet to increase an athlete's glucose reserves could be achieved by :
   6 marks for six from :
- ❑ Carbo-loading (or glycogen loading) before the event (modern method).
- ❑ This consists of tapering of training, whilst eating 50% CHO diet.
- ❑ Partially depletes glycogen stores.
- ❑ Therefore energy levels are not compromised.
- ❑ And glycogen synthase activity is increased.
- ❑ Then, gradually increase CHO intake to 70% of diet.
- ❑ With light training.
- ❑ Day of rest and 70% CHO diet.
- ❑ Repletes glycogen stores on day of marathon.
- ❑ Taking in isotonic fluids during the event will top up blood glucose levels during the event.

8) b)
Control of body temperature during a marathon can be achieved by :
   4 marks for four from :
- ❑ Replace body fluids to prevent dehydration and over heating.
- ❑ Wear suitable clothing such as mesh running vest.
- ❑ That allows air to circulate.
- ❑ Hence body is cooled by evaporation of sweat, convection and radiation.
- ❑ Use sponge stations to cool down body parts.

OXYGEN CONSUMPTION / FITNESS MEASURES

9) a) i)
- ❑ $\dot{V}O_{2max}$ represents the greatest rate / amount of oxygen used / consumed by an individual per unit of time.
- ❑ Measured in (cm^3) or ml kg^{-1} min^{-1}.

9) a) ii)
   See graph on right, 1 mark each for any two points correctly made :
- ❑ Title, x and y axes chosen correctly.
- ❑ Axes correctly labelled.
   Sensible scale.
- ❑ Points marked correctly.
   Male and female lines indicated.
- ❑ Points plotted correctly.
   Good clean lines drawn.

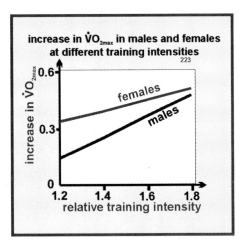

increase in $\dot{V}O_{2max}$ in males and females at different training intensities

OXYGEN CONSUMPTION / FITNESS MEASURES - ANSWERS QUESTION 9 (continued)

9) b) i)
The relationship between relative training intensity and $\dot{V}O_{2max}$ for males and females over whole range :
- As the relative training intensity is increased the $\dot{V}O_{2max}$ is increased.
- Males show a faster rate (females slower) of increase in $\dot{V}O_{2max}$.

9) b) ii)
- The increase in $\dot{V}O_{2max}$ is greater in females at the same relative intensity.
- This difference decreases with increasing relative training intensity.

9) c)
As compared with males, females have :
   3 marks for three from (the reverse statement could be used, then males have ....) :
- Greater % body fat than males.
- Smaller hearts / cardiac output / faster heart rate / smaller stroke volume.
- Lower % haemoglobin / RBC.
- Less muscle mass.

9) d) i)
Relative training intensity is :
- The training level / effort being used as compared with another different level of effort that could have been used or % effort used.

How relative training intensity could be measured : (2 marks for two from) :
- By measuring the increase in heart rate when increasing the relative intensity.
- By the onset of blood lactate accumulation (OBLA).
- Increase in O_2 consumption.
- Increase in minute ventilation.

9) e)
Other factors involved in the effectiveness of training programmes : (4 marks for four from) :
- Frequency of training sessions.
- Duration of training session.
- Use of adequate recovery between intervals.
- Type of training activity / specificity / variance.
- Genetic limitations.
- Use of warm-up / cool-down.
- Number of repetitions / sets used.
- Progressive overload.
- Rest days.
- Periodisation.
- Injury.

FITNESS TESTING

10) a) i)
- Reliability means that the test will give consistent results over a number of trials.
- Validity means that the test does measure what it claims to measure.

10) a) ii)
Definitions of maximal and submaximal : **(**3 marks for three from) :
- Maximal means that the subject makes 'all-out' effort or a test to exhaustion.
- For example : during maximal effort, measurements are taken at 'all-out' effort stage, in anaerobic work 1RM represents one repetition maximum, 30 metre sprint, Wingate 30 second cycle ergometer test. Alternatively, examples of maximal aerobic tests are the NCF multi-stage shuttle run test, Cooper's 12 minute run test.
- Submaximal means that the subject exercises below maximum effort.
- In sub-maximal work, extrapolation is used to estimate maximum capacities. Examples are the PWC-170 test & the Queen's College step test, Fitech step test (depend on heart rate recovery as a fitness indicator).

10) b) i)
   Disadvantages of maximal tests : 2 marks for two from :
- Difficulty in ensuring the subject is exerting maximum effort.
- Possible dangers of over-exertion and injury.
- Dependent on level of motivation (arousal levels).

10) b) ii)
   Disadvantages of sub-maximal tests :
- Depend on projection / extrapolation being made to unknown maximum.
- Therefore small inaccuracies / uncontrolled variables can result in large discrepancies as a result of magnification of results.

FITNESS TESTING - ANSWERS Question 10 continued

10) c) i)
The 'step test' could be criticised for :
  5 marks for five from :
❏ The methodology relies on the subject raising body weight against gravity at a set rate.
❏ Reliability and validity of the test depend on the correct stepping technique being used.
❏ This technique could be difficult to maintain.
❏ And could change during exercise period.
❏ Stepping technique can be affected by length and proportion of subject's legs.
❏ Or failure to achieve correct leg extension.
❏ The surface top for stepping on may vary from soft to hard.
❏ Having different proportion of body fat which are not accounted for in expressing results in kg of body weight.
❏ Difficulty in recording pulse / heart rates with accuracy.
❏ Specificity of test activity favours performers of sports which also make endurance demands on leg muscle groups (runners, cyclists).

10) c) ii)
  See graph on right, 3 marks given for :
❏ Labelled axes
❏ Correctly shaped curve
❏ Steady state illustrated and labelled.
  2 marks for two from (explanation) :
❏ Steady state implies that the demands of the body for O_2
❏ Is balanced by O_2 uptake.
❏ Hence plateau or constant level as shown on graph.

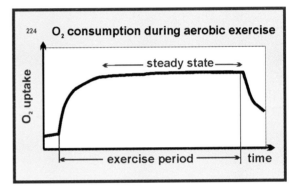

224 **O₂ consumption during aerobic exercise**

10) c) iii)
Greater accuracy of the cycle ergometer test arises from :
  2 marks for two from :
❏ Pedalling rate more accurately controlled than stepping rate.
❏ Cycling technique involves fewer variables than step test.
❏ Examples, relatively still upper body allows accuracy in the measurement of changes of heart rate.
❏ Body mass or weight not directly involved.
❏ Adjustable seat height for leg length.

10) d)
Greater usefulness of sport specific tests arises from :
  4 marks for four from :
❏ Better reflection of the physiological demands of the sport.
❏ For example, aerobic capacity is determined by the combination of cardio-respiratory systems with specific working muscles.
❏ Anaerobic power measures depend entirely on the anaerobic efficiency of the specific working muscles.
❏ Specificity of testing matches demands of that particular sport, for example, cycle ergometer test for cyclist, treadmill testing for road runner.
❏ Problems of using shuttle run test for a swimmer will give a predicted $\dot{V}O_{2max}$ result.
❏ But does not give a true reflection of the physiological demands of the sport, for example, swim training.

STRENGTH TRAINING / FITNESS COMPONENTS

11) a)
❏ 1RM represents the heaviest resistance.
❏ That can be used for one complete repetition of an exercise.
You could assess an athlete's strength using :
  1 mark for one from :
❏ Sargeant jump (height achieved).
❏ Maximal weight lifted.
❏ Use of dynamometer that can measure the force of a selected muscular contraction.

STRENGTH TRAINING / FITNESS COMPONENTS - ANSWERS QUESTION 11 (continued)

11) b) i)
Important training principles would be :
  4 marks for four from :
❑ Warm-up, which raises body temperature / redistributes blood to active tissues / reduces blood viscosity.
❑ Overload, which stresses body systems so that physiological adaptations occur.
❑ Specificity, in which training relevant to the needs of specific activity is undertaken.
❑ Repetition, which enhances skill learning and leads to physiological adaptation.
❑ Cool-down, which maintains blood supply to active tissues enabling waste products to be removed.
❑ Individual response, a coach would tailor a programme to meet an individual's needs.
❑ Variance, in which the programme is varied to prevent staleness.
❑ Moderation, not overtraining or doing too much, which would prevent injury.

11) b) ii)
The activities during a strength training session could be :
❑ Any one from the list : use of weights / circuits / hill sprints / sprinting with resistance such as dragging a tyre
   along the track or harness work.
  3 marks for three from :
❑ Indication of loading in excess of 80%.   ❑ Use of sets.   ❑ Repetitions.
❑ Rest relief, for example, bench press 5 x 40kg (in excess of 80% of max.) 60 sec. between sets.
❑ Selection of a variety of exercises, for example, leg press, sit ups, back hyperextensions.
❑ Alternative example : 8 x 60 metre hill sprints (100% effort) walk back recovery for the rest relief.

11) b) iii)
ATP is regenerated during maximal strength work :
  3 marks for :
❑ Alactic anaerobic energy (ATP/PC) system.
❑ ATP is resynthesised via phosphocreatine.
❑ Coupled reaction between PC and ADP.
  OR 3 marks for coupled reaction equations :

$$PC \xrightarrow{\text{creatine kinase}} P_i + C + Energy$$

❑ $Energy + ADP + P_i \Longrightarrow ATP + C$
❑ $PC + ADP \Longrightarrow ATP + C$ Net effect of coupled reaction.

11) c) i)
Causes of muscle soreness :
  2 marks for two from :
❑ Effects of waste products such as the build up of blood lactate (accumulation of H^+).
❑ This creates a low pH which acts upon pain receptors to produce muscle soreness.
❑ Damage to muscle tissue i.e. micro tears within muscle fibres.
❑ Damage to connective tissues such as tendons and muscle sheaths.
Prevention of muscle soreness :
  2 marks for two from :
❑ Effect of cool-down which is to maintain elevated heart / respiratory rates.
❑ Cool-down has the effect of flushing out waste products by oxidation of lactic acid.
❑ Use of rest days to allow any damage to repair itself.

11) d)
The physiological gains made from a programme of strength training would be :
  6 marks for six from :
❑ 1RM increases significantly.
❑ Largest strength gains take place early on in the training programme.
❑ This would be due to improved coordination and motor units recruited.
❑ Increased muscle fibre size will give overall power and strength increases (muscle hypertrophy).
❑ And also give increased Peak Power.
❑ This peak power will be achieved sooner during maximal anaerobic work.
❑ This is due to significant increases in PC stores in fast twitch motor units.
❑ And improved motor unit recruitment.
❑ Fatigue reduces as toleration to lactic acid increases.
❑ And anaerobic capacity increases.
❑ As thresholds between energy systems are delayed.

2.24 Exercise Physiology

STRENGTH TRAINING / FITNESS COMPONENTS - ANSWERS QUESTION 11 (continued)

11) e)

1 mark for :
- ❏ Co-ordination : practice any open skill, for example, hitting a tennis ball against a wall.
  Adaptive response : 1 mark for :
- ❏ Improvement in neuro-muscular co-ordination or improved recruitment of neural firing patterns of motor units.
  1 mark for :
- ❏ Flexibility : could be passive / active / ballistic / PNF or combinations of these types of training.
  Adaptive response : 1 mark for one from :
- ❏ Improvement in ability of antagonist to relax.
- ❏ Improvement in agonist muscle to lengthen under tension.
- ❏ Effect of residual stretching : muscle does not return to original resting state.
  1 mark for :
- ❏ Endurance : any form of aerobic exercise that raises heart rate to in excess of 120 bpm, for example, steady state 3 mile run.
  Adaptive responses : 1 mark for one from :
- ❏ Improved capillarisation of muscle bed i.e. new blood capillaries are created within the muscle.
- ❏ More efficient use of existing blood capillaries within the muscle.
- ❏ Adaptive response of fast twitch fibres type IIa.
- ❏ Increased mitochondrial density.
- ❏ Increased amounts of muscle myoglobin.
- ❏ Increased oxidative enzymes.

INTERVAL TRAINING

12) a)

4 marks for four from :
- ❏ A 'set' is a group of work / exercise intervals.
- ❏ Separated from one another by a rest period.
- ❏ Which allows a degree of recovery between sets.
- ❏ Thus increasing the number of work intervals.
- ❏ Whilst maintaining quality.
- ❏ Hence optimising on improvements in fitness.

12) b)

The important information missing from the outline interval sessions :

3 marks for three from :
- ❏ The pace at which the work intervals should be performed.
- ❏ The duration of the rest between work intervals.
- ❏ The duration of the rest between sets.
- ❏ The terrain over which the work intervals are to be carried out.

12) c)

A maximum of 8 marks given for four points each from two of the three sections below :

Alactic anaerobic :
- ❏ Many short efforts of 50 metres repeatedly deplete ATP-PC stores.
- ❏ Which conditions the metabolic pathways.
- ❏ And develops fast twitch motor units.
- ❏ Therefore training the ability to develop muscular power.

Lactic anaerobic :
- ❏ Fewer longer efforts of 400 metres repeatedly generate lactic acid.
- ❏ Hence reducing the 'slowing' effects of local muscular fatigue.
- ❏ And develops fast twitch motor units.
- ❏ Therefore trains speed endurance over relatively short distances.

Aerobic :
- ❏ Fewer longer efforts of 1000 metres are mainly aerobic.
- ❏ Which conditions the respiratory system.
- ❏ And cardiovascular systems.
- ❏ Therefore increasing the efficiency of the delivery of oxygen to working tissues (i.e. enhanced $\dot{V}O_{2max}$).
- ❏ Therefore trains aerobic endurance.

INTERVAL TRAINING - ANSWERS QUESTION 12 (continued)

12) d)
  5 marks for five from :
❑ The three energy systems are not really distinct from each other in a game activity such as football.
❑ All three energy systems show overlap in meeting the demands of a 'game' activity of this kind (page 2.1).
❑ Some bursts of energy will be relatively short stressing the alactic anaerobic component (ATP / PC system).
❑ Whilst at other times and towards the end of the game there will be demands made on the lactic anaerobic component.
❑ Both these components will make the main demand on the fast twitch motor units.
❑ During more restful stages of the game and recovery, slow twitch motor units will be active.
❑ Thus making demands on the aerobic system.

PRINCIPLES OF TRAINING : REVERSIBILITY, WARM-UP, COOL-DOWN

13) a) i)
An organised fitness programme produces :
❑ The schedule of work produces an overload demand on the body's systems.
❑ To which the body responds with increased efficiency.

13) a) ii)
Reversibility means :
❑ Gains previously made from training are lost.
❑ When the training stimulus is not maintained.

13) b) i)
When training stops, the cardiovascular system undergoes reversibility because :
  7 marks for seven from :
❑ Pumping action of the heart decreases in efficiency.
❑ Capillarisation of cardiac muscle decreases.
❑ Mitochondria of cardiac muscle decrease in size and number.
❑ Ventricular size decreases.
❑ Therefore stroke volume decreases.
❑ Contractility of cardiac muscle decreases.
❑ Therefore cardiac output decreases.
❑ Thickness of ventricular wall decreases.
❑ Therefore overall hypertrophy of heart is reduced.
❑ Resting heart rate is increased.
❑ Resting blood pressure increases.
❑ Blood volume decreases.
❑ Therefore red blood cell decreases.
❑ Which in turn reduces the oxygen carrying capacity of red blood cells.
❑ Decreased capillaries per muscle fibre.
❑ Therefore less effective blood redistribution to active tissues.
❑ Reduced venous tone.
❑ Therefore increased blood pooling in venous system.

13) b) ii)
Notes :
Stimulation of skeletal muscle can either be direct via the alpha motor neurones which innervate the muscle fibres or indirectly via the muscle spindles.
Muscles and the nervous system show reversible effects when training ceases because of :
  5 marks for five from :
❑ Loss of hypertrophy of fast twitch muscle fibres / motor units.
❑ This leads to a reduction in resting stores of phospho-creatine (PC).
❑ There is a deconditioning of neural pathways involved in direct (alpha) stimulation.
❑ And a deconditioning of neural pathways involved in reciprocal inhibition of antagonistic muscles.
❑ This slows down the speed of response.
❑ Lack of involvement in the game and relevant coaching / practice sessions can also result in a loss of powers of concentration.
❑ It is a combination of these outcomes that can result in a player being 'slower off the mark' in the game situation.

PRINCIPLES OF TRAINING : REVERSIBILITY, WARM-UP, COOL-DOWN - ANSWERS QUESTION 13 (continued)

13) c)

The benefits of rest on training effects are :

4 marks for four from :

- ❏ Enforced rest as a result of injury.
- ❏ Allows recovery period during which essential nutrients and stores can replenish.
- ❏ After which body systems can respond positively to the training stimulus.
- ❏ As compared with continuous / excessive training and insufficient recovery.
- ❏ This causes a decrease in performance / over-use injuries.
- ❏ Hence continuous training can cause 'staleness' which rest following injury overcomes.

13) d)

From a physiological standpoint, explain why warm-up and cool-down are important within an exercise regime.

Warm-up : 4 marks for four from :

- ❏ Raises body temperature.
- ❏ Increases metabolic rate.
- ❏ Raises energy release.
- ❏ Reduces response times.
- ❏ This increase in temperature reduces blood viscosity.
- ❏ And therefore increases blood flow to working muscles.
- ❏ Slightly increasing demand for oxygen will increase heart rate and breathing volumes.
- ❏ Which makes more oxygen available to working tissue.
- ❏ Blood supply is redistributed to working tissue (vascular shunt).
- ❏ A warm-up prepares the body for skill demands of the activity - reducing the risk of injury.

Cool-down : 4 marks for four from :

- ❏ Continued low level exercise and stretching keeps the capillary beds open within active (muscle) tissue.
- ❏ This enables the flushing out of waste products such as lactic acid from the metabolic processes.
- ❏ Enabling the body's systems to gradually return to its resting state.
- ❏ Which limits muscle soreness (DOMS).
- ❏ And enhances recovery from the exercise period.

PERIODISATION

14) a)

Discuss the concept of periodisation and outline its particular application to a strength-training programme for your particular sport.

2 marks for two from :

- ❏ Periodisation is a concept which is centred around a cyclical load design principle.
- ❏ Which enables the coach / athlete to vary intensity, duration and frequency of chosen activity in a structured plan.
- ❏ Strength training for chosen sport - example: sprint swimming (up to 100 metres) must be based on specific physiological requirements of the sport.
- ❏ And therefore the development of power via maximal strength work stressing the ATP-PC (alactic) energy system.
- ❏ And muscular (speed) endurance stressing the Lactic acid (lactate) system.
- ❏ Competition phase to be identified in answer i.e. December - May.

Single periodised year is divided into three periods:

3 marks for three from :

- ❏ A. Preparatory period - macrocycles :
- ❏ 1: July /August   - aerobic conditioning (4 weeks).
- ❏ 2: August / Sept   - speed endurance (lactate work, 6 weeks).
- ❏ 3. October / November   - maximum strength work (alactic, 6 weeks) including pre-competition phase.

3 marks for three from :

- ❏ B. Competition period - macrocycles
- ❏ 1: December   - speed endurance (lactate work, 4 weeks).
- ❏ 2: January / February - strength maintenance work (8 weeks).
- ❏ 3: March - mesocycle i) - maximum strength work tapered for major competition.
-          - mesocycle ii: - major competition peaks.
- ❏ 4: April   - maximum strength work (4 weeks).
- ❏ 5: May   - strength maintenance work (4 weeks).

PERIODISATION - ANSWERS QUESTION 14) a) (continued)

14) a)
2 marks for two from :
- ❑   C. Transition period - macrocycle
- ❑   1: June   - rest.
- ❑   2: July   - exercise other than that programmed within swimming schedule.

14) b)
Why is it important to vary the loading patterns for each of the periods you have identified.
5 marks for five from :
- ❑   Physiological adaptations should take place over a period of months.
- ❑   Without undue stress.
- ❑   To reduce the risk of injury, staleness and / or overtraining.
- ❑   Hence the idea of cyclical loading that incorporates increases in workloads.
- ❑   Followed by decreases in workloads between and within each period.
- ❑   This concept is also known as step loading and reverse step loading.
- ❑   In the preparatory period, the aim is to show an overall increase in speed endurance and maximal strength.
- ❑   In the competition phase, the aim is to maintain or plateau strength gains achieved in the preparatory phase.
- ❑   And to taper strength work prior to major competition so that peak performance is attained.
- ❑   In the transition phase, the swimmer has time to mentally and physically recover from hard swim training.
- ❑   And has the opportunity to play other sports that he / she would not normally have time for.

ERGOGENIC AIDS AND PHYSICAL PERFORMANCE

15) a) i)
Explain the word 'acclimatisation' and describe the physiological preocesses as an elite athlete adapts to altitude.
2 marks for :
- ❑   Acclimatisation consists of reversible physiological changes.
- ❑   Which occur as a result of continued exposure to a different climate (changes in altitude, hot or cold).

8 marks for eight from:
Respiratory response :
- ❑   Hypoxia stimulates central and peripheral chemoreceptors.
- ❑   This causes increased breathing rate and tidal volume.
- ❑   Which leads to increased fluid loss
- ❑   Which reduces plasma volume.
- ❑   This decreases pCO_2, thereby elevating blood pH.
- ❑   Hence urine becomes more alkaline.
- ❑   Respiratory response stabilises after first week.

Vascular response :
- ❑   Increases in red blood cell manufacture (polycythemia).
- ❑   And hence increased blood haemoglobin concentration.
- ❑   Thereby $\dot{V}O_{2max}$ increasing beyond normal values found at sea level.

Cardiac response :
- ❑   Initially increases in HR and SV due to reduced pO_2.
- ❑   And reduced O_2 supply to myocardial tissue.

Cellular response :
- ❑   Long-term, increased myoglobin, mitochondria and oxidative enzymes.
- ❑   Therefore increased cellular respiration beyond normal values found at sea level.

15) a) ii)
How is aerobic training affected by altitude and by a subsequent return to sea level?
4 marks for four from:
- ❑   At altitude, hypoxia significantly reduces oxygen availability.
- ❑   Due to reduced $\dot{V}O_{2max}$ (by up to 15%).
- ❑   Therefore during first week of stay, athlete is advised to train submaximally.
- ❑   Example, easy steady state 30 minute runs / walks.
- ❑   Slower than pace achieved at sea level.
- ❑   To reduce stress on cardio / vascular / respiratory systems.
- ❑   To reduce lactic acid levels (since glycolysis is higher at altitude for the equivalent workload at sea level).
- ❑   During the second week, training levels are increased as respiratory system returns to sea level functioning.
- ❑   And the benefits of increased Hb levels kick in.
- ❑   But athlete is still performing below sea level aerobic capacity.

ERGOGENIC AIDS AND PHYSICAL PERFORMANCE - ANSWERS QUESTION 15) a) ii) (continued)

15) a) ii)
2 marks for two from:
- On return to sea level, aerobic performance is enhanced.
- Due to improved and elevated $\dot{V}O_{2max}$.
- And improved aerobic working capacity of muscle.
- Gained during acclimatisation phase.
- Reversibility of altitude gains occur within 2 weeks after descent.

15) b)
What is an ergogenic aid? Briefly provide a summary of the role that nutritional supplements play in improving performance.
2 marks for :
- An ergogenic aid is defined as any means of improving the efficiency .
- And enhancing the quality of sporting performance.

6 marks for six from :
- Creatine supplementation increases PC levels.
- Thereby enhancing ATP-PC energy system.
- Glutamine supplementation reduces the risk of infection by boosting the body's immune system.
- Vitamin supplementation (C & E) act as antioxidants, thereby enhancing recovery from exercise.
- Isotonic Sports Drinks prevent dehydration.
- And supplement energy reserve.
- Hypotonic sports drinks replenish blood glucose levels.
- And top up glycogen stores after exercise has finished.
- Caffeine ingestion increases mental alertness.

15) c) i)
Describe the method of blood doping and its potential for improving endurance performance.
2 marks for two from:
- Blood doping involves the removal, storage.
- And subsequent re-infusion of a small quantity of blood after 5-6 weeks.

2 marks for two from:
- Aim is to increase the numbers of red blood cells (polycythemia).
- And hence the oxygen-carrying capacity of the sportsperson's blood.
- Thereby leading to improved $\dot{V}O_{2max}$ and cellular respiration.

15) c) ii)
Discuss the health issues that are associated with the use of rEPO in sport.
4 marks for four from:
- Elevation of red blood cell production that can reach toxic life-threatening levels.
- Blood clots form more readily.
- This is due to increased blood viscosity.
- This increases the danger of a stroke or coronary thrombosis.
- During exercise dehydration magnifies the risks identified above.
- Resting heart rate can fall to dangerously low levels.

EXERCISE and HEALTH

16) a)
1 mark for each explanation :
- Nerve conduction velocity reduces slightly due to reduced myelinated sheaths surrounding neurones.
- Loss of neurones that are non-renewable therefore increased reaction time.
- Basal metabolic rate reduces slightly due to an overall reduction in energy requirements of body systems.
- Cardiac index reduces due to a decline in HR_{max} (HR_{max} = 220 - age).
- Vital capacity reduces dramatically due to loss of elasticity of alveoli walls.
- Also due to reduced strength of respiratory muscles.

16) b)
Decline in bone mass with age is more pronounced in women because :
3 marks for :
- Reduction in female hormone oestrogen levels in blood following menopause.
- Possibly diet related : inadequate calcium intake.
- Females are more likely not to take regular physical exercise.

EXERCISE AND HEALTH - ANSWERS QUESTION 16 (continued)

16) c) i)
The causes of middle age spread :
❒ Lack of physical activity.
❒ Over eating or positive energy balance.

16) c) ii)
The health risks associated with middle age spread : 2 marks for two from :
❒ Hypertension.   ❒ CHD coronary heart disease.
❒ Limited mobility of joints.   ❒ Poor strength to weight ratio.

16) d) i)
Example week's programme for 4 marks for activity / 4 marks for fitness components :

	Activity	**Fitness Component(s)**
Monday	❒ 45 min continuous aerobic swim.	❒ flexibility / body composition.
Tuesday	❒ 1 hr Modern Dancing.	❒ flexibility / endurance.
Wednesday	rest day.	
Thursday	❒ 20 min fitness trail.	❒ muscular strength.
Friday	rest day.	
Saturday	❒ 2 hr mountain hike.	❒ muscular endurance / body composition.
Sunday	rest day.	

16) d) ii)
The effects of aerobic and anaerobic exercise on older people are :
3 marks for aerobic adaptations from :
❒ The effects of training has been shown to increase endurance capacity and strength.
❒ Due to improvements in $\dot{V}O_{2max}$ values.
❒ Gains in muscle oxidative enzyme activity (and not increases in cardiac output).
❒ Since a reduction in HR_{max} appears to be similar in both sedentary and highly trained ageing persons.
❒ Although stroke volume can be maintained when older adults continue to train intensely.
❒ Improvements in coronary circulation (capillaries within the heart muscle remain efficient).
❒ Peripheral blood flow decreases with ageing, even though capillary density in the muscles remains unchanged.
❒ Control of hypertension.
❒ This appears to be compensated for by a greater $a\text{-}\bar{v}O_2$diff (i.e. more oxygen uptake by the exercising muscles).
❒ Therefore, overall evidence appears to suggest that peripheral factors play a greater role in aerobic adaptations.
❒ Than central factors such as heart rate.
❒ Aerobic exercise reduces the loss of elasticity from the lungs and chest wall.
❒ As a result, endurance trained older athletes have only a slight decrease in pulmonary ventilation capacity.
❒ Improved recovery following exercise.
❒ Reduced body fat and blood glucose levels, therefore reduced risk of obesity and diabetes.
❒ Reduced ratio of low density lipoproteins (LDL cholesterol) to high density lipoproteins (HDL cholesterol), therefore reducing the risk of CHD and atherosclerosis.

3 marks for anaerobic adaptations from :
❒ Anaerobic exercise maintains muscle hypertrophy.
❒ And reduces decline in reflex responses and reaction times.
❒ Because fibre-type composition remains unchanged.
❒ This is because fast twitch motor units continue to be innervated.
❒ And protein synthesis maintained.
❒ Reduces decline in ATP / PC stores, hence helps maintain maximum power output.
❒ And maintains alatic / lactic threshold.
❒ Reduces decline in glycolysis (lactic acid system), which maintains tolerance to muscle fatigue.
❒ Anaerobic exercise strengthens bone tissue and joints.

Jan Roscoe

2.30 Exercise Physiology

SELECTED BIBLIOGRAPHY

ADAM	1999	Interactive Physiology Multipack CDROMs. Benjamin / Cummings.
Adams, G.M.	1998	Exercise Physiology Laboratory Manual 3e. McGraw-Hill.
Beashel, P.	1996	Advanced Studies in Physical Education and Sport. Thomas Nelson.
Boulton & Hawker.	1988	Exercise Physiology, Video Sports Science Series. University of Western Australia.
Clegg, C.	1995	Exercise Physiology. Feltham Press.
	1996	Measurement and Testing of Physical Performance. Feltham Press.
	2000	Graphs for Exercise Physiology. Feltham Press.
Davis, R.J. et.al.	2000	Physical Education and the Study of Sport 4e. Mosby.
Dick, F.	1991	Training Theory. BAF.
Gallligan, F. et al.	2000	A level PE for Edexcel. Heinemann.
Honeybourne, J. et.al.	2000	Advanced Physical Education and Sport 2e. Nelson Thornes.
	2001	Advanced Physical Education and Sport 2e - Teachers' Resource Pack. Nelson Thornes.
McArdle, W.D.	2000	Essentials of Exercise Physiology 2e. Lippincott, Williams and Wilkins.
Mottram, D.R.	1996	Drugs in Sport 2e. E & F.N. Spon.
Paish, W.	1990	Nutrition for Sport. Crowood Press.
Powers, S.K.	2000	Exercise Physiology, Theory and Applications 4e. McGraw-Hill.
Prentice, W.	1998	Fitness and Wellness for Life 6e. McGraw-Hill.
Roscoe, J.	2000	Teachers' Guide to Physical Education and the Study of Sport 4e. Exercise Physiology. Jan Roscoe Publications.
Sharkey, B.J.	1997	Fitness and Health 4e. Human Kinetics.
Wesson, K. et.al.	2000	Sport and PE. A Complete Guide to Advanced Level Study 2e. Hodder & Stoughton.
Wilmore, J.M.	2000	Physiology of Sport and Exercise 2e. Human Kinetics.
Wirhed, R.	1997	Athletic Ability and the Anatomy of Motion 2e. Mosby.

LINEAR MOTION - Position, Distance and Displacement

BIOMECHANICS

POSITION
- This is a way of explaining where a point is relative to some fixed point.

- Position is usually expressed in terms of coordinates (x and y) like a graph in maths.

- For example, the centre forward takes a shot from a position 20 m out from the goal line, and 10m to the left of the left hand post.

- The left hand post is the fixed point or origin of measurement.
- 20 m and 10 m are the coordinates of the position of the centre forward relative to that point.

DISTANCE means the total path length moved by a body.

- Example, a 10,000 m race is run round and round the track, 25 times 400 m, starting and finishing POSITION are the same, but distance travelled is 10,000 m.

- Unit the metre m.

DISPLACEMENT
- This means the vector distance from a fixed point (starting point or origin).

- This is the actual 'as the crow flies' distance between start and finish (with direction included).

- Example, the start and finish of a long distance race (Stage 5 of the Tours de France) may be 190 km apart due West, but the distance travelled may be 250 km!

- Unit the metre m.

LINEAR MOTION - Speed Velocity & Acceleration

ACCELERATION $= \dfrac{\text{change of velocity}}{\text{time taken to change}}$ $a = \dfrac{v - u}{t}$
- Unit ms^{-2}.

- An object changing direction is accelerating, since the velocity changes.
- Example, swerving rugby player.
- Direction of acceleration is along the radius of the curve (path of player).
- This is a radial acceleration.
- Deceleration is negative acceleration (slowing down).
- Acceleration in same direction as net force.
- Acceleration is a vector (has direction).

VELOCITY / TIME graph
- Gradient of graph is acceleration.
- Area under graph is distance travelled.

SPEED $= \dfrac{\text{distance moved}}{\text{time taken}}$ $v = \dfrac{s}{t}$ unit ms^{-1}.
   = scalar (no direction)

VELOCITY = speed in a given direction.
   = vector.

DISTANCE / TIME graph.
- Gradient of graph is velocity.

VECTORS

- A VECTOR has DIRECTION as well as SIZE (magnitude or value).

- A vector can be represented by a line on a piece of paper (graph paper).
- The length of the line represents the size (say the value of a force in newtons).
- The angle of the line to the horizontal represents the direction.

- Examples of vectors are force, acceleration, velocity, weight, momentum.

- A SCALAR has SIZE (value) only.

- Examples of scalars are mass, temperature, energy, speed, distance, volume, pressure, power.

ADDING VECTORS
- This is a process which involves finding the size and direction of a resultant of 2 or more vectors.
- Complete the parallelogram as shown in the example above.
- The resultant is the diagonal of the parallelogram.

- The resultant of two vectors at right angles found by completing the rectangle.
- $F^2 = F_1^2 + F_2^2$
- $\theta = \tan^{-1}(F_2/F_1)$.

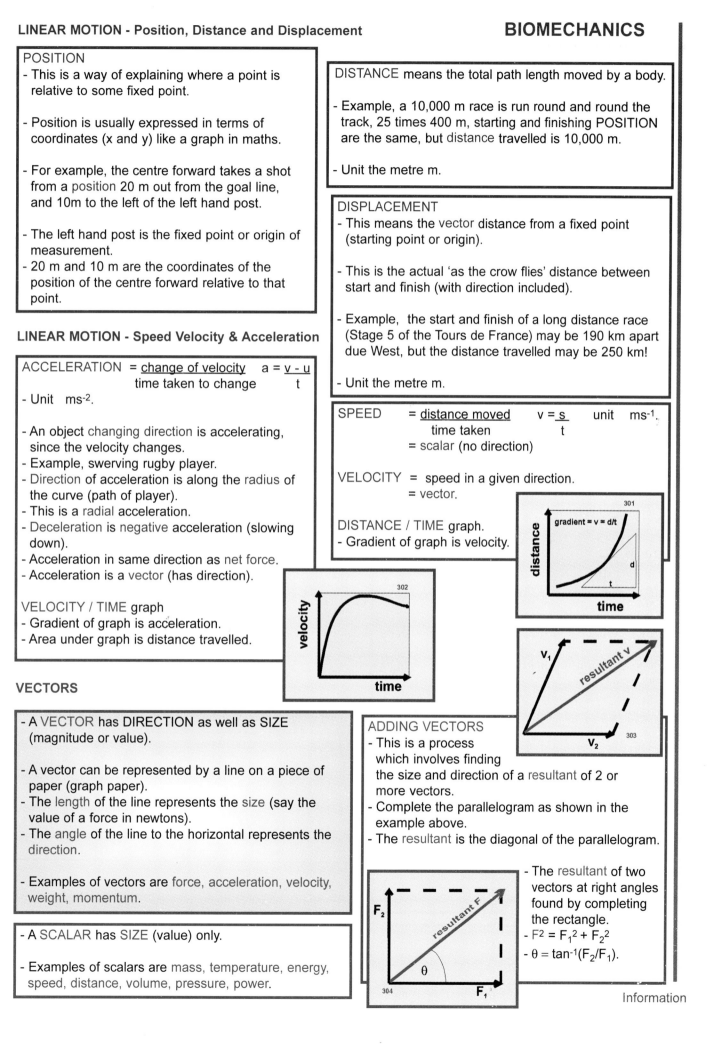

Information

COMPONENTS of a VECTOR

- A VECTOR can be RESOLVED into COMPONENTS which must be at right angles.

- This is done by completing a rectangle with the original vector as the diagonal.

- The vertical and horizontal sides of the rectangle are called the horizontal and vertical components of the original vector.

- $F_h = F.\cos \theta$ and $F_v = F.\sin \theta$.

- Components of the VELOCITY of an object in flight would look like :

- Solid black arrows represent the components.
- Solid red arrows represent the velocity vector

FORCE

FORCE is push or pull.

- Unit of force is the Newton (10 N is approximately the weight of 1 kg).

- Force changes the state of motion of an object.
- The link of force with acceleration (or deceleration).
- The more force exerted, the bigger the acceleration produced (Newton's Second law of motion).

FORCE is a VECTOR

- Force has size (magnitude) and direction
- Resultant of many forces acting in different directions.
- Example :

- The drawing of pin men diagrams.
- Showing forces acting.
- Note the point of action of a force.
- And the direction of a force.
- And the resultant of several forces (black arrow).

GRAVITY and WEIGHT

GRAVITY

- Gravity is a force field produced between any two objects which have mass
- The two objects would attract each other, and for example a mutual force of attraction holds the moon in orbit around the Earth.
- In sport, the main effect of gravity is to pull your body downwards.
- The forces between two people due to gravity are very tiny and can be ignored!

NEWTON'S LAW of GRAVITATION

- This law says that the force due to gravity (on a body or object) is proportional to its mass.
- This force also depends on the distance apart of the objects exerting the force of gravity one on the other (for example, Earth pulls on you as a sportsperson).

- This means that gravity gets less the further away from the centre of the Earth you are.
- And that for each kilogramme of mass the Earth pulls with a force of 9.81 Newtons (usually approximated to 10 N).

WEIGHT and MASS are DIFFERENT

MASS

- Mass is the same everywhere and is related to amount of matter and inertia (inertia is the property of mass which means that it is hard to get a massive body moving, and also hard to stop it once it is moving).

- Measured in kilogrammes kg.

WEIGHT

- Weight is produced by the gravitational force field acting on objects / bodies.
- It is a force which acts downwards towards the centre of the Earth.

- Weight is the predominant force experienced by objects moving freely through air.
- Flight of thrown object is a parabola if no air resistance.

- Your weight would be approximately the same everywhere on Earth (value 10 Newtons per kilogramme).
- Variations occur between poles and equator, and at altitude (less weight at altitude means slightly further jumps and throws).

WEIGHT

- Measured in newtons N.

Information

NEWTON'S LAWS OF MOTION

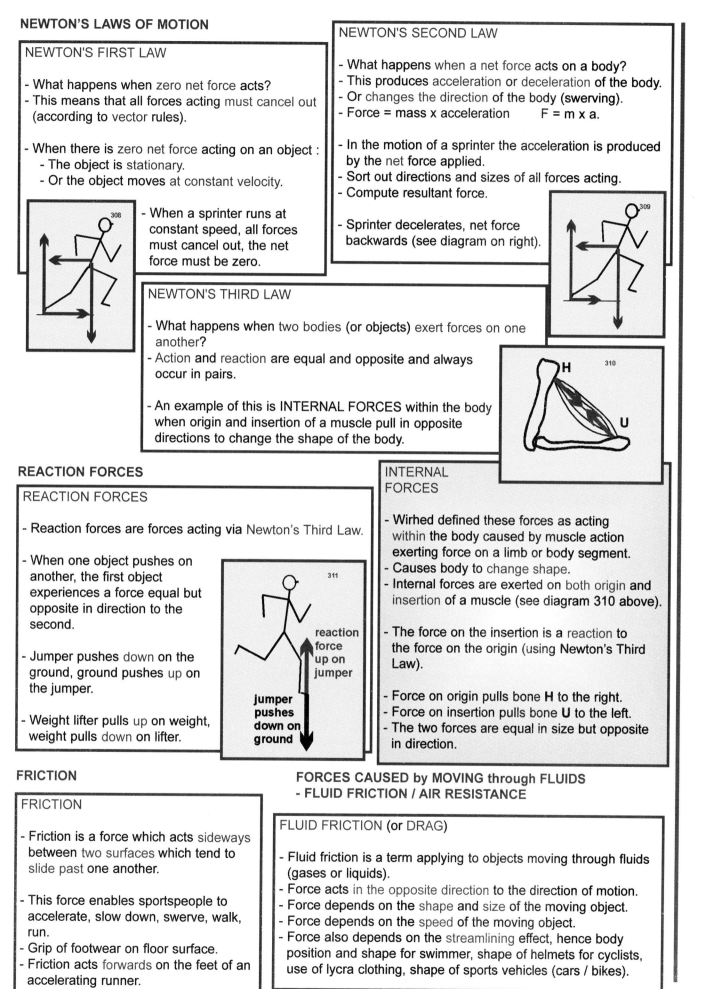

NEWTON'S FIRST LAW

- What happens when zero net force acts?
- This means that all forces acting must cancel out (according to vector rules).

- When there is zero net force acting on an object :
  - The object is stationary.
  - Or the object moves at constant velocity.

- When a sprinter runs at constant speed, all forces must cancel out, the net force must be zero.

NEWTON'S SECOND LAW

- What happens when a net force acts on a body?
- This produces acceleration or deceleration of the body.
- Or changes the direction of the body (swerving).
- Force = mass x acceleration $F = m \times a$.

- In the motion of a sprinter the acceleration is produced by the net force applied.
- Sort out directions and sizes of all forces acting.
- Compute resultant force.

- Sprinter decelerates, net force backwards (see diagram on right).

NEWTON'S THIRD LAW

- What happens when two bodies (or objects) exert forces on one another?
- Action and reaction are equal and opposite and always occur in pairs.

- An example of this is INTERNAL FORCES within the body when origin and insertion of a muscle pull in opposite directions to change the shape of the body.

REACTION FORCES

REACTION FORCES

- Reaction forces are forces acting via Newton's Third Law.

- When one object pushes on another, the first object experiences a force equal but opposite in direction to the second.

- Jumper pushes down on the ground, ground pushes up on the jumper.

- Weight lifter pulls up on weight, weight pulls down on lifter.

reaction force up on jumper

jumper pushes down on ground

INTERNAL FORCES

- Wirhed defined these forces as acting within the body caused by muscle action exerting force on a limb or body segment.
- Causes body to change shape.
- Internal forces are exerted on both origin and insertion of a muscle (see diagram 310 above).

- The force on the insertion is a reaction to the force on the origin (using Newton's Third Law).

- Force on origin pulls bone **H** to the right.
- Force on insertion pulls bone **U** to the left.
- The two forces are equal in size but opposite in direction.

FRICTION

FRICTION

- Friction is a force which acts sideways between two surfaces which tend to slide past one another.

- This force enables sportspeople to accelerate, slow down, swerve, walk, run.
- Grip of footwear on floor surface.
- Friction acts forwards on the feet of an accelerating runner.

FORCES CAUSED by MOVING through FLUIDS - FLUID FRICTION / AIR RESISTANCE

FLUID FRICTION (or DRAG)

- Fluid friction is a term applying to objects moving through fluids (gases or liquids).
- Force acts in the opposite direction to the direction of motion.
- Force depends on the shape and size of the moving object.
- Force depends on the speed of the moving object.
- Force also depends on the streamlining effect, hence body position and shape for swimmer, shape of helmets for cyclists, use of lycra clothing, shape of sports vehicles (cars / bikes).

BERNOULLI EFFECT (FORCE)

BERNOULLI EFFECT
- This is the effect that enables aerofoils to fly.

- Caused by reduction in pressure on surface across which a fluid moves.
- The greater the speed, the bigger the pressure difference, the greater the force.
- The Magnus Effect is this effect applied to spinning (swerving) balls, see diagram.
- Direction of swerve of spinning ball is the same sense as the direction of spin.
- Lift is a force depending on the shape of the moving object sometimes linked to Bernoulli (inverse lift - downforce on racing cars - has the same cause).

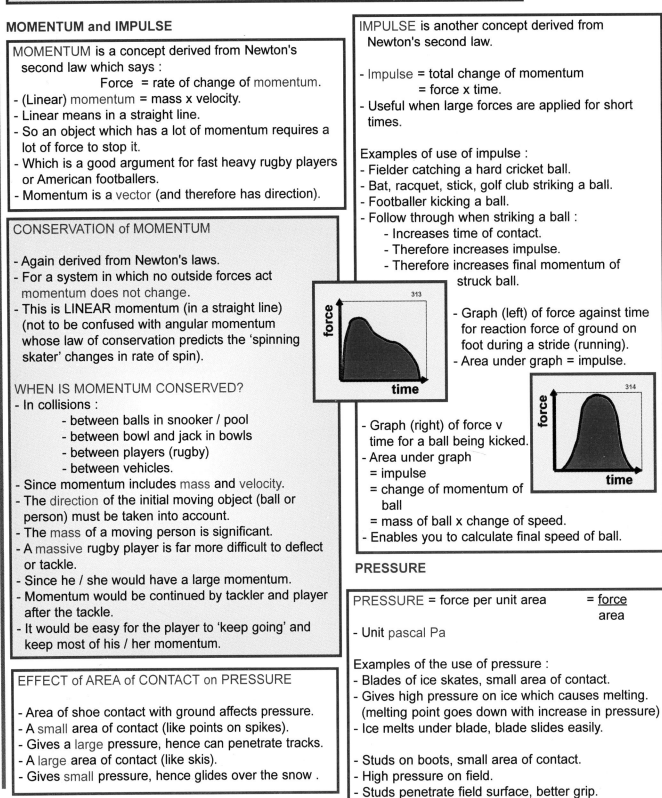

direction of spin   312
direction of motion
direction of swerve

MOMENTUM and IMPULSE

MOMENTUM is a concept derived from Newton's second law which says :
$$\text{Force} = \text{rate of change of momentum}.$$
- (Linear) momentum = mass x velocity.
- Linear means in a straight line.
- So an object which has a lot of momentum requires a lot of force to stop it.
- Which is a good argument for fast heavy rugby players or American footballers.
- Momentum is a vector (and therefore has direction).

CONSERVATION of MOMENTUM

- Again derived from Newton's laws.
- For a system in which no outside forces act momentum does not change.
- This is LINEAR momentum (in a straight line) (not to be confused with angular momentum whose law of conservation predicts the 'spinning skater' changes in rate of spin).

WHEN IS MOMENTUM CONSERVED?
- In collisions :
        - between balls in snooker / pool
        - between bowl and jack in bowls
        - between players (rugby)
        - between vehicles.
- Since momentum includes mass and velocity.
- The direction of the initial moving object (ball or person) must be taken into account.
- The mass of a moving person is significant.
- A massive rugby player is far more difficult to deflect or tackle.
- Since he / she would have a large momentum.
- Momentum would be continued by tackler and player after the tackle.
- It would be easy for the player to 'keep going' and keep most of his / her momentum.

EFFECT of AREA of CONTACT on PRESSURE

- Area of shoe contact with ground affects pressure.
- A small area of contact (like points on spikes).
- Gives a large pressure, hence can penetrate tracks.
- A large area of contact (like skis).
- Gives small pressure, hence glides over the snow .

IMPULSE is another concept derived from Newton's second law.

- Impulse = total change of momentum
           = force x time.
- Useful when large forces are applied for short times.

Examples of use of impulse :
- Fielder catching a hard cricket ball.
- Bat, racquet, stick, golf club striking a ball.
- Footballer kicking a ball.
- Follow through when striking a ball :
    - Increases time of contact.
    - Therefore increases impulse.
    - Therefore increases final momentum of struck ball.

force   313
time

- Graph (left) of force against time for reaction force of ground on foot during a stride (running).
- Area under graph = impulse.

force   314
time

- Graph (right) of force v time for a ball being kicked.
- Area under graph
    = impulse
    = change of momentum of ball
    = mass of ball x change of speed.
- Enables you to calculate final speed of ball.

PRESSURE

PRESSURE = force per unit area $= \dfrac{\text{force}}{\text{area}}$
- Unit pascal Pa

Examples of the use of pressure :
- Blades of ice skates, small area of contact.
- Gives high pressure on ice which causes melting. (melting point goes down with increase in pressure)
- Ice melts under blade, blade slides easily.

- Studs on boots, small area of contact.
- High pressure on field.
- Studs penetrate field surface, better grip.

PROJECTILES

FACTORS AFFECTING RANGE of PROJECTILE

- Speed of release.
- Angle of release.
- Height of release (compared to landing height).

- The motion of most thrown or struck objects is affected by :
    - Air resistance.
    - Sometimes air flow (Bernoulli effect).
- Examples include badminton shuttle, table tennis ball, discus, javelin, american football, golf ball.
- Without air resistance (shot, hammer) flight path would be a symmetric curve called a parabola.

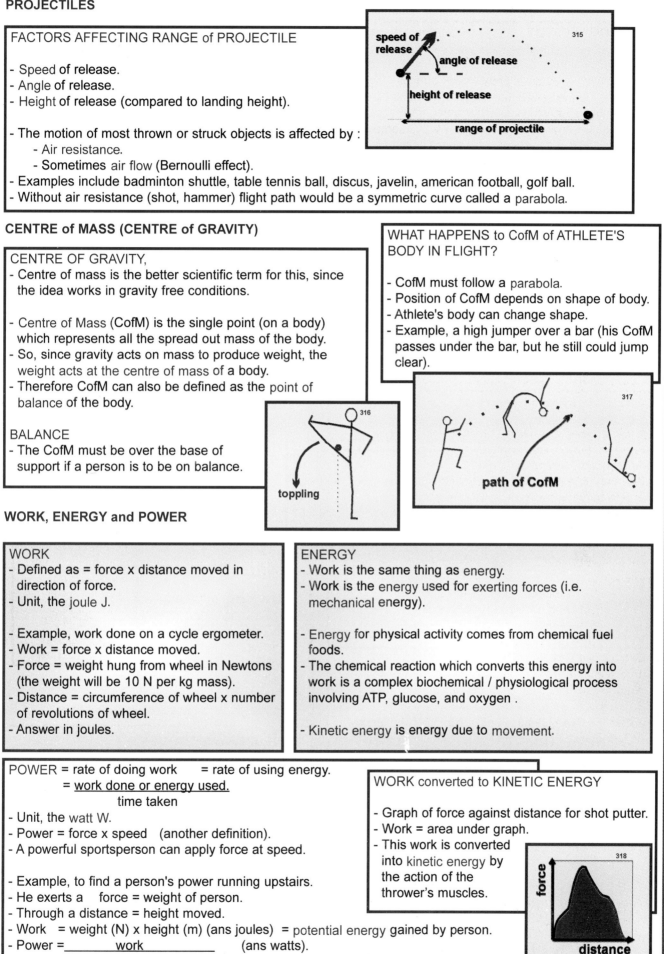

CENTRE of MASS (CENTRE of GRAVITY)

CENTRE OF GRAVITY,
- Centre of mass is the better scientific term for this, since the idea works in gravity free conditions.

- Centre of Mass (CofM) is the single point (on a body) which represents all the spread out mass of the body.
- So, since gravity acts on mass to produce weight, the weight acts at the centre of mass of a body.
- Therefore CofM can also be defined as the point of balance of the body.

BALANCE
- The CofM must be over the base of support if a person is to be on balance.

WHAT HAPPENS to CofM of ATHLETE'S BODY IN FLIGHT?

- CofM must follow a parabola.
- Position of CofM depends on shape of body.
- Athlete's body can change shape.
- Example, a high jumper over a bar (his CofM passes under the bar, but he still could jump clear).

toppling

path of CofM

WORK, ENERGY and POWER

WORK
- Defined as = force x distance moved in direction of force.
- Unit, the joule J.

- Example, work done on a cycle ergometer.
- Work = force x distance moved.
- Force = weight hung from wheel in Newtons (the weight will be 10 N per kg mass).
- Distance = circumference of wheel x number of revolutions of wheel.
- Answer in joules.

ENERGY
- Work is the same thing as energy.
- Work is the energy used for exerting forces (i.e. mechanical energy).

- Energy for physical activity comes from chemical fuel foods.
- The chemical reaction which converts this energy into work is a complex biochemical / physiological process involving ATP, glucose, and oxygen .

- Kinetic energy is energy due to movement.

POWER = rate of doing work = rate of using energy.
$$= \frac{\text{work done or energy used.}}{\text{time taken}}$$
- Unit, the watt W.
- Power = force x speed (another definition).
- A powerful sportsperson can apply force at speed.

- Example, to find a person's power running upstairs.
- He exerts a force = weight of person.
- Through a distance = height moved.
- Work = weight (N) x height (m) (ans joules) = potential energy gained by person.
- Power = $\dfrac{\text{work}}{\text{time taken to run upstairs}}$ (ans watts).

WORK converted to KINETIC ENERGY

- Graph of force against distance for shot putter.
- Work = area under graph.
- This work is converted into kinetic energy by the action of the thrower's muscles.

Information

ROTATIONAL / ANGULAR MOTION

ANGULAR VELOCITY = angle turned through per second

$$\omega = \frac{\text{angle turned through}}{\text{time taken}} = \frac{\theta}{t}$$

ω = Greek letter omega.

- This is rate of spin, most easily understood as revolutions per second (revs per sec).
- Revs per sec would have to be converted to the unit radians per second for calculations.
1 rev per second = 2 x π = 6.28 rs⁻¹.

- Rates of spin apply to :
  - Tumbling gymnasts, trampolinists and divers (piked straight and tucked somersaults), discus and hammer throwers, spinning skaters, skiers turning and twisting between slalom gates.

ACTION of FORCES in MUSCLES at JOINTS - LEVERS

LEVERS

- Levers have an effort, pivot (fulcrum) and load.
- And are a means of applying forces at a distance from the source of the force.

CLASSIFICATION OF LEVERS

- Class 1 lever :
  See-saw lever found rarely in the body, e.g. triceps.

- Class 2 lever :
  Wheelbarrow lever, load bigger than effort, e.g. calf muscle.

- Class 3 lever :
  Mechanical disadvantage, effort bigger than load, most common system found in body, e.g. biceps.

JOINTS as LEVERS - EXAMPLES

- Find forces in several different muscles (groups).
- Look at size of muscle and relate to the force it exerts.
- Does the force change with the angle of the limbs?
- What are the implications for the physiology of muscle tissue?

ANGLE (angular displacement)

- To be scientifically correct angle should not be measured in degrees, but in RADIANS (r).
- Angle $= \dfrac{\text{arc length}}{\text{radius of arc}} = \dfrac{l}{r}$
- 360 degrees = 2 x π radians = 6.28 radians
- 180⁰ = π r = 3.14 r
- 90⁰ = 1/2 π r = 1.57 r
- 30⁰ = 1/6 π r = 0.52 r
- And so on (see maths text book for more).

ANGULAR ACCELERATION
- Rate of change of angular velocity.
- Angular acceleration

$$= \frac{\text{change of angular velocity}}{\text{time taken}}$$

$$A = \frac{\omega_2 - \omega_1}{t}$$

- (Note similarity of formula with linear motion).

- Used when rates of spin increase or decrease.
- Example, hammer thrower.

MOMENT of a FORCE (TORQUE)

= force x distance from pivot to line of action of force
- Unit   newton metre Nm.
- Example (above diagram) moment = F x **d**.
- **d** measured at right angles to **F**.

PRINCIPLE of MOMENTS

- This law applies when a lever is balanced.
- (When the arms of the lever are not accelerating).
- Moments tend to turn a lever arm :
  clockwise (CW) or anticlockwise (ACW).

- ANTICLOCKWISE MOMENT
            = CLOCKWISE MOMENT.

FORCES in MUSCLES

- Examples from :
- Biceps muscle acting on elbow joint.
- Triceps muscle acting on elbow joint.
- Quadriceps acting on knee joint.
- Gastrocnemius muscle acting on ankle joint via the achilles tendon.

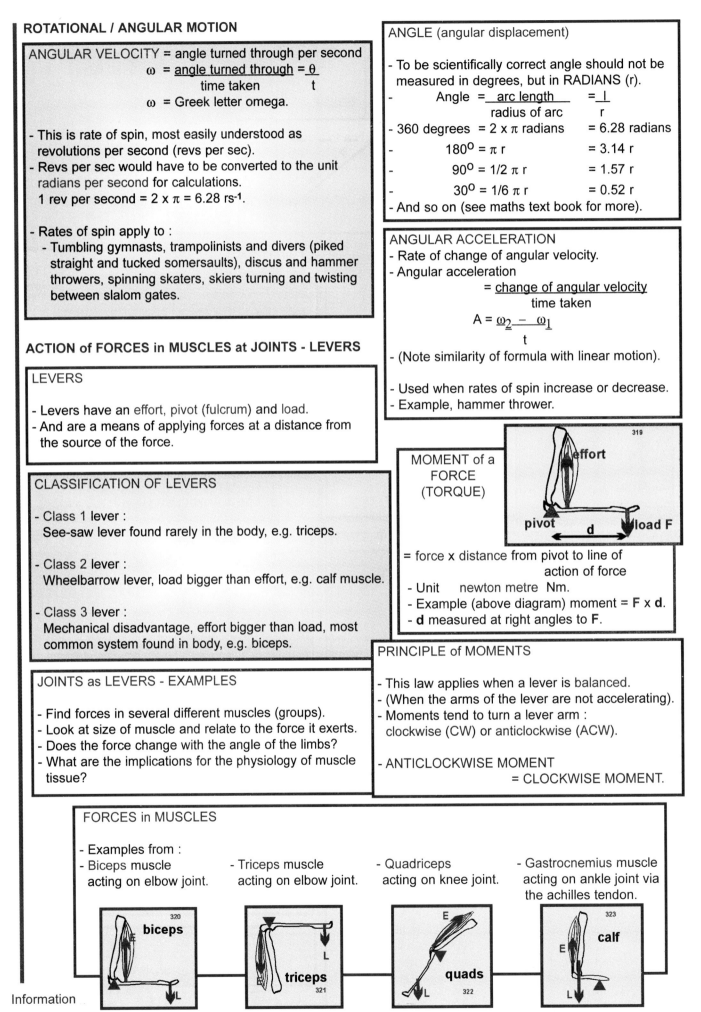

FORCE IN TRICEPS MUSCLE

FORCE IN TRICEPS MUSCLE a worked example.

- Load (weight in hand is 16 kg) = 16 x 10 (each kg weighs 10 N) = 160 N.
- Distance of load to pivot (hand to elbow joint) = 0.3 m.
- Anticlockwise moment (of load) = 160 x 0.3. = 48 Nm.
- Distance of effort from pivot (triceps muscle insertion to elbow joint) = 0.02 m.
- Clockwise moment (of effort) = effort x 0.02.
- ACW moment = CW moment
  48 Nm = effort x 0.02
- Therefore effort = $\frac{48}{0.02}$ = 2400 N = force in triceps muscle.

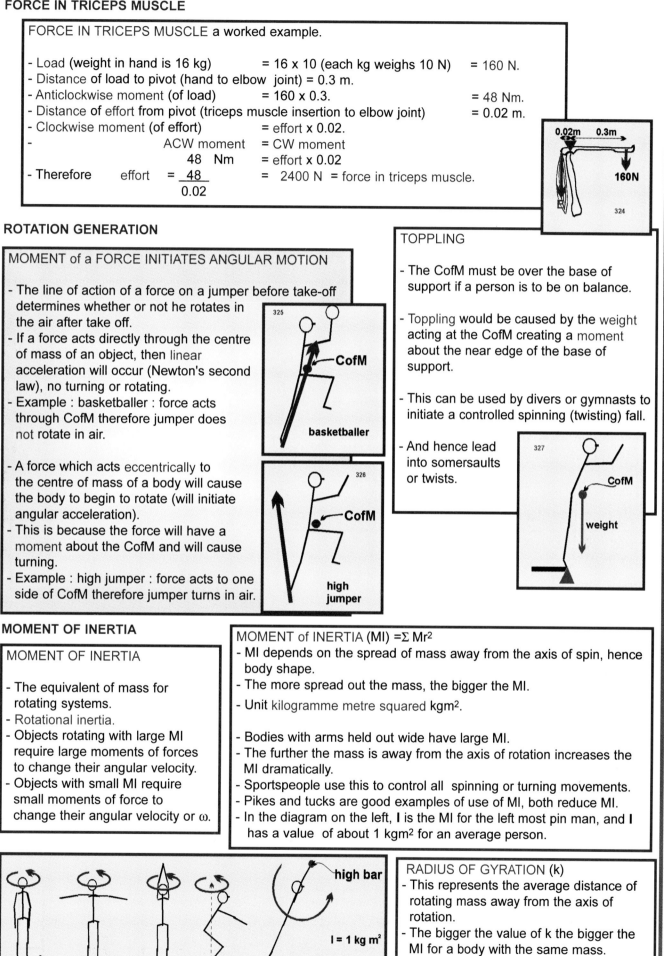

ROTATION GENERATION

MOMENT of a FORCE INITIATES ANGULAR MOTION

- The line of action of a force on a jumper before take-off determines whether or not he rotates in the air after take off.
- If a force acts directly through the centre of mass of an object, then linear acceleration will occur (Newton's second law), no turning or rotating.
- Example : basketballer : force acts through CofM therefore jumper does not rotate in air.

- A force which acts eccentrically to the centre of mass of a body will cause the body to begin to rotate (will initiate angular acceleration).
- This is because the force will have a moment about the CofM and will cause turning.
- Example : high jumper : force acts to one side of CofM therefore jumper turns in air.

TOPPLING

- The CofM must be over the base of support if a person is to be on balance.

- Toppling would be caused by the weight acting at the CofM creating a moment about the near edge of the base of support.

- This can be used by divers or gymnasts to initiate a controlled spinning (twisting) fall.

- And hence lead into somersaults or twists.

MOMENT OF INERTIA

MOMENT OF INERTIA

- The equivalent of mass for rotating systems.
- Rotational inertia.
- Objects rotating with large MI require large moments of forces to change their angular velocity.
- Objects with small MI require small moments of force to change their angular velocity or ω.

MOMENT of INERTIA (MI) $= \Sigma Mr^2$
- MI depends on the spread of mass away from the axis of spin, hence body shape.
- The more spread out the mass, the bigger the MI.
- Unit kilogramme metre squared kgm^2.

- Bodies with arms held out wide have large MI.
- The further the mass is away from the axis of rotation increases the MI dramatically.
- Sportspeople use this to control all spinning or turning movements.
- Pikes and tucks are good examples of use of MI, both reduce MI.
- In the diagram on the left, I is the MI for the left most pin man, and I has a value of about 1 kgm^2 for an average person.

RADIUS OF GYRATION (k)
- This represents the average distance of rotating mass away from the axis of rotation.
- The bigger the value of k the bigger the MI for a body with the same mass.

MOMENT of INERTIA - continued

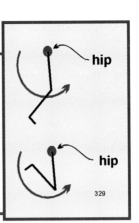

The SPRINTER'S LEG
- When the leg is straight, the leg has high MI about hip as axis.
- Therefore requires large force in groin muscle to swing leg.

- On the other hand when fully bent the leg has low MI.
- Therefore requires low force in groin muscle to swing leg.
- So a sprinter tends to bring the leg through as bent as possible (heel as close to backside as possible).
- This is easier and faster the more bent the leg.

ANGULAR MOMENTUM

ANGULAR MOMENTUM (H)
- Angular Momentum = Moment of Inertia x Angular Velocity.
- $H = I \times \omega$.

CONSERVATION of ANGULAR MOMENTUM
- Angular momentum of a spinning body remains the same (provided no external forces act).
- A body which is spinning / twisting / tumbling will keep its value of H once the movement has started.
- Therefore if MI (I) changes by changing body shape.
- Then ω must also change to keep angular momentum (H) the same.
- Strictly, this is only exactly true if the body has no contact with its surroundings, as for example a high diver doing piked or tucked somersaults in the air.
- But it is almost true for the spinning skater!
- If MI (I) increases (body spread out more) then ω must decrease (rate of spin gets less).

EXAMPLES

- Spinning skater, arms wide - spin slowly, arms narrow - spin quickly.

- Tumbling gymnast, diver, or trampolinist, tuck - spin fast, straight body - spin slowly.
- Dancer executing spin jump, arms held close - spin rapidly.

- Slalom skier crouches on approach to gate, as he / she passes the gate he / she stands straight up (reducing MI) - so turns rapidly past the gate, then crouches again (increasing MI) - to resume slow turn between gates.

QUESTIONS

LINEAR MOTION

1) The table shows the speed of an 19 year old male sprinter during a 200 m race.
a) **i)** Plot a graph of speed against time during this race.   (5 marks)
   ii) When does he reach maximum speed and what happens to his speed between 8 and 22 seconds?   (2 marks)
   iii) Use the graph to establish his speed at 0.5 seconds and 1.5 seconds and calculate the average acceleration between 0.5 and 1.5 seconds.   (3 marks)
   iv) If his mass was 60 kg, what was the net forward force acting on him between 0.5 and 1.5 seconds? What is the nature of this force?   (3 marks)
   v) Sketch pin diagrams of the athlete to show the forces acting on him at the start and at the end of the race.   (5 marks)
b) What physiological reason could you give for the fact that he begins to slow down from about 7 seconds after the start, assuming that he is going 'flat out' all the way?   (2 marks)
c) A hockey player at constant speed is able to swerve and change direction.
   i) Sketch a diagram to show the direction of the force acting on her which would have this effect. (Show on your diagram the direction of the force relative to the direction of travel.) What is the nature of this force?   (3 marks)
   ii) What factors would enable her to swerve more effectively?   (2 marks)

Table - Data for 200 metres sprint	
speed/ms^{-1}	time/seconds
0.0	0
6.0	1
7.5	2
8.2	3
8.4	4
8.5	5
8.5	7
8.4	8
8.3	10
8.2	13
8.1	18
8.0	22

LINEAR MOTION - QUESTIONS (continued)

2) a) Sketch a pin man drawing of a person standing still showing all the forces acting on him.   (2 marks)
b) Sketch a second diagram showing the vertical forces acting an a high jumper just before take-off. Represent the relative sizes of any forces you show by the length of force arrow on your diagram.   (2 marks)
c) Use this second diagram and your understanding of Newton's Laws of motion to explain why the high jumper is able to take off. If the vertical upward ground reaction force on the jumper is 2000 N, and the weight of the jumper is 800N, estimate the net upward force acting on him.   (4 marks)
d) The mass of the jumper is 80 kg, calculate his upward acceleration during this part of the jump.   (2 marks)
e) Successful games players are often able to change their velocity rapidly in the game situation. Explain the bio-mechanics behind this ability using examples from a game of your choice.   (6 marks)

3) a)   i) Define the term velocity.
ii) For movements that take place along a single line of motion, what is the significance of positive and negative velocity values?   (2 marks)
b) The diagram (on the right) shows a linear velocity curve (of the centre of gravity - centre of mass) for a basketballer during the take-off ground contact phase of a vertical jump. Examine the curve and explain what is happening to the jumper at points **A**, **B**, **C**, and **D**.   (8 marks)
c) Copy the diagram and sketch a continuation of the graph to show what would happen to the players velocity during the period of flight.   (4 marks)
d) If it assumed that air resistance is negligible, identify which forces will be causing the changes in velocity when the jumper is :
i) On the ground.   **ii)** In the air.   (4 marks)
e) Identify and explain the points on the graph where the net force acting on the jumper is zero.   (4 marks)

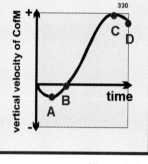

VECTORS - FORCES

4) a) What characterises a vector quantity?   (2 marks)
b) Sketch a diagram to show the flight path of the shot from the moment it leaves the putter's hand to the moment it lands.   (1 mark)
c) State and briefly explain three factors (excluding air effects) which should be used by the putter to optimise the distance thrown.   (6 marks)
d) Explain why the turn in a discus throw produces greater horizontal range than the standing throw.   (3 marks)

5) a) A sprinter uses her calf muscles to push hard on the blocks at the start of a run. Explain, using Newton's Laws, how this enables her to accelerate forwards out of the blocks.   (5 marks)
b) The force diagram on the right shows the forces acting on the runner at the start of the race.
i) Use a vector diagram to show how you could work out the resultant force acting.   (3 marks)
ii) If the resultant force was 300 Newtons and the runner's mass was 60 kg, what would be her acceleration?   (2 marks)
iii) What would be the speed of the runner after 1.5 seconds, assuming that the acceleration is the same over that period of time?   (2 marks)
c) A squash player drives forward into a forehand stroke. Show how Newton's Third Law of motion explains his ability to do this.   (3 marks)

AIR RESISTANCE AND FLUID FRICTION

6) a) What is the effect of air resistance on the flight path of an object?   (4 marks)
b) Explain the effect of air resistance on the flight of two badminton shuttles, one of which has been struck hard and the other gently.   (10 marks)
c) Briefly explain why the flight path of a shot in athletics is so different from the flight of a badminton shuttle.   (4 marks)

AIR RESISTANCE AND FLUID FRICTION (continued)

7)) a) Identify three physical factors (not skill factors) which govern a swimmer's speed and explain how one of these occurs.   (3 marks)
b) Describe the factors which determine the amount of fluid friction acting on a swimmer.   (4 marks)
c) Explain how you would minimise turbulent flow (high drag) of the water past the swimmers body.   (2 marks)
d) Give three examples, each from a different sporting context, to show
how fluid friction affects the sportsperson.   (3 marks)
e) How would you attempt to reduce fluid friction?   (3 marks)
f) Look at figure 332 on the right showing the vertical forces acting on a
swimmer during a stroke. Explain why it is difficult for a swimmer to keep
a horizontal floating position.   (4 marks)

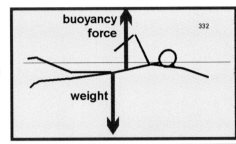

BERNOULLI / MAGNUS EFFECT

8) a) The Bernoulli effect states that a faster flowing liquid or gas exerts
less pressure than a slower moving liquid or gas. Using the diagram on the right,
show how the Bernoulli effect explains the swerve of a spinning ball.   (4 marks)
b) Use diagrams to show how your explanation relates to the flight of a table
tennis ball with side, back and top spin.   (3 marks)
c) Sketch a vector diagram of all forces acting on a table tennis ball in flight with
back spin, and explain how the resultant force on the ball predicts the actual
acceleration of the ball.   (4 marks)
d) Identify one sport other than a ball game, in which the Bernoulli effect plays a part.   (1 mark)
e) When a spinning ball bounces, it exerts forces on the ground. Explain with a diagram what happens to a
bouncing ball with backspin.   (2 marks)

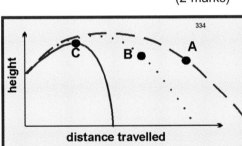

AIR EFFECTS

9) a) The chart on the right shows the flight paths of three different
types of struck or thrown objects found in sport.
   A represents the flight path of a tennis ball with backspin.
   B represents the flight path of a shot in athletics.
   C represents the flight path of a badminton shuttle.

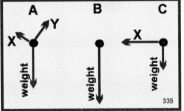

The force diagrams on the left represent the forces acting on the objects at the
point in the path marked with a large dot in the graph above.
     i) Describe the nature of the forces labelled **X** and **Y** in the diagrams.
                                                                       (2 marks)
     ii) Explain why each object has a different flight path.   (6 marks)
b) The diagram (lower right) illustrates the forces acting on a javelin. Force **L** is
the lift force caused by aerodynamic forces acting on the javelin as a whole. Force **W** is the weight of the javelin.
   i) How would the two forces affect the orientation of the javelin as it
   continues its flight?   (4 marks)
   ii) If the weight of the javelin cannot be changed, how could you alter
   the forces acting on the javelin other than throw it harder?   (4 marks)

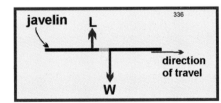

IMPULSE - MOMENTUM

10) a) In the case of a tennis ball being struck, the ball arrives with an incoming velocity of 20 ms^{-1}, and leaves
the racquet with an outgoing velocity of 30 ms^{-1}. The mass of the ball is 150 g = 0.15 kg and time of contact
between between ball and racquet = 0.1 s
     i) Calculate the incoming momentum of the ball (remember momentum = m x v)   (2 marks)
     ii) Calculate the outgoing momentum of the ball.   (2 marks)
     iii) Calculate the change of momentum of the ball.   (2 marks)
b) Using the formula : F x t = change of momentum, calculate the average Force of Impact between ball and
racquet.   (3 marks)
c) A Hockey player strikes a ball.
     i) Sketch a graph of the force applied to the ball against time.   (2 marks)
     ii) Explain the importance of follow through in striking a hockey or cricket ball.   (4 marks)

IMPULSE - MOMENTUM (continued)

11) a) The four man bobsleigh develops a large momentum during the first few seconds of its run.

i) Explain the meaning of the term momentum, and explain why the four man bobsleigh travelling at a speed of 28 m s^{-1} has a different momentum to a skier moving at the same speed. (2 marks)

ii) Explain using Newton's Laws of motion how the bobsleigh acquires its large momentum during the first part of a run. (4 marks)

iii) If the total force generated by the men pushing the bobsleigh is 6000 N over 25m in 6.0 seconds, calculate the work done and power generated by the men for this period. (4 marks)

b) Fluid friction is a force which acts on the bobsleigh once it is moving.

i) Identify the nature of the fluid friction in this case and explain how this might limit the maximum speed of the bob. (3 marks)

ii) Explain the term 'turbulent flow', and how the bobsleigh is used to minimise this factor. (3 marks)

c) Look at the speed time graph in figure 337 below of the motion of a bobsleigh during its run.

i) What is happening at points **Y** and **Z** on the graph? (2 marks)

ii) Sketch a diagram of the bob showing all forces acting on it at the points **X** and **Y** on the graph. (4 marks)

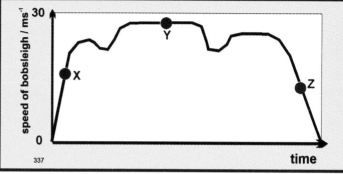

JOINTS AS LEVERS

12) a) Research the human joint complexes, and classify the lever class of as many muscle groups on the joints as you can. (5 marks)

b) The diagram on the right shows an elbow joint of a person performing an exercise. Work out the clockwise moment provided by the force of 200 Newtons about the elbow as a pivot / fulcrum, then, assuming the arm is stationary, use the principle of moments to calculate the force E exerted by the biceps muscle. Show your working. (6 marks)

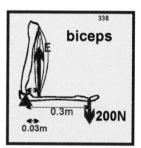

c) The results from an experiment on various joints and muscles of the same person are given in the table on the left

Table - Data for force in different muscle groups		
	force exerted by muscle / N	cross sectional area of muscle / cm^2
biceps	2000	40
gastrocnemius	2400	50
triceps	1500	30
quads	3000	70

i) Plot a graph of force exerted by muscle against cross sectional area of muscle. (3 marks)

ii) What is the physiological reason for the shape of this graph? (2 marks)

d) What feature of the ankle joint and its associated calf muscles enables it to be more efficient in exerting force on the body than almost any other joint in the body? (2 marks)

13) a) Figure 3 shows the elbow joint and the position of the triceps muscle in relation to it when supporting a load behind the head. Draw a simplified sketch to show the lever system, indicating the various forces operating. (4 marks)

b) Using the values shown in the diagram, calculate the load. Neglecting the mass of the ulna, estimate the effort needed to balance the system. (Take the gravitational force on 1 kg to be 10 N). (4 marks)

c) What anatomical factors would affect the value of the maximum load this system could support, given that the angle between the long bones does not change? (3 marks)

d) How would you expect the load to change as the arm extends, and briefly explain how this change of load affects the use of the arm in a sporting situation. (2 marks)

e) Sketch two other types of lever system within the body, labelling the effort, fulcrum and load in each case. (6 marks)

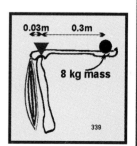

JOINTS AS LEVERS - QUESTIONS (continued)

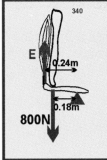

14) a) The diagram on the right shows a diagram of a sportsperson's foot pivoting at a point under the ball of the foot. Use your knowledge of the principle of moments applied to this lever to calculate force **E**. Show all your working. (4 marks)
b) Sketch the lever system which would represent the action of the biceps muscle in flexing the arm. (3 marks)
c) Explain why the biceps / radius lever system is much less efficient at exerting force on the surroundings than the ankle / calf muscle lever system. (3 marks)

CENTRE of MASS

15) a) Explain the concept of centre of mass (centre of gravity). Illustrate your answer using sketches of the human body. (2 marks)
b) Describe an experiment you could use to determine the position of the centre of mass of a person adopting a sporting pose. (4 marks)
c) What effects do changes in body position have on the location of the centre of mass? (2 marks)
d) Explain with drawings how a high jumper changes the position of his / her centre of mass by changing body shape after take-off. (3 marks)

16) a) Sport performers adopt strategies to improve height in situations such as basketball tip-off, rugby line-out, and soccer header.
    i) State the shape of the flight path of the centre of mass of the jumper once he / she has taken off, and briefly explain why this cannot change once he / she is in the air (assume air resistance is so small as to be negligible). (3 marks)
    ii) Explain how a jumper can maximise the height jumped once he / she has taken off. (3 marks)
b) The size and direction of forces applied before take-off can affect the subsequent flight, sketch diagrams or briefly explain how this is done in the case of a high jumper and a basketballer executing a jump shot. (4 marks)

ROTATION

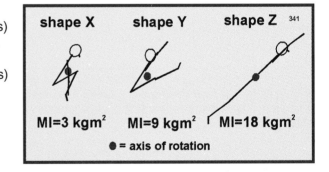

17) a) Define the term Angular Velocity. (2 marks)
b) A diver can make a number of different shapes in the air. The diagram on the right shows three of these. Explain the meaning of moment of inertia (MI) in this context. (4 marks)
c) During a dive a diver goes through the shapes shown in the table below.

Table - Data for shapes of diver during flight		
phase of dive	body shape	time during flight
1	Z	0 - 0.5 s
2	Y	0.5 - 0.7s
3	X	0.7 - 1.0s
4	Z	1.0 - 1.1s
entry		1.1s

i) Explain how the rate of spinning (angular velocity) would change through the dive. (5 marks)
ii) Sketch a graph of this rate of spinning against time. Your sketch need only be approximate. (4 marks)

d)   **i)** State the relationship between Angular Momentum, Moment of Inertia and Angular Velocity. (2 marks)
    ii) Name the law of conservation which accounts for these variations in rate of spin. (1 mark)
    iii) Explain and sketch the arc described by the diver as he / she falls. (3 marks)
e)   **i)** Describe in detail the body shape and movement within another sporting situation where rates of spin are affected by body shape. (6 marks)
    ii) How would you stop the spinning in this situation? (2 marks)

ROTATION - QUESTIONS (continued)

18) a) During the long jump flight phase, a jumper has to adjust body shape and make movements in order to acquire the best body position for landing.

    i) Sketch a pin man diagram showing forces acting on the jumper just before take-off, and explain why these forces would cause a forward angular motion during flight.   **(4 marks)**

    ii) Explain at least one of the techniques which jumpers adopt in order to overcome the problem of forward angular momentum during flight.   **(6 marks)**

b) Briefly explain why there is a difference between the mechanics of take-off of long jumper and triple jumper.   **(4 marks)**

19) a) The diagram below shows a gymnast undertaking a forward somersault following a run up. Sketch three traces on a single graph to represent any changes in Angular Momentum, Moment of Inertia and Angular Velocity for the period of activity between positions 2 and 9.   **(3 marks)**

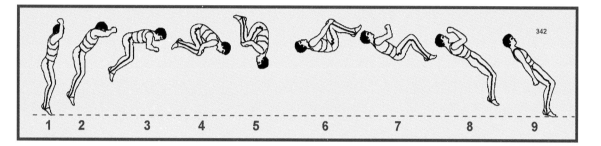

b) Explain the shapes of the traces on the sketch graph that you have drawn.   **(6 marks)**

c) The chart on the right shows a table which sets out measurements of angular velocities (rates of spin) of the gymnast at successive frames from the start of the somersault. Estimate from the chart the ratio of angular velocities at times **X** and **Y**.   **(1 mark)**

d) If the Moment of Inertia of the gymnast is 8 kgm² at time **X**, estimate the Moment of Inertia at time **Y**, using data from the table in the chart.   **(2 marks)**

Table - Data for angular velocity of gymnast		
	frame	angular velocity / degrees s^{-1}
	1	650
X	2	750
	3	850
	4	1100
	5	1400
Y	6	1500
	7	1000
	8	850
	9	650

e) During the landing (from position 9 onwards), what conditions must exist if the gymnast is to cancel out his / her existing forward angular motion effectively? **(2 marks)**

f) Draw a diagram which shows the characteristics of the ground reaction force that you would expect to be present for position 9.   **(3 marks)**

20) a) How can the notion of angular momentum be used to explain the variations in motion of a high diver or a gymnast tumbler (diagrams optional)?   **(4 marks)**

b) The diagram on the right shows a spinning skater in various positions. Under each diagram is an approximate value for the moment of inertia of the skater spinning about his / her central vertical axis. The angular velocity of the skater in position **W** is 2.0 revolutions per second.

    i) What is the formula for calculating the skater's angular velocity? Calculate the angular velocity for the skater in position **Z**.   **(2 marks)**

    ii) Sketch a figure showing a possible position which could cause the skater to attain an angular velocity of 3.0 revolutions per second and calculate what the Moment of Inertia of this shape must be. **(2 marks)**

c) Principles of angular momentum can be used to improve performance in a variety of sports. With the use of diagrams explain :

    i) How a slalom skier turns through the gates at maximum speed.   **(4 marks)**

    ii) How a dancer manages to complete a triple spin in the air before touching the ground.   **(4 marks)**

ROTATION - QUESTION 20 (continued)

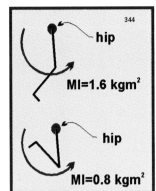

20) d) The diagram on the right shows a sportsperson's leg in two different positions. The values quoted are the moment of inertia of the leg as it rotates about the hip joint (shown as a red dot on each diagram). Explain the implications of these data for the efficiency of running style in a sprinter and long distance runner.   (7 marks)

ANSWERS

The answer for each mark awarded is notated by the ❑ symbol - where there are more ❑ symbols than there are marks available, marks would be given for any choice up to the maximum available. Usually, the precise wording specified in an answer would not be required - answers with the same meaning would be acceptable. In Science areas, sometimes the precise words used in terminology would be required (for example, **Impulse** has the precise definition as Force multiplied by time for an action).

LINEAR MOTION

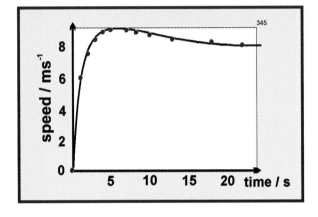

1) a) i)
       See speed / time graph on right, 5 marks for :
❑   Horizontal axis correctly scaled and labelled.
❑   Vertical axis correctly scaled and labelled.
❑ ❑ 2 marks for points plotted correctly.
❑   Curve drawn correctly.
1) a) ii)
       2 marks for :
❑   Maximum speed is reached between 5 - 7 seconds.
❑   After 8 seconds there is a gradual slowing down.
1) a) iii)
       3 marks for :
❑   At 0.5 seconds, speed = 3.0 ms^{-1} (allow + or - 0.2).
❑   At 1.5 seconds, speed = 6.8 ms^{-1} (allow + or - 0.3).
❑   Acceleration = change of speed per second = 6.8 - 3.0 (in 1 second) = 3.8 ms^{-2}.
1) a) iv)
       3 marks for :
❑   Accelerating force is given by Newton' Second Law of motion,
               force = mass x acceleration.
❑   Therefore   force = 60kg x 3.8ms^{-2} = 228 Newtons.
❑   The nature of the force is friction between footwear and ground.

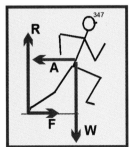

1) a) v)
Pin man diagrams showing forces acting at start and end of race :
       At start diagram on left shows (3 marks for) :
❑   Weight **W**.
❑   Normal Reaction force **R**.
❑   Forward Friction force **F**.
       Near the end of the run, diagram on right shows (2 marks for) :
❑   Weight Reaction and Friction forces.
❑   Air resistance force **A** - in opposite direction to forward motion.

1) b)
The physiological reason for slowing down after 7 seconds :
       2 marks for two from :
❑   She has reached the alactic acid threshold.
❑   She has used up her phosphocreatine stores.
❑   She has moved from ATP-PC system to the lactic system of ATP (energy) regeneration.

LINEAR MOTION - ANSWERS QUESTION 1 (continued)

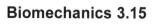

1) c) i)
The direction and nature of the force acting during swerving :
    See diagram on right. 3 marks for :
- ☐ Direction of force.
- ☐ At right angles to direction of motion of swerver.
- ☐ Nature of force is friction between footwear and ground.

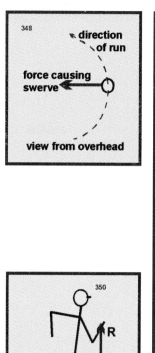

1) c) ii)
The factors enabling more effective swerving :
    2 marks for :
- ☐ Nature of ground and surface (loose, muddy, wet, firm, dry).
- ☐ Footwear (studs, spikes, flats).

2) a)
All forces acting on a man standing at rest :

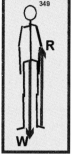

    See diagram on left, 2 marks for :
- ☐ Note that the force arrows are equal indicating that the forces cancel out - there is zero net force.
- ☐ The upward reaction force **R** acts at the feet, the weight **W** acts at the centre of mass.

2) b)
The vertical forces acting on a high jumper just before takeoff :
    See diagram on right, 2 marks for :
- ☐ The upward reaction force **R** acts at the take off foot, **W** acts at the centre of mass.
- ☐ Note that the upward arrow is bigger than the downward arrow, which means that there is a net upward force acting on the jumper.

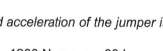

2) c)
The high jumper is able to take off because :
    4 marks for :
- ☐ Newton's second law of motion says that acceleration is linked to net force
- ☐ So since here there is a net upward force, there will be an upward acceleration.
- ☐ Which of course will give him / her a vertical upward velocity which will enable the jumper to take off.
- ☐ Net upward force F = 2000 - 800 = 1200 N.

2) d)
From Newton's second law, and the mass of the jumper being 80 kg, the upward acceleration of the jumper is :
    2 marks for :
- ☐ Newton's Second law gives :   Force = mass x acceleration,   Force = 1200 N, mass = 80 kg.
    therefore   1200 = 80 x acceleration
- ☐   acceleration = $\dfrac{1200}{80}$ = 15 ms^{-2}.

2) e)
The biomechanics behind the ability to change velocity rapidly is :
    6 marks for six from :
- ☐ The force applied to the person is that betwen footwear and ground - friction.
- ☐ The factors which govern the size of the friction force are the weight of the individual, and the nature of the surface and footwear used.
- ☐ Newton's 3rd Law applies between foot and ground.
- ☐ The sportsperson pushes on the ground (the action force), the ground pushes back with a reaction force (which is equal in size but opposite in direction to the action force) on on the person.
- ☐ Acceleration = rate of change of velocity, velocity includes the direction.
- ☐ Newton's 2nd Law tells us how much acceleration is produced by the force acting.
- ☐ Force = mass x acceleration enables you to work out the acceleration
- ☐ Hence the bigger the force (the stronger the person) the greater the change in velocity.
- ☐ If the force is sideways to the direction of motion at the time, then the direction is changed.
- ☐ A sideways force causes swerving (change of direction but no change of speed).
- ☐ A force in the direction of motion causes increase or decrease in speed.

LINEAR MOTION - ANSWERS (continued)

3) a) i) and ii)
  2 marks for :
☐ Velocity = distance moved per second in a given direction.
☐ Positive values of velocity mean in a forwards direction, negative values in a backwards direction.

3) b)
What is happening to the jumper at the point on the graph?
  8 marks for :
☐ At **A** the player's CoM is moving downwards at its biggest downward value of speed.
☐ And the CoM is sinking as the jumper flexes his legs.
☐ At **B** the player's CoM is at its lowest point.
☐ As the athlete starts his upward drive.
☐ At **C** the player's CoM (and hence body) is moving at its maximum vertical upwards speed.
☐ And he is at the end of his upwards acceleration phase.
☐ Between **C** and **D** the jumper actually slows down slightly just before take-off.
☐ And at **D**, his take-off speed is slightly lower than the maximum which his CoM achieved during the upwards acceleration phase.

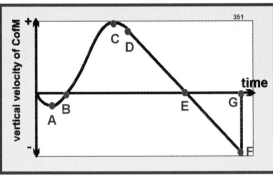

3) c)
Extend the diagram to continue what happens after take-off.
  See diagram on right : 4 marks for four from :
☐ A straight line from the take-off point (**D**) down through the horizontal axis - athlete falls under gravity only.
☐ Between **D** and **E** the jumper is moving upwards, but decelerating to the peak of his flight at time **E**.
☐ Between **E** and **F** the jumper is falling back to earth (moving downwards - hence negative velocity).
☐ Equal portions of the graph to the left and right of the crossing point - time **DE** = time **EF**.
☐ At point **F**, he lands, and his velocity quickly drops to zero (at **G**).

3) d) i) and ii)
Identify the forces causing change of velocity on the ground and in the air.
  4 marks for :
☐ Up to **A**, (while in contact with the ground) gravity causes the downward motion of the jumper's CoM.
☐ Between **A** and **C**, (ground) an upward reaction force causes the change in upward speed.
☐ The jumper pushes down on the ground, the ground pushes up on the jumper with a reaction force equal in value to that which he pushes down (Newton's Third Law).
☐ In the air, (after **D**) gravity (the jumpers weight) causes the downward change in velocity.

3) e)
The points on the graph where net force acting on the jumper is zero :
  4 marks for :
☐ Points **A** and **C** are points at which the net force acting on the jumper is zero.
☐ This is because the rate of change of velocity at these points is zero.
☐ Therefore acceleration is zero.
☐ Therefore force must be zero since Newton's second law links force and acceleration.

FORCES - VECTORS

4) a)
What characterises a vector quantity?
  2 marks for :
☐ A vector has size (or value or magnitude).
☐ And direction. For example, force. velocity, acceleration, weight.

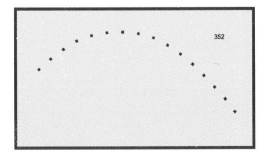

4) b)
The flight path of a shot :
☐ See diagram on right. Flight path a parabola not a circle.

FORCES - VECTORS - ANSWERS QUESTION 4 (continued)

4) c)

Factors affecting distance thrown :
    6 marks for :
- ❐ Speed of release.
- ❐ The faster the shot is released the further it will go.
- ❐ Angle of release.
- ❐ The optimum angle depends on height of release, but would be between 42º and 45º.
- ❐ Height of release.
- ❐ The higher the release, the further the shot will travel.

4) d)

The discus turn produces a longer throw than a standing throw because:
    3 marks for three from :
- ❐ Forces are applied to the discus over a larger distance.
- ❐ Since work = force x distance, this means that more energy is given to the discus, which therefore will have more kinetic energy on release.
- ❐ Or, the forces are applied over a longer time.
- ❐ Therefore the force x time (impulse) is bigger, and the change of momentum bigger.
- ❐ So the discus has a higher speed at release.
- ❐ Or, the discus is accelerated to some degree before the standing throw position is reached, and hence the turn produces extra velocity over and above the standing throw.

5) a)

Use Newton's laws to explain why a sprinter accelerates from the blocks :
    5 marks for five from :
- ❐ Using Newton's 3rd law of motion.
- ❐ Which states that action and reaction are equal and opposite in direction.
- ❐ If she pushes down and back on the ground.
- ❐ The ground pushes up and forward on her.
- ❐ Newton's 2nd law of motion.
- ❐ Says that if a force is exerted, then this produces an acceleration.
- ❐ In the same direction as the force - i.e. forwards.

5) b) i)

The vector diagram from which resultant force could be calculated :
    3 marks for :
- ❐ See diagram on right.
- ❐ Note that the parallelogram rule is used to estimate the resultant.
- ❐ The resultant is horizontal, showing that the net force is forwards.

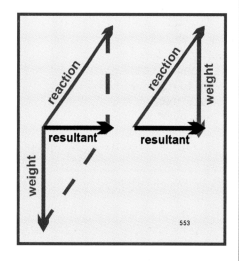

5) b) ii)

Calculate the sprinter's acceleration.
    2 marks for two from :
- ❐ Newton's 2nd law gives   force = mass x acceleration.
- ❐ Therefore :   300 N   = 60 kg x acceleration.
- ❐ Hence :   acceleration = $\dfrac{300}{60}$ = 5 ms^{-2}.

5) b) iii)

How fast is the sprinter travelling after 1.5 seconds?
    2 marks for :
- ❐ Speed changes by 5 ms^{-1} each second.
- ❐ Therefore total change of speed in 1.5 seconds = 7.5 ms^{-1}.

5) c)

Newton's 3rd law of motion explains the ability of a squash player to drive forward into a forehand stroke :
    3 marks for three from :
- ❐ Newton's 3rd Law says that for every action there is an equal and opposite reaction.
- ❐ In this case the action is the force exerted by the player pushing backwards on the ground (squash court).
- ❐ The reaction is the forward force exerted by the ground on the player.
- ❐ This forward force enables the player to drive forwards.
- ❐ See diagram 354 on right.

AIR RESISTANCE AND FLUID FRICTION

6) a)
- ❏ The effect of air resistance is to deviate the path from the symmetric shape known as a parabola.
- ❏ Air resistance force acts in a direction opposite to the direction of motion of the object.
- ❏ Therefore it will always be moving more slowly (than if there were no air resistance).
- ❏ The bigger the air resistance compared to the weight, the bigger the asymmetry of the flight path.

6) b)
Badminton shuttle struck hard - see diagram 355 on upper right :
   5 marks for five from :

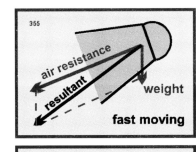

- ❏ A rapidly moving badminton shuttle will have a very large value for air resistance at the beginning of its flight.
- ❏ Compared to the weight of the shuttle.
- ❏ Therefore the resultant force (see diagram) is almost in the same direction as the air resistance.
- ❏ Later in the flight, the shuttle would have slowed considerably.
- ❏ Hence the air resistance value will have dropped.
- ❏ Until the weight is much bigger than the air resistance.
- ❏ Then the shuttle would fall as if under gravity only.
- ❏ Hence a path which differs markedly from the symmetric parabolic path which would be observed if there were zero or very little air resistance.
- ❏ See lower diagram 356 on upper right.

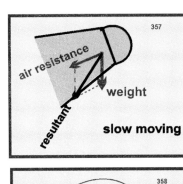

Badminton shuttle struck gently - see diagram 357 on upper left :
- ❏ Here the weight is the predominant force.
- ❏ Because the shuttle is moving slowly, air resistance is small.
- ❏ Hence resultant force is almost that of the weight only.
- ❏ And the flight is almost parabolic.
- ❏ See diagram 358 lower left.

6) c)
Shot in flight - see diagram 359 on right :
- ❏ Resultant force is almost in the same direction as the weight.
- ❏ Hence the flight of the shot is similar to gravity only.

Badminton shuttle in flight :
- ❏ Resultant force is almost in the same direction as air resistance.
- ❏ Opposite to the direction of motion hence marked deceleration and asymmetric path.

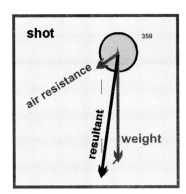

7) a)
Three factors which govern a swimmer's speed :
   3 marks for three from :
- ❏ Thrust on the water (force exerted by hands and feet on the water).
- ❏ Body shape (which best allows smooth flow of water past the body).
- ❏ Surface effects (like hair / shiny swimsuits / skullcap etc) which change the water flow past the body.
- ❏ Dive entry / thrust on bath side on turning.

7) b)
Factors which determine the amount of fluid friction on a swimmer :
   4 marks for four from :
- ❏ Speed of the swimmer.
- ❏ Forward cross section (size of the person as viewed from the forward direction).
- ❏ Body shape / surface effects (smooth flow).
- ❏ Surface area in contact with the water (big person as opposed to small person).
- ❏ Avoidance of water surface effects (like for example swimming underwater after a turn).

AIR RESISTANCE AND FLUID FRICTION - ANSWERS QUESTION 7 (continued)

7) c)
Turbulent flow would be minimised :
    2 marks for two from :
☐   By shaving body hair.
☐   By wearing a swim cap.
☐   Swimwear surface (shiny or directionally flocked) and shape (high neck to avoid drag at neckline).

7) d)
Fluid friction affects the sportsperson in the following contexts : (3 marks for three from) :
☐   Air resistance involving performer (athlete running, skier, cyclist, parachutist).
☐   Air resistance involving sports vehicle (racing car, glider, cyclist).
☐   Air resistance involving projectile (badminton shuttle, ball).
☐   Water resistance involving performer (swimmer).
☐   Water resistance on sports vehicle (water skis, canoeing, rowing, sailing, speedboats).

7) e)
The sportsperson would attempt to reduce fluid friction by :
    3 marks for :
☐   Reducing forward cross sectional area by crouching. Cyclist - special bike shape to help with this, skiing.
☐   Removing resistance from surface. Special clothing (lycra), shaving head, bathing cap, removing protruding
    bits of cycle or boat.
☐   Reduce area of contact. Boat, windsurfer, water skis (aquaplaning).

7) f)
Explain why it is difficult for a swimmer to keep a horizontal floating position.
    4 marks for :
☐   The two forces (weight and buoyancy force) do not act through the same point.
☐   The forces are eccentric (are not in line).
☐   This causes a turning effect, in this case the body is turned by these forces anticlockwise.
☐   With the swimmer's feet falling downwards relative to the head.

BERNOULLI / MAGNUS EFFECT

8) a)
The Bernoulli effect explains the swerve of a ball :
    4 marks for four from :
☐   The ball moving through the air causes the air flow to separate, with air flowing further past the lower half of
    the ball.
☐   In the same time as the air flow over the top of the ball (the air is a fixed entity - the ball moves through it).
☐   Therefore the air flows faster past the lower half of the ball.
☐   Therefore there is less pressure on the bottom of the ball.
☐   Hence the ball will experience a force downwards.

8) b)
How does a spinning table tennis ball swerve?
    Side spin : (1 mark for) :
☐   See diagram to right.
    Back spin : (1 mark for one from) :
☐   See diagram.
☐   Note tendency of ball to travel straighter.
☐   Or even lift.
    Top spin : (1mark for one from) :
☐   See diagram.
☐   Note pronounced curve downwards (dip).

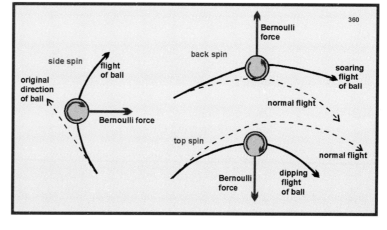

BERNOULLI / MAGNUS EFFECT - ANSWERS QUESTION 8 (continued)

8) c)
The vector diagram of all forces acting on a table tennis ball with back spin :
   See diagram 361 on upper right - 4 marks for four from :
❑ Note that the Bernoulli effect force is upwards, weight downwards, and air resistance (fluid friction) in a direction opposite to the direction of motion of the ball.
❑ Bernoulli effect force is equal or bigger than the weight.
❑ Resultant would therefore be upwards and to the left of the diagram.
❑ Acceleration of the ball (deceleration) is in the same direction as the resultant force, i.e. upwards and to the left.
❑ Hence the path upwards and to the left of original direction.

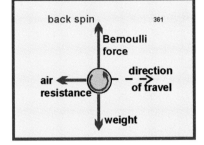

8) d)
   One sport in which Bernoulli effect plays a part.
   1 mark for one from :
❑ Ground effects in racing cars.
❑ Wing effects on gliding / flying / kites.
❑ Effects on ski jumping.
❑ Effects on hand shape in swimming (enables greater thrust on water).

8) e)
A bouncing ball with backspin :
   See diagram 362 lower right :
❑ Ball will kick backwards from its anticipated flight after bouncing.
❑ Friction between ground and ball is increased because of relative motion of surfaces (ball and ground) in contact.

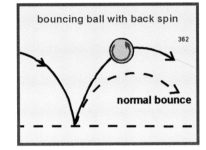

9) a) i)
The nature of the forces labelled is :
❑ **X** = air resistance which acts opposite to direction of motion.
❑ **Y** = Bernoulli (or Magnus) effect caused by backspin.

9) a) ii)
Each object has a different flight path because :
   6 marks for six from :

A (ball with backspin)	**B** (shot)	**C** (shuttle)
❑ Magnus / Bernoulli effect.	❑ Weight is much larger than any other forces acting.	❑ Air resistance is much larger than the weight.
❑ Causes ball to deviate upwards from parabola.	❑ Therefore flight is parabolic.	❑ So shuttle rapidly slows down.
	❑ Very little air resistance (compared to weight).	

9) b) i)
How would the two forces affect the orientation of the javelin in flight?
❑ The forces are not in line.   ❑ Therefore the 2 forces create a moment or torque.
❑ Tending to turn the javelin clockwise.   ❑ Making its point tilt downwards.

9) b) ii)
The forces acting on the javelin could be altered as follows : (4 marks for four from) :
❑ Arrange the lift force nearer the Centre of Mass.   ❑ So that the clockwise moment is less.
❑ Or, arrange for a larger lift force.   ❑ By having a different shape of javelin.
❑ So that the flight deviates upwards more from the parabolic curve.

IMPULSE - MOMENTUM

10) a) i)
To calculate the incoming, outgoing, and change of momentum of the ball :
   2 marks for each section :
❑ Incoming momentum of the ball   = - 0.15 x 20.   ❑   = - 3 kg ms^{-1}.
❑ The minus sign is because the ball is coming towards the player, the positive direction will be away from the player.

10) a) ii)
❑ Outgoing momentum of the ball   = 0.15 x 30.   ❑   = 4.5 kg ms^{-1}.

10) a) iii)
❑   Change of momentum   = outgoing momentum - incoming momentum.
                                  = 4.5 - (- 3).   ❑   = 7.5 kg ms^{-1}.

IMPULSE - MOMENTUM - ANSWERS QUESTION 10 (continued)

10) b)
- ❑ Average force (of impact) x time of contact between ball and racquet.
  = change of momentum of ball on impact.
- ❑   force = $\dfrac{\text{change of momentum}}{\text{time of contact}}$ = $\dfrac{7.5}{0.1}$.

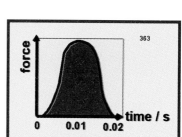

- ❑   So, average force (of impact) = 75 Newtons.

10) c) i)
  See sketch graph on right. Marks given for :
- ❑ Inverted U shape.
- ❑ The idea that a very short period of time elapses (0.01 to 0.1 s).

10) c) ii)
The importance of follow through in striking a ball :
- ❑ Follow through increases time of contact between bat and ball.
- ❑ Which therefore increases impulse applied to ball,   impulse = force x time of contact.
- ❑ This therefore increases outgoing momentum of ball,   impulse = change of momentum of ball.
- ❑ Hence outgoing velocity of ball is increased.
- ❑ Also direction of outgoing ball is controlled by follow through.
- ❑ Another way of looking at this is to use the work principle,   work = force x distance.
- ❑ Therefore force applied over a bigger distance means more work is done.
- ❑ This work would be translated into Kinetic Energy (motion energy), hence the ball would have a higher KE.
- ❑ Hence a higher final velocity   (KE = $\frac{1}{2}$ m v²).

11) a) i)
Explain the meaning of the term momentum, and explain why the four man bobsleigh travelling at a speed of 28 m s^{-1} has a different momentum to a skier moving at the same speed.
  2 marks for :
- ❑ Momentum = mass x velocity, and is therefore a combination of mass and velocity.
- ❑ A four man bob has four people in it and therefore (approximately) four times the mass of a lone skier. Hence the momentum of the bob when full of its men will be (approximately) four times that of the skier at the same speed.

11) a) ii)
Explain using Newton's Laws of motion how the bobsleigh acquires its large momentum.
  4 marks for four from :
- ❑ The force applied to the bob comes via Newton's 3rd Law.
- ❑ Which says that action and reaction are equal in size but opposite in direcftion.
- ❑ The four bobmen push hard on the ground backwards (action), and the ground pushes hard forwards on the men (and the bob) (reaction).
- ❑ The force is linked to the change of momentum (or acceleration) of the bob by Newton's 2nd Law.
- ❑ This says that Force = rate of change of momentum (= mass x acceleration).
- ❑ So large forces give large changes of momentum (or acceleration or change of velocity).

11) a) iii)
If the total force generated by the men pushing the bobsleigh is 6000 N over 25m in 6.0 seconds, calculate the work done and power generated by the men for this period.
  4 marks for four from :
- ❑ The work done   = force applied x distance travelled in the direction of the force.
- ❑ Therefore work done   = 6000 x 25   = 150000 joules   = 150 kJ.
- ❑ The power   = $\dfrac{\text{work done}}{\text{time taken}}$ = work done per second = rate of working.
- ❑ Therefore power   = $\dfrac{150000}{6.0}$ = 25000 watts   = 25 kW.

11) b) i)
Identify the nature of the fluid friction in this case and explain how this might limit the maximum speed of the bob.
  3 marks for three from :
- ❑ The fluid friction in this case is air resistance / drag.
- ❑ This increases if turbulent flow occurs, or if streamlining breaks down.
- ❑ This increases if the size of the bob (and its occupants) is larger than it could be (by for example a bobman putting his head out of the top of the bob).
- ❑ As the speed increases. the fluid friction force gets bigger, until it matches the weight component down the track, then the bob couldn't go any faster.

IMPULSE - MOMENTUM - ANSWERS QUESTION 11 (continued)

11) b) ii)
Explain the term 'turbulent flow', and how the bobsleigh is used to minimise this factor.
    3 marks for three from :
❏ At low speeds, air flow past a moving object is laminar, which means the air flows in layers.
❏ When this flow is interrupted either by going too fast or by a protrusion (which upsets the streamlined shape), then the air is thrown out into vortices, the layers mix up, and this is turbulent flow.
❏ In order to minimise turbulent flow, the bob has to be as streamlined as possible (so that flow is as laminar as possible).
❏ This is done by having a specially designed streamlined shape to the bob.
❏ And by having no protrusions from the bob while in motion - handles, heads of bobmen (this is why the bobmen crouch down once in the bob after the start.

11) c) i)
In the speed time graph what is happening at points Y and Z?
    2 marks for :
❏ At point Y the bob is moving at its maximum speed, and is moving at approximately contant speed.
❏ At point Z the bob is decelerating rapidly (presumably after the finish line).

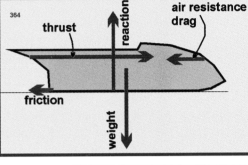

11) c) ii)
Sketch a diagram of the bob showing all forces acting on it at the points X and Y on the graph.
    4 marks for :
❏ At point **X**, see figure 364 upper right, showing vertical forces (weight downwards, reaction force upwards) equal in size.
❏ Thrust (from the pushing bobmen) acting forwards bigger than both of air resistance, and friction with the track acting backwards.
❏ At point **Y**, see figure 365 on the lower right, again in which vertical forces cancel out.
❏ But now the component of weight down the sloping track cancels out the small combined effect of air resistance and friction with the track. There would be exact cancelling out of forces when the bob moves at constant speed.

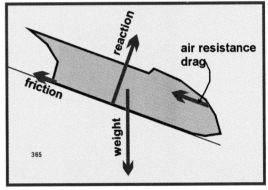

JOINTS AS LEVERS

12) a)
Classify as many joint complexes as you can : (5 marks for any five from) :
Class 1 : ❏ Neck muscles / neck vertebrae - as in a nodding movement.   ❏ Triceps / elbow joint.
           ❏ Abdominals / hip joint.
Class 2 : ❏ Calf / ankle joint.
Class 3 : ❏ Pectoral muscles / shoulder joint.   ❏ Quadriceps / knee.
           ❏ Gluteus maximus / hip joint.   ❏ Hamstrings / knee.
           ❏ Forearm muscles which control fingers and grip / wrist and fingers. ❏ Biceps / elbow.

12) b)
Calculate the force in the biceps muscle : (6 marks for six from) :
❏   0.3m   = elbow joint to hand distance.
❏   Clockwise moment = 200 x 0.3 = 60 Nm.
❏ Principle of moments is   'clockwise moment = anticlockwise moment'.
❏ This applies when the system is in equilibrium i.e. nothing is unbalanced or moving.
❏   Distance from fulcrum to muscle insertion = 0.03m.
❏   Anticlockwise moment = force in muscle x 0.03.
❏ Therefore   force in muscle x 0.03 = 60 (this is the value of the clockwise moment from above).
❏ Therefore   force in muscle   =   60   = 2000 N
                                               0.03

JOINTS AS LEVERS - ANSWERS QUESTION 12 (continued)

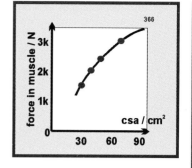

12) c) i)

   See sketch graph to the right. 3 marks for :
- ❏ Correct points plotted.
- ❏ Correct linear axes.
- ❏ Appropriate average line.

12) c) ii)

The physiological reason for the shape of the graph :
   3 marks for :
- ❏ The bigger the cross sectional area (or bulk) of muscle.
- ❏ The more muscle fibres there are likely to be within the muscle.
- ❏ Hence it would be stronger.

12) d)

The feature of the ankle joint which enables it to be more efficient than others is : (2 marks for two from) :
- ❏ It is a class 2 lever.
- ❏ In which the effort (force in the muscle) is smaller than the load.
- ❏ Hence large forces can be exerted on the ground by using a relatively small force in a muscle.

13) a)

The simplified sketch of the triceps / elbow lever system is :
   See diagram to the right, 4 marks given for :
- ❏ Note the position of the fulcrum at the elbow.
- ❏ The forces at the triceps and hand act downwards.
- ❏ The effort acts at the triceps.
- ❏ The load acts at the hand.

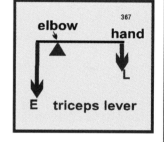

13) b)

   4 marks for four from :
- ❏ The load = 8 kg x gravitational field strength (g)   = 8 x 10 = 80 N.
- ❏ Principle of moments :   clockwise moment   = anticlockwise moment.
- ❏ Therefore load x distance of load from fulcrum   = effort x distance of effort from fulcrum.
- ❏ Hence :   80 N x   0.3 m   = effort x   0.03 m (approximately).
- ❏ Therefore :   effort   = $\frac{80 \times 0.3}{0.03}$ = 800 Newtons (approximately).

- ❏ The approximate calculations refer to the fact that the angle between the effort and the lever arm will not be exactly 90°, and since the measurement of the distance when working out the moment is at right angles to the line of action of the force, the distance 0.03 m will therefore only be approximate.

13) c)

Anatomical factors would be :
   3 marks for :
- ❏ The length of the ulnar or radius.
- ❏ The distance of the point of the elbow (line of action of the triceps tendon) to the fulcrum.
- ❏ The strength of the triceps muscle.

13) d)

The load would change if the arm were to extend because : (2 marks for two from) :
- ❏ There would be no change if the lines of action of effort and load were to remain parallel.
- ❏ But when the arm is straight, the perpendicular distance from load to elbow is least.
- ❏ Whereas the triceps tendon remains at a fixed distance from the fulcrum (the triceps tendon rolls round the end of the elbow).
- ❏ Therefore, when the arm is straight the load would be at a maximum.
- ❏ This explains why the arm is much stronger when straight as in gymnastic vaults or weight lifter locking arms overhead, and weaker when the arm is bent or away from the body.

13) e)

   See diagrams 368and 369 for examples of a class 3 lever - effort between fulcrum and load.
   See diagram 370 for an example of a
   class 2 lever - load between effort and fulcrum.
   3 marks for each of two figures for :
- ❏ The load correctly marked.
- ❏ The effort correctly marked.
- ❏ The fulcrum correctly marked.

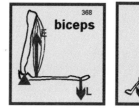
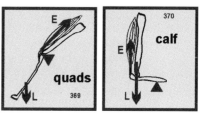

JOINTS AS LEVERS - ANSWERS (continued)

14) a)

Calculate the force in the calf muscle.

  4 marks for four from :

❑ The load = the weight of the sportsperson = 800 N.
   The effort is provided by the force of contraction of the calf muscles (F) and will be calculated as follows :

❑ The principle of moments says that :

        clockwise moment   = anticlockwise moment.

❑ Anticlockwise moment   = load x distance of line of action of load to fulcrum
                            = 800 N x 0.18 m = 144 Nm.

❑   Clockwise moment = effort (E) x 0.24m.

❑   Therefore :   E x 0.24 = 112 Nm.

            And :   E   = $\frac{112}{0.24}$ = 600 N.

14) b)

  See diagram on right, marks for :

❑ Position of load at hand.

❑ Position of effort in biceps muscle.

❑ Position of fulcrum at elbow.

14) c)

❑ The calf muscle ankle system is a class 2 lever in which the load is between the effort and the fulcrum.

❑ This means that the effort will always be less than the load, therefore the force in the calf muscle will be less than the load.

❑ The biceps elbow system is a class 3 lever in which the effort is between the load and the fulcrum.

❑ This means that the effort will always be bigger than the load, and the force in the biceps muscle will be more than the load.

❑ Therefore, for a given muscle force, the calf system will be able to exert more force on the surroundings than the biceps system.

CENTRE of MASS

15) a)

❑ Centre of mass of a body is the point at which the whole mass of the body appears to act.

❑ The CoM lies below the point of suspension of the body.

❑ And would be an amalgamation of all body parts (see diagram to right).

15) b)

A method for finding the CoM of a sportsperson : (4 marks for four from) :

❑ One method would be to suspend the sportsperson from 2 different points on the body (a hand, then a foot).

❑ In each case a plumb line would fall through the centre of mass.

❑ The centre of mass would then lie on the point of intersection of the 2 lines.

❑ Practical difficulties would include the difficulty of holding a sporting pose while the plumb line was taken.

❑ For example, it would take a very strong athlete to hold a piked position while suspended from one foot.

❑ A more practical method which would need more sophisticated equipment, would be to lie the sportsperson on a board placed on 2 sensitive scales or balances (bathroom scales might suffice).

❑ The ratio of distance from each balance to the centre of mass position would be inverse to the reading on the balance.

❑ For example, if the scales were 2 m apart, and scale 1 read 200N and scale 2 read 400N, then the position of the centre of mass would be 1.33m from scale 1 and 0.67 m from scale 2.

15) c)

❑ See diagram as answer to **15 a)** above.

❑ The most significant point is that the centre of mass can lie outside the body.

15) d)

A high jumper can change the position of his / her CoM by :

  See diagram on right, 3 marks for :

❑ The dot showing the centre of mass in each shape varies its position depending on the position of the person's arms, legs, torso.

❑ Note that at the highest point, where the body is in an inverted U position, the centre of mass is below the body.

❑ And it is possible for a skilful jumper to clear a bar while his centre of mass passes underneath the bar.

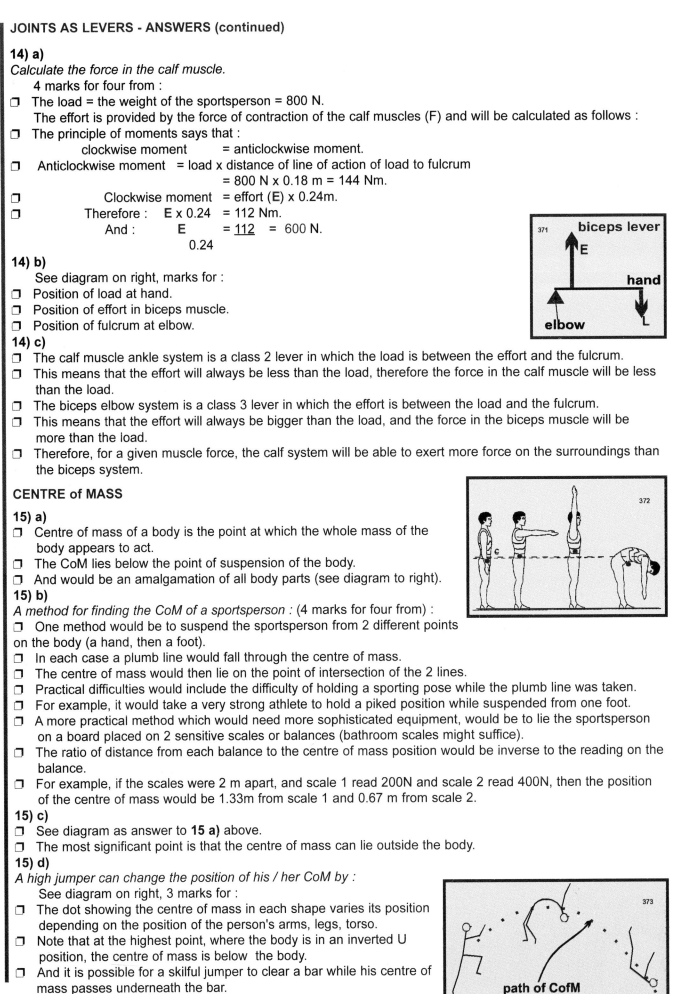

CENTRE of MASS - ANSWERS (continued)

16) a) i)
State the shape of the flight path of the CoM after take off, and explain why this shape cannot change.
   3 marks for :
❏ The shape of the flight path of the centre of mass of the jumper after take off is a parabola.
❏ Once the jumper is airborne, the major force acting is his / her weight acting vertically downwards.
❏ Unless other forces act (by collision with another athlete for example) the shape of the
   flight path would be the same as if a shot were thrown. See diagram 373 page 3.24.

16) a) ii)
Explain how a jumper can maximise the height jumped once he / she has taken off.
   3 marks for three from :
❏ On take-off, the jumper projects arms and free leg as high as possible.
❏ The CoM then follows a parabola - its maximum height being determined by forces just before take-off, and
   the upward velocity at take-off.
❏ Just before the top of the flight, the jumper moves all free arms / legs downwards.
❏ This has the effect of lowering the CoM relative to the jumpers head.
❏ This means that the jumper's head will be higher relative to the CoM than it otherwise would have been.
❏ Hence the jumper appears to jump higher - or keep higher longer during the flight.

16) b)
How do the size and direction of forces applied before take off affect subsequent flight?
   4 marks for :

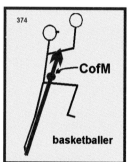

❏ In the diagrams on the right of the jumper before take-off, the basketball player (374)
   has the resultant (of reaction and friction) force of the ground on the jumper acting in a
   direction through the centre of mass, whereas the high jumper (375) has this force
   acting in a direction to the left of the centre of mass.
❏ The effect of this is for the basketball player to keep the same body orientation
   throughout the jump, whereas the high jumper's body rotates in a clockwise direction.
❏ In the case of the high jumper this is because the net force has a moment about the
   jumper's centre of mass, which will cause rotation about this point as a fulcrum or axis
   of rotation.
❏ Once the jumper has taken off, then the path of the centre of mass has been
   determined and cannot be changed.

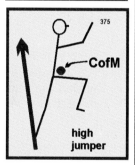

ROTATION

17) a)
❏ Angular velocity is the rate of spin or turning of a body.
❏ Or the angle turned through per second, angular velocity = <u>angle turned through</u>.
   time taken to turn

17) b)
The meaning of moment of inertia in the context of the tumbling diver : (4 marks for four from) :
❏ Moment of inertia (MI) is the rotational inertia of a body, the equivalent of mass for a rotating body.
❏ MI can be thought of as resistance to rotational motion, the tendency to remain stationary or continue to
   rotate at constant rate of spin.
❏ Large MI requires large turning forces (moments) to act on the body to start or stop it spinning.
❏ MI depends on the distribution of mass away from the axis of rotation.
❏ MI = the sum of the masses of all body parts multiplied by the distance squared from the axis of rotation.
❏ This means that the further a mass (body part) is away from the axis, the more effect it has on the MI.
❏ MI $= \Sigma\, m\, r^2$.
❏ Also MI = <u>angular momentum</u>
                  angular velocity

17) c) i)
The rate of spinning would change throughout the flight of the diver as follows :
   5 marks for :
❏ Phase 1 - very slow rate of spin.
❏ Phase 2 - rate of spin about twice that of phase 1.
❏ Phase 3 - fastest rate of spin, about 6 times that of phase 1.
❏ Phase 4 - very slow rate of spin (same as phase 1).
❏ Mark awarded for numerical estimates of rates of spin.

ROTATION - ANSWERS QUESTION 17 (continued)

17) c) ii)
The graph of rate of spinning against time for the diver would be :
    See diagram 376 on right, 4 marks for :
- ❏ Axes correctly scaled and labelled.
- ❏ Same value at start and finish.
- ❏ Value approximately double phase 1 for phase 2.
- ❏ Value approximately six times phase 1 for phase 3.

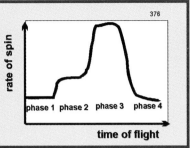

17) d) i)
    2 marks for :
- ❏ Angular momentum is a combination of moment of inertia and angular velocity.
- ❏ Angular momentum = moment of inertia x angular velocity.

17) d) ii)
State the law which governs the changes in rates of spin throughout the dive.
- ❏ The law of conservation of angular momentum.

17) d) iii)
    3 marks for :
- ❏ See diagram 377 to right.
- ❏ The path of the centre of mass of the diver would be a parabola.
- ❏ Which is the arc described by all bodies falling under gravity.

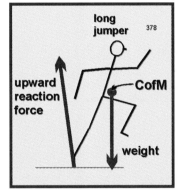

17) e) i)
Another sporting context in which rates of spin change with body shape :
    6 marks for :
- ❏ Mark given for appropriate choice of sport - skating, skiing, discus, gymnastics, trampolining.
- ❏ Slow rate of spinning with extended body position.
- ❏ For example, arms held out wide in skating.
- ❏ Rapid rate of spinning with narrow body position.
- ❏ For example, arms held overhead for spinning skater.
- ❏ No forces must act on surroundings during the spinning.

17) e) ii)
Explain how you would stop the spinning of a dancer or skater etc.
    2 marks for two from :
- ❏ You would stop the spinning by applying force.
- ❏ To the surroundings.
- ❏ By the landing process, or putting your feet in contact with the ground.

18) a) i)
Sketch a pin man diagram showing forces acting on the jumper just before take off, and explain why these forces would cause a forward angular motion during flight.
    See diagram 378 on the right, 4 marks for :
- ❏ The upward reaction force and weight are eccentric (do not act through the same line or point).
- ❏ This means that they will cause a forward toppling or angular motion (spinning).
- ❏ Once in the air, this forward angular motion will continue.
- ❏ Because angular momentum is conserved for a spinning body which has no interaction with its surroundings.

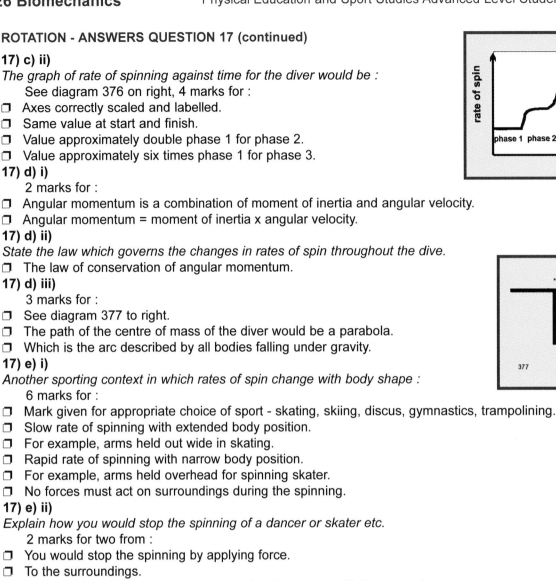

18) a) ii)
Explain at least one of the techniques which jumpers adopt in order to overcome the problem of forward angular momentum during flight.
    6 marks for six from :
- ❏ From the above answer, this means that the jumper would fall forward on his / her face unless a technique is adopted to counteract the motion.
- ❏ This foward spinning angular momentum **cannot** be changed once in flight.
- ❏ So the jumper has to spin parts of his body rapidly forward (in the same direction as the toppling).
- ❏ An example of this is the running hitch kick - the jumper cycles his / her legs forward (cycling or running motion) - which takes up the forward angular momentum.
- ❏ This means that the forward toppling momentum is taken up by this new motion.
- ❏ And the jumpers trunk and legs will not topple as much as they would without this motion.
- ❏ Hopefully the jumper will be able to land feet forward to reach out for maximum possible distance.

ROTATION - ANSWERS (continued)

18) b)
Briefly explain why there is a difference between the mechanics of take-off of long jumper and triple jumper.
   4 marks for four from :
❑ The long jumper needs to have maximum height from take-off to acheive maximum distance.
❑ This means that the upward reaction force is usually vertical and behind the centre of mass of the jumper, which leads to the foward toppling discussed above.
❑ The triple jumper has to land on his / her feet in an upright (approximately) position.
❑ And therefore the jumper has to adjust the upward drive to a more forward one (where the reaction force would lie as near as possible to the centre of mass).
❑ This would ensure that toppling would occur less than in the long jump, and the jumper would be able to land on his / her feet and control the next two phases of the jump better.

19) a)
Sketch 3 traces on a graph showing angular momentum, MI, and angular velocity.
   See diagram 379 on the right, 3 marks for :
❑ Angular momentum = constant.
❑ Angular velocity starts slow, speeds up during the tucked phase then slows down again as he opens out and lands.
❑ Moment of inertia starts high (body straight), becomes low (tucked position) then high again (straight and landing).

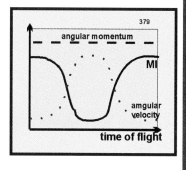

19) b)
Explain the shapes of the traces on the graph.
   6 marks for six from :
❑ Angular momentum - remains constant throughout the flight (this is a universal law obeyed everywhere provided no forces act on the body), so the graph would be a horizontal line.
❑ Moment of inertia changes with body shape.
❑ MI value high when body position straight (take-off and landing).
❑ MI value low when tucked or piked (mid-flight).
❑ Angular velocity (rate of spin) changes in the opposite sense to MI.
   Since angular momentum = MI x angular velocity = constant in value throughout the flight.
❑ So as MI goes down (from straight to tucked), angular velocity must increase - rate of spinning increases.
❑ Later in the flight, as MI increases again (from tucked to straight), rate of spin reduces.

19) c)
Estimate from the chart in the question the ratio of angular velocities at times X and Y.
   1 mark for one from :
❑ The ratio of angular velocities at X and Y is 750 : 1500 , i.e. 1 : 2.
❑ The angular velocity doubles when going from X to Y.

19) d)
   2 marks for two from :
❑ From b) above, the ratio of rates of spin at X : Y is 1 : 2, therefore the ratio of MI from X : Y must be 2 : 1.
❑ If the rate of spin doubles when going from X to Y, the MI must halve when going from X to Y.
❑ So, the MI at X = 8 kgm², therefore the MI at Y = 4 kgm².

19) e)
The conditions which must exist if the gymnast is to cancel out the forward rotation are :
   2 marks for two from :
❑ The gymnast is spinning clockwise, therefore an anticlockwise torque or moment of force must be applied to stop this.
❑ So, a force from the ground on the gymnast must act upwards and forwards of his centre of mass.
❑ Hence an anticlockwise moment would be exerted on him about the centre of mass.

19) f)
The ground reaction force exerted at the moment of landing would be :
   3 marks for three from :
❑ See diagram 380 on right, marks awarded for :
❑ Resultant ground reaction force (**R**) to the right of the centre of mass of the gymnast (which would stop his forward rotation as discussed above).
❑ Vertical component of ground reaction force (**N**) bigger than his weight - this would mean a net upward force acting.
❑ Which in turn would cause vertical deceleration as he lands.
❑ Horizontal component of ground reaction force (**F**) backwards which would cause horizontal deceleration as he lands (stop him moving forwards).

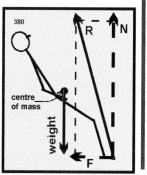

ROTATION - ANSWERS QUESTION 20 (continued)

20) a)
How can the notion of angular momentum be used to explain variations in motion of a diver / gymnast.
- ❏ Angular momentum = moment of inertia (MI) x angular velocity (rate of spin).
- ❏ The law of conservation of angular momentum explains the variations of motion of a gymnast, which says that moment of inertia x rate of spin remains constant throughout the tumble.
- ❏ Straight position gives the gymnast's body a high MI and therefore a low rate of spin.
- ❏ Whereas a tucked or piked position gives him a low MI and therefore a high rate of spin.

20) b) i)
*The formula for calculating angular velocity, and the angular velocity of the skater in position **Z** :*
  2 marks for two from :
- ❏   MI x rate of spin (angular velocity) = new MI x new rate of spin.
- ❏ Or angular velocity = <u>angular momentum</u> = <u>   (MI x angular velocity) at any point in the movement   </u>.
                MI   MI (at the point at which you wish to know the angular velocity)
- ❏ (Or angular velocity = <u>angle turned through</u>).
               time taken to turn
- ❏ Angular velocity for the skater in position **Z**
              = <u>MI in position W x angular velocity in position W</u> = <u> 1 x 2 </u>
                        MI in position Z   6
          = 0.33 revs per second.

20) b) ii)
The shape which must be adopted if the skater were to spin at 3.0 revs per second :
  3 marks for :
- ❏ In order to spin faster, the skater must adopt a tighter shape, see diagram 381 on the right.
- ❏ The skater spins at 3.0 revolutions per second when the MI is 1.0 kgm². Therefore the angular momentum   = MI x spin rate
               =1.0 x 3.0   = 3.0.
- ❏   So the new MI   = <u>angular momentum</u> = <u>3.0</u>   = 0.75 kgm².
                    new rate of spin   4.0

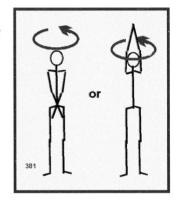

381

20) c) i)
A slalom skier turns through the gates at maximum speed by :
  See diagram 382 middle right. 4 marks for :
- ❏ Angular momentum is conserved (only approximately because of contact with snow).
- ❏ So MI x rate of spin remains the same.
- ❏ Skier crouches (large MI) hence slow rate of turning - between gates.
- ❏ Skier straightens (small MI) hence rapid rate of turning - at a gate.

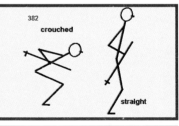

382
crouched
straight

20) c) ii)
A dancer is able to complete a triple spin after take off by :
  See diagram 383 on lower right. 4 marks for :
- ❏ The movement is initiated with arms held wide - highest possible MI.
- ❏ Once she has taken off, angular momentum is conserved.
- ❏ Flight shape has arms tucked across chest - lowest possible MI.
- ❏ Therefore highest possible rate of spin.

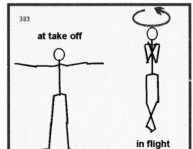

383
at take off
in flight

ROTATION - ANSWERS QUESTION 20 (continued)

20) d)
The implications of the values of MI for bent and straight legs for the running action of various runners are :
    7 marks for seven from :
❐ Moment of inertia (MI) as inertia requires torque (in groin muscle) to achieve acceleration of leg.
❐ Larger MI of leg (as in straight leg shape) needs more pull from groin muscles to achieve a given angular acceleration of the leg.
❐ The pull (turning force) on the leg is provided by abdominal hip flexor muscles acting on hip joint.
❐ A bigger force in these muscles will give a bigger turning force (torque or moment) on the leg.
❐ A sprinter needs to bring the leg through fastest (i.e. with the most acceleration), and therefore needs the leg to have the least possible MI, hence bent leg shape.
❐ An endurance runner doesn't need to bring the leg through quickly, less energy is required, and less force in the muscles needed, hence a larger MI would be possible (i.e. there is no need for a small MI) - and straighter leg shape would be possible.
❐ So for the endurance runner, the efficiency of leg action is better if the leg is straighter, and since speed is not required this will do.
❐ Bent leg shape is more efficient for a sprinter because there is less MI.
❐ Or, for a sprinter, a low value of MI means a high angular velocity and hence speed of movement.

Dennis Roscoe.

SELECTED BIBLIOGRAPHY

Bartlett, R.   1997   Introduction to Sports Biomechnics.   E & FN Spon.

Beashel, P.   1996   Advanced Studies in Physical Education.   Thomas Nelson

Boulton and Hawker   1988   Video 2, Sports Science Series, Biomechanics. University of Western Australia.

Boulton and Hawker   1998   CDROM, Body Systems 2e.   University of Western Australia.

Carr, G.   1997   Mechanics of Sport, A Practitioner's Guide.   Human Kinetics.

Davis, R.J. et.al.   2000   Physical Education and the Study of Sport 4e.   Mosby

Davis, and Kimmet.   1986   Physical Education Theory and Practice.   MacMillan.

Galligan, F.   2000   Advanced PE for Edexcel.   Heinemann.

Hay, J.G.   1988   Anatomy, Mechanics and Human Motion.   Prentice Hall.

Hay, J.G.   1993   The Biomechanics of Sports Techniques.   Prentice Hall.

Roscoe, D.A.   2000   Teachers' Guide to Physical Education and the Study of Sport 4e
                                                        Biomechanics.   Jan Roscoe Publications.

Thompson, C.W.   1998   Manual of Structural Kinesiology 13e.   McGraw-Hill.

Wesson, K. et.al.   2000   PE and Sports Studies. A Complete Guide to A Level Study.
                                                        Hodder and Stoughton.

Walder, P   1995   Mechanics and Sports Performance.   Feltham Press.

Wirhed, R.   1997   Athletic Ability and the Anatomy of Motion 2e.   Mosby.

CHARACTERISTICS OF SKILL

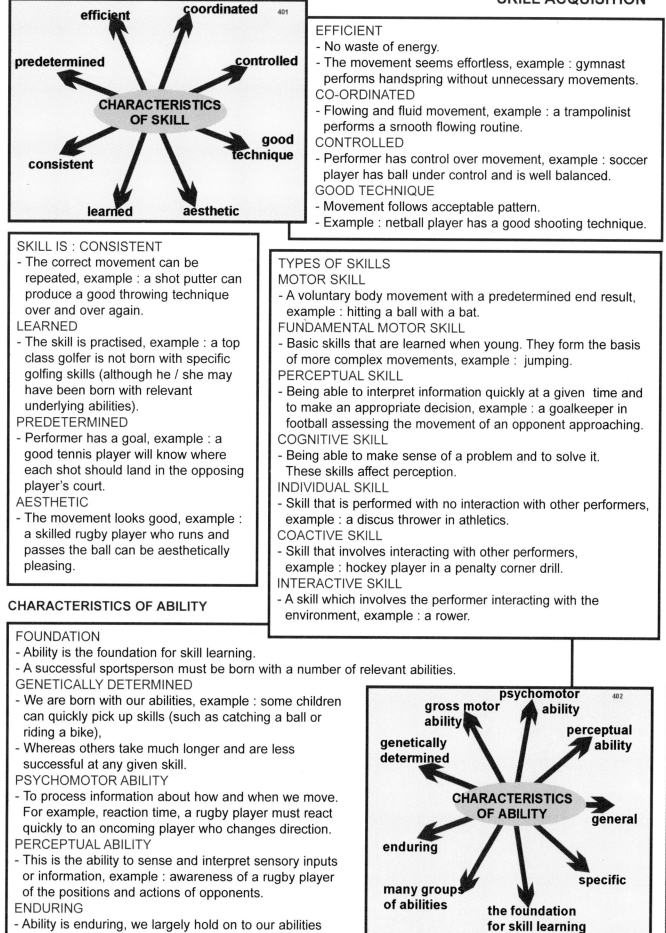

SKILL ACQUISITION

EFFICIENT
- No waste of energy.
- The movement seems effortless, example : gymnast performs handspring without unnecessary movements.
CO-ORDINATED
- Flowing and fluid movement, example : a trampolinist performs a smooth flowing routine.
CONTROLLED
- Performer has control over movement, example : soccer player has ball under control and is well balanced.
GOOD TECHNIQUE
- Movement follows acceptable pattern.
- Example : netball player has a good shooting technique.

SKILL IS : CONSISTENT
- The correct movement can be repeated, example : a shot putter can produce a good throwing technique over and over again.
LEARNED
- The skill is practised, example : a top class golfer is not born with specific golfing skills (although he / she may have been born with relevant underlying abilities).
PREDETERMINED
- Performer has a goal, example : a good tennis player will know where each shot should land in the opposing player's court.
AESTHETIC
- The movement looks good, example : a skilled rugby player who runs and passes the ball can be aesthetically pleasing.

TYPES OF SKILLS
MOTOR SKILL
- A voluntary body movement with a predetermined end result, example : hitting a ball with a bat.
FUNDAMENTAL MOTOR SKILL
- Basic skills that are learned when young. They form the basis of more complex movements, example : jumping.
PERCEPTUAL SKILL
- Being able to interpret information quickly at a given time and to make an appropriate decision, example : a goalkeeper in football assessing the movement of an opponent approaching.
COGNITIVE SKILL
- Being able to make sense of a problem and to solve it. These skills affect perception.
INDIVIDUAL SKILL
- Skill that is performed with no interaction with other performers, example : a discus thrower in athletics.
COACTIVE SKILL
- Skill that involves interacting with other performers, example : hockey player in a penalty corner drill.
INTERACTIVE SKILL
- A skill which involves the performer interacting with the environment, example : a rower.

CHARACTERISTICS OF ABILITY

FOUNDATION
- Ability is the foundation for skill learning.
- A successful sportsperson must be born with a number of relevant abilities.
GENETICALLY DETERMINED
- We are born with our abilities, example : some children can quickly pick up skills (such as catching a ball or riding a bike),
- Whereas others take much longer and are less successful at any given skill.
PSYCHOMOTOR ABILITY
- To process information about how and when we move. For example, reaction time, a rugby player must react quickly to an oncoming player who changes direction.
PERCEPTUAL ABILITY
- This is the ability to sense and interpret sensory inputs or information, example : awareness of a rugby player of the positions and actions of opponents.
ENDURING
- Ability is enduring, we largely hold on to our abilities throughout our lives, for example, riding a bike.

CHARACTERISTICS OF ABILITY (continued)

GROSS MOTOR ABILITY
- To be able to move using muscle movements, example : being able to run or ride a bike.

GENERAL ABILITY
- Does not really exist
- We have specific abilities.

SPECIFIC ABILITIES
- Skills require different abilities.
- Example : gymnastics involves balance, strength and flexibility.

GROUPS OF ABILITIES
- A good sportsperson may have many different groups of abilities.
- Example : a good all round sportsman could have different specific abilities such as good hand eye coordination and balance which could be transferred to lots of different sports activities.

SKILL CLASSIFICATION

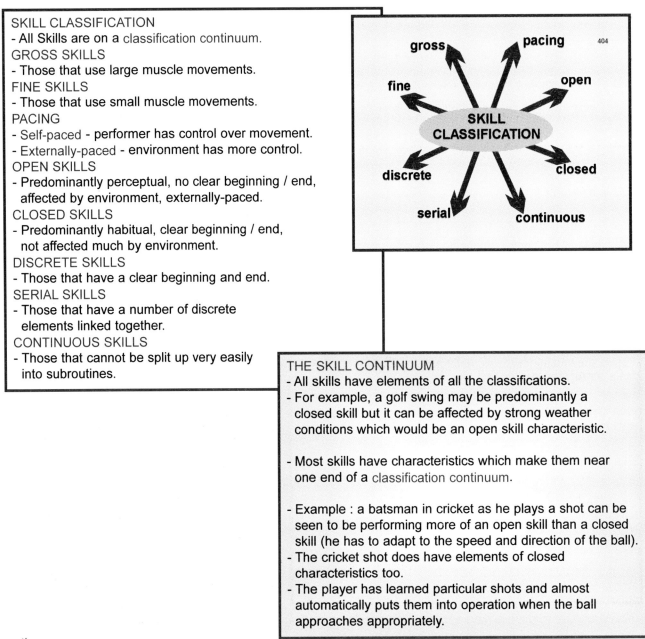

SKILL CLASSIFICATION
- All Skills are on a classification continuum.

GROSS SKILLS
- Those that use large muscle movements.

FINE SKILLS
- Those that use small muscle movements.

PACING
- Self-paced - performer has control over movement.
- Externally-paced - environment has more control.

OPEN SKILLS
- Predominantly perceptual, no clear beginning / end, affected by environment, externally-paced.

CLOSED SKILLS
- Predominantly habitual, clear beginning / end, not affected much by environment.

DISCRETE SKILLS
- Those that have a clear beginning and end.

SERIAL SKILLS
- Those that have a number of discrete elements linked together.

CONTINUOUS SKILLS
- Those that cannot be split up very easily into subroutines.

THE SKILL CONTINUUM
- All skills have elements of all the classifications.
- For example, a golf swing may be predominantly a closed skill but it can be affected by strong weather conditions which would be an open skill characteristic.

- Most skills have characteristics which make them near one end of a classification continuum.

- Example : a batsman in cricket as he plays a shot can be seen to be performing more of an open skill than a closed skill (he has to adapt to the speed and direction of the ball).
- The cricket shot does have elements of closed characteristics too.
- The player has learned particular shots and almost automatically puts them into operation when the ball approaches appropriately.

SKILL CLASSIFICATION (continued)

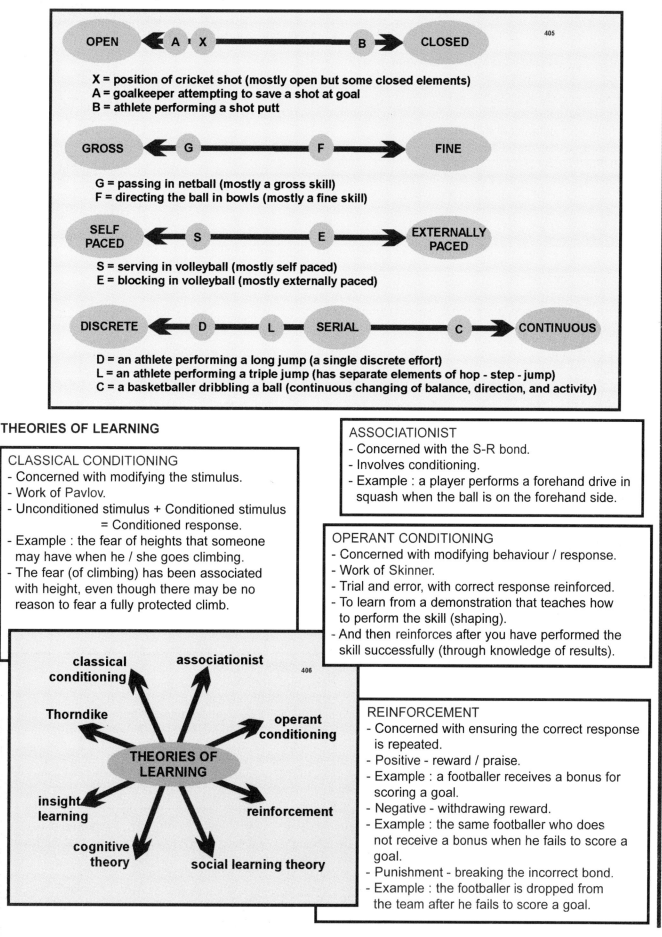

X = position of cricket shot (mostly open but some closed elements)
A = goalkeeper attempting to save a shot at goal
B = athlete performing a shot putt

G = passing in netball (mostly a gross skill)
F = directing the ball in bowls (mostly a fine skill)

S = serving in volleyball (mostly self paced)
E = blocking in volleyball (mostly externally paced)

D = an athlete performing a long jump (a single discrete effort)
L = an athlete performing a triple jump (has separate elements of hop - step - jump)
C = a basketballer dribbling a ball (continuous changing of balance, direction, and activity)

THEORIES OF LEARNING

CLASSICAL CONDITIONING
- Concerned with modifying the stimulus.
- Work of Pavlov.
- Unconditioned stimulus + Conditioned stimulus
    = Conditioned response.
- Example : the fear of heights that someone
  may have when he / she goes climbing.
- The fear (of climbing) has been associated
  with height, even though there may be no
  reason to fear a fully protected climb.

ASSOCIATIONIST
- Concerned with the S-R bond.
- Involves conditioning.
- Example : a player performs a forehand drive in
  squash when the ball is on the forehand side.

OPERANT CONDITIONING
- Concerned with modifying behaviour / response.
- Work of Skinner.
- Trial and error, with correct response reinforced.
- To learn from a demonstration that teaches how
  to perform the skill (shaping).
- And then reinforces after you have performed the
  skill successfully (through knowledge of results).

REINFORCEMENT
- Concerned with ensuring the correct response
  is repeated.
- Positive - reward / praise.
- Example : a footballer receives a bonus for
  scoring a goal.
- Negative - withdrawing reward.
- Example : the same footballer who does
  not receive a bonus when he fails to score a
  goal.
- Punishment - breaking the incorrect bond.
- Example : the footballer is dropped from
  the team after he fails to score a goal.

THEORIES OF LEARNING (continued)

INSIGHT LEARNING
- See learning as a problem to be solved by the performer.
- The more you understand why a movement is to be performed, the better the learning.
- Example : hockey players being encouraged to think about marking strategies against twin centre forwards.
- A problem to be solved which gives the players more insight and eventual understanding of the problem.

COGNITIVE THEORY
- Concerned with understanding and insight.
- Work of Gestaltists / German scientists who showed importance of perceiving a problem in its entirety.
- And the use of intervening variables.
- Example : a badminton player will understand the necessity of performing a 'clear' to wrong foot opponent.

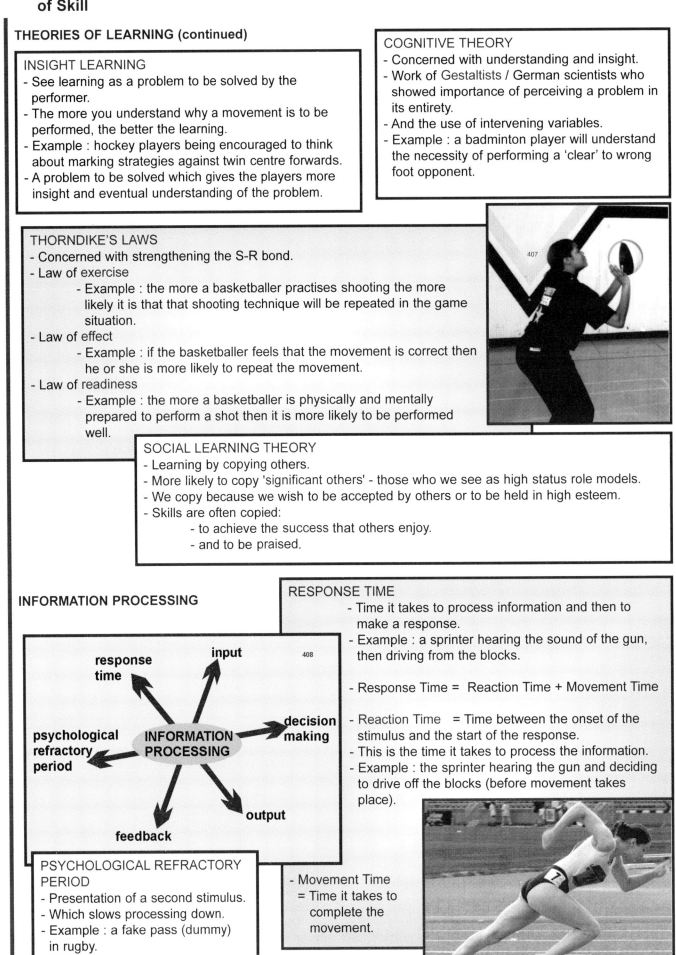

THORNDIKE'S LAWS
- Concerned with strengthening the S-R bond.
- Law of exercise
    - Example : the more a basketballer practises shooting the more likely it is that that shooting technique will be repeated in the game situation.
- Law of effect
    - Example : if the basketballer feels that the movement is correct then he or she is more likely to repeat the movement.
- Law of readiness
    - Example : the more a basketballer is physically and mentally prepared to perform a shot then it is more likely to be performed well.

SOCIAL LEARNING THEORY
- Learning by copying others.
- More likely to copy 'significant others' - those who we see as high status role models.
- We copy because we wish to be accepted by others or to be held in high esteem.
- Skills are often copied:
    - to achieve the success that others enjoy.
    - and to be praised.

INFORMATION PROCESSING

response time — input — decision making — output — feedback — psychological refractory period — **INFORMATION PROCESSING**

RESPONSE TIME
- Time it takes to process information and then to make a response.
- Example : a sprinter hearing the sound of the gun, then driving from the blocks.

- Response Time = Reaction Time + Movement Time

- Reaction Time = Time between the onset of the stimulus and the start of the response.
- This is the time it takes to process the information.
- Example : the sprinter hearing the gun and deciding to drive off the blocks (before movement takes place).

PSYCHOLOGICAL REFRACTORY PERIOD
- Presentation of a second stimulus.
- Which slows processing down.
- Example : a fake pass (dummy) in rugby.

- Movement Time = Time it takes to complete the movement.

INFORMATION PROCESSING (continued)

INPUT
- Display involves information from the environment.
- Information enters brain via sense organs.
- Example : before catching a ball, the catcher sees the ball and is aware of the thrower's movement.

DECISION MAKING
- Involves the perceptual process which selects appropriate information, uses memory and formulates a motor plan.
- Example : other information (which is irrelevant) is ignored by the catcher of the ball.
- Previous experiences are drawn from to decide how to catch the ball.

OUTPUT
- Involves the effector mechanism and muscle movement.
- The nerves send messages to the muscles which move in order for the ball to be caught.

FEEDBACK
- Information which is used during and after movement.
- Intrinsic / internal - Kinaesthesis.
- This is the feeling that the catcher gets as the ball is caught or the feeling of balance that a gymnast gets when she performs a leap on the beam.
- Extrinsic / external / augmented - Knowledge of results.
- The catcher of the ball is aware that the ball is safely caught or the round of applause that the gymnast gets after completing her beam sequence.

ATTENTION
- Attentional wastage can inhibit performance.
- Concentration is required to make skill performance more effective.
- Focus on cues are crucial for success.

NEDEFFER (1976) - 'ATTENTIONAL FOCUS'
- Seen as two continua:
    - Broad / Narrow Focus
    - Broad - the netball player is taking into account all the players in front of her.
    - Narrow - the netball player is concentrating on the goal to shoot.
    - External / Internal Focus
    - External - the netball player is watching the body movements of her opponent.
    - Internal - the netball player is focusing on keeping calm in an important situation.

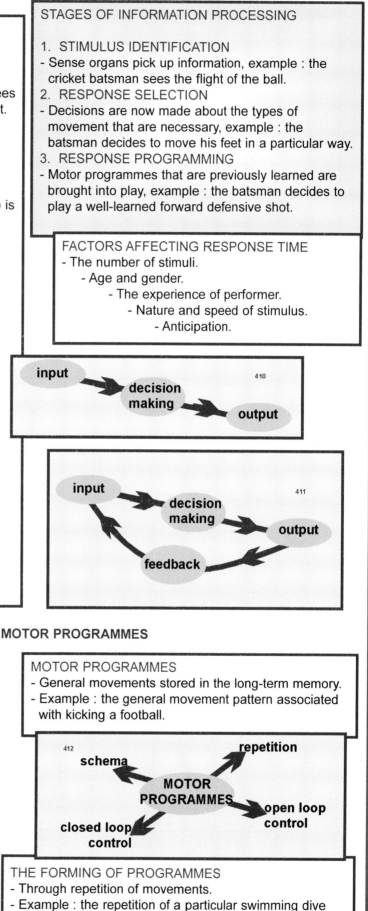

STAGES OF INFORMATION PROCESSING

1. STIMULUS IDENTIFICATION
- Sense organs pick up information, example : the cricket batsman sees the flight of the ball.
2. RESPONSE SELECTION
- Decisions are now made about the types of movement that are necessary, example : the batsman decides to move his feet in a particular way.
3. RESPONSE PROGRAMMING
- Motor programmes that are previously learned are brought into play, example : the batsman decides to play a well-learned forward defensive shot.

FACTORS AFFECTING RESPONSE TIME
- The number of stimuli.
    - Age and gender.
        - The experience of performer.
            - Nature and speed of stimulus.
                - Anticipation.

input → decision making → output   410

input → decision making → output → feedback →   411

MOTOR PROGRAMMES

MOTOR PROGRAMMES
- General movements stored in the long-term memory.
- Example : the general movement pattern associated with kicking a football.

412   schema — MOTOR PROGRAMMES — repetition / open loop control / closed loop control

THE FORMING OF PROGRAMMES
- Through repetition of movements.
- Example : the repetition of a particular swimming dive will eventually cause the swimmer to perform the dive with little conscious control.

MOTOR PROGRAMMES (continued)

OPEN LOOP CONTROL
- Programmes stored can be retrieved by making one decision. For example, throw, catch or kick.
- It is almost automatic and there is too little time for feedback.

CLOSED LOOP CONTROL
- This occurs when there is **intrinsic** or **internal** feedback, via proprioceptors.
- Example : the kinaesthetic sense (via the nervous system) that a trampolinist gets when he or she performs a somersault.
- If there is an error during the movement, this is detected and possibly corrected by the trampolinist during the movement.

MEMORY

MEMORY
- Plays an important part in the performance of skills.
- We use past experiences to help us perform skills.
- We also use parts of our memories to process information.

SHORT-TERM SENSORY STORE (STSS)
- Information is passed through this store where it is filtered.
- This is where **selective attention** takes place.
- Example : a tennis player will select only the **ball** from the display which includes the other player, the crowd, and other movements behind the ball.

SCHEMA
- Items of information in the long-term memory that update and modify programmes.

RECALL SCHEMA
- Information about producing the movement.
- Example : aspects of the environment.

RECOGNITION SCHEMA
- Information about judging the movement.
- Example : kinaesthetic feedback.

SCHEMA INFORMATION
- 1. **Knowledge of environment**.
- Example : a basketballer who is aware of how far he / she is away from the basket.
- 2. **Response specifications**.
- Example : the basketballer recognising that he / she must carry out a jump shot because of an opponent.
- 3. **Sensory consequences**.
- Example : the basketballer intrinsically aware of his / her body movements as the jump shot is being performed.
- 4. **Response outcomes**.
- Example : the basketballer being aware of whether or not the shot has succeeded.

SHORT-TERM MEMORY (STM)
- The 'engine room', where all information that has been filtered passes through.
- Only stores small amounts of information (7 pieces ±2).
- Example : in table tennis, the player who is to receive a serve uses his / her STM to remember the position of the opposing player as the serve commences, his / her own position, and any other information that is less than one minute old.

- Amounts of information can be extended by 'chunking' (grouping / organising together information).
- Example : a rugby player may remember a set play at a lineout by memorising a number.

LONG-TERM MEMORY (LTM)
- Limitless capacity.
- Storing or remembering achieved through : repetition; association; novelty; meaningfulness.
- Motor programmes / schema stored here.
- Retrieved information from here is used in skill performance.

- Example : a hockey player who is experienced has information stored such as motor programmes related to stopping and hitting the ball, and strategies such as how to tackle effectively.

MEMORY

short-term sensory store → short-term memory ↔ long-term memory ↔ perception → decision making

413

MENTAL REHEARSAL (MENTAL PRACTICE)
- This is the process of mentally visualising the movements in motor skill performance.
- This gives greater understanding, causes fewer errors, improves confidence and lowers arousal.
- The acquisition of skills can be quicker and more effective if mental practice is employed.
- Mental rehearsal technique should be practised away from competition and should be an important element of training.
- The finer the detail of the imagery the more effective the technique.
- Combine with distributed practice techniques.

Information

PHASES OF SKILL LEARNING

PHASES OF SKILL LEARNING
- Learning is a complex process, but there is general agreement that the learning of skills occurs in stages.

cognitive stage 414

⬇

associative stage

⬇

autonomous stage

STAGE 1 : COGNITIVE STAGE
- **Trial and error** / trying to find out how to perform the skill.
- When success is experienced and reinforced, the next stage is reached.
- Accurate **information** / **demonstrations** are important for modelling.
- Example : a beginner learning to pass at hockey will be shown how to pass by the teacher.
- The beginner watches the demonstration and understands what needs to be done.

STAGE 2 : ASSOCIATIVE STAGE
- The practice stage. Much **internal** / **external** feedback.
- Errors are detected and corrected.
- Normally there is much improvement.
- Often the performer stays in this stage.
- Example : the novice hockey player will now practise the pass, perhaps by practising the subroutines. The teacher will give feedback.

STAGE 3 : AUTONOMOUS STAGE
- The skill is now performed without much conscious control.
- Motor programmes are run in this stage.
- This stage is only reached by the very skilful.
- Example : the hockey pass has been learnt, and the player can now pass with little conscious effort.

typical 418

performance / number of trials

LEARNING CURVES
- These reflect the relationships which exist between trials of a skill and the success or performance rate.
- Learning curves show performances but can give a good indication of learning.
- Useful for goal setting and recognising the actual ability level of the performer.

- S shaped is a typical curve of learning of a gross motor skill.
- Positive acceleration
- Poor early performances but improves later.
- Linear
- Performance is directly proportional to the number of practice trials.
- Negative
- Good early performances but poorer performances in later trials.
- Plateau
- Not much change if at all in performances over a number of trials.

- To avoid a plateau:
    - Give new goals that can be reached.
    - Give praise that is deserved.
    - Ensure that there are regular rest intervals.
    - Maintain motivation and employ positive cognitive techniques.

positive acceleration 419

performance / number of trials

linear 420

performance / number of trials

negative 421

performance / number of trials

plateau 422

performance / number of trials

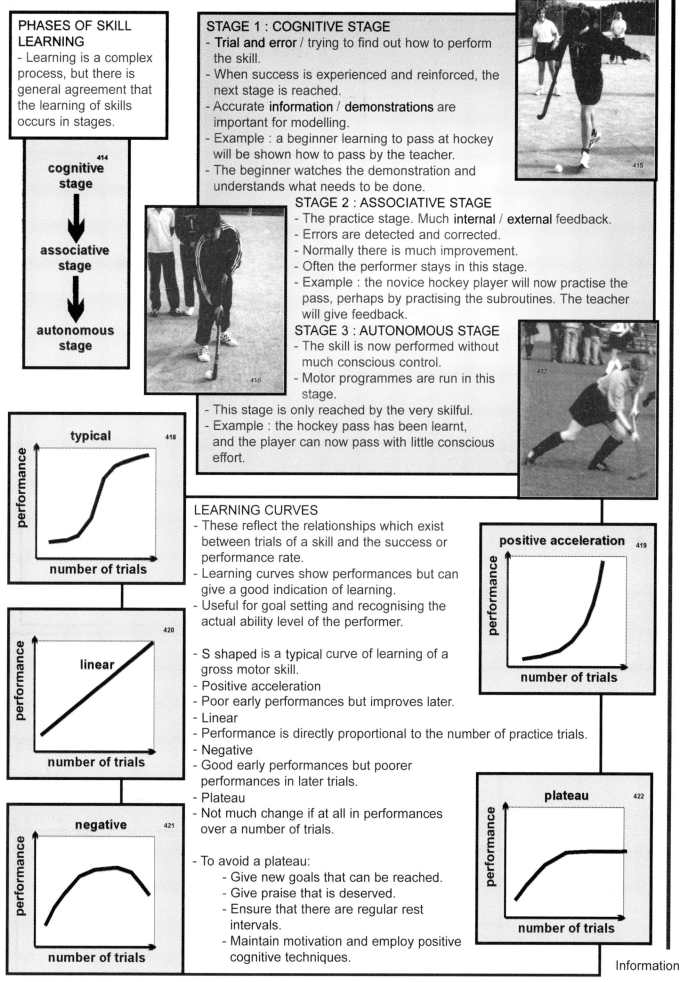

TRANSFER

TRANSFER
- Influence of one skill on the performance of another.

RETROACTIVE TRANSFER
- Influence of one skill on a skill that has previously been learned.
- Example : a hockey player learns the flicking skill which may have a negative effect on the previously learned push (the push pass may be lifted unnecessarily).

PROACTIVE TRANSFER
- Influence of one skill on a skill yet to be learned.
- Example : having learned the forehand drive in tennis, the action is then modified to the forehand drive with top spin.

POSITIVE TRANSFER
- One skill helping the learning / performance of another.
- Example : throwing a tennis ball over the net overarm may positively influence the player's arm action in the serve.
- Takes place if :
    - Skills are similar.
    - Skills performed in similar environment.
- Information processing is similar.
- Previous skill must be thoroughly learned.

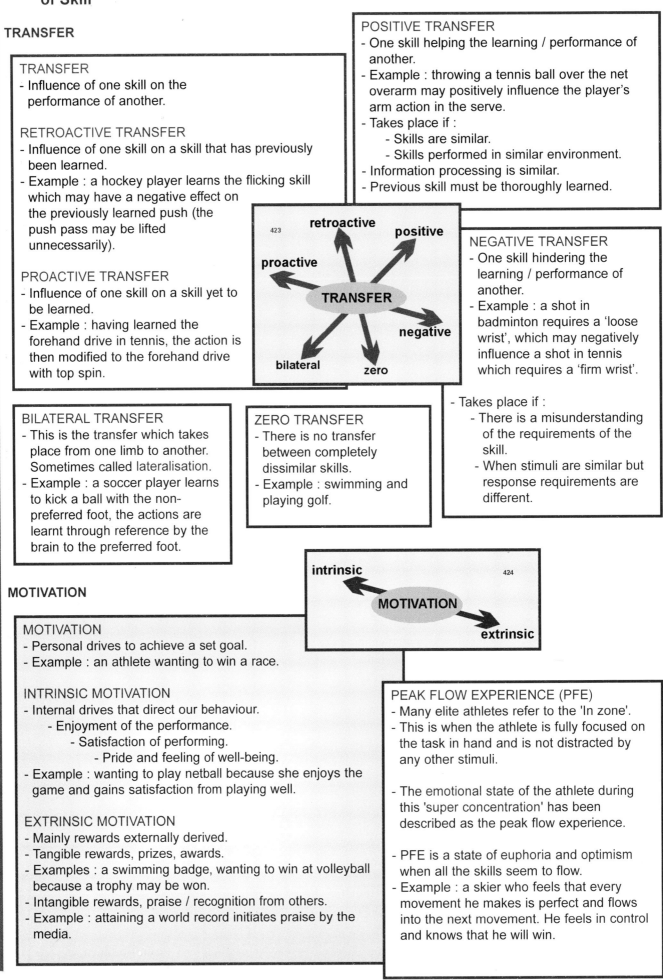

NEGATIVE TRANSFER
- One skill hindering the learning / performance of another.
- Example : a shot in badminton requires a 'loose wrist', which may negatively influence a shot in tennis which requires a 'firm wrist'.

- Takes place if :
    - There is a misunderstanding of the requirements of the skill.
    - When stimuli are similar but response requirements are different.

BILATERAL TRANSFER
- This is the transfer which takes place from one limb to another. Sometimes called lateralisation.
- Example : a soccer player learns to kick a ball with the non-preferred foot, the actions are learnt through reference by the brain to the preferred foot.

ZERO TRANSFER
- There is no transfer between completely dissimilar skills.
- Example : swimming and playing golf.

MOTIVATION

MOTIVATION
- Personal drives to achieve a set goal.
- Example : an athlete wanting to win a race.

INTRINSIC MOTIVATION
- Internal drives that direct our behaviour.
    - Enjoyment of the performance.
        - Satisfaction of performing.
            - Pride and feeling of well-being.
- Example : wanting to play netball because she enjoys the game and gains satisfaction from playing well.

EXTRINSIC MOTIVATION
- Mainly rewards externally derived.
- Tangible rewards, prizes, awards.
- Examples : a swimming badge, wanting to win at volleyball because a trophy may be won.
- Intangible rewards, praise / recognition from others.
- Example : attaining a world record initiates praise by the media.

PEAK FLOW EXPERIENCE (PFE)
- Many elite athletes refer to the 'In zone'.
- This is when the athlete is fully focused on the task in hand and is not distracted by any other stimuli.

- The emotional state of the athlete during this 'super concentration' has been described as the peak flow experience.

- PFE is a state of euphoria and optimism when all the skills seem to flow.
- Example : a skier who feels that every movement he makes is perfect and flows into the next movement. He feels in control and knows that he will win.

MOTIVATION (continued)

AROUSAL LEVELS
- The levels of inner drives.
- Arousal needs to be under control and at the right level depending upon the task.

DRIVE THEORY
- The higher the arousal level, the more likely the dominant response occurs.
- Example : a top class tennis player who plays in front of a large crowd, will pull off her best possible shots.

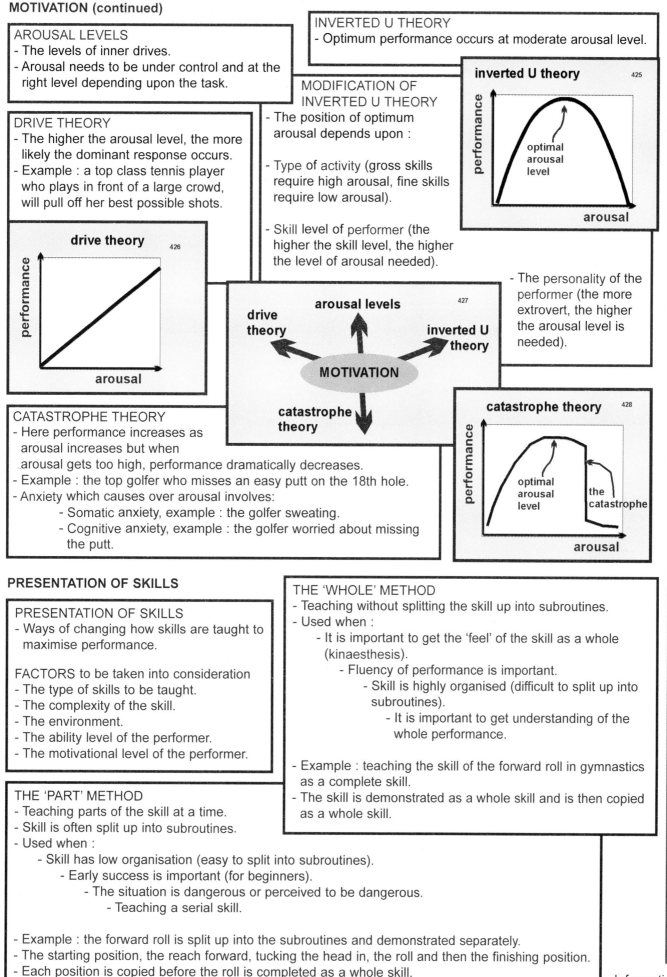

drive theory 426

INVERTED U THEORY
- Optimum performance occurs at moderate arousal level.

inverted U theory 425

MODIFICATION OF INVERTED U THEORY
- The position of optimum arousal depends upon :

- Type of activity (gross skills require high arousal, fine skills require low arousal).

- Skill level of performer (the higher the skill level, the higher the level of arousal needed).

- The personality of the performer (the more extrovert, the higher the arousal level is needed).

MOTIVATION 427
- drive theory
- arousal levels
- inverted U theory
- catastrophe theory

CATASTROPHE THEORY
- Here performance increases as arousal increases but when arousal gets too high, performance dramatically decreases.
- Example : the top golfer who misses an easy putt on the 18th hole.
- Anxiety which causes over arousal involves:
    - Somatic anxiety, example : the golfer sweating.
    - Cognitive anxiety, example : the golfer worried about missing the putt.

catastrophe theory 428
- optimal arousal level
- the catastrophe

PRESENTATION OF SKILLS

PRESENTATION OF SKILLS
- Ways of changing how skills are taught to maximise performance.

FACTORS to be taken into consideration
- The type of skills to be taught.
- The complexity of the skill.
- The environment.
- The ability level of the performer.
- The motivational level of the performer.

THE 'WHOLE' METHOD
- Teaching without splitting the skill up into subroutines.
- Used when :
    - It is important to get the 'feel' of the skill as a whole (kinaesthesis).
        - Fluency of performance is important.
            - Skill is highly organised (difficult to split up into subroutines).
                - It is important to get understanding of the whole performance.

- Example : teaching the skill of the forward roll in gymnastics as a complete skill.
- The skill is demonstrated as a whole skill and is then copied as a whole skill.

THE 'PART' METHOD
- Teaching parts of the skill at a time.
- Skill is often split up into subroutines.
- Used when :
    - Skill has low organisation (easy to split into subroutines).
        - Early success is important (for beginners).
            - The situation is dangerous or perceived to be dangerous.
                - Teaching a serial skill.

- Example : the forward roll is split up into the subroutines and demonstrated separately.
- The starting position, the reach forward, tucking the head in, the roll and then the finishing position.
- Each position is copied before the roll is completed as a whole skill.

Information

PRESENTATION OF SKILLS (continued)

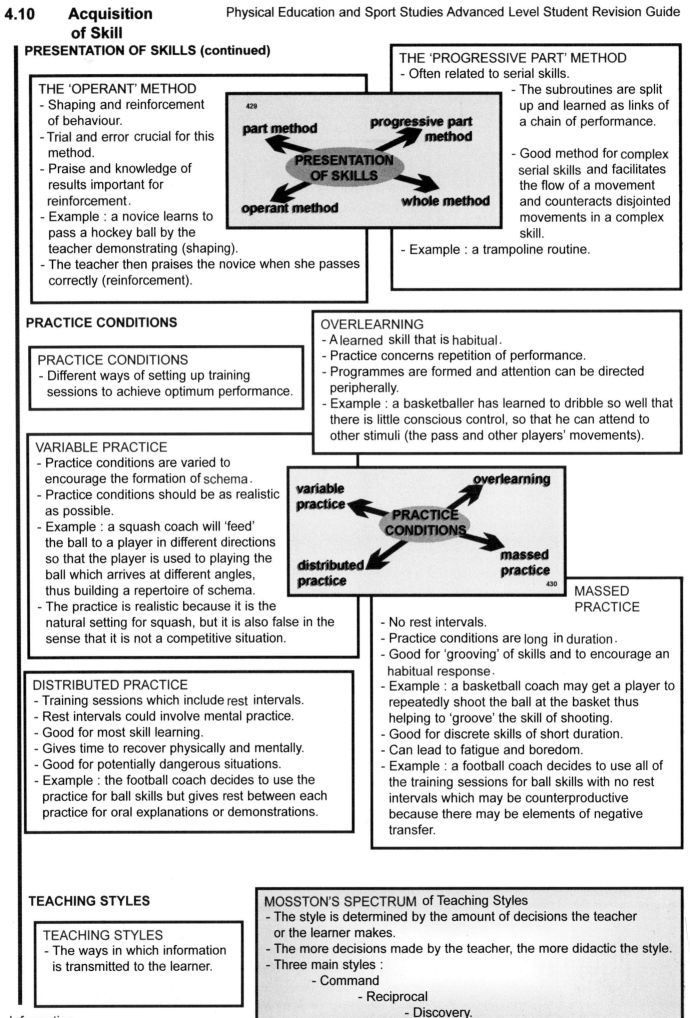

THE 'OPERANT' METHOD
- Shaping and reinforcement of behaviour.
- Trial and error crucial for this method.
- Praise and knowledge of results important for reinforcement.
- Example : a novice learns to pass a hockey ball by the teacher demonstrating (shaping).
- The teacher then praises the novice when she passes correctly (reinforcement).

THE 'PROGRESSIVE PART' METHOD
- Often related to serial skills.
- The subroutines are split up and learned as links of a chain of performance.
- Good method for complex serial skills and facilitates the flow of a movement and counteracts disjointed movements in a complex skill.
- Example : a trampoline routine.

PRACTICE CONDITIONS

PRACTICE CONDITIONS
- Different ways of setting up training sessions to achieve optimum performance.

OVERLEARNING
- A learned skill that is habitual.
- Practice concerns repetition of performance.
- Programmes are formed and attention can be directed peripherally.
- Example : a basketballer has learned to dribble so well that there is little conscious control, so that he can attend to other stimuli (the pass and other players' movements).

VARIABLE PRACTICE
- Practice conditions are varied to encourage the formation of schema.
- Practice conditions should be as realistic as possible.
- Example : a squash coach will 'feed' the ball to a player in different directions so that the player is used to playing the ball which arrives at different angles, thus building a repertoire of schema.
- The practice is realistic because it is the natural setting for squash, but it is also false in the sense that it is not a competitive situation.

MASSED PRACTICE
- No rest intervals.
- Practice conditions are long in duration.
- Good for 'grooving' of skills and to encourage an habitual response.
- Example : a basketball coach may get a player to repeatedly shoot the ball at the basket thus helping to 'groove' the skill of shooting.
- Good for discrete skills of short duration.
- Can lead to fatigue and boredom.
- Example : a football coach decides to use all of the training sessions for ball skills with no rest intervals which may be counterproductive because there may be elements of negative transfer.

DISTRIBUTED PRACTICE
- Training sessions which include rest intervals.
- Rest intervals could involve mental practice.
- Good for most skill learning.
- Gives time to recover physically and mentally.
- Good for potentially dangerous situations.
- Example : the football coach decides to use the practice for ball skills but gives rest between each practice for oral explanations or demonstrations.

TEACHING STYLES

TEACHING STYLES
- The ways in which information is transmitted to the learner.

MOSSTON'S SPECTRUM of Teaching Styles
- The style is determined by the amount of decisions the teacher or the learner makes.
- The more decisions made by the teacher, the more didactic the style.
- Three main styles :
    - Command
        - Reciprocal
            - Discovery.

Information

TEACHING STYLES (continued)

COMMAND
- Style which involves mostly the teacher making the decisions.
- Authoritarian and didactic.
- Example : in a hockey small game situation, the coach calls 'freeze' to preserve pitch position.

- Good for : novices, quick responses, dangerous situations, hostile groups, large groups.

- Not good for : high level performers, social interaction and creativity.

RECIPROCAL
- Style which involves learners becoming teachers of others.
- Example : the coach teaches the skill of a tumble turn to some of the swimmers, who in turn then teach others.
  - Good for :
    - social interaction
    - giving responsibility
    - personal development
    - feedback.
  - Not good for :
    - discipline
    - correct information delivered.
    - beginners
    - those who have poor communication skills.

command ← TEACHING STYLES → reciprocal ↓ discovery 431

DISCOVERY
- Style involving decision making by the performer / learner.
- Example : the coach tells players in a hockey team to work out for themselves the strategies for a penalty corner.
- Good for : creativity, motivation, high level performer.
- Not good for : efficiency, learning correct habits, motivation if things go wrong.

GUIDANCE METHODS

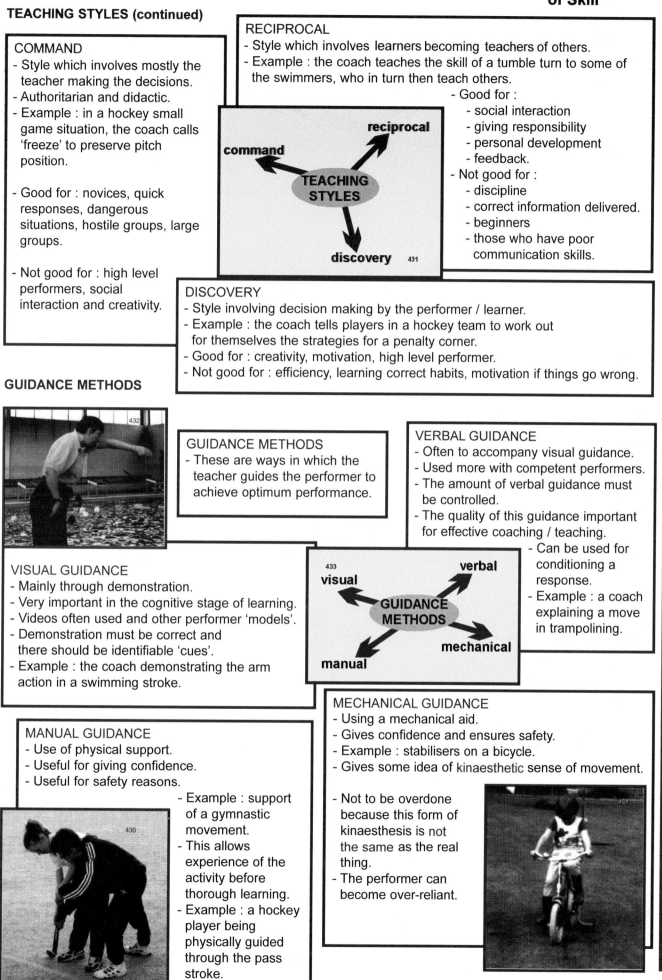

GUIDANCE METHODS
- These are ways in which the teacher guides the performer to achieve optimum performance.

VERBAL GUIDANCE
- Often to accompany visual guidance.
- Used more with competent performers.
- The amount of verbal guidance must be controlled.
- The quality of this guidance important for effective coaching / teaching.
  - Can be used for conditioning a response.
  - Example : a coach explaining a move in trampolining.

VISUAL GUIDANCE
- Mainly through demonstration.
- Very important in the cognitive stage of learning.
- Videos often used and other performer 'models'.
- Demonstration must be correct and there should be identifiable 'cues'.
- Example : the coach demonstrating the arm action in a swimming stroke.

visual ← GUIDANCE METHODS → verbal, mechanical, manual   433

MANUAL GUIDANCE
- Use of physical support.
- Useful for giving confidence.
- Useful for safety reasons.
  - Example : support of a gymnastic movement.
  - This allows experience of the activity before thorough learning.
  - Example : a hockey player being physically guided through the pass stroke.

MECHANICAL GUIDANCE
- Using a mechanical aid.
- Gives confidence and ensures safety.
- Example : stabilisers on a bicycle.
- Gives some idea of kinaesthetic sense of movement.

- Not to be overdone because this form of kinaesthesis is not the same as the real thing.
- The performer can become over-reliant.

Information

QUESTIONS

CHARACTERISTICS OF SKILL

1) If you were watching a number of performers in sport, what characteristics would you expect the movements of a skilled performer to have? (4 marks)

2) By using examples from Physical Education, explain what is meant by fundamental motor skills and why they are so important. (4 marks)

ABILITY

3) You are observing a number of tennis players being coached. There are a mixture of abilities.
a) What is meant by ability? (3 marks)
b) Give two types of abilities that are important to play tennis effectively. (2 marks)
c) Why is it wrong to assume that there is such a thing as natural ability? (2 marks)

CLASSIFICATION OF SKILLS

4) a) Why is the tennis serve often regarded as a closed skill? (2 marks)
b) Using passing skills in a team game, explain what is meant by an open skill. (4 marks)
c) Give one example from sport of each of the following and state why you have chosen your example :
continuous skills; serial skills; discrete skills. (3 marks)

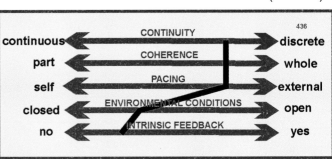

5) The diagram on the right shows a profile for the racing start in swimming scaled across five different continua representing the skill characteristics of the movement.
a) Referring to the profile, describe the swim racing start in terms of each of the five characteristics shown. (5 marks)
b) **i)** Using this same profile chart, sketch a profile which would describe the characteristics of a tennis serve. (3 marks)
ii) Explain why you have chosen your particular characteristic for coherence and environmental conditions. (5 marks)

iii) Explain how your profile for the tennis serve might assist a coach in planning practices for players learning this skill. (7 marks)

THEORIES OF LEARNING

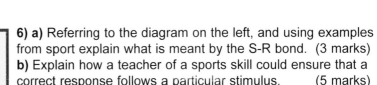

6) a) Referring to the diagram on the left, and using examples from sport explain what is meant by the S-R bond. (3 marks)
b) Explain how a teacher of a sports skill could ensure that a correct response follows a particular stimulus. (5 marks)
c) What is meant by operant conditioning? Show how you would use operant conditioning to teach a named sports skill. (5 marks)
d) State what is meant by reinforcement and give examples of different types. (4 marks)
e) Explain what is meant by classical conditioning and give an example from sport. (4 marks)

INFORMATION PROCESSING

7) a) Give the three main receptor systems used by a performer in sport. (3 marks)
b) Where is the filtering mechanism found in an information processing model? Explain what happens with information as it passes through this mechanism. (2 marks)
c) What is the difference between reaction time and response time?
What advice would you give to a sprinter to cut down on reaction time at the start of a race? (4 marks)
d) Define the term feedback, and briefly describe three functions of feedback. (5 marks)
e) Look at the diagram on the right which illustrates two ways of classifying sources of feedback. Where possible explain the kinds of feedback available to a performer which would be classified as **W**, **X**, **Y**, and **Z**. (4 marks)
f) How would you make feedback effective when teaching a motor skill? (5 marks)

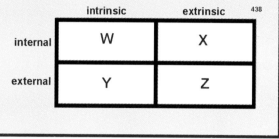

	intrinsic	extrinsic	438
internal	W	X	
external	Y	Z	

8) a) Name the three main stages in information processing and use a practical example to illustrate what happens in each stage. (6 marks)
b) Nedeffer (1976), identified two types of attention in sports performance. Name one attentional focus and give a practical example showing its importance. (2 marks)

MOTOR PROGRAMMES

9) a) State what is meant by a motor programme and give an example. (2 marks)
b) How can a programme become a subroutine? (2 marks)
c) How is closed loop control used to make a movement more skilful? (3 marks)

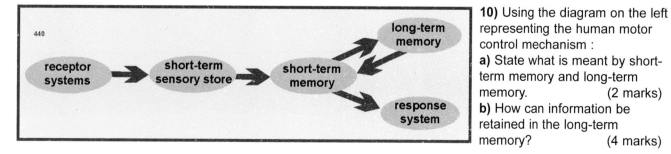

439

d) Looking at the diagram above, list six major subroutines of the executive programme for throwing. (6 marks)
e) Using examples from sport, identify four items of information stored as schema. (4 marks)
f) Comparing the skills of throwing the javelin and taking a free throw at basketball, explain how the skills are related using schema theory. (4 marks)
g) Briefly explain how the analysis of skills will influence a coach in organising training for javelin throwing as compared with basketball free throw. (4 marks)

MEMORY

440

receptor systems → short-term sensory store → short-term memory → long-term memory

short-term memory → response system

10) Using the diagram on the left representing the human motor control mechanism :
a) State what is meant by short-term memory and long-term memory. (2 marks)
b) How can information be retained in the long-term memory? (4 marks)

MEMORY QUESTIONS (continued)

10 c) Using the example of a table tennis player receiving a serve :
i) What information would be held in the short-term sensory store, and for how long? (2 marks)
ii) Name and describe the purpose of the process by which information is transferred from the short-term sensory store to the short-term memory. (4 marks)
iii) What types of information would you use (if you were a table tennis player receiving a serve) from your short-term memory? (3 marks)
iv) And your long-term memory? (3 marks)

PHASES OF SKILL LEARNING

11) a) Name the three phases of learning and put them into a practical context. (6 marks)
b) Explain the third stage of learning associated with advanced performers. (4 marks)
c) How might the type of mental practice change in the last phase of learning? (2 marks)
d) Figure 441 illustrates the amount of learning of a simple motor skill that has taken place over a number of trial periods. Explain the fluctuations in performance shown. (5 marks)

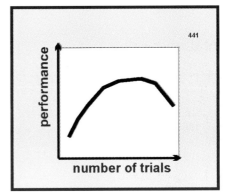

TRANSFER

12) a) Using a practical example, explain what is meant by the term transfer in skill learning. (3 marks)
b) How can transfer be detrimental to performance? Give a practical example. (3 marks)
c) How can a teacher or a coach ensure that as much positive transfer takes place as possible in a training session? (5 marks)

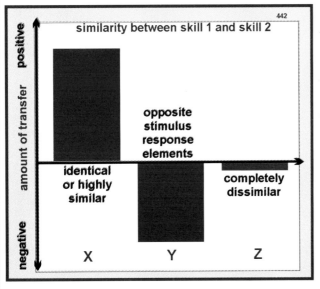

13) a) Define the terms positive transfer and negative transfer in the context of someone learning a sport skill. (2 marks)

b) Chart 442 on the left shows different amounts of transfer in different situations labelled **X**, **Y**, and **Z**. For each of these situations give examples of one pair of games type skills which illustrate the kinds of transfer indicated. Explain the reasons for your choice. (10 marks)

MOTIVATION

14) a) What is meant by intrinsic and extrinsic motivation? Give practical examples to illustrate your answer. (4 marks)
b) How can extrinsic motives affect intrinsic motivation? (2 marks)
c) What sort of motivation methods would you use to motivate a beginner in gymnastics? (4 marks)
d) How would the motivation methods used for a skilled performer differ from that used for a beginner? (3 marks)
e) Many elite athletes identify an emotional response called the peak flow experience that is associated with success. Describe what is meant by peak flow experience and give reasons why it might occur. (5 marks)

PRESENTATION OF SKILLS

15) a) What must be taken into account before any decision can be made about how to teach a skill? (6 marks)
b) Generally a skill should be taught as a whole as far as possible, give reasons for this. (3 marks)
c) Some skills need to be split up into subroutines to be taught effectively. What are the advantages and disadvantages of this type of skill presentation? (6 marks)

PRACTICE CONDITIONS

16) a) Define massed and distributed practice. (2 marks)
b) Justify the choice of practice conditions for a training session of a sport of your choice. (8 marks)

TEACHING STYLES

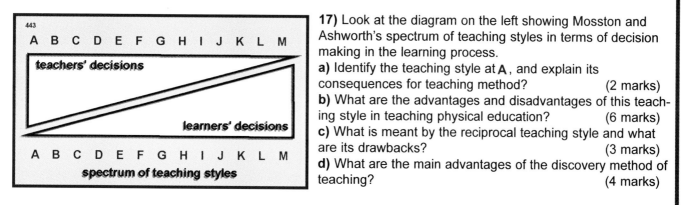

443
A B C D E F G H I J K L M
teachers' decisions
learners' decisions
A B C D E F G H I J K L M
spectrum of teaching styles

17) Look at the diagram on the left showing Mosston and Ashworth's spectrum of teaching styles in terms of decision making in the learning process.
a) Identify the teaching style at **A**, and explain its consequences for teaching method? (2 marks)
b) What are the advantages and disadvantages of this teaching style in teaching physical education? (6 marks)
c) What is meant by the reciprocal teaching style and what are its drawbacks? (3 marks)
d) What are the main advantages of the discovery method of teaching? (4 marks)

GUIDANCE METHODS

18) a) Other than visual guidance, what other main methods of guidance are there? Give a practical example for each. (6 marks)
b) How would you optimise the use of visual guidance in teaching motor skills? What are the drawbacks of this method? (4 marks)

ANSWERS

The answer for each mark awarded is notated by the ❐ symbol - where there are more ❐ symbols than there are marks available, marks would be given for any choice up to the maximum available. Usually, the precise wording specified in an answer would not be required - answers with the same meaning would be acceptable.

CHARACTERISTICS OF SKILL

1)
If you were watching a number of performers in sport, what characteristics would you expect the movements of a skilled performer to have?
    4 marks for four from :
❐ Movement seems effortless.
❐ There are many correct movements consistently performed.
❐ The movement follows a technical model.
❐ The movement is aesthetically pleasing.
❐ The movement is controlled and well co-ordinated.

2)
By using examples from Physical Education, explain what is meant by fundamental motor skills and why they are so important.
    4 marks for four from :
❐ Jumping; catching; throwing etc.
❐ Basis for the development of other skills.
❐ Learned through early experiences usually via play.
❐ Important because can draw on them for lifetime sports / healthy lifestyles.
❐ Helps personal development / self-esteem.

4.16 Acquisition of Skill

ABILITY

3) a)

What is meant by ability?

3 marks for three from :
- ❐ Ability is a trait / innate / you are born with certain abilities.
- ❐ There are two types of ability - Perceptual and Motor.
- ❐ Perceptual ability is related to processing spatial information.
- ❐ Perceptual ability is concerned with judgement and interpretation of information.
- ❐ Motor ability is concerned with proficiency of movement patterns.

3) b)

Give two types of abilities that are important to play tennis effectively.

2 marks for two from :
- ❐ Good reactions to stimuli.
- ❐ Speed of movement.
- ❐ Explosive strength.
- ❐ Good body balance.
- ❐ Good timing for hitting the ball and moving into position.
- ❐ Good degree of body suppleness / flexibility.

3) c)

Why is it wrong to assume that there is such a thing as natural ability?
- ❐ Abilities are not all-encompassing, they are specific.
- ❐ Specific movements / skills require different abilities.

CLASSIFICATION OF SKILLS

4) a)

Why is the tennis serve often regarded as a closed skill?

2 marks for two from :
- ❐ Tends to be an habitual response.
- ❐ Little reference to the environment.
- ❐ There is a definite beginning and end.
- ❐ More self-paced than externally-paced.

4) b)

Using passing skills in a team game, explain what is meant by an open skill.

4 marks from four examples of passing skills and explanations :
- ❐ When passing a soccer ball you need to take into account any challenge from your opponents.
- ❐ You need to refer to where your team mate is when passing a netball.
- ❐ You need to process a great deal of information regarding speed of passing the ball in hockey and the direction of the pass.
- ❐ When passing the ball in rugby the speed at which you pass is often dictated by how quickly you are being closed-down.

4) c)

Give one example from sport of each of the following and state why you have chosen your example : continuous skills; serial skills; discrete skills.
- ❐ Continuous skill = Cycling - because the subroutines of the pedalling action are not easily separated.
- ❐ Serial skill = Triple jump - because there are a number of discrete elements linked together to make up the whole skill.
- ❐ Discrete skill = Forward roll - because there is a definite beginning and a definite end to the skill.

5) a)

Referring to the chart, describe the swim racing start in terms of each of the five characteristics.
- ❐ Continuity - the start is shown as being discrete, it has a distinct beginning and end.
- ❐ Coherence - the start is shown as being whole, it cannot be meaningfully broken down into sub-parts for practice.
- ❐ Pacing - the start is shown as being externally paced, the swimmer has to react to the external stimulus of the gun or hooter.
- ❐ Environmental conditions - the start is shown as a closed skill, although the swimmer reacts to an external signal, no interpretation of that stimulus is required, and only the one response (movement from the start box) relevant.
- ❐ Intrinsic feedback - the start is shown as providing very little intrinsic feedback, the information arising directly from the movement itself (kinaesthetic) would not tell the swimmer much about the quality of the start in the context of the race.

Answers

CLASSIFICATION OF SKILLS - ANSWERS QUESTION 5 (continued)

5) b) i)

Sketch a profile which would describe the characteristics of a tennis serve.

See chart on the right, marks awarded for :

☐ 1 mark for 1 element.

☐ 2 marks for 3 correct.

☐ 3 marks for 5 correct (approximate answers acceptable).

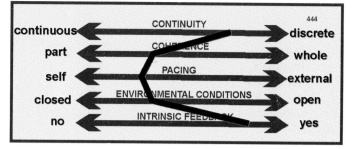

5) b) ii)

Explain why you have chosen your particular characteristic for coherence and environmental conditions.

5 marks for five from :

Coherence :

☐ The serve is a part of a skill, it can meaningfully broken down into subparts for practice.

☐ Subparts could be : approach, backswing, throw up of the ball, strike phase, follow through, recovery.

☐ This approach would not be appropriate at a later more autonomous level of learning or skill development.

Environmental conditions :

☐ The serve is a fairly closed skill, then player uses a well learned technique.

☐ However, a player must be able to use more than one movement pattern in order to be able to use a safer serve for a second serve situation.

☐ At higher levels of skill, there may be a degree of openness in the selection of a specific serve action.

☐ A player will 'read' the receiver's positions on court and / or his / her strength at returning different types of serve, and hence choose appropriately.

5) b) iii)

Explain why your profile might assist a coach in planning practices for players learning the skill.

7 marks for seven from :

☐ The coach should look at the position of the skill in each continuum to see if it will tell him / her something about how to organise the practices.

Continuity :

☐ Because the skill is discrete, it can be practised in isolation from other aspects of the game.

☐ It should be practised sufficiently to enable accuracy / consistency to develop.

Coherence :

☐ Coach will be able to analyse the appropriate parts of the skill.

☐ (Any two from) stance, throw up, backswing, strike phase, follow through.

☐ And set separate practices for each element.

☐ Before integrating the elements later.

Pacing :

☐ Because the skill is internally paced, the coach should encourage beginners to take their own time in executing the skill.

☐ And to adopt a set routine / mental set for the technique.

Environmental conditions :

☐ Although the serve is relatively 'closed', it can be affected by a cross wind, temperature, pressure, and sun in the eyes.

☐ Which means that the player should be exposed to practice in this variety of environmental conditions in order to be best prepared for them in the competitive situation.

Intrinsic feedback :

☐ The coach should encourage the learner to try to repeat the 'feeling' of a good serve.

THEORIES OF LEARNING

6) a)

By using examples from sport explain what is meant by the S-R bond.

☐ A certain response is connected to a certain stimulus, for example, a forehand is hit by a right-handed player because the ball appears on the right hand side of the player's body.

☐ The stimulus acts as a cue to be associated with a response, for example, in volleyball a player will jump to block a ball being smashed across the net by the opposition.

☐ The response is almost automatic because the bond is so great between stimulus and response. For example, a 'reflex' save by a goalkeeper to a shot on goal.

THEORIES OF LEARNING - ANSWERS QUESTION 6 (continued)

6) b)

Explain how a teacher of a sports skill could ensure that a correct response follows a particular stimulus.

5 marks for five from :

❑ Give **praise** / positive reinforcement.

❑ Give **feedback** / give direct knowledge about what to do.

❑ Give **satisfaction** if movement is correct (Thorndike's Law of Effect).

❑ Give **negative** reinforcement if movement is incorrect.

❑ Give **punishment** if movement is incorrect.

❑ **Repeat** the correct movement to establish a motor programme.

6) c)

What is meant by operant conditioning and show how you would use it to teach a named sports skill?

5 marks for five from :

❑ **Operant conditioning** is shaping behaviour by reinforcement.

❑ For example, to teach a high long serve in badminton.

❑ Give demonstration (**shaping**).

❑ Get opponent to stand in service box opposite with racket held high (**shaping**).

❑ Give targets to aim for (**shaping**).

❑ Give knowledge of results (**reinforcement**).

❑ Give feedback about performance (**reinforcement**).

❑ Give praise (**reinforcement**).

6) d)

State what is meant by reinforcement and give examples of different types.

❑ **Reinforcement** is the manipulation of a stimulus to ensure that a response reoccurs.

❑ For example, **positive** reinforcement - giving praise when a swimmer wins a race.

❑ For example, **negative** reinforcement - taking away the praise if the swimmer subsequently loses.

❑ For example, **punishment** - telling the swimmer off for not trying very hard if he / she loses the race.

6) e)

Explain what is meant by classical conditioning and give an example from sport.

❑ Classical conditioning is the manipulation of the stimulus to get a certain response.

❑ Classical conditioning is the pairing of an unconditioned stimulus with a conditioned stimulus to get a conditioned response.

❑ For example, if a young child is frightened of the water, this may be due to classical conditioning.

❑ This is because the child has learnt to pair the sight of water with the emotion of fear.

INFORMATION PROCESSING

7) a)

Give the three main receptor systems used by a performer in sport.

❑ Visual.

❑ Auditory.

❑ Proprioceptors.

7) b)

Where is the filtering mechanism found in an information processing model? Explain what happens with information as it passes through this mechanism.

2 marks for two from :

❑ The filtering mechanism is found in the short-term sensory store.

❑ Helps with selective attention.

❑ Makes irrelevant information redundant.

❑ Helps to concentrate effort on information that is important.

7) c)

What is the difference between reaction time and response time? What advice would you give to a sprinter to cut down on reaction time at the start of a race?

4 marks for four from :

❑ Reaction time = time between onset of stimulus and the initiation of the response.

❑ Response time is reaction time plus movement time / it is the time between the onset of the stimulus and the completion of the response.

❑ Coach concentration / focusing.

❑ Teach mental rehearsal.

❑ Lower arousal level of athlete via cognitive / somatic strategies.

❑ Ignore external stimuli other than the starting gun / selective attention.

❑ Teach strategies of driving from the blocks / practise responding to the gun.

INFORMATION PROCESSING - ANSWER QUESTION 7 (continued)

7) d)

Define the term feedback, and describe three functions of feedback.

Feedback (2 marks for two from) :

❐ Any kind of information received by a learner as a result of a particular response or act.

❐ This information would be available during and after the movement had been completed.

❐ And would be brought into the system both during the course of the movement and after the movement had been completed.

Functions of feedback (3 marks) :

❐ **Motivational** - success or failure, clear goals, inspires the performer to continue striving for perfection.

❐ **Reinforcing** - increases the chance of the performer repeating the performance.

❐ **Informational** - the outcome of the performance, is it correct or incorrect?

7) e)

Explain the kinds of feedback available to a performer for the different classifications.

❐ **W** represents feedback that is perceived (by proprioception, the feeling of muscle tension).

❐ **X** represents feedback that might be due to a crowd noise reacting to a game situation, or seeing other performers.

❐ **Y** represents augmented or extrinsic feedback in which verbal or non-verbal information about the performance is given to the performer, otherwise known as knowledge of performance.

❐ **Z** represents feedback concerning the outcome - whether the performer has been successful or has failed, distance or time achieved (as in a race or throw or jump), otherwise known as knowledge of results.

7) f)

How would you make feedback effective when teaching a motor skill?

5 marks for five from :

❐ Feedback must be accurate and well-informed.

❐ Knowledge of results is important.

❐ Be specific and selective with information / not too much information at a time.

❐ Make the feedback interesting to hold attention and aid retention.

❐ Information should be understood by the performer.

❐ Feedback should be given straight after the performance.

❐ Encourage intrinsic feedback / the feel of the movement / kinaesthesis.

8) a)

Name the three main stages in information processing and use a practical example to illustrate what happens in each stage.

❐ Stimulus identification.

❐ A rounders fielder gets ready to catch the ball by watching it.

❐ Response selection.

❐ A rounders fielder makes decisions to enable the catch to take place - decides to move her feet and to get her hands ready for the catch.

❐ Response programming.

❐ A rounders fielder starts to move, putting her decisions into practice.

8) b)

Nedeffer (1976), identified two types of attention in sports performance. Name one attentional focus and give a practical example showing its importance.

❐ Broad / Narrow or External / Internal.

❐ Broad - volleyball player will focus on the opponents and the position of his own players.

❐ Narrow - volleyball player will focus on the ball as it approaches.

❐ External - volleyball player will focus on his opponents' positions.

❐ Internal - volleyball player will focus on his own feelings of aggression and determination.

MOTOR PROGRAMMES

9) a)

State what is meant by a motor programme and give an example.

1 mark for one from :

❐ A set of movements stored in the long-term memory.

❐ Movements are so well-learned they are almost automatic.

❐ One decision can stimulate the onset of a programme.

1 mark for :

❐ Examples : a basketball dribble, throwing a ball, cycling.

| MOTOR PROGRAMMES - ANSWERS QUESTIONS 9 (continued)

9) b)

How can a programme become a subroutine?

2 marks for two from :

❏ The programme is so well-learned / habitual / overlearned.

❏ That it becomes part (subroutine) of a more complex movement.

❏ For example, a basketball dribble becomes a subroutine of the lay-up shot.

9) c)

How is closed loop control used to make a movement more skilful?

3 marks for three from :

❏ Proprioception / intrinsic feedback gives information about errors and / or correct movements.

❏ This information can then be used to correct errors or reinforce correct movement.

❏ Information is sent via the command mechanism / effector mechanism for muscular control.

❏ There has to be little conscious attention during closed loop control.

9) d)

List six major subroutines of the executive programme for throwing.

6 marks for six from :

❏ Grip on implement.

❏ Initial body / arm / feet / head position.

❏ Action of right leg (right handed thrower).

❏ Action of trunk during throw.

❏ Action of right arm during throw.

❏ Sequence of legs - trunk - arm during throw.

❏ Position and action of left side / leg / arm before delivery.

❏ Position of head / eyes (view) during delivery.

9) e)

Using examples from sport, identify four items of information stored as schema.

❏ Knowledge of the environment, for example, knowing how far away you are from the basket before you shoot in basketball.

❏ Response specifications, for example, knowing what you have to do to score.

❏ Sensory consequences, for example, what the movement feels like as you are shooting.

❏ Response outcomes, for example, the end result which would be either success or failure.

9) f)

Comparing the javelin and free throw at basketball, explain the relationship of the skills using schema theory.

❏ Knowledge of the environment - awareness of the foul line and the need to complete the throw behind it (javelin), awareness of side line again with the need to complete the throw outside the court proper (basketball).

❏ Response specifications - knowing that you have to throw as far as possible into the field (javelin), knowing that you have to throw to a colleague on the court (basketball).

❏ Sensory consequences - the feeling of the movement of throwing (both).

❏ Response outcomes - distance thrown (javelin), correct receipt of the ball by colleague (basketball).

9) g)

Explain how the analysis of skills will help a coach organise training for javelin throwing.

❏ The breaking down of the skill into subroutines will enable the coach to analyse the movements objectively.

❏ And thereby set a programme for practice of the individual subroutines.

❏ As drills or individual skill practices which are made separately.

❏ Which would then be incorporated into the motor programme as a whole.

MEMORY

10) a)

State what is meant by short-term memory and long-term memory.

2 marks for two from :

❏ Long-term and short-term memories are part of multi-store model of memory.

❏ All information passes through STM.

❏ STM uses information immediately if presented within about 1 minute.

❏ LTM has almost limitless capacity.

❏ LTM stores information over a long period of time.

❏ LTM stores are used if information is over 1 minute old.

MEMORY - ANSWERS QUESTION 10 (continued)

10) b)

How can information be retained in the long-term memory?

4 marks for four from :

❑ Through repetition of the stimuli.

❑ Through having meaning to the performer.

❑ Information is novel.

❑ Stored here if associated with another piece of stored information.

❑ If stimuli are emotionally intense.

❑ If information is perceived to be important / relevant.

10) c) i)

What information would be held in the short-term sensory store, and for how long?

2 marks for two from :

❑ Information held would be local and temporary, pertaining to the immediate surroundings of the player and his / her opponent.

❑ This would be retained for up to 1/4 seconds or sooner if the display changes, and new more relevant information replaces it.

❑ Examples would be from : position of the ball, placement of opponents hands / bat, placement of opponent relative to table.

10) c) ii)

Name and describe the process by which information is transferred from the short-term sensory store to the short-term memory.

4 marks for four from :

❑ The process is called selective attention.

❑ And is caused by the individual selecting from the many (thousands) of bits of information which flow through the short-term sensory store each second.

❑ Those items which are relevant.

❑ And avoiding items which would distract the player (such as the crowd, other movements behind the ball).

❑ An example could be the retaining of the ready position of the opponent once the serve has begun.

10) c) iii)

What types of information would you use (if you were a table tennis player) from your short-term memory?

3 marks for three from :

❑ Position of player.

❑ Speed of the ball.

❑ Trajectory of ball.

❑ Spin of ball.

❑ Score.

❑ Previous point / rally.

10) c) iv)

From your long-term memory?

3 marks for three from :

❑ Previous points over 1 minute old.

❑ Previous experiences, for example, with this player.

❑ Your own strengths and weaknesses.

❑ The opponent's strengths and weaknesses.

❑ Any other relevant information over 1 minute old.

PHASES OF SKILL LEARNING

11) a)

Name the three phases of learning and put them into a practical context.

❑ Cognitive phase.

❑ For example, a beginner watching a demonstration.

❑ Associative phase.

❑ For example, a gymnast practising a floor routine.

❑ Autonomous phase.

❑ For example, a skilled athlete running in a hurdles race.

PHASES OF SKILL LEARNING - ANSWERS QUESTION 11 (continued)

11) b)
Explain the third stage of learning associated with advanced performers.
    4 marks for four from :
- ❐ Almost automatic in movements.
- ❐ Seems confident / has predetermined goals.
- ❐ More likely to complete complex movements.
- ❐ Is successful consistently.
- ❐ Less likely to lose concentration / is focused.
- ❐ Advanced performers will only stay in this phase if they keep referring back to the associative phase / keep practising.

11) c)
How might the type of mental practice change in the last phase of learning?
    2 marks for two from :
- ❐ Concentrating on only very few stimuli / very selective in attention.
- ❐ Less about skill performance, more on keeping calm.
- ❐ Visualising success more than other phases.
- ❐ Thinking more about tactics / strategies.

11) d)
The figure illustrates the amount of learning of a simple motor skill that has taken place over a number of trial periods. Explain the fluctuations in performance shown.
- ❐ Low at first because skill is being learned / cognitive phase.
- ❐ Sharp increase due to rapid learning because skill is simple and trials likely to be successful.
- ❐ Sharp increase due to good motivation levels.
- ❐ Plateau because lack of motivation / goals reached / lack of fitness / reactive inhibition.
- ❐ Fall in performance because of lack of motivation / fatigue / lack of experience.

TRANSFER

12) a)
Using a practical example, explain what is meant by the term transfer in skill learning.
- ❐ Transfer - the influence of the learning or performance of one skill on the learning / performance of another skill.
- ❐ If you perform one skill and then perform another the second may well be affected by the first.
- ❐ For example, you perform a push pass in hockey and then you perform a flick, the actions of the first skill may help that of the second (positive transfer).

12) b)
How can transfer be detrimental to performance? Give a practical example.
- ❐ The performance of one skill may well hinder the performance of another.
- ❐ Because there may well be inappropriate movements / information processing which could confuse the performer.
- ❐ For example, a badminton player may play tennis immediately after playing badminton and the forehand in tennis may be far too 'wristy' because of the confusion in the response.

12) c)
How can a teacher or a coach ensure that as much positive transfer takes place as possible in a training session?
    5 marks for five from :
- ❐ The coach uses as many different practices as possible in training.
- ❐ To ensure the building of schema.
- ❐ Make sure training is relevant to the 'real' game.
- ❐ Tell performers about transfer to heighten awareness.
- ❐ Avoid confusing practises to avoid negative transfer.
- ❐ Ensure that skills are thoroughly learned before moving on to other skills.
- ❐ Give distributed practice sessions / rest intervals for mental assimilation.

TRANSFER - ANSWERS (continued)

13) a)

Define the terms positive transfer and negative transfer in the context of someone learning a sport skill.

❏ Positive transfer refers to the enhancement of performance of a skill being learned as a result of the previous learning of one or more other skills. Context example : learning an overhead volleyball serve having already learnt a tennis serve.

❏ Negative transfer refers to the impairment of performance of a skill due to the previous learning of another skill or skills. Context example : the attempted learning of a volley in badminton (loose wrist), having learned a tennis volley (firm wrist).

13) b)

For each situation give examples of a pair of skills which illustrate the kinds of transfer shown.

   10 marks for ten from :

   Situation **X** :

❏ Positive transfer is likely where two skills / movements have highly similar forms.

❏ And are dependent on similar psychomotor abilities.

❏ The similarities are such that the two skills are complementary.

   Games examples (one example from) :

❏ Shooting at goal at soccer, and taking a place kick at rugby.

❏ Tennis serve, volleyball serve.

❏ Receiving serve at squash, facing a fast bowler at cricket.

   Situation **Y** :

❏ Negative transfer is likely where the two skills / movements have similar but not identical movement patterns.

❏ Both skills are dependent upon similar psychomotor abilities.

❏ But are used in a slightly different way.

❏ Such that one interferes with the other.

   Games examples (one example from) :

❏ Volleying in tennis, volleying at badminton (the wrist problem).

❏ Playing at hockey and shinty (different rules for use of stick).

❏ Throwing the javelin, and round arm throwing (cricket).

   Situation **Z** :

❏ Zero transfer is likely where the two skills have different forms or movement patterns.

❏ Both skills would be dependent upon different psychomotor abilities.

❏ Hence the two skills do not interact at all.

   Games examples (one example from) :

❏ Swimming race start, and running sprint start.

❏ Golf drive, and basketball dribbling.

❏ Passing a rugby ball, and high jump.

MOTIVATION

14) a)

What is meant by intrinsic and extrinsic motivation? Give practical examples to illustrate your answer.

❏ Intrinsic : motivation from within / personal drives towards achieving a goal.

❏ For example, a surfer goes surfing because he derives enjoyment from the sport.

❏ Extrinsic : motivation through external reward / external drive from others.

❏ For example, a swimmer goes swimming just to gain a distance swimming badge.

14) b)

How can extrinsic motives affect intrinsic motivation?

   2 marks for two from :

❏ End up just doing the activity for the reward.

❏ Lose the enjoyment / play element of the activity.

❏ If the rewards stop, then participation is likely to stop.

| MOTIVATION - ANSWERS Question 14 (continued)

14) c)
What sort of motivation methods would you use to motivate a beginner in gymnastics?
    4 marks for four from :
- ❑ Give achievable goals / give success.
- ❑ Reinforce through praise or success.
- ❑ Only praise when it is deserved.
- ❑ Verbal encouragement.
- ❑ Vicarious processes / give models of similar ability.
- ❑ Introduce a small element of competition.
- ❑ But keep competition to a minimum.
- ❑ Emphasise personal progress.
- ❑ Raise status of the activity.

14) d)
How would the motivation methods used for a skilled performer differ from that used for a beginner?
    3 marks for three from :
- ❑ Give more demanding goals / just beyond reach.
- ❑ Larger extrinsic rewards.
- ❑ Reinforce success.
- ❑ Attribute to internal factors.
- ❑ Emphasise results / comparisons play bigger part.
- ❑ Use of audience / presence of others.
- ❑ Reinforce tactical aspects.

14) e)
Many elite athletes identify an emotional response called the peak flow experience that is associated with success. Describe what is meant by peak flow experience and give reasons why it might occur.
- ❑ Emotional response of pleasure / fulfilment / euphoria.
- ❑ The 'in zone' with full concentration.
- ❑ Confidence is high / relaxed / optimistic.
- ❑ Occurs because of firmly established motor programmes / considerable amount of training.
- ❑ Good powers of selective attention.
- ❑ If the athlete enjoys the activity, PFE is more likely to occur.
- ❑ Determination and self belief can lead to PFE.

PRESENTATION OF SKILLS

15) a)
What must be taken into account before any decision can be made about how to teach a skill?
    6 marks for six from :
- ❑ The perceptual / decision making requirements of the skill.
- ❑ What margin of error there is.
- ❑ The complexity of the skill.
- ❑ The transferability of the skill.
- ❑ How organised the skill is.
- ❑ Knowledge of the ability of the performer.
- ❑ Preferences of the performer.
- ❑ Strengths of the coach / teacher.
- ❑ Environmental factors.
- ❑ The number of performers to be taught.
- ❑ The age / gender / physique / any disability of the performer.

15) b)
Generally a skill should be taught as a whole as far as possible, give reasons for this.
    3 marks for three from :
- ❑ The performer can appreciate skill in its entirety.
- ❑ Has overall kinaesthetic sense of the skill.
- ❑ The flow of the skill is not interfered with.
- ❑ Much more efficient in skill learning / quicker to learn.
- ❑ Can help understanding / cognitive development of the performer.

PRESENTATION OF SKILLS - ANSWER QUESTION 15 (continued)

15) c)
What are the advantages and disadvantages of presenting skills split up into subroutines?
Advantages (3 marks for three from) :
❑ Useful if skill is dangerous / to lower fear level.
❑ Good for complex / difficult skills.
❑ Good for serial skills.
❑ Gives success at each stage / less likely to fail overall skill.
❑ Helps confidence and motivation.
Disadvantages (3 marks for three from) :
❑ Transfer of movements from the part skill to the whole may not work.
❑ Some skills cannot be split up into subroutines very easily.
❑ Loses the overall kinaesthetic sense.
❑ Loses the flow of the skill.
❑ Takes up too much time.

PRACTICE CONDITIONS

16) a)
Define massed and distributed practice.
❑ Massed - no rest intervals / practice conditions of long duration.
❑ Distributed - rest intervals at regular periods of time during a session.
16) b)
Justify the choice of practice conditions for a training session of a sport of your choice.
8 marks from eight relevant answers depending on choice of sport :
Massed :
❑ To ensure motor programmes are learned / for overlearning.
❑ To encourage an habitual response.
❑ To cut down on response / reaction time.
❑ Good for learning discrete skills.
❑ Good for skills performed over a short duration, for example, basketball shots.
❑ But can lead to fatigue / boredom / demotivation.
Distributed :
❑ To give physical rest / recuperation.
❑ To give mental rest / gather thoughts.
❑ To relieve stress.
❑ Provides safety for dangerous activities.

TEACHING STYLES

17) a)
Identify style A, and explain its consequences for teaching method.
1 mark for :
❑ Command / Autocratic / authoritarian style.
1 mark for one from :
❑ Teacher makes most of the decisions.
❑ Learner takes little or no responsibility for the progress of the learning process.
17) b)
What are the advantages and disadvantages of this method in teaching physical education?
6 marks for six from :
Advantages :
❑ More control / discipline.
❑ Good if time is short / efficient.
❑ Good for dangerous situations.
❑ Effective for large groups / teams.
Disadvantages :
❑ No individual feedback.
❑ No participation in decision making.
❑ No social interaction.
❑ Creativity of performer not taken into account.

TEACHING STYLES - ANSWERS QUESTION 17 (continued)

17) c)
What is meant by the reciprocal teaching style and what are its drawbacks?
    1 mark for :
❐ Reciprocal style = teacher develops pupils as teachers.
    2 marks for two from :
    Drawbacks :
❐ Lack of control.
❐ May be false information passed on.
❐ Lack of credibility of teacher-pupils.
❐ If communication skills poor, then teaching ineffective.

17) d)
What are the main advantages of the discovery method of teaching?
    4 marks for four from :
❐ Facilitates creativity.
❐ Sense of ownership over your own learning.
❐ Great deal of satisfaction if success is experienced.
❐ Work can be undertaken at the learner's own pace.
❐ Many experiences can build a large store of schema.
❐ Learning is more long-lasting / more meaningful.

GUIDANCE METHODS

18) a)
Other than visual guidance, what other main methods of guidance are there? Give a practical example for each.
❐ Verbal.
❐ For example, instructions to an athlete before a race.
❐ Manual.
❐ For example, supporting a gymnast doing a handspring.
❐ Mechanical.
❐ For example, a child using stabilisers on a bicycle.

18) b)
How would you optimise the use of visual guidance in teaching motor skills? What are the drawbacks of this method?
    2 marks for two from :
❐ The coach or teacher would use an accurate demonstration.
❐ Cueing the performer to important elements.
❐ Use immediately before performance.
❐ If visual guidance is used as feedback, it must be used immediately after the performance.
❐ Make sure it is supplemented with verbal guidance.
❐ If models / videos are used, ensure relevance to the learner.
❐ Make sure the model presented is attainable.
    2 marks for two from :
    Drawbacks :
❐ Confusion if too much visual guidance is shown at a time.
❐ Model / demonstration may be inaccurate.
❐ If videos are used, these may be boring / demotivating.
❐ Model seen may be perceived as unattainable.

John Honeybourne

SELECTED BIBLIOGRAPHY

Biddle, S.J.   1996   Psychology of PE and Sport - a Teachers' Guide.   FIT Systems.

Beashel, P.   1996   Physical Education at Advanced Level.   Thomas Nelson.

Boulton & Hawker   1996   The Learning of Skills.   Video Education Australasia.

Christina, R.W.   1988   Coaches Guide to Teaching Sport Skills.   Human Kinetics.

Cox, R.H.   1999   Sports Psychology 4e.   WCB / McGraw Hill.

Davis, R.J. et. al.   2000   Physical Education and the Study of Sport 4e.   Mosby Wolfe.

Davis, Kimmet, Auty   1986   Physical Education, Theory and Practice.   MacMillan.

Galligan, F. et al   2000   Advanced PE for Edexcel.   Heinemann.

Gill, D.   2000   Psychological Dynamics of Sport 2e.   Human Kinetics.

Gross, R.D.   1992   Psychology : The Science of Mind and Behaviour.   Hodder and Stoughton.

Honeybourne, J. et.al.   2000   Advanced Physical Education and Sport 2e.   Nelson Thornes.
                         2000   Advanced Physical Education and Sport 2e - Teacher Resource Pack
                                                                  .   Nelson Thornes.
                         2000   Advanced Physical Education & Sport for AS level.   Nelson Thornes.

Honeybourne, J. et.al.   1998   PE for you   Stanley Thornes.

Mace, R et al   2001   CD ROM Switch on to Skill in Sport.   Sport in Mind.

Magill, R.A.   2000   Motor Learning, Concepts and Applications 6e.   McGraw-Hill.

Roberts, G.C.   1999   Learning Experiences in Sports Psychology 2e.   Human Kinetics.

Roscoe, D.   2000   Teacher's Guide to Physical Education and the Study of Sport 4e
                                                  Skill Acquisition.   Jan Roscoe Publications.

Schmidt, R.A.   2000   Motor Learning and Performance 2e.   Human Kinetics.

Sharp, B.   1992   Acquiring Skill in Sport.   Sports Dynamics.

Webster, S.J.   1996   Sport Psychology - An A Level Guide for Teachers and Students.
                                                                  Jan Roscoe Publications.

Wesson, K. et. al.   2000   Sport and PE, A Complete Guide to A Level Study 2e.   Hodder and Stoughton.

PSYCHOLOGY of SPORT

PERSONALITY

PERSONALITY
- The unique characteristics of an individual.
- No particular personality is suited for a particular sport.
- Knowledge about personality is important to ensure optimum performance.
- Example : a coach or teacher who knows what an individual is like in different situations, will know how to deal with that individual and to get the best out of him / her.

STABLE
- Behaviour is predictable.
- Example : a golfer who has an even temperament in most situations.

NEUROTIC
- Behaviour is unpredictable, often involving mood swings.
- Example : a soccer player who tends to fly off the handle if things are not going his way.

TRAIT APPROACH
- Innate characteristics.
- Enduring characteristics that individuals take to all situations.
- Example : the work of Eysenck.

SOCIAL LEARNING
- Behaviour is learned from others that are significant.
- Example : the work of Bandura.
- A soccer player might learn on the field behaviour (diving to obtain a penalty, or strutting and exhibitionism after scoring) from observing top players.

INTERACTIONIST
- A mixture of trait and social learning.
- B = f (p,e).
- (Behaviour is a result of the interaction of personality traits and the environment).
- Example : a soccer player may be an introvert after the game but reveals extrovert qualities during the game.

TYPE A
- Higher levels of stress, this person lacks tolerance and patience.
- Example : a gymnast who seems very anxious in most situations and does not suffer fools gladly.

TYPE B
- More relaxed, this person has low personal stress.
- Example : a volleyballer who tends to be calm in most situations and seems unflappable.

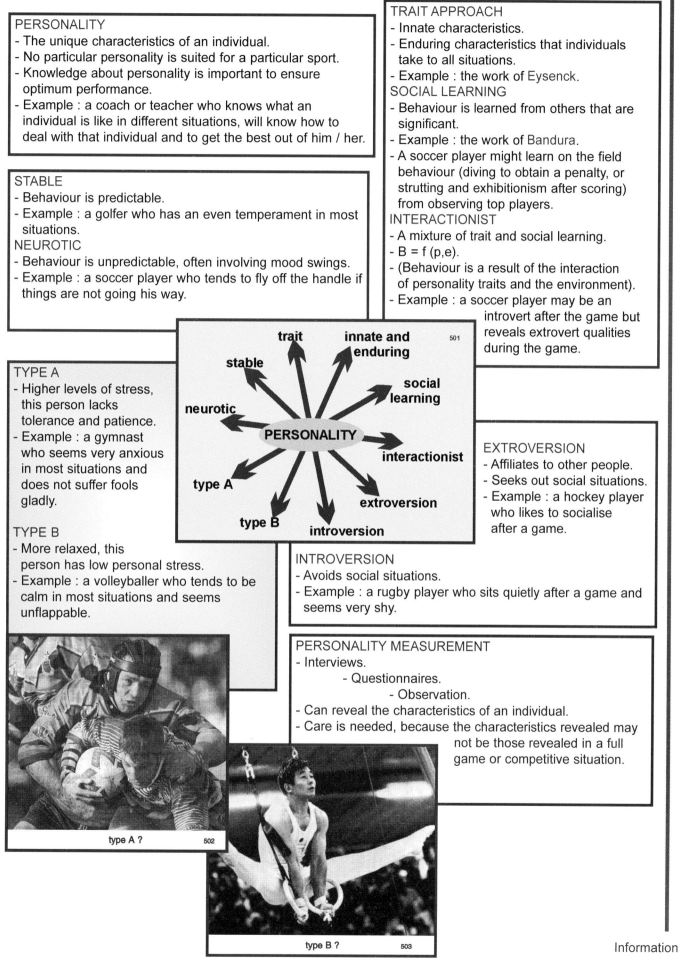

EXTROVERSION
- Affiliates to other people.
- Seeks out social situations.
- Example : a hockey player who likes to socialise after a game.

INTROVERSION
- Avoids social situations.
- Example : a rugby player who sits quietly after a game and seems very shy.

PERSONALITY MEASUREMENT
- Interviews.
  - Questionnaires.
    - Observation.
- Can reveal the characteristics of an individual.
- Care is needed, because the characteristics revealed may not be those revealed in a full game or competitive situation.

type A ?   502

type B ?   503

Information

PERSONALITY (continued)

HOLLANDER'S PERSONALITY STRUCTURE
- PSYCHOLOGICAL CORE
- Beliefs and values that remain fairly permanent.
- Example : the value of fair play in sport.
- TYPICAL RESPONSES
- The way in which we usually respond in certain situations.
- Example : stopping when we hear the referee's whistle.
- ROLE RELATED BEHAVIOUR
- In certain situations we may behave quite differently.
- Example : we may argue with the referee.
- SOCIAL ENVIRONMENT
- The behaviour and expectations of others affect our role
  related behaviour.
- Example : we argue because we have seen others get away with it.

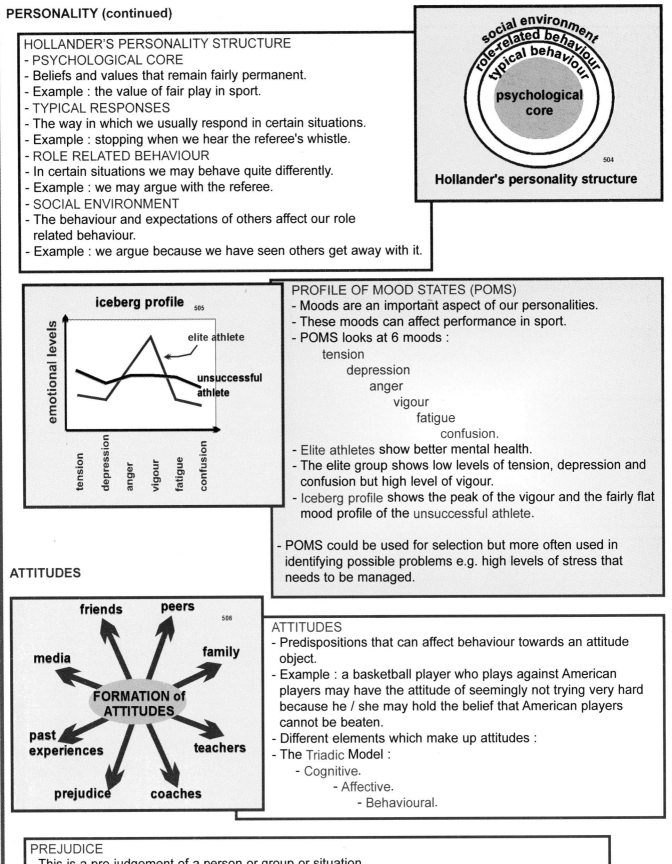

Hollander's personality structure

iceberg profile 505

PROFILE OF MOOD STATES (POMS)
- Moods are an important aspect of our personalities.
- These moods can affect performance in sport.
- POMS looks at 6 moods :
        tension
            depression
                anger
                    vigour
                        fatigue
                            confusion.
- Elite athletes show better mental health.
- The elite group shows low levels of tension, depression and
  confusion but high level of vigour.
- Iceberg profile shows the peak of the vigour and the fairly flat
  mood profile of the unsuccessful athlete.

- POMS could be used for selection but more often used in
  identifying possible problems e.g. high levels of stress that
  needs to be managed.

ATTITUDES

FORMATION of ATTITUDES 506

ATTITUDES
- Predispositions that can affect behaviour towards an attitude
  object.
- Example : a basketball player who plays against American
  players may have the attitude of seemingly not trying very hard
  because he / she may hold the belief that American players
  cannot be beaten.
- Different elements which make up attitudes :
- The Triadic Model :
    - Cognitive.
        - Affective.
            - Behavioural.

PREJUDICE
- This is a pre-judgement of a person or group or situation.
- Judgement based on small amount of experience and inadequate information.
- Some judgements based on information that is incorrect but is passed on to reinforce stereotypes
  and therefore prejudice.
- Example : gender prejudice in sport when a woman tries to join a golf club and finds difficulty in
  gaining full membership, whereas a man of similar ability is accepted.

ATTITUDE (continued)

COGNITIVE
- The belief aspect.
- Example : you have a positive attitude to sport because you believe that it is good for you.

AFFECTIVE
- The emotional aspect.
- Example : you have a positive attitude to sport because you enjoy sport.

BEHAVIOURAL
- The way in which we act towards an attitude object.
- Example : you have a positive attitude to sport because you regularly participate.

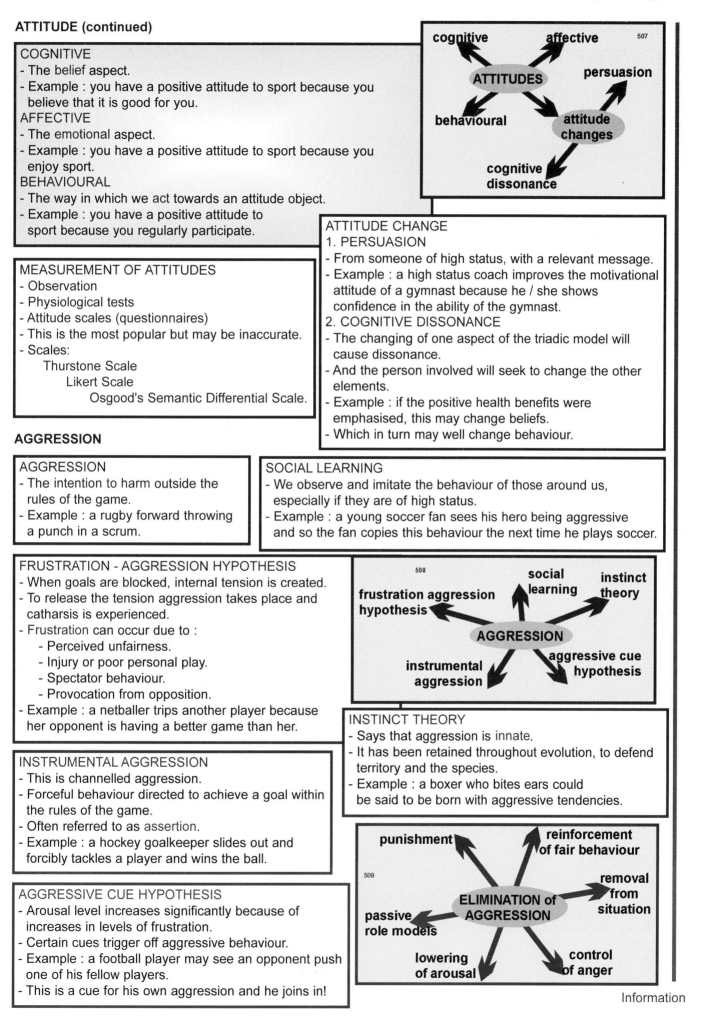

MEASUREMENT OF ATTITUDES
- Observation
- Physiological tests
- Attitude scales (questionnaires)
- This is the most popular but may be inaccurate.
- Scales:
  - Thurstone Scale
  - Likert Scale
  - Osgood's Semantic Differential Scale.

ATTITUDE CHANGE
1. PERSUASION
- From someone of high status, with a relevant message.
- Example : a high status coach improves the motivational attitude of a gymnast because he / she shows confidence in the ability of the gymnast.
2. COGNITIVE DISSONANCE
- The changing of one aspect of the triadic model will cause dissonance.
- And the person involved will seek to change the other elements.
- Example : if the positive health benefits were emphasised, this may change beliefs.
- Which in turn may well change behaviour.

AGGRESSION

AGGRESSION
- The intention to harm outside the rules of the game.
- Example : a rugby forward throwing a punch in a scrum.

SOCIAL LEARNING
- We observe and imitate the behaviour of those around us, especially if they are of high status.
- Example : a young soccer fan sees his hero being aggressive and so the fan copies this behaviour the next time he plays soccer.

FRUSTRATION - AGGRESSION HYPOTHESIS
- When goals are blocked, internal tension is created.
- To release the tension aggression takes place and catharsis is experienced.
- Frustration can occur due to :
  - Perceived unfairness.
  - Injury or poor personal play.
  - Spectator behaviour.
  - Provocation from opposition.
- Example : a netballer trips another player because her opponent is having a better game than her.

INSTRUMENTAL AGGRESSION
- This is channelled aggression.
- Forceful behaviour directed to achieve a goal within the rules of the game.
- Often referred to as assertion.
- Example : a hockey goalkeeper slides out and forcibly tackles a player and wins the ball.

INSTINCT THEORY
- Says that aggression is innate.
- It has been retained throughout evolution, to defend territory and the species.
- Example : a boxer who bites ears could be said to be born with aggressive tendencies.

AGGRESSIVE CUE HYPOTHESIS
- Arousal level increases significantly because of increases in levels of frustration.
- Certain cues trigger off aggressive behaviour.
- Example : a football player may see an opponent push one of his fellow players.
- This is a cue for his own aggression and he joins in!

Information

ACHIEVEMENT MOTIVATION

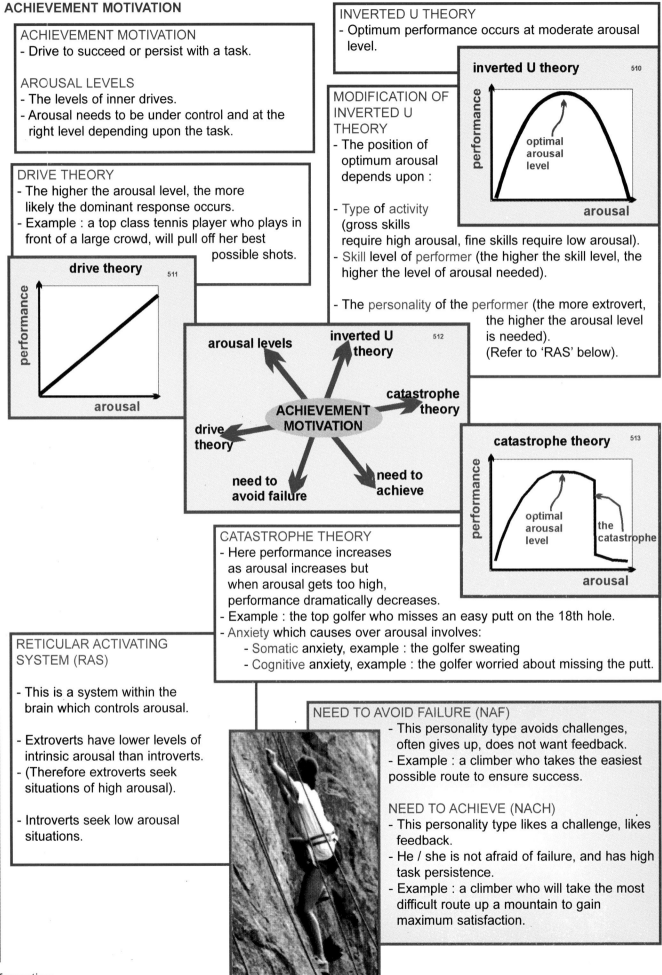

ACHIEVEMENT MOTIVATION
- Drive to succeed or persist with a task.

AROUSAL LEVELS
- The levels of inner drives.
- Arousal needs to be under control and at the right level depending upon the task.

DRIVE THEORY
- The higher the arousal level, the more likely the dominant response occurs.
- Example : a top class tennis player who plays in front of a large crowd, will pull off her best possible shots.

drive theory 511

INVERTED U THEORY
- Optimum performance occurs at moderate arousal level.

inverted U theory 510

MODIFICATION OF INVERTED U THEORY
- The position of optimum arousal depends upon :

- Type of activity (gross skills require high arousal, fine skills require low arousal).
- Skill level of performer (the higher the skill level, the higher the level of arousal needed).

- The personality of the performer (the more extrovert, the higher the arousal level is needed).
  (Refer to 'RAS' below).

arousal levels   **inverted U theory** 512
ACHIEVEMENT MOTIVATION
drive theory   **catastrophe theory**
need to avoid failure   **need to achieve**

catastrophe theory 513

CATASTROPHE THEORY
- Here performance increases as arousal increases but when arousal gets too high, performance dramatically decreases.
- Example : the top golfer who misses an easy putt on the 18th hole.
- Anxiety which causes over arousal involves:
  - Somatic anxiety, example : the golfer sweating
  - Cognitive anxiety, example : the golfer worried about missing the putt.

RETICULAR ACTIVATING SYSTEM (RAS)

- This is a system within the brain which controls arousal.

- Extroverts have lower levels of intrinsic arousal than introverts.
- (Therefore extroverts seek situations of high arousal).

- Introverts seek low arousal situations.

NEED TO AVOID FAILURE (NAF)
- This personality type avoids challenges, often gives up, does not want feedback.
- Example : a climber who takes the easiest possible route to ensure success.

NEED TO ACHIEVE (NACH)
- This personality type likes a challenge, likes feedback.
- He / she is not afraid of failure, and has high task persistence.
- Example : a climber who will take the most difficult route up a mountain to gain maximum satisfaction.

ATTRIBUTION

ATTRIBUTION
- Giving reasons for our behaviour.
- This can affect levels of motivation.
- Example : a reason could be : 'I performed badly in my trampoline routine because I had a bad ankle'.

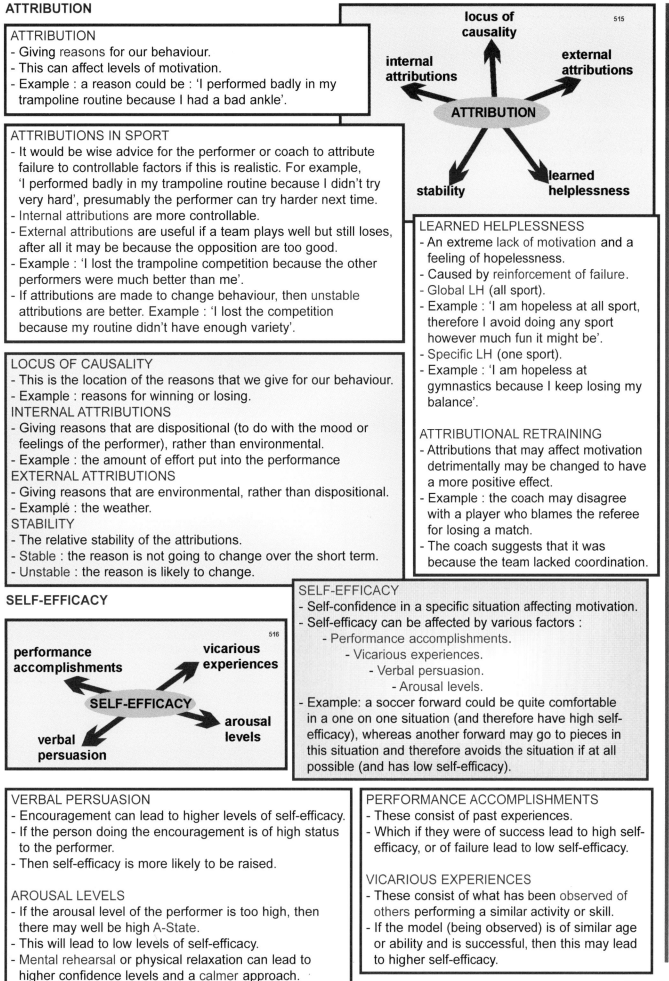

ATTRIBUTIONS IN SPORT
- It would be wise advice for the performer or coach to attribute failure to controllable factors if this is realistic. For example, 'I performed badly in my trampoline routine because I didn't try very hard', presumably the performer can try harder next time.
- Internal attributions are more controllable.
- External attributions are useful if a team plays well but still loses, after all it may be because the opposition are too good.
- Example : 'I lost the trampoline competition because the other performers were much better than me'.
- If attributions are made to change behaviour, then unstable attributions are better. Example : 'I lost the competition because my routine didn't have enough variety'.

LOCUS OF CAUSALITY
- This is the location of the reasons that we give for our behaviour.
- Example : reasons for winning or losing.

INTERNAL ATTRIBUTIONS
- Giving reasons that are dispositional (to do with the mood or feelings of the performer), rather than environmental.
- Example : the amount of effort put into the performance

EXTERNAL ATTRIBUTIONS
- Giving reasons that are environmental, rather than dispositional.
- Example : the weather.

STABILITY
- The relative stability of the attributions.
- Stable : the reason is not going to change over the short term.
- Unstable : the reason is likely to change.

LEARNED HELPLESSNESS
- An extreme lack of motivation and a feeling of hopelessness.
- Caused by reinforcement of failure.
- Global LH (all sport).
- Example : 'I am hopeless at all sport, therefore I avoid doing any sport however much fun it might be'.
- Specific LH (one sport).
- Example : 'I am hopeless at gymnastics because I keep losing my balance'.

ATTRIBUTIONAL RETRAINING
- Attributions that may affect motivation detrimentally may be changed to have a more positive effect.
- Example : the coach may disagree with a player who blames the referee for losing a match.
- The coach suggests that it was because the team lacked coordination.

SELF-EFFICACY

SELF-EFFICACY
- Self-confidence in a specific situation affecting motivation.
- Self-efficacy can be affected by various factors :
  - Performance accomplishments.
  - Vicarious experiences.
  - Verbal persuasion.
  - Arousal levels.
- Example: a soccer forward could be quite comfortable in a one on one situation (and therefore have high self-efficacy), whereas another forward may go to pieces in this situation and therefore avoids the situation if at all possible (and has low self-efficacy).

VERBAL PERSUASION
- Encouragement can lead to higher levels of self-efficacy.
- If the person doing the encouragement is of high status to the performer.
- Then self-efficacy is more likely to be raised.

AROUSAL LEVELS
- If the arousal level of the performer is too high, then there may well be high A-State.
- This will lead to low levels of self-efficacy.
- Mental rehearsal or physical relaxation can lead to higher confidence levels and a calmer approach.

PERFORMANCE ACCOMPLISHMENTS
- These consist of past experiences.
- Which if they were of success lead to high self-efficacy, or of failure lead to low self-efficacy.

VICARIOUS EXPERIENCES
- These consist of what has been observed of others performing a similar activity or skill.
- If the model (being observed) is of similar age or ability and is successful, then this may lead to higher self-efficacy.

SOCIAL LEARNING

SOCIAL LEARNING
- Is important in the process of socialisation (adopting the norms and values of your culture).
- Example : a child will watch his / her mother's behaviour and copy it.
- Learning how to behave appropriately.
- Example : a player responding in a controlled way to an unfavourable refereeing decision.

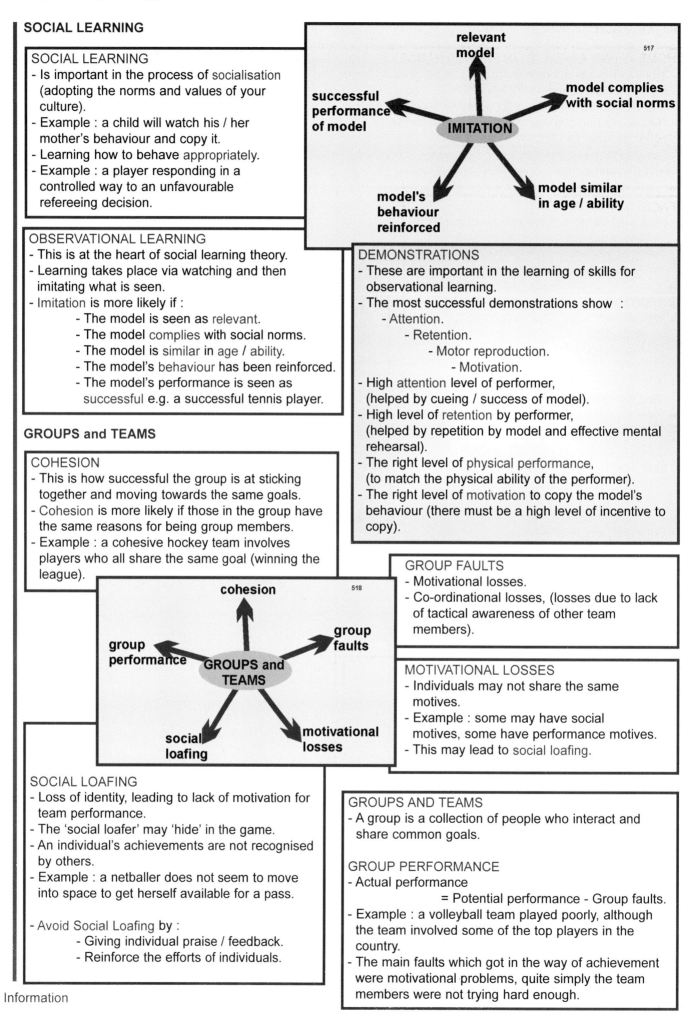

OBSERVATIONAL LEARNING
- This is at the heart of social learning theory.
- Learning takes place via watching and then imitating what is seen.
- Imitation is more likely if :
    - The model is seen as relevant.
    - The model complies with social norms.
    - The model is similar in age / ability.
    - The model's behaviour has been reinforced.
    - The model's performance is seen as successful e.g. a successful tennis player.

DEMONSTRATIONS
- These are important in the learning of skills for observational learning.
- The most successful demonstrations show :
    - Attention.
        - Retention.
            - Motor reproduction.
                - Motivation.
- High attention level of performer, (helped by cueing / success of model).
- High level of retention by performer, (helped by repetition by model and effective mental rehearsal).
- The right level of physical performance, (to match the physical ability of the performer).
- The right level of motivation to copy the model's behaviour (there must be a high level of incentive to copy).

GROUPS and TEAMS

COHESION
- This is how successful the group is at sticking together and moving towards the same goals.
- Cohesion is more likely if those in the group have the same reasons for being group members.
- Example : a cohesive hockey team involves players who all share the same goal (winning the league).

GROUP FAULTS
- Motivational losses.
- Co-ordinational losses, (losses due to lack of tactical awareness of other team members).

MOTIVATIONAL LOSSES
- Individuals may not share the same motives.
- Example : some may have social motives, some have performance motives.
- This may lead to social loafing.

SOCIAL LOAFING
- Loss of identity, leading to lack of motivation for team performance.
- The 'social loafer' may 'hide' in the game.
- An individual's achievements are not recognised by others.
- Example : a netballer does not seem to move into space to get herself available for a pass.

- Avoid Social Loafing by :
    - Giving individual praise / feedback.
    - Reinforce the efforts of individuals.

GROUPS AND TEAMS
- A group is a collection of people who interact and share common goals.

GROUP PERFORMANCE
- Actual performance
                = Potential performance - Group faults.
- Example : a volleyball team played poorly, although the team involved some of the top players in the country.
- The main faults which got in the way of achievement were motivational problems, quite simply the team members were not trying hard enough.

Information

SOCIAL FACILITATION

HOME / AWAY EFFECTS ON PERFORMANCE
- More teams win at home than away, although there are incidences of the reverse effect.
- The crowd / audience may be judged as supportive or hostile.
- High levels of anxiety caused by hostility may hinder performance.
- The environment is familiar to home teams and therefore this limits anxiety caused by an alien environment.

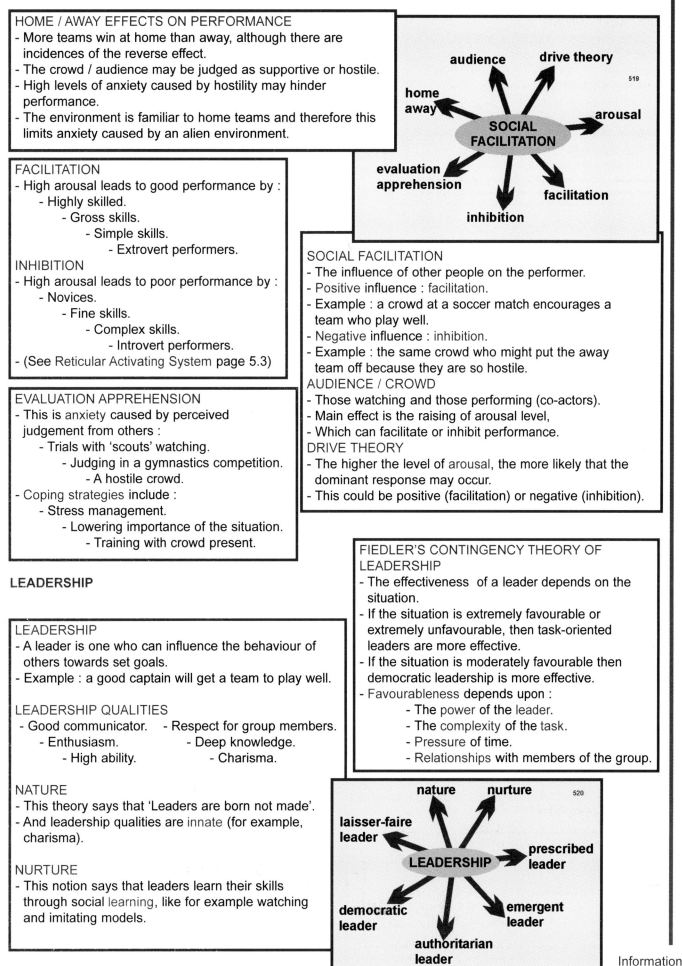

FACILITATION
- High arousal leads to good performance by :
    - Highly skilled.
        - Gross skills.
            - Simple skills.
                - Extrovert performers.

INHIBITION
- High arousal leads to poor performance by :
    - Novices.
        - Fine skills.
            - Complex skills.
                - Introvert performers.
- (See Reticular Activating System page 5.3)

EVALUATION APPREHENSION
- This is anxiety caused by perceived judgement from others :
    - Trials with 'scouts' watching.
        - Judging in a gymnastics competition.
            - A hostile crowd.
- Coping strategies include :
    - Stress management.
        - Lowering importance of the situation.
            - Training with crowd present.

SOCIAL FACILITATION
- The influence of other people on the performer.
- Positive influence : facilitation.
- Example : a crowd at a soccer match encourages a team who play well.
- Negative influence : inhibition.
- Example : the same crowd who might put the away team off because they are so hostile.

AUDIENCE / CROWD
- Those watching and those performing (co-actors).
- Main effect is the raising of arousal level,
- Which can facilitate or inhibit performance.

DRIVE THEORY
- The higher the level of arousal, the more likely that the dominant response may occur.
- This could be positive (facilitation) or negative (inhibition).

LEADERSHIP

LEADERSHIP
- A leader is one who can influence the behaviour of others towards set goals.
- Example : a good captain will get a team to play well.

LEADERSHIP QUALITIES
- Good communicator.   - Respect for group members.
    - Enthusiasm.   - Deep knowledge.
        - High ability.   - Charisma.

NATURE
- This theory says that 'Leaders are born not made'.
- And leadership qualities are innate (for example, charisma).

NURTURE
- This notion says that leaders learn their skills through social learning, like for example watching and imitating models.

FIEDLER'S CONTINGENCY THEORY OF LEADERSHIP
- The effectiveness of a leader depends on the situation.
- If the situation is extremely favourable or extremely unfavourable, then task-oriented leaders are more effective.
- If the situation is moderately favourable then democratic leadership is more effective.
- Favourableness depends upon :
    - The power of the leader.
    - The complexity of the task.
    - Pressure of time.
    - Relationships with members of the group.

LEADERSHIP (continued)

EMERGENT LEADERS
- Those that are chosen by the group from within the group.
- Example : a swimming team may vote for its captain.

PRESCRIBED LEADERS
- Those who are appointed by an external body to a group.
- Example : the team is told who their captain is by the management committee.

STYLES
- Depend on :
    - Situation.
        - Leader's personality.
            - Group members' personalities.

LEADERSHIP STYLES

AUTHORITARIAN
- This style is task-oriented, and is best for team motivation, large groups, hostile groups, dangerous situations and when time is short.
- Example : the coach who shouts instructions during a game.

DEMOCRATIC
- This style is person-oriented, and is best for individual performers, those who are highly skilled, and when problems need to be solved.
- Example : a team coach who asks the opinions of his team members so that collective decisions can be made.

LAISSEZ-FAIRE
- This is when no real leader position exists, and is best for highly motivated and skilled performers.
- Example : a coach who does not hold any type of meeting, and lets players play as they wish.

STRESS

STRESS
- Levels of stress depend upon our perception of demands and our abilities to cope with the demands.

POSITIVE ASPECTS
- Will drive us to achieve more.
- Human nature to challenge the body / mind.
- Can help to avoid dangerous situations.
- Example : the athlete who runs faster if he is frightened of the consequences of losing.

STRESS RESPONSE
- General Adaptation Syndrome (GAS) :
    - Alarm reaction.
        - Resistance.
            - Exhaustion.

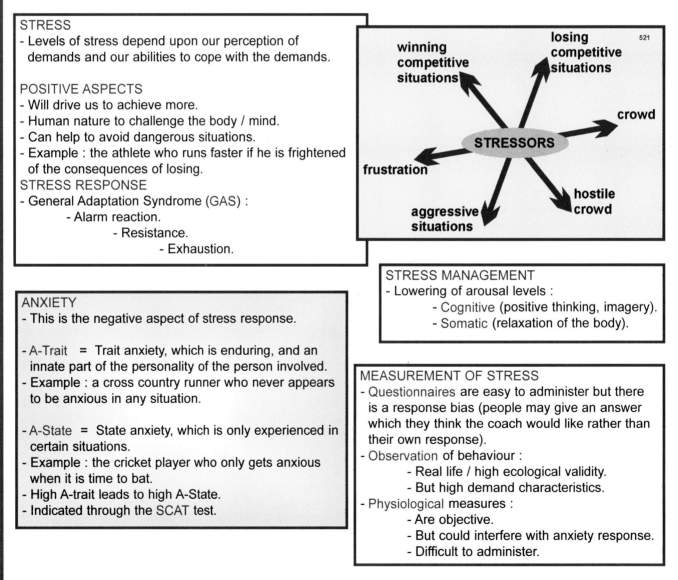

STRESS MANAGEMENT
- Lowering of arousal levels :
    - Cognitive (positive thinking, imagery).
    - Somatic (relaxation of the body).

ANXIETY
- This is the negative aspect of stress response.

- A-Trait = Trait anxiety, which is enduring, and an innate part of the personality of the person involved.
- Example : a cross country runner who never appears to be anxious in any situation.

- A-State = State anxiety, which is only experienced in certain situations.
- Example : the cricket player who only gets anxious when it is time to bat.
- High A-trait leads to high A-State.
- Indicated through the SCAT test.

MEASUREMENT OF STRESS
- Questionnaires are easy to administer but there is a response bias (people may give an answer which they think the coach would like rather than their own response).
- Observation of behaviour :
    - Real life / high ecological validity.
    - But high demand characteristics.
- Physiological measures :
    - Are objective.
    - But could interfere with anxiety response.
    - Difficult to administer.

GOAL SETTING

GOAL SETTING
- Can increase motivation and control stress / anxiety.
- Example : a golfer sets a target of shots to be played around a course, this may well motivate him to play well.

TYPES OF GOALS
- Outcome - this would be the end result of the activity.
- Example : a goal for a swimmer could be to win a race.
- Performance - judging against other performances.
- Example : a goal for a swimmer may be to beat his or her best time.
- Process - this would be related to techniques or the way in which the activity is undertaken.
- Example : the goal might be to improve the swimmer's leg kick action.

FACTORS AFFECTING GOAL SETTING
- Set goals that are achievable but challenging.
- Goals must be clear and specific and relevant.
- They need to progress from short-term to long-term.
- They need to be measured as time goes on.
- They also need to be evaluated and modified if necessary.
- Goals that are shared between performer and the coach are more effective.

SHORT-TERM GOALS
- These are more process oriented and lead on to long-term aims.
- Example : a sprinter tries to improve her start technique.

LONG-TERM GOALS
- These are more product oriented and are to be achieved over a long period of time.
- They must be attainable to be motivating.
- Example : the sprinter aims to get into the British Olympic Team.

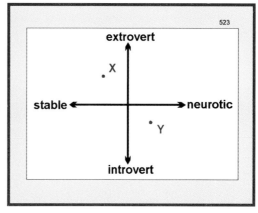

QUESTIONS

PERSONALITY

1) **a)** What do we mean by the term personality? Why is it important for sports psychologists to know about personality? (3 marks)
b) Eysenck identified two dimensions of personality as in diagram 523 on the right. Describe the trait approach to personality. What do the traits extroversion and stability mean? (4 marks)
c) From the diagram describe the characteristics of players **X** and **Y**. (4 marks)
d) By using an example from sport, outline the social learning approach to personality. (3 marks)
e) What do we mean by the interactionist approach? (2 marks)

2) **a)** Hollander (1971) viewed personality as a structure with layers of influence. Using examples from sport, explain Hollander's structure of personality. (8 marks)
b) What is the iceberg profile and how does it relate to the personalities of elite athletes? (4 marks)

ATTITUDES

3) **a)** What do we mean by the term attitude? (1 mark)
b) We often refer to someone as having a positive attitude in sport. Using the triadic model describe the characteristics of a positive attitude. (3 marks)
c) What factors influence our attitudes? (4 marks)
d) If you wished to change a young person's negative attitude to sport into a positive one, what strategies would you employ? Use psychological theory to back up your answer. (4 marks)
e) What do we mean by the term prejudice and how does it manifest itself in sport? (4 marks)
f) Observing behaviour is one method of measuring attitudes. What are the advantages and disadvantages of such a method? (4 marks)

AGGRESSION

4) a) What do we mean by the term aggression in sports psychology? Give an example from a sport or game which would illustrate your answer.   (2 marks)
b) How would you distinguish between aggression and assertion?   (2 marks)
c) Some team players display unwanted aggression. What are the possible causes of such aggression?
                                                                                              (4 marks)
d) Explain in more detail what is meant by social learning when applied to aggression.   (4 marks)
e) How can aggressive tendencies be eliminated in a sports situation?   (4 marks)
f) The aggressive cue hypothesis (Berkowitz 1969), is a theory which explains why aggression may be experienced by sports performers. Using an example from sport describe the aggressive cue hypothesis.   (4 marks)

ACHIEVEMENT MOTIVATION

5) a) Describe the characteristics of the positive motive : 'the need to achieve'.   (4 marks)
b)   **i)** Describe an example from sport of someone who has a high motive to avoid failure.
         ii) Identify factors which could affect the use of motives to achieve and to avoid failure in sporting
         situations.   (3 marks)
c) How would you promote the need to achieve motive, rather than the need to avoid failure?   (8 marks)

ATTRIBUTION

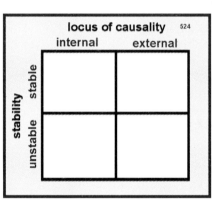

6) a) Diagram 524 on the right partly illustrates Weiner's model of attribution. Define the term attribution by using a sporting situation.   (1 mark)
b) Explain the terms locus of causality and stability when applied to attribution theory.   (4 marks)
c) Redraw the model and place on it relevant attributions for each of the four boxes.   (4 marks)
d) What attributions would you encourage if your team were playing well but often losing?   (5 marks)

7) a) Many young people claim to be hopeless at gymnastics. Suggest three reasons why these youngsters might have a negative attitude to gymnastics.   (3 marks)
b) What is meant by learned helplessness and how is it caused?   (3 marks)
c) How would you attempt to attract beginners to a gymnastics class, and then change any negative attitudes to the sport which they might have?   (3 marks)

SELF-EFFICACY

8) a) What is meant by the term self-efficacy when applied to sports psychology?   (1 mark)
b) What factors influence self-efficacy? Use practical examples from sport to illustrate your answer.   (8 marks)
c) As a coach of a sports team, how would you raise an individual's level of self-efficacy?   (4 marks)

SOCIAL LEARNING / OBSERVATIONAL LEARNING

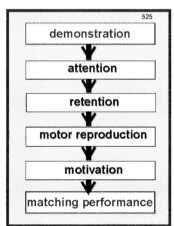

9) a) What is meant by the term socialisation and how can it be explained within t9e context of sport?   (3 marks)
b) By using Bandura's model of observational learning shown in diagram 525 on the right, explain the importance of an effective demonstration in the learning of motor skills.   (10 marks)
c) Videos are often used in the teaching and refining of motor skills as well as illustrating tactical strategies in sport. How would you use a video to encourage participation and to motivate performers in sport?   (6 marks)

GROUPS AND TEAMS

10) a) What is meant by cohesion in the context of teams? (4 marks)
b) What factors stop a team ever performing to their true potential? (6 marks)
c) Explain what is meant by social loafing by using examples from sport. (3 marks)
d) What advice would you give a coach of a team to ensure maximum productivity? (5 marks)

SOCIAL FACILITATION

11) a) What is meant by social facilitation and what is its main effect? (3 marks)
b) What effects can be experienced by an individual if there is an audience present? (6 marks)
c) What is meant by evaluation apprehension? (2 marks)
d) As a coach of an individual who is affected adversely by the presence of an audience, how would you help him or her to overcome the negative influences? (4 marks)

	group 1 no audience	group 2 with audience
average time held in seconds	46.5	50.5

12) Two groups of male sportspeople (of the same age) undertook an arms length weight hold endurance test. Success at this exercise was measured by the length of time the weight was held. The table on the left shows the average times for group 1 (who did the exercise alone) and group 2 (who did the exercise in the presence of an audience).

a) What effect (if any) did the audience have on the performance of the exercise? (1 mark)
b) How would you account for this effect (or lack of effect)? (4 marks)
c) The audience in this exercise (for group 2) was not known to the participants. Explain any effect you think there would be if the audience was known to the group. (6 marks)

LEADERSHIP

13) a) What is meant by a leader and what sort of qualities would you expect to see in a leader within the context of sport? (4 marks)
b) Using psychological theories describe how an individual becomes a leader. (4 marks)
c) Name three leadership styles. (3 marks)
d) What factors should be taken into consideration when deciding upon which leadership style to adopt? (6 marks)

14) a) Look at diagram 526 on the right of a multidimensional model of leadership. Explain each part of the model using examples from sport. (8 marks)
b) Discuss the statement 'Good leaders are born not made', and explain whether you agree or disagree in the light of psychological theory. (5 marks)

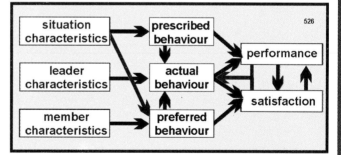

STRESS AND STRESS MANAGEMENT

15) a) What is meant by the term stress? (2 marks)
b) Explain two psychological symptoms of stress. (2 marks)
c) Identify three main stressors in the context of sport. (3 marks)
d) What is the difference between state and trait anxiety? (2 marks)
e) What coping strategies should the anxious performer draw upon? (5 marks)

16) a) Describe three techniques used to measure stress. (3 marks)
b) Give one advantage and one disadvantage of each technique. (6 marks)
c) Discuss the possible relationships between anxiety and performance in sporting activities. (7 marks)
d) High levels of arousal have often been linked with stress. Sketch a graph showing the relationship between the performance of a complex skill and level of arousal. (2 marks)
e) Add a second curve to your graph showing how the performance of a simple skill might be affected by arousal. (1 mark)

GOAL SETTING

17) a) What are the main positive effects of setting goals in sport?   (2 marks)
b) Show what is meant by short-term goals and long-term goals by using examples from sport.   (4 marks)
c) As a coach how would you ensure that your goal setting was as effective as possible?   (6 marks)

ANSWERS

The answer for each mark awarded is notated by the ❐ symbol - where there are more ❐ symbols than there are marks available, marks would be given for any choice up to the maximum available. Usually, the precise wording specified in an answer would not be required - answers with the same meaning would be acceptable.

PERSONALITY

1) a)
What do we mean by the term personality? Why is it important for sports psychologists to know about personality?
     3 marks for three from :
❐ Personality involves the unique characteristics of an individual.
❐ Personality involves consistent behaviour patterns.
❐ Individuals behave in different ways, so it is important to understand them.
❐ Better understanding can lead to better motivational / training strategies.
❐ Performers will relate better to those that understand them.

1) b)
Describe the trait approach to personality. What do the traits extroversion and stability mean?
❐ The trait approach sees the personality of the performer as genetic or innate.
❐ Traits are the enduring characteristics of an individual.
❐ Extroversion - the sportsperson seeks social situations or is sociable.
❐ Stable - The performer has a level personality, and is predictable or steady.

1) c)
Describe the characteristics of players X and Y (from the diagram).
     Player **X** - stable extrovert (2 marks for) :
❐ Extrovert - sociable / outgoing / talkative / easy-going.
❐ Stable - fairly even tempered / reliable / controlled.
     Player **Y** - neurotic introvert (2 marks for) :
❐ Introvert - passive / quiet / peaceful / thoughtful / shy.
❐ Neurotic - moody / anxious / pessimistic / unstable.

1) d)
By using an example from sport, outline the social learning approach to personality.
     3 marks for three from :
     Practical examples expressing :
❐ Observation of others who are around.
❐ Imitation of others.
❐ Social learning is more likely if those being observed are 'significant' or of high status.
❐ Personality is learned from others.

1) e)
What do we mean by the interactionist approach?
     2 marks for two from :
❐ A mix of trait and social learning.
❐ An individual adapts his or her personality according to the environment.
❐ Behaviour is determined by the interaction of a person with his / her environment.
❐ This approach explains why people seemingly have different personalities in different situations.

PERSONALITY - ANSWERS (continued)

2) a)

Hollander (1971) viewed personality as a structure with layers of influence. Using examples from sport, explain Hollander's structure of personality.

- ❑ Essentially a trait approach.
- ❑ Psychological core / inner layer not affected by the environment / basis beliefs.
- ❑ Example : a hockey player who believes in fair play / value of physical exercise.
- ❑ Typical response layer / middle layer which represents are typical responses.
- ❑ Example : a hockey player usually turns up for training.
- ❑ Role-related behaviour layer / outer layer which represents our responses that are affected by circumstances.
- ❑ Example : hockey player may not take part fully in training because of lack of motivation on that day.
- ❑ Social environment / surrounding layer representing social influences / expectations.
- ❑ Example : hockey player may not take part in training because there are pressures from friends to do other activities.

2) b)

What is the iceberg profile and how does it relate to the personalities of elite athletes?

- ❑ Profile from POMS research / questionnaire / profile of mood states, see chart 527 on the right.
- ❑ Shows high values related to vigour and assertion / anger in elite athletes.
- ❑ Shows low values in tension / depression / fatigue / confusion.
- ❑ Shows positive health of elite.
- ❑ As opposed to negative of unsuccessful athletes.

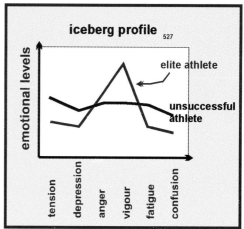

ATTITUDES

3) a)

What do we mean by the term attitude?

   1 mark for one from :

- ❑ A predisposition (an opinion held because of previous experiences) towards an attitude object.
- ❑ An attitude is made up of beliefs, feelings and behaviour.

3) b)

We often refer to someone as having a positive attitude in sport. Using the triadic model describe the characteristics of a positive attitude.

- ❑ Cognitive aspects   - The sportsperson has a belief in the activity as worthwhile.
- ❑ Affective aspects   - The sportsperson has positive emotions or enjoyment or enthusiasm.
- ❑ Behavioural aspects - The sportsperson participates or spectates regularly.

3) c)

What factors influence our attitudes?

   4 marks for four from :

- ❑ Past experiences.
- ❑ Education.
- ❑ Media.
- ❑ Other group members or peers.
- ❑ Cultural norms.
- ❑ Parental influences.
- ❑ Perceived need for health or exercise.

3) d)

If you wished to change a young person's negative attitude to sport into a positive one, what strategies would you employ? Use psychological theory to back up your answer.

   4 marks for four from :

- ❑ Use cognitive dissonance.
- ❑ Persuasion.
- ❑ Change one aspect of the triadic model to create dissonance.
- ❑ Attribute early failure to controllable factors (like the need to try harder or change an aspect of technique).
- ❑ Give success or positive reinforcement when the performer achieves partial success.
- ❑ Use of appropriate role models.
- ❑ Show the benefits to health.
- ❑ Emphasise positive body image.
- ❑ Promote awareness of self or emphasise personal satisfaction.

ATTITUDES - ANSWERS (continued)

3) e)
What do we mean by the term prejudice and how does it manifest itself in sport?
- ❐ Pre-judgement of individual / group.
- ❐ Based on narrow experience / usually unfair.
- ❐ Crowd behaviour against individual / team.
- ❐ Racism - with example in sport.
- ❐ Team members valuing their own group over others.
- ❐ Age / gender with examples.
- ❐ Disability - lack of access to sports venues etc.

3) f)
Observing behaviour is one method of measuring attitudes. What are the advantages and disadvantages of such a method?
Advantages:
- ❐ Observe subjects in natural environment.
- ❐ More natural behaviour / true to life.

Disadvantages:
- ❐ Subjects aware of observation therefore attitudes may be false / demand characteristics.
- ❐ Interpretation of observer is subjective / observational bias.

AGGRESSION

4) a)
What do we mean by the term aggression in sports psychology? Give an example from a sport or game which would illustrate your answer.
   1 mark for :
- ❐ This is the intention or expectation to harm someone else outside the rules of the competition.
   1 mark for one from :
- ❐ An example - foul tackling where the intention is to injure the opponent rather than to prevent a goal.
- ❐ Spectator aggression - displaced from the action on the field, aggression between rival supporters.

4) b)
How would you distinguish between aggression and assertion?
   2 marks for two from :
- ❐ Assertion is (goal directed) robust play within the rules of the game, whereas aggression deals with foul play outside the rules of the game.
- ❐ Assertion could be described as instrumental aggression / channelled aggression / balanced tension.
- ❐ A suitable games example would be for assertion : legitimate yet hard or robust tackling, and for aggression : punching or hitting an opponent (at rugby / hockey / soccer).

4) c)
Some team players display unwanted aggression. What are the possible causes of such aggression?
   4 marks for four from :
- ❐ Frustration or perceived unfairness.
- ❐ High level of competition / the importance of the event / expectations of victory.
- ❐ Losing a competition / sense of failure / loss of self-esteem.
- ❐ An innate feeling which cannot be helped or is instinctive.
- ❐ Physical contact in the game.
- ❐ Influences outside the game.

4) d)
Explain in more detail what is meant by social learning when applied to aggression.
   4 marks for four from :
- ❐ The observation and copying of others.
- ❐ If what is observed is reinforced, then it is more likely to be copied.
- ❐ It is more likely that the learner will copy others with high status.
- ❐ Media which highlights aggression makes it seem normal or the expected thing in the situation.
- ❐ May be adopted by the performer to be accepted in a group or to avoid rejection from the group.
- ❐ Live aggression is more likely to be copied than aggression recorded and played back later.
- ❐ Aggression is more likely to be copied if male watches male (or female watches female) - similar role models.
- ❐ If the situation is realistic when modelled, then it is more likely to be copied.

AGGRESSION - ANSWERS Question 4 (continued)

4) e)
How can aggressive tendencies be eliminated in a sports situation?
> 4 marks for four from :
- ❐ Positively reinforce non-aggressive behaviours.
- ❐ Give negative feedback to aggression.
- ❐ Punish.
- ❐ Remove the offending player from the aggressive situation.
- ❐ Suggest that the performer undertakes physical relaxation / control of arousal.
- ❐ Promote cognitive strategies or temper control.
- ❐ Give non-aggressive role models.

4) f)
The aggressive cue hypothesis (Berkowitz 1969), is a theory which explains why aggression may be experienced by sports performers. Using an example from sport describe the aggressive cue hypothesis.
> 4 marks for :
- ❐ The individual is frustrated - the football player is having a bad game.
- ❐ There is an increase in arousal levels / intensity of behaviour - the football player gets a physiological and psychological arousal response.
- ❐ The player not playing very well becomes the cue for aggression.
- ❐ This cue if repeated may well result in further aggression.

ACHIEVEMENT MOTIVATION

5) a)
Describe the characteristics of the positive motive : 'the need to achieve'.
> 4 marks for four from :
- ❐ The performer will be enthusiastic or will like the challenge.
- ❐ He / she will persist with the task / will keep trying / training.
- ❐ The performer will take personal responsibility for his / her actions.
- ❐ He / she wants to complete the task.
- ❐ The performer is not afraid of failing / sees failing as a step towards success.
- ❐ He / she likes feedback.

5) b) i)
Describe an example from sport of someone who has a high motive to avoid failure.
> 1 mark for one from (must have a sporting example) :
- ❐ Rock climbing - the climber takes an easy route up the rock.
- ❐ Soccer / hockey / rugby - the player gives up when trying to chase a ball.
- ❐ A player will hide (social loafing) in a game situation.

5) b) ii)
Identify factors which could affect the use of motives to achieve and to avoid failure in sporting situations.
> 3 marks for three from :
- ❐ Player perception of probability of success.
- ❐ The player's own ability level or the ability of an opponent.
- ❐ Previous experience of the task.
- ❐ Importance of the task or the level of competition.
- ❐ Level of motivation of the player.
- ❐ Player personality trait may predetermine which motive is used.

5) c)
How would you promote the need to achieve motive, rather than the need to avoid failure motive?
> 8 marks for eight from :
- ❐ Give early success to the learner.
- ❐ Raise self-efficacy / confidence levels (as a result of early success).
- ❐ Attribute success to internal and controllable factors (such as ability, talent, or effort, tactics).
- ❐ Give rewards to the learner.
- ❐ Promote intrinsic rewards, the satisfaction of personal bests.
- ❐ If failure occurs encourage it to be seen as important for eventual success.
- ❐ Redefine success / decrease importance of a failure if needed.
- ❐ Avoid comparison with others if it is likely to lower self-esteem.
- ❐ Show successful and attainable models.
- ❐ Highlight success in media - with others who have achieved.
- ❐ Control anxiety / arousal levels.

ATTRIBUTION

6) a)
Define the term attribution by using a sporting situation.
   1 mark for one from :
❏   The reasons that we give for our behaviour.
❏   The reasons can be dispositional (due to the performer's mood or feelings) or environmental and they can affect his / her motivation.

6) b)
Explain the terms locus of causality and stability when applied to attribution theory.
   4 marks for four from :
❏   Locus of causality = location of causes / reasons for the performer's behaviour.
❏   Internal causes are dispositional, the reasons are from within the group or an individual and are due to his / her mood or state of mind.
❏   External causes are environmental, the reasons are out of the individual's control.
❏   The stability dimension refers to how changeable the reasons / attributions are over the short term.
❏   If stable - not very changeable.
❏   If unstable - very changeable.

6) c)
Redraw the model and place on it relevant attributions for each of the four boxes.
   1 mark for each box - see diagram 528 on right
❏   ❏   ❏   ❏

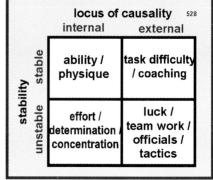

6) d)
What attributions would you encourage if your team were playing well but often losing?
   5 marks for five from :
❏   Attribute the losing to external factors.
❏   Attribute the fact of losing to the superiority of the opposition or the task difficulty.
❏   Emphasise that tactics could be changed.
❏   Losing could be due to unlucky events within the game or competition.
❏   And team members could be wrongly treated by officials if this was the case.
❏   Emphasise the positive aspects of their play.
❏   Reinforce their efforts / commitment.
❏   Encourage unstable attributions such as team work or tactics which could be changed.

7) a)
Many young people claim to be hopeless at gymnastics. Suggest three reasons why these youngsters might have a negative attitude to gymnastics.
   3 marks for three from :
❏   The perceived high difficulty or complexity of gymnastics.
❏   The media highlights the perceived difficulty of gymnastics (only expert performers are ever shown on TV).
❏   The beginner has had early failure or a negative past experience at gymnastics.
❏   The beginner may be fearful of gymnastics as a dangerous activity or one with high risk.
❏   He / she may have fear of the unknown (no past experience).
❏   The beginner may have high motive to avoid failure or have negative personality / trait factors.
❏   He / she may have been told that he / she is useless at gymnastics.
❏   There may be a race / gender / age constraint (boys think that its a girls sport or there is peer group pressure against the activity).
❏   He / she may attribute (attribution theory) past failure to lack of ability (I tried it before and failed).
❏   The beginner may have performance goals (to achieve a complex move) rather than a learning goal (to achieve a satisfaction through learning something which is achievable).

7) b)
What is meant by learned helplessness (LH) and how is it caused?
   3 marks for three from :
❏   LH is a lack of motivation due to a feeling of hopelessness.
❏   LH can be specific (to a single sport or activity) or global (to all sport).
❏   LH is caused by reinforcement of failure.
❏   If LH is reinforced by the high status of others who are succeeding, then new peers can be found who are roughly equal in ability.
❏   Previous experiences are perceived as failing and are internally attributed.

ATTRIBUTION - ANSWERS QUESTION 7 (continued)

7) c)

How would you attempt to attract beginners to a gymnastics class, and then change any negative attitudes?

❐ One mark given for any description of a strategy to attract newcomers : open days / advertising / displays, which portray a positive image, using desirable role models and so on.

3 marks for three from :

❐ The coach may attribute early failures to controllable factors.
❐ Attribution retraining / 'you can put right what went wrong'.
❐ The coach could explain early failure.
❐ The coach would give early success experiences.
❐ And redefine success.
❐ By stressing personal improvement (or health or fitness or image) rather than competition.
❐ Make the activity enjoyable (coach must have a positive personality to encourage this).

SELF-EFFICACY

8) a)

What is meant by the term self-efficacy when applied to sports psychology?

1 mark for :

❐ Self-efficacy is the level of self-confidence an individual has in a given situation (also called state confidence).

8) b)

What factors influence self-efficacy? Use practical examples from sport to illustrate your answer.

8 marks for :

❐ Self-efficacy can be enhanced by performance accomplishments.
❐ Example, the learner tried the butterfly stroke in swimming and was successful (hence high self-efficacy).
❐ Vicarious experiences affect self-efficacy.
❐ Example, the learner may have seen another swimmer perform the butterfly.
❐ Verbal persuasion.
❐ Example, a teacher shouting encouragement to a pupil attempting a high jump.
❐ Emotional arousal.
❐ Example, an athlete feeling anxious just before a race.

8) c)

As a coach of a sports team, how would you raise an individual's level of self-efficacy?

4 marks for :

❐ Ensure the performer experiences success.
❐ Show the performer a model of similar age / ability being successful.
❐ Encourage the performer / persuade the performer that success is attainable.
❐ Calm the performer down if anxiety is high.

SOCIAL LEARNING / OBSERVATIONAL LEARNING

9) a)

What is meant by the term socialisation and how can it be explained within the context of sport?

3 marks for three from :

❐ Socialisation is the adoption of a culture's norms and values.
❐ Sport often mirrors a culture's conventions.
❐ Example, fair play and courtesy are part of British culture.
❐ Playing by the rules.
❐ Leadership roles.
❐ Behaviour is copied both within and outside sport.
❐ Sport can help self-discipline, and this can then be transferred to the outside world.

9) b)

Using Bandura's model of observational learning, show the importance of demonstration in motor skill learning.

10 marks for :

❐ Attention.
❐ Example, demonstration must encourage concentration and be accurate or exciting.
❐ Retention.
❐ Example, demonstration must facilitate storage in LTM (must be memorable).
❐ Motor Reproduction.
❐ Example, the performer must be able enough to copy the demonstration.
❐ Motivation.
❐ Example, the performer must want to copy the demonstration.
❐ Matching Performance.
❐ Example, the performer then has to try to imitate what has been seen.

SOCIAL LEARNING / OBSERVATIONAL LEARNING - ANSWERS QUESTION 9 (continued)

9) c)
Videos are often used in the teaching and refining of motor skills as well as illustrating tactical strategies in sport. How would you use a video to encourage participation and to motivate performers in sport?
    6 marks for six from :
- Use accurate models which give a high level for encouragement or excitement.
- Use video of the same age group or ability if confidence is low.
- Use only short clips and then put these into context.
- Draw attention to important aspects of the video.
- Repeat important sections.
- Encourage copying of behaviour straight after the viewing.
- Use negative aspects of the video to reinforce positive behaviours.

GROUPS AND TEAMS

10) a)
What is meant by cohesion in the context of teams?
    4 marks for four from :
- Individuals in a team must have common goals.
- Players in a team must interact effectively.
- Players in a team must communicate effectively.
- Motives for playing must be similar within a team.
- Similarity of interests / outlook ensures cohesion.
- Social cohesion encourages cohesion within the game.

10) b)
What factors stop a team ever performing to their true potential?
    6 marks for six from :
- Social loafing.
- Loss of individuality.
- Differences in values / motives.
- Lack of co-ordination.
- Conflict of motives.
- Social conflict.
- Lack of an effective leader.
- Lack of perceived team ability.
- Too many lost games / lack of success / lack of recognition.
- Wrong strategies / tactics.

10) c)
Explain what is meant by social loafing by using examples from sport.
    3 marks for : (must use practical examples)
- Loss of motivation. Example, an individual does not try very hard in a game of netball.
- Lack of individuality. Example, an individual player is 'lost' within a team or does not get recognition.
- Lack of perceived external evaluation. Example, a player does not feel that he / she is being judged and therefore is not accountable for lack of effort.

10) d)
What advice would you give a coach of a team to ensure maximum productivity?
    5 marks for five from :
- Encourage cohesion.
- By social mixing or sharing of experiences.
- Give individuals encouragement as well as the team.
- Give praise / reinforce success / give incentives / rewards.
- Attribute failure to controllable factors.
- Attribute success to internal factors.
- Encourage peer support.
- Develop co-ordination through training, for example, small sided games.
- Develop a person-oriented leadership approach (democratic leadership).

SOCIAL FACILITATION

11) a)

What is meant by social facilitation and what is its main effect?

3 marks for three from :

- ❐ Social facilitation means the effects of the presence of others on performance.
- ❐ This can be the effect of an audience or co-actors (members of the performer's own team or the opposition).
- ❐ Social facilitation can be positive or negative.
- ❐ If negative it is often called social inhibition.
- ❐ The main effect of social facilitation is to raise arousal level.

11) b)

What effects can be experienced by an individual if there is an audience present?

6 marks for six from :

- ❐ Raising of the performer's arousal level.
- ❐ More mistakes could be made by the performer.
- ❐ Feeling of being evaluated or judged (evaluation apprehension).
- ❐ Physiological arousal effects / heart rate high.
- ❐ The dominant response (a practised activity) is more likely to occur (linked with higher arousal), Drive Theory.
- ❐ Inverted U Theory says that the effect can be positive up to a point (moderate arousal level).
- ❐ If the performer is experienced, the audience could spur him / her on to high levels of performance.
- ❐ If the performer is extrovert, the audience could facilitate performance (showing off to the audience).
- ❐ If the performer is introvert, the audience could inhibit performance (shy in front of the audience).
- ❐ The effect of an audience on a performer depends on the type of task being performed.
- ❐ Gross / simple skills could facilitate performance.
- ❐ Fine / complex skills could inhibit performance.

11) c)

What is meant by evaluation apprehension?

2 marks for :

- ❐ This means a high level of anxiety / negative stress / arousal levels are experienced by the performer.
- ❐ Which would be caused by perceived external judgement or evaluation by others.

11) d)

As a coach of an individual who is affected adversely by the presence of an audience, how would you help him or her to overcome the negative influences?

4 marks for four from :

- ❐ Decrease the importance of the event.
- ❐ Selective attention, focus on technique or tactics instead of the audience (ignore distractions).
- ❐ Use an audience in training.
- ❐ Use the audience to get behind you in an event.
- ❐ Get the performer to use relaxation or somatic strategies.
- ❐ Get the performer to use cognitive stress management / positive thinking or imagery.

12) a)

What effect (if any) did the audience have on the performance of the exercise?

1 mark for :

- ❐ The audience had the effect of improving performance.

12) b)

How would you account for this effect (or lack of effect)?

4 marks for four from :

- ❐ Social facilitation.
- ❐ The mere presence of an audience has a positive effect on a well-learned skill.
- ❐ The group wants to impress the audience or is worried by not impressing the audience.
- ❐ Adrenaline (or hormonal effects) induced by the presence of the audience would have a positive effect.
- ❐ Positive effects are attributed to presence of an evaluative audience.
- ❐ An audience has an effect on level of arousal and thus increases a performance up to the optimum level.
- ❐ Distraction by the audience may have a negative effect.

SOCIAL FACILITATION - ANSWERS QUESTION 12 (continued)

12) c)
The audience in this exercise (for group 2) was not known to the participants. Explain any effect you think there would be if the audience was known to the group.

6 marks for six from :
- ❏ Cottrell's evaluation effect.
- ❏ The group might perceive the evaluation by the audience as being greater than if the audience was unknown.
- ❏ Subjects may not wish to perform well in front of friends.
- ❏ Subjects may seek praise from friends or fear ridicule from friends.
- ❏ Subjects may lose concentration due to presence of an audience known to them.
- ❏ Performance might be increased by an atmosphere of competition within the group.
- ❏ The subjects may have the motive to do well (achieve) or avoid failure in front of this audience.

LEADERSHIP

13) a)
What is meant by a leader and what sort of qualities would you expect to see in a leader within the context of sport?

4 marks for four from :
- ❏ A leader is one who can influence the behaviour of others towards a set goal.
  Qualities of a leader :
- ❏ High ability / knowledge levels.
- ❏ Good communicator / socially adept.
- ❏ Enthusiastic / good motivator.
- ❏ Has respect for group members.
- ❏ Charisma / naturally a leader.
- ❏ Has a repertoire of styles.

13) b)
Using psychological theories describe how an individual becomes a leader.

4 marks for four from :
- ❏ The individual is born a good leader, or has innate characteristics which make him / her a good leader.
- ❏ The leader has learned leadership behaviour via social learning.
- ❏ The leader has copied behaviour from others of high status.
- ❏ The leader has emerged via group agreement.
- ❏ The leader has been prescribed via an external agent (a governing body or team management).

13) c)
Name three leadership styles.

3 marks for :
- ❏ Autocratic / authoritarian / task-oriented.
- ❏ Democratic / person-oriented.
- ❏ Laissez Faire / passive style.

13) d)
What factors should be taken into consideration when deciding upon which leadership style to adopt?

6 marks for six from :
- ❏ Size of group.
- ❏ Large group : task-oriented leader. Small group : democratic leader.
- ❏ Nature of group / hostility of group / group conservatism.
- ❏ Personality of the leader / confidence of leader.
- ❏ The experience of the leader.
- ❏ The danger presented by the situation.
- ❏ The importance of the event.
- ❏ Time factors.
- ❏ The complexity of the task.
- ❏ The expectation of others.

LEADERSHIP - ANSWERS (continued)

14) a)

Explain each part of the model using examples from sport.

3 marks for three from :

☐ The model predicts that behaviour (is dependent on a leader).

☐ The model predicts that satisfaction from performance (is dependent on a leader).

☐ The model predicts that (behaviour and satisfaction from performance) depend on leader characteristics and other factors.

☐ Situational characteristics (pressure of a game or crowds) affect leadership relationships.

☐ Leadership characteristics (the type of person the leader is, his / her personality, temperament, experience).

☐ Member characteristics with reference to the group or individual involved (personalities / cohesion / experience / expertise / beliefs).

Behaviour of the group associated with leadership can be viewed from three perspectives :

3 marks for :

☐ Prescribed behaviour, what does the situation require a leader to do (explained through a sporting example)?

☐ Actual behaviour, what the leader actually does in a situation which may be rational / accountable.

☐ Preferred behaviour, what style of leadership does the group want (autocratic / democratic)?

2 marks for :

☐ Explanation of resultant performance (linked with a sporting example).

☐ Explanation of resultant satisfaction (linked with a sporting example).

14) b)

Discuss the statement 'Good leaders are born not made', and explain whether you agree or disagree in the light of psychological theory.

5 marks for five from :

☐ Trait theory.

☐ This is the great man or person theory.

As opposed to :

☐ Situation or interaction theories.

☐ Behaviour is a function of person and the environment (or B = f(p,e)).

☐ Environmental or behavioural influences can be associated with leadership.

☐ Being taught how to communicate.

☐ Learning through one's social interactions / environmental influences / upbringing / education how to be a leader.

Other supporting comments :

☐ Personality characteristics associated with leadership.

☐ Having the ability to perceive relationships.

STRESS AND STRESS MANAGEMENT

15) a)

What is meant by the term stress?

2 marks for :

☐ Stress means our perceptions of the demands of a task or situation.

☐ And the perceived ability to cope with those demands.

15) b)

Explain two psychological symptoms of stress.

2 marks for two from :

☐ Worry / feeling overwhelmed / feeling out of control.

☐ Inability to make decisions.

☐ Inability to concentrate or direct attention, confusion.

☐ Narrowing of attention.

☐ Irritability.

STRESS AND STRESS MANAGEMENT - ANSWERS QUESTION 16 (continued)

15) c)
Identify three main stressors in the context of sport.
 3 marks for three from :
- ➁ Stressors are factors or situations which can cause stress, for example, competition against self.
- ➁ Competition against others.
- ➁ The expectancy of others.
- ➁ The event being perceived as important.
- ➁ The hostility of others / the crowd.
- ➁ Feeling of frustration caused by injury / poor play / officials' decisions.

15) d)
What is the difference between state and trait anxiety?
 2 marks for :
- ➁ State : feeling of apprehension / stress in a specific situation.
- ➁ Trait : general stress levels / innate anxiety / anxiety you take to all situations.

15) e)
What coping strategies should the anxious performer draw upon?
 5 marks for five from :
- ➁ Cognitive strategies, for example, imagery / mental rehearsal / selective attention.
- ➁ Positive thinking / negative thought stopping.
- ➁ Hypnotism.
- ➁ Somatic strategies, for example, relaxation.
- ➁ Or yoga.
- ➁ Attainable goal setting.
- ➁ Decreasing the perceived importance of the event.
- ➁ Raising self-efficacy / increasing confidence.
- ➁ Positive reinforcement.
- ➁ Give success.
- ➁ Attributional factors.
- ➁ Redefine success.

16) a)
Describe three techniques used to measure stress.
 3 marks for :
- ➁ Self-report / questionnaire.
- ➁ Observation of behaviour.
- ➁ Physiological factors, for example, taking blood pressure or heart rate.

16) b)
Give one advantage and one disadvantage of each technique.
 2 marks for one advantage and one disadvantage (self-report / questionnaire) :
 Advantages :
- ➁ Easy to administer / often quick to score.
- ➁ Can be used in large groups.
- ➁ The data can be normative (related to data from large test groups which will give a standardised score).
 Disadvantages :
- ➁ The subject might fake the test or be subject to bias, or the test may not be suitable for that individual.
- ➁ The results may be open to misinterpretation by non experts.
- ➁ The results may not be sensitive to small changes in anxiety.
- ➁ Written tests would not be possible in most real sport settings (would interfere with actual anxiety response).

 2 marks for one advantage and one disadvantage (behavioural observation) :
 Advantages :
- ➁ This is real life behaviour monitored in a sporting situation.
- ➁ It would be possible to compare behaviour across different situations.
- ➁ In depth analysis would be possible with one person.
 Disadvantages :
- ➁ It could be difficult to say whether behaviour reflects real anxiety (the observation would be subjective).
- ➁ It would be difficult to observe large groups of sportspeople.
- ➁ It would be difficult to quantify responses (to obtain a score or ranking).

STRESS AND STRESS MANAGEMENT - ANSWERS Question 16) b) continued

16) b)

2 marks for one advantage and one disadvantage (physiological indices) :

Advantages :

❏ Such measurements would be an objective measure of physical reactions (a definite value or score could be given).

❏ It would be possible to assess during a sporting performance.

Disadvantages :

❏ Measurements could interfere with the anxiety response.

❏ Not all individuals react with the same physiological response which may or may not be linked with anxiety.

16) c)

Discuss the possible relationships between anxiety and performance in sporting activities.

7 marks for seven from :

❏ Anxiety is an aspect of arousal (arousal is required or evident in most sport performance).

❏ Inverted U theory links arousal and performance in sport.

Marks given for sketch graph (see figure on right) showing inverted U theory,

     ❏ Showing low performance at low arousal.

     ❏ Showing high performance at medium arousal.

     ❏ Showing low performance at high arousal.

❏ Small amount of anxiety suggests that the performer is casual / inattentive, therefore unlikely to perform at his / her best (i.e. produce a low performance).

❏ High anxiety / arousal can cause over-excitement or disruption of concentration / attention / control.

❏ Moderate levels of anxiety / arousal is optimal and makes a performer ready for action.

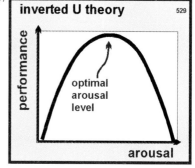

❏ Differences depend on the type of activity, for example, high arousal may be required for contact games, and low arousal or calmness for gymnastics.

❏ Differences may also be due to the personality of the performer, for example to perform well extroverts need high anxiety, and introverts need low arousal / anxiety.

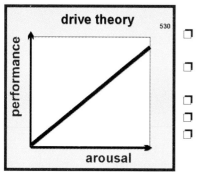

❏ Drive theory (see figure on left), mark given for linear relationship between arousal and performance.

❏ Drive theory (also called Hull's theory) can explain what happens for simple skills.

❏ The more arousal, the better the performance.

❏ Performance can be explained by P = H x D (performance = habit x drive).

❏ This means that the dominant response is accentuated by high arousal levels (the higher the arousal the better the performance).

16) d)

High levels of arousal have often been linked with stress. Sketch a graph showing the relationship between the performance of a complex skill and level of arousal.

See figure 525 above right for the inverted U graph, 2 marks given for :

❏ Inverted U shape.

❏ Optimum performance at moderate arousal levels.

16) e)

Add a second curve to your graph showing how the performance of a simple skill might be affected by arousal.

See graph on right, 1 mark given for one from :

❏ Graph showing optimum performance at high arousal level (red line on graph).

❏ Or Drive theory, linear relationship between performance and arousal, or the higher the arousal the better the performance (dashed red line on graph).

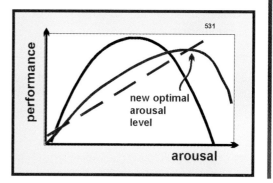

GOAL SETTING

17) a)
What are the main positive effects of setting goals in sport?
- ❐ Raising motivation levels.
- ❐ Controlling anxiety or stress.

17) b)
Show what is meant by short-term goals and long-term goals by using examples from sport.
  2 marks for two from :
- ❐ Short-term - process oriented goals.
- ❐ Which affect aspects of performance.
- ❐ For example, the goal of following through into court after a serve in tennis.
  2 marks for two from :
- ❐ Long-term goals - product oriented.
- ❐ Which affect the result or future aim.
- ❐ For example, to beat your personal best in athletics or to win the league at soccer.

17) c)
As a coach how would you ensure that your goal setting was as effective as possible?
  6 marks for six from :
- ❐ Goals must be attainable / within your reach.
- ❐ Goals which are challenging are more motivating.
- ❐ Set goals which are positive rather than negative.
- ❐ Goals should involve individual as well as team targets.
- ❐ Goals should be measurable.
- ❐ Target dates are important so that the performer is accountable.
- ❐ Goals should be negotiable.
- ❐ Goals should have shared ownership.
- ❐ Goals should be a mixture of process and product.

John Honeybourne.

Answers

SELECTED BIBLIOGRAPHY

Backley, S.	1996	The Winning Mind. Aurum Press.
Beashel, P.	1996	Advanced Studies in Physical Education and Sport. Thomas Nelson.
Biddle, S.J.	1996	Psychology of PE and Sport - A Practical Guide for Teachers. FIT Systems.
Bull, S.	1997	Sport Psychology. Crowood Press.
Bull, S.	1996	The Mental Game Plan - Getting Psyched for Sport. Sports Dynamics.
Butler, R.J.	1996	Sports Psychology in Action. Butterworth / Heinemann.
Cox, R.	1999	Sport Psychology : Concepts and Applications 4e. McGraw-Hill.
Davis, R. et. al.	2000	Physical Education and the Study of Sport 4e. Mosby.Wolfe.
Galligan, F. et al	2000	Advanced PE for Edexcel. Heinemann.
Gill, D.	2000	Psychological Dynamics of Sport 2e. Human Kinetics.
Gould, D.	2000	Study Guide to Foundations of Sport and Exercise Psychology (Weinberg). Human Kinetics.
Honeybourne, J. et.al.	2000 2000	Advanced Physical Education & Sport for A level 2e. Nelson Thornes. Advanced Physical Education & Sport 2e - Teacher Resource Pack . Nelson Thornes.
Honeybourne, J. et.al.	1998	PE for you Stanley Thornes.
Mace, R et al	1999	CD ROM Switch on to Sports Psychology. Sport in Mind.
Martens, R.	1987	Coaches Guide to Sport Psychology. Human Kinetics.
Martens, R.	1990	Competitive Anxiety in Sport. Human Kinetics.
Morris, T.	1995	Sport Psychology. Wiley.
Roberts, G.C.	1999	Learning Experiences in Sport Psychology 2e. Human Kinetics.
Roberts, G.C.	1992	Motivation in Sport and Exercise Science. Human Kinetics.
Roscoe, D.	2000	Teacher's Guide to Physical Education and the Study of Sport 4e Sport Psychology. Jan Roscoe Publications.
Webster, S.	1997	Sport Psychology - An A Level guide for Teachers and Students. Jan Roscoe Publications.
Weinberg, R.S.	1999	Foundations of Sport and Exercise Psychology. Human Kinetics.
Wesson, K. et.al.	2000	Sport and PE. A Complete Guide to A Level Study 2e. Hodder and Stoughton.
Wood, B.	1998	Applying Psychology to Sport. Hodder & Stoughton.

CONTEMPORARY STUDIES

LEISURE AND RECREATION

LEISURE
- Leisure is time in which there is opportunity for choice (Arnold).
- Leisure consists of relatively self-determining activity-experiences which fall into one's economically free-time roles (Kaplan).

LEISURE
- We can recognise it because it is an activity (apart from obligations).
- This involves :   free time
                    choice
                    opportunity.

LEISURE
- It functions as activity (as a positive attempt to allow) :
        free development
        relaxation
        re-creation.
- Leisure is more than an activity, it is a valuable experience.
- Leisure is potentially : self-realising
                            socialising
                            culturally civilising.

watching & listening

playing games & competing

daydreaming & relaxing

visiting & communicating

gardening & constructing

LEISURE ACTIVITIES

dancing & romancing

reading & writing

playing instruments & painting

walking & jogging

inventing & discovering

LEISURE
- Different theories exist regarding leisure as :
        a spare time activity
        an economic condition
        a form of social control
        a basis for creative fulfilment.

RECREATION
- Recreation is a positive aspect of leisure and is widely described as active leisure.

- Recreation carries the individual away from usual concerns and problems.
- The attitudes derived from this are those involving feelings of relaxation.
- Contentment not complacency might best describe an attitude which is a product of a recreative experience. (Van der Swaag)

CONCEPTS and THEORIES of PLAY

CONCEPTS of PLAY

- Play consists of activities from which you get immediate pleasure without ulterior motive.

- Time and space are freely decided.

- Play has intrinsic value and is spontaneous.

- Play is non-serious and is enjoyment oriented.

- Play for a child increases mastery over reality.
- While an adult steps aside from reality.

PLAY
- Play is an activity which proceeds within certain limits of time and space.
- In a visible order according to rules freely accepted.
- Outside the sphere of necessity or material utility.
- The play mood is one of rapture and enthusiasm.
- This play mood is sacred or festive in accordance with the occasion.
- A feeling of exultation and tension accompanies the action.
- Mirth and relaxation follow (Huizinga).

PLAY

PLAY
- Is a voluntary experience : it is freedom.
- Is not ordinary or real life.
- Is a temporary world.
- Creates order.
- Is sharing a common experience.

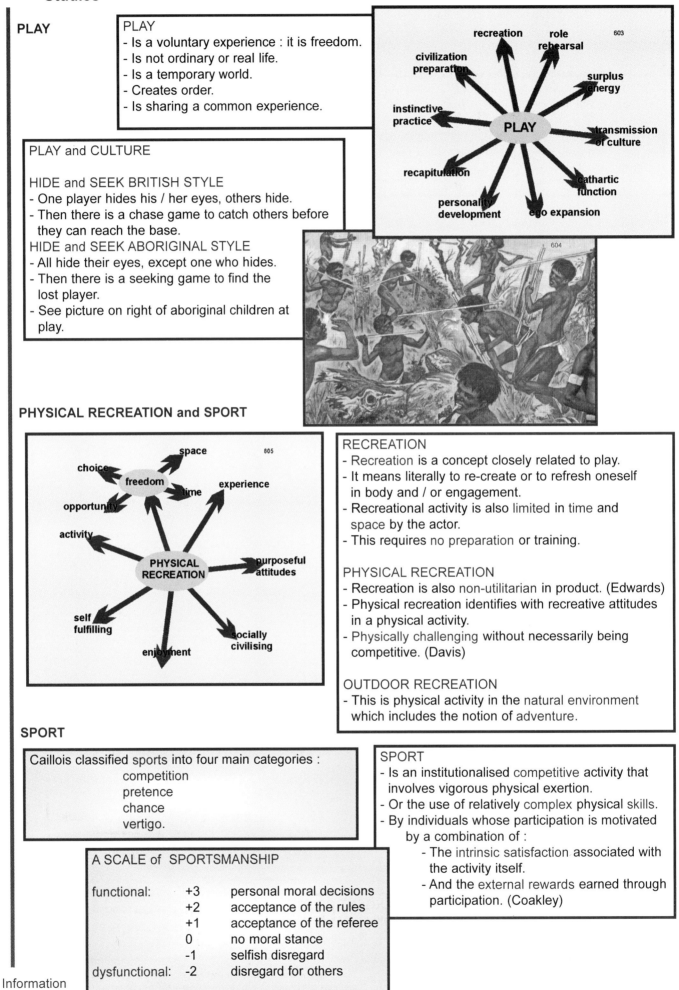

PLAY and CULTURE

HIDE and SEEK BRITISH STYLE
- One player hides his / her eyes, others hide.
- Then there is a chase game to catch others before they can reach the base.

HIDE and SEEK ABORIGINAL STYLE
- All hide their eyes, except one who hides.
- Then there is a seeking game to find the lost player.
- See picture on right of aboriginal children at play.

PHYSICAL RECREATION and SPORT

RECREATION
- Recreation is a concept closely related to play.
- It means literally to re-create or to refresh oneself in body and / or engagement.
- Recreational activity is also limited in time and space by the actor.
- This requires no preparation or training.

PHYSICAL RECREATION
- Recreation is also non-utilitarian in product. (Edwards)
- Physical recreation identifies with recreative attitudes in a physical activity.
- Physically challenging without necessarily being competitive. (Davis)

OUTDOOR RECREATION
- This is physical activity in the natural environment which includes the notion of adventure.

SPORT

Caillois classified sports into four main categories :
competition
pretence
chance
vertigo.

SPORT
- Is an institutionalised competitive activity that involves vigorous physical exertion.
- Or the use of relatively complex physical skills.
- By individuals whose participation is motivated by a combination of :
  - The intrinsic satisfaction associated with the activity itself.
  - And the external rewards earned through participation. (Coakley)

A SCALE of SPORTSMANSHIP

functional:	+3	personal moral decisions
	+2	acceptance of the rules
	+1	acceptance of the referee
	0	no moral stance
	-1	selfish disregard
dysfunctional:	-2	disregard for others

CHARACTERISTICS of SPORT

CHARACTERISTICS of SPORT

- Any physical activity which has the character of play and which takes the form of a struggle with oneself or involves competition with others is a sport.

- If this activity involves competition, then it should always be performed with a spirit of sportsmanship. There can be no true sport without the idea of fair play.

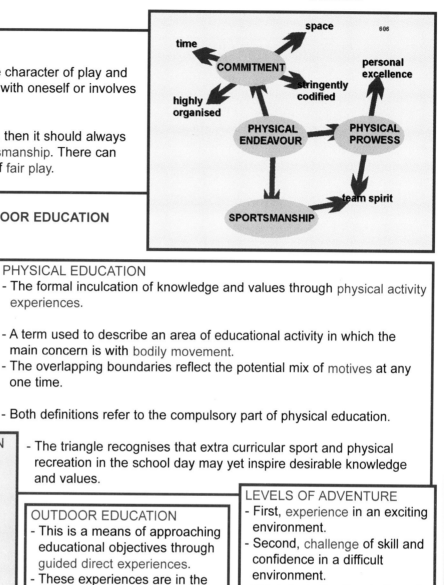

PHYSICAL EDUCATION and OUTDOOR EDUCATION

PHYSICAL EDUCATION
- The formal inculcation of knowledge and values through physical activity experiences.

- A term used to describe an area of educational activity in which the main concern is with bodily movement.
- The overlapping boundaries reflect the potential mix of motives at any one time.

- Both definitions refer to the compulsory part of physical education.

- The triangle recognises that extra curricular sport and physical recreation in the school day may yet inspire desirable knowledge and values.

VALUES IN PHYSICAL EDUCATION

PHYSICAL
- Health and fitness.
- Skills and tactics.
- Sports and pastimes.
PERSONAL
- Self-realisation and socialization.
- Decision-making and ethics.
- Emotional experience.
PREPARATION
- Active leisure.
- Sporting opportunity.
- Career potential.
QUALITATIVE
- Creativity and appreciation.
- Commitment and vitality.

OUTDOOR EDUCATION
- This is a means of approaching educational objectives through guided direct experiences.
- These experiences are in the natural environment using its resources as learning materials.

LEVELS OF ADVENTURE
- First, experience in an exciting environment.
- Second, challenge of skill and confidence in a difficult environment.
- Third, test of self and others in a frontier experience.
- Fourth, misadventure in a dangerous environment.

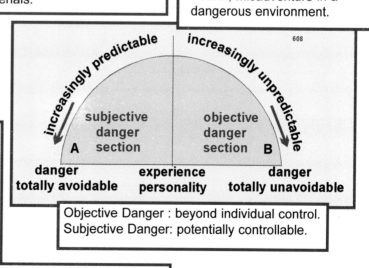

Objective Danger : beyond individual control.
Subjective Danger: potentially controllable.

SPORT AND CULTURE

ETHNIC SPORTS AND PASTIMES
Survival - related to warfare.
   Economic.
      Social - related to ritual.
COLONIAL CONQUEST AND IMPOSITION
  Military.
    Diplomatic.
      Economic.
        Rational sports.
          Missionary.
POST-COLONIAL EMERGENCE
Adaptation - (Samoan Rugby).
  Reversion - (Trobriand Cricket).
    Adoption - (Bungee Jumping).

EMERGENT COUNTRIES
- Nation building.
   Integration.
     Health.
       Social control.

Information

SPORT and CULTURE (continued)

SPORT AND EMERGENT CULTURE
- Many countries have progressed beyond their tribal origins and as 'Third World Countries' are striving to improve the quality of life.
- This is where sport is seen as a way of satisfying the needs of the people and achieving exposure for the country.
- There is a process of nation building and integration together with a need for improved health and social control.
- The process chosen is elitist, where disproportionate support for one sport is used to achieve world recognition.
- Examples of this include West Indian Cricket, Kenyan Athletics, Nigerian Boxing, Indonesian Badminton and Brazilian Soccer.
- Success has led to other sports being expanded in each country.
- And elitist principles being at least partly relaxed.
- As success in a sport has led to exposure on the world stage.
- And broader status being given to the significance of sport.

SPORT AND TRIBAL CULTURE
- There are still many tribal communities such as the Polynesians, Eskimos and Aborigines, where the original tribal sports and pastimes can still be found.
- They reflect the needs of the community in terms of survival in the natural world.
- But also ritual and festival elements which bound the community together.
- The advent of Colonialism led to subjugation, ritual curtailment and social conditioning through colonial education and sports.
- Today we find a re-emergence of the old culture where European games have gone through adaptation, reversion and adoption.

DISPROPORTIONATE FUNDING
Elitism.
  Selectivity.
    Occupational.
      Excellence.
INTERNAL APPEASEMENT / EXTERNAL EXPOSURE
Role models.   World arena.
  Opportunity.   Fundings return.
    Provision.   Talent pay-back.

SPORT IN ADVANCED CULTURES: EAST - WEST
- In looking at advanced industrialised countries, identifiable as the G8.
- There is a political and socio-economic polarisation from the American extreme of multi-party democracy and capitalism, identifiable as the 'American Dream'.
- To the old Soviet Union and countries like China (authoritarian single party control exists in a Marxist-socialist society), identifiable in the 'Shop Window'.
- Most West European countries lie between these two, as alternative conservative - socialist governments working within a mixed economy.
- In the US model, sport exists as a social institution, where technical, managerial and corporate organisation are present.
- And as a social situation where sport occurs at a producer and consumer level.
- In the case of the capitalist model, commercialism and the professionalisation of sport is uppermost.
- Whereas the socialist model has a political agenda.
- In both cases mass participation & sporting excellence is endorsed at voluntary, public and private levels.
- But varying in terms of the domination of one of these.

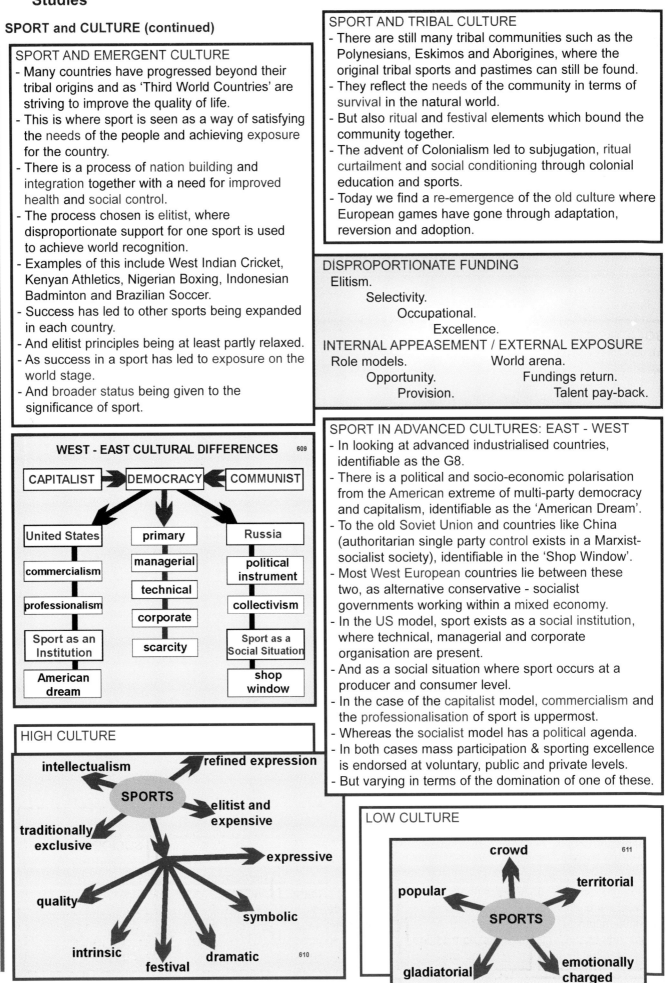

WEST - EAST CULTURAL DIFFERENCES 609

CAPITALIST → DEMOCRACY ← COMMUNIST

United States / primary / Russia
commercialism / managerial / political instrument
technical
professionalism / collectivism
corporate
Sport as an Institution / scarcity / Sport as a Social Situation
American dream / shop window

HIGH CULTURE
intellectualism — refined expression — SPORTS — elitist and expensive — traditionally exclusive — expressive — quality — symbolic — intrinsic — festival — dramatic 610

LOW CULTURE
crowd 611 — popular — territorial — SPORTS — gladiatorial — emotionally charged

SPORT and CULTURE (continued)

SPORT AND CULTURE : HIGH - LOW

- Western democracies have societies with social advantage built into specific sub-cultures.
- In Europe this is normally a social class variable.
- But in the USA it tends to be based on race.
- In both cases there are gender variables.

- Behaviour expectations reflect these status divisions.
- The higher groups tend to identify with a high culture.
- This culture is one in which sports are supported on aesthetic and intellectual grounds and behaviour expectations are those of a respectable audience.

- Whereas low cultural groups or popular culture has a behaviour pattern based on excessive emotionalism.
- And anti-social behaviour based on the expectations of a large crowd.

HIGH - LOW CULTURE

- These two groups tend to follow different sports as a tradition.
- Where the elite sports have a history of being exclusive and the popular sports of a history of being violent.

- However, there are sports and pastimes which are common to both groups.
- And with increasing emphasis on law and order, popular sports are becoming more rationalised.
- Significantly, this is very much the result of commercial interests making respectability important.
- And the increased income of professional players.

SOCIETAL ISSUE
MASS PARTICIPATION IN SPORT

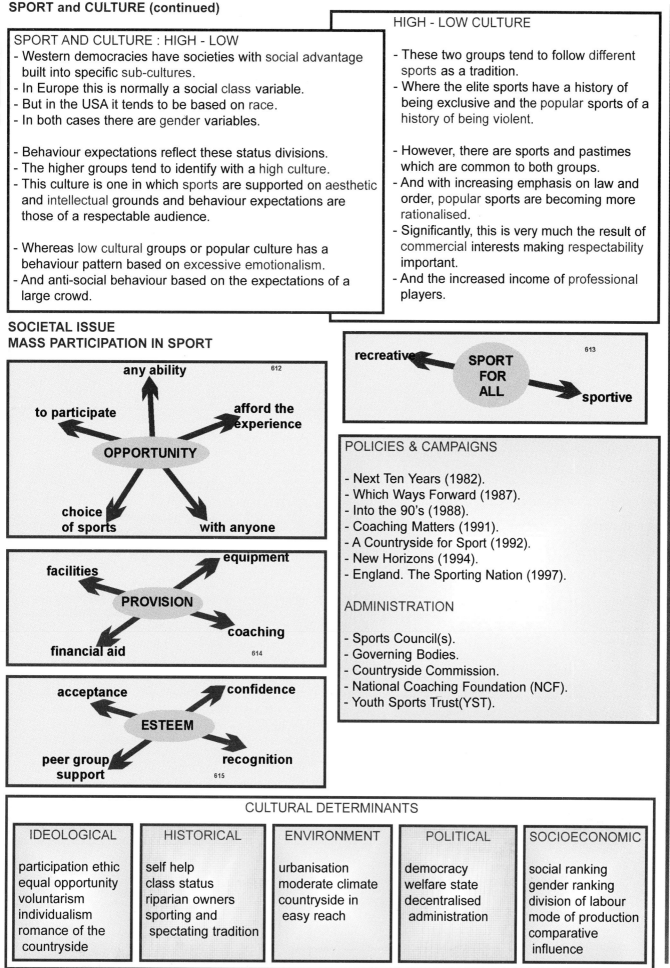

OPPORTUNITY
- any ability
- to participate
- afford the experience
- choice of sports
- with anyone
612

SPORT FOR ALL
- recreative
- sportive
613

PROVISION
- equipment
- facilities
- coaching
- financial aid
614

ESTEEM
- acceptance
- confidence
- peer group support
- recognition
615

POLICIES & CAMPAIGNS

- Next Ten Years (1982).
- Which Ways Forward (1987).
- Into the 90's (1988).
- Coaching Matters (1991).
- A Countryside for Sport (1992).
- New Horizons (1994).
- England. The Sporting Nation (1997).

ADMINISTRATION

- Sports Council(s).
- Governing Bodies.
- Countryside Commission.
- National Coaching Foundation (NCF).
- Youth Sports Trust(YST).

CULTURAL DETERMINANTS

IDEOLOGICAL	HISTORICAL	ENVIRONMENT	POLITICAL	SOCIOECONOMIC
participation ethic	self help	urbanisation	democracy	social ranking
equal opportunity	class status	moderate climate	welfare state	gender ranking
voluntarism	riparian owners	countryside in	decentralised	division of labour
individualism	sporting and	easy reach	administration	mode of production
romance of the	spectating tradition			comparative
countryside				influence

Information

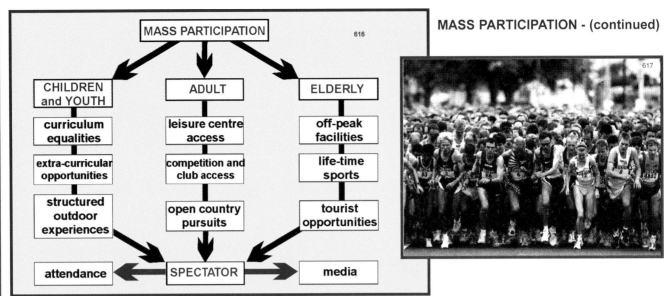

MASS PARTICIPATION - (continued)

SOCIETAL ISSUE - EXCELLENCE IN SPORT

EXCELLENCE IN SPORT - The Issue :
- There is a major debate in a world which places sport high as a barometer of the international political and economic success of a country.
- There are a number of different ways of achieving this.
- All recognise that the international standards of performance are now so high that disproportionate funding has become a fundamental necessity.
- In all cases the process can only be achieved through a pyramid process of getting promising performers to the top.
- But the shape of that pyramid depends on the extent to which elitism is operating, through necessity or design.

performance pyramid

excellence

performance

participation

foundation

EXCELLENCE
- A poor tribal society is likely to select a single sport with which to identify itself.
- One which is natural to the people, cheap to develop and unsophisticated, for example, marathon running in Ethiopia.

- An emerging country may start like that, as in Kenya, but broaden their programme as a result of role model success and exposure to the world.
- Their focus now is on nation-building and integration.

- Finally, advanced countries (for example the G8 top industrialised countries) like the UK and USA would be looking for a much broader pyramid of opportunity, provision for all and self-esteem for all minorities to participate.

- To achieve these targets disproportionate funding is necessary for Olympic success.

EXCELLENCE and PROFESSIONALISATION
- The significance of extrinsic and intrinsic values leads to a balance between professional administrative standards and required levels of sportsmanship.

- Each of the five levels of participation shown need to be fully professionalised to establish excellence.

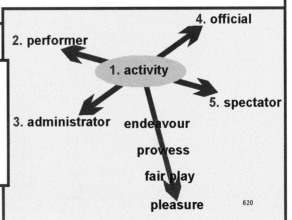

EXCELLENCE in SPORT continued

FUNDING and EFFECTIVE PERFORMANCE
- A Welfare State with a market economy.
- Where funding occurs at all three levels.
- But the balance must allow all to participate fully.

PRIVATE	VOLUNTARY	PUBLIC
commercial	governing bodies	government aid
sponsorship	private clubs	local gov. aid
benefactors	subscriptions	National Lottery
media exposure		

AGENCIES AND INITIATIVES

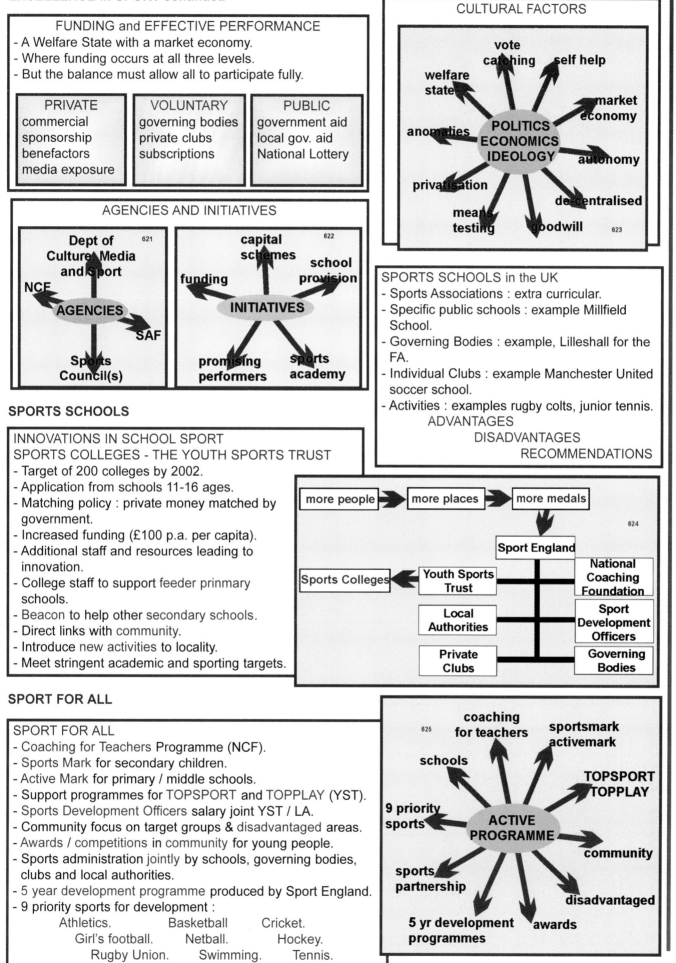

CULTURAL FACTORS

POLITICS ECONOMICS IDEOLOGY

vote catching · self help · welfare state · market economy · anomalies · autonomy · privatisation · de-centralised · means testing · goodwill

623

SPORTS SCHOOLS in the UK
- Sports Associations : extra curricular.
- Specific public schools : example Millfield School.
- Governing Bodies : example, Lilleshall for the FA.
- Individual Clubs : example Manchester United soccer school.
- Activities : examples rugby colts, junior tennis.
  ADVANTAGES
  DISADVANTAGES
  RECOMMENDATIONS

SPORTS SCHOOLS

INNOVATIONS IN SCHOOL SPORT
SPORTS COLLEGES - THE YOUTH SPORTS TRUST
- Target of 200 colleges by 2002.
- Application from schools 11-16 ages.
- Matching policy : private money matched by government.
- Increased funding (£100 p.a. per capita).
- Additional staff and resources leading to innovation.
- College staff to support feeder prinmary schools.
- Beacon to help other secondary schools.
- Direct links with community.
- Introduce new activities to locality.
- Meet stringent academic and sporting targets.

more people → more places → more medals

Sport England

Youth Sports Trust → Sports Colleges

Local Authorities

Private Clubs

National Coaching Foundation

Sport Development Officers

Governing Bodies

624

SPORT FOR ALL

SPORT FOR ALL
- Coaching for Teachers Programme (NCF).
- Sports Mark for secondary children.
- Active Mark for primary / middle schools.
- Support programmes for TOPSPORT and TOPPLAY (YST).
- Sports Development Officers salary joint YST / LA.
- Community focus on target groups & disadvantaged areas.
- Awards / competitions in community for young people.
- Sports administration jointly by schools, governing bodies, clubs and local authorities.
- 5 year development programme produced by Sport England.
- 9 priority sports for development :

Athletics.	Basketball	Cricket.
Girl's football.	Netball.	Hockey.
Rugby Union.	Swimming.	Tennis.

ACTIVE PROGRAMME

coaching for teachers · sportsmark activemark · schools · TOPSPORT TOPPLAY · 9 priority sports · community · sports partnership · disadvantaged · 5 yr development programmes · awards

625

SUB-CULTURAL ISSUES - SPORT & MINORITIES

626

GENDER - the HISTORICAL PERSPECTIVE

- Victorian attitudes to women led to females being excluded from rational sport on the grounds that it was too manly and could endanger childbirth.
- Fashions among the upper and middle classes prevented freedom of movement.
- Prevailing attitudes discouraged women from vigorous activity, any activity which brought their femininity into question, such as competition, sweating, displaying their bodies.
- Upper class women excluded themselves from this and developed selective sports on their own private land and in private schools.
- Lower class women were obliged to work to supplement their husband's wages as well as bring up their families and so had no time for sport.

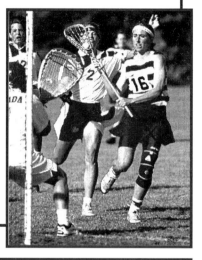

GENDER - RIGHTS or PRIVILEGES?

- Modern feminist movements have advanced the rights of women to sport, but this is still resisted by many men and women.

- Only a minority of games involve women on equal terms and combat sports like boxing and wrestling for women are generally deemed undesirable.

AGE

YOUNG

- It is clearly necessary that young children must start to specialise if they are going to reach the top in certain sports.
- They are open to abuse, losing their chance to experience a range of sports.
- They are not physically ready for some training regimes and skills.
- Young people's bodies cannot always stand the years of stress.
- And they can become burnt out while still young.

ELDERLY

- The presumption is that to be elderly is to be senile and incapable of physical activity.
- Sport for the elderly is most valuable to them and their morale.
- Many sports (governing bodies) are improving their veteran policy.
- Access is a major problem, but non-peak periods during the day are used.
- The main problem is the esteem of elderly females brought up as non-participants in sport.
- Aerobics has grown in popularity with this group of women.

RACE and BLACK ISSUES

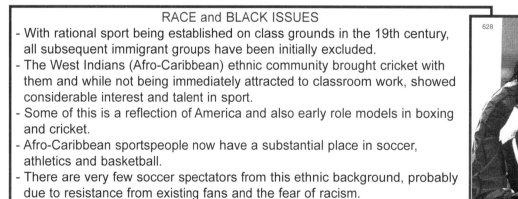

628

- With rational sport being established on class grounds in the 19th century, all subsequent immigrant groups have been initially excluded.
- The West Indians (Afro-Caribbean) ethnic community brought cricket with them and while not being immediately attracted to classroom work, showed considerable interest and talent in sport.
- Some of this is a reflection of America and also early role models in boxing and cricket.
- Afro-Caribbean sportspeople now have a substantial place in soccer, athletics and basketball.
- There are very few soccer spectators from this ethnic background, probably due to resistance from existing fans and the fear of racism.
- Afro-Caribbean females are also very interested in sport.

SUB-CULTURAL ISSUES - SPORT and MINORITIES (continued)

RACE and ETHNIC DIFFERENCES
- The Asian community from Kenya have made considerable social advances, but have not regarded sport as a career route.
- Many from the Indian sub-continent have been too busy surviving and coping with the language.
- In some areas, however, Asian soccer and cricket leagues are producing good players.
- Many Asians are Moslems and this limits female participation in sport.

DISABILITY

DISABILITY
- There has always been a conflict of attitude between ability and disability in the context of sport.
- Opportunity is often limited by the attitudes of the able-bodied.
- And also limited by the self-esteem of many who suffer from impairments.
- The main problem which is being tackled is access, where public sport facilities are now required to have ramps and wide doorways to allow wheelchair access.
- The Paraplegic Games and numerous marathons have highlighted their potential success at world level.

DISABILITY
IMPAIRMENTS :
- Loss of faculty or use of part of the body.

DISABILITIES :
- Loss of ability in certain activities due to impairment.

HANDICAP :
- Physical and social barriers as a result of disability.

TYPES :
- Mental, visual, hearing, C.P., les autres, quadriplegic, paraplegic, amputees.

DRUGS and SPORT

TYPES of DRUGS	EFFECTS
Stimulants	Increase alertness, reduce fatigue, increase competitiveness and hostility.
Narcotics / Analgesics	Management of severe pain.
Anabolic Steroids	Increase muscle strength and bulk, promote aggressiveness.
Diuretics	Reduce weight quickly, reduce concentration of substances by diluting urine.
Peptide & Glycoprotein Hormones & Analogues	Growth hormone and regulation of red blood cell production (example : rEPO, HGH).
Creatine & Supplements	Not drugs but health risks with excessive use.

TESTING PROCEDURES
- Random tests.
- Admission to all sports and performers.
- Sophisticated procedures.
- Which drugs are being taken?

CONCERNS ABOUT DRUGS in SPORT

Performance Enhancement
- Part of the win ethic and the right to excel.

Health Risk
- There has been little research into long-term damage.

Cheating
- It isn't fair for the unscrupulous to take advantage.

Illegal
- Some drugs are against the law, others against sporting regulations.

Role models
- Young people can be attracted to these unethical, dangerous drugs because their heroes take them, thus ceasing to be only a personal decision.

PUNISHMENT
- Temporary or permanent bans of performers.
- Punishment of coaches and ability to identify guilty officials.
- Punishment of governing bodies and Governments.

ADVERTISING and the SPORTS STAR

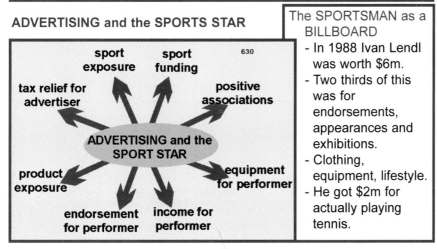

sport exposure
sport funding
630
tax relief for advertiser
positive associations
ADVERTISING and the SPORT STAR
product exposure
equipment for performer
endorsement for performer
income for performer

The SPORTSMAN as a BILLBOARD
- In 1988 Ivan Lendl was worth $6m.
- Two thirds of this was for endorsements, appearances and exhibitions.
- Clothing, equipment, lifestyle.
- He got $2m for actually playing tennis.

QUESTIONS

LEISURE and RECREATION

1) a) Leisure is a time in which there is opportunity for choice. Explain this definition of Leisure by Arnold, using your own examples. (4 marks)
b) There are four different theories on the place of leisure in various cultures. Details of these are to be found in Davis et al, PE and the Study of Sport.
    i) Briefly explain the implications of each of these. (8 marks)
    ii) Explain the relative importance of each one in this country. (4 marks)
c) What is implied when Kaplan suggests that leisure is more than an activity, it is also a worthwhile experience? (4 marks)
d) Select a recreation and explain its positive function in your life. (5 marks)

CONCEPTS and THEORIES of PLAY

2) a) Explain the concept of play using Huizinga's definition and the characteristics drawn from it. (5 marks)
b) Play can be described as a number of different things :
    i) Having observed a group of children at play, discuss freedom, reality, temporary significance, order and sharing. (5 marks)
    ii) Select an example from children's play and adult play and explain the different function of play in these two cases. (4 marks)
    iii) Use the picture of aboriginal children to explain play and display and explain this as an activity and as an experience. (4 marks)
c) There are many theories offered to explain play. Select any two of these theories and use a play activity to explain them. (3 marks)
d) Discuss the function behind children playing hide and seek in Britain as against an Aboriginal community in the Australian bush. (4 marks)

PHYSICAL RECREATION and SPORT

3) a) Use Edward's definition and the Physical Recreation model to:
    i) Explain the dimensions at which freedom operates in a physical recreation of your choice. (4 marks)
    ii) Describe Physical Recreation in the context of activity, experience and purposeful attitudes. (3 marks)
b) Select four activities to explain Caillois' classification of sports. (4 marks)
c) Coakley suggests that the definition of sport hinges on activity characteristics, organisational stringency and committed attitudes. Use his definition and the supporting model to discuss this theory. (6 marks)
d) There can be no sport without sportsmanship.
    i) Explain the meaning of a functional - dysfunctional continuum. (2 marks)
    ii) Use this concept to suggest ways in which a game tests the ability of a player to play fair. (6 marks)

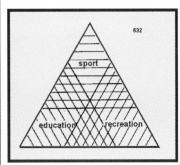

PHYSICAL EDUCATION and OUTDOOR RECREATION

4) a) i) Use the institutional pyramid to explain its three administrative sections. (3 marks)
    ii) Explain the three values, educative, sportive and recreative. (3 marks)
    iii) What is the significance of presenting this with the three triangles overlapping? (2 marks)
b) Discuss the extent to which the two definitions contradict the pyramid theory. (2 marks)
c) Select one of the core activities you have been taught on the PE curriculum and explain how physical, personal, preparation and qualitative values were likely to have been achieved. (8 marks)
d) i) Use the model on the right of Outdoor Education to explain the ways in which perceived risk is encouraged and real risk avoided whenever possible. (3 marks)
    ii) Take the example of a canoe trip or a mountain walk and explain levels of adventure which might occur. (4 marks)

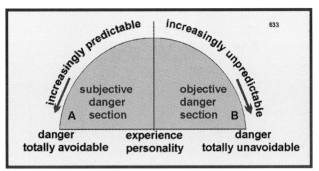

SPORT and CULTURE

5) a) Tribal cultures tend to retain a functional view of their sport. Explain why Western Samoan rugby is an adaptation of colonial rugby in a Polynesian style. (6 marks)
b) Kenyan athletics started as an extreme version of elitist sport.
    i) Explain the levels at which this elitism existed. (3 marks)
    ii) Link the development of this sport with the needs of an emergent nation. (4 marks)
c) Use the organisation of ice hockey in the USA and Russia to explain the differences between sport in each country. (6 marks)
d) Use the identified characteristics of high culture and low culture in the best behaviour to be found in rugby union and the worst behaviour to be found in professional soccer. (6 marks)

The CONTEMPORARY ISSUE of MASS PARTICIPATION in SPORT

6) a)   **i)** Use the diagram on the right to explain the transition of motives from recreative to sporting in the concept of Sport for All. (3 marks)
    ii) Use the diagram below left to explain the place of Sport for All in this pyramid and describe what should be happening at each level as far as mass participation in sport is concerned. (4 marks)

recreative ← SPORT FOR ALL → sportive *634*

b) Sport for All remains Sport for Some in the UK.
    i) Explain this statement in the context of opportunity. (3 marks)
    ii) Discuss the principle of access in terms of provision. (2 marks)
    iii) Explain the problem that certain groups of people lack the self-esteem to take a full part in sport. (3 marks)

performance pyramid *635*
excellence
performance
participation
foundation

c) Describe some of the campaigns adopted by the Countryside Commission to encourage a wider involvement in outdoor recreation. (4 marks)
d) Cultural factors may have determined the relative success of the Sport for All campaign. Link self-help, voluntarism and social ranking as factors which may have handicapped the development of mass participation in sport in this country. (6 marks)

SOCIETAL ISSUE: EXCELLENCE in SPORT

7) a) Many nations in the world recognise the value of sport in terms of national prestige by producing Olympic gold medals. Explain the existence of elitism in Ethiopia, Kenya and the UK. (6 marks)
b) Rugby Union has recently been professionalised.
    i) Identify the different types of participant in this process and explain the need for each to be professionalised. (4 marks)
    ii) Explain ways in which such values as endeavour, prowess, fair play and pleasure might be affected by the changes to professionalism. (5 marks)
c) Explain ways in which an agency like the National Coaching Foundation might influence recent initiatives. (4 marks)
d) Discuss the possible need to change the balance of private, voluntary and public funding for high level sport in this country. (6 marks)

8) Sport England with its Active Sports programmes has energised school sport.
a) Differentiate between the types of sports schools which have existed in the UK for a number of years, giving examples where possible. (6 marks)
b) Describe the main features of the sports college in England. (8 marks)
c) Explain the Active Sport programme in the context of schools, community and sport. (6 marks)
d) Discuss the role of different agencies in the promotion of Active Sport. (5 marks)

SUBCULTURAL ISSUES - SPORT and MINORITIES

9) a) Suggest reasons why rugby football is still only played by a small proportion of women. (4 marks)
b)   **i)** Explain the popularity of track and field athletics to Afro-Caribbean performers. (4 marks)
    ii) Explain the term 'stacking' in professional soccer in Britain and explain the absence of black supporters on the terraces. (5 marks)
c)   **i)** Discuss the problems which have arisen with young American tennis stars over the last decade. (4 marks)
    ii) The lowest participant gender age-group is women over 47. Explain this problem and suggest ways of overcoming it. (4 marks)
d) What are your views on able-bodied athletes playing wheelchair basketball? (4 marks)

SPECIFIC ISSUES in PE and SPORT

10) a)   **i)** Drug taking is a major issue in international sport. Select two types of drug used in sport and explain how they advantage performers who take them.

(6 marks)

ii) Explain four reasons why drugs should not be allowed in sport. (4 marks)

b)   **i)** We have an incomplete sports school system in the UK. What are the advantages of having a sports school system? (4 marks)

ii) Identify the types of sport school operating in this country and suggest their weaknesses. (4 marks)

c)   **i)** Some professional performers are little more than billboards. What are the benefits of advertising to the performer? (3 marks)

ii) Explain the positive and negative associations between sport and a product like tobacco. (4 marks)

ANSWERS

The answer for each mark awarded is notated by the ❏ symbol - where there are more ❏ symbols than there are marks available, marks would be given for any choice up to the maximum available. Usually, the precise wording specified in an answer would not be required - answers with the same meaning would be acceptable.

LEISURE and RECREATION

1) a)
Leisure is a time in which there is the opportunity for choice. Explain this definition of Leisure by Arnold, using your own examples.
   4 marks for :
❏ Free time is a fundamental element of leisure.
❏ Where you decide what to do and how long to do it.
❏ Opportunity to engage in a leisure situation is a central factor and although provision for leisure may exist, it must exist for you.
❏ Choices must be yours whether to engage in leisure or not, what activity you want to do, and who you want to share it with.

1) b) i)
There are four different theories on the place of leisure in various cultures.
Briefly explain the implications of these.
   2 marks for two points made on the theory : Leisure as a spare time Activity.
❏ Work is high status and leisure is low.
❏ Intellectual and purposeful activities are important and practical leisure activities not serious.
❏ Recreation is unimportant.
❏ Inactivity leads to laziness and temptations.
   2 marks for two points made on the theory : Leisure as an Economic Condition.
❏ Traditional class stratification of society.
❏ Leisured class has the right to leisure.
❏ Working class has to work to win the right to leisure.
❏ Basis of productivity and status in the work-place.
❏ Disadvantages extended into disadvantaged sub-cultures, for example, working class women.
   2 marks for two points made on the theory : Leisure as a form of Social Control.
❏ A purposeful interpretation of leisure.
❏ Development of a society influenced by leisure patterns.
❏ As reflected in equal social status or political rights or cultural identity.
❏ As a social process available for each citizen.
❏ Enabling increased production or healthy living or social control.
   2 marks for two points made on the theory : Leisure as a basis of Creative Fulfilment.
❏ Personal freedom to have choices.
❏ Personal development in terms of self-realisation.
❏ Socialization arising out of the leisure experience.
❏ Cultural awareness increasing the quality of life.

LEISURE and RECREATION - ANSWERS QUESTION 1 (continued)

1) b) ii)

Explain the relative importance of each one in this country.

4 marks for :

❏ Leisure as a spare time activity is traditional in the UK, reflecting the Protestant work ethic or life in an industrialised society.

❏ Leisure as an economic condition is also traditional reflecting the British class system.

❏ Leisure as a form of social control while part of our Welfare State has lost ground with the demise of socialism and the rise of market economics and materialism.

❏ Leisure as a basis for creative fulfilment is an ideal strived for by radical politicians, social reformers and educators, but limited by traditional policies and values.

1) c)

What is implied when Kaplan suggests that leisure is more than an activity, it is also a worthwhile experience?

4 marks for :

❏ Activity implies that it is something you do...an action word.

❏ It facilitates, giving an individual opportunity or a vehicle which allows experience to occur.

❏ Experience is the human element where changes occur as a result of participation.

❏ It has the potential to be worthwhile because learning takes place which can be valuable.

1) d)

Select a recreation and explain its positive function in your life.

❏ 1 mark for selecting a suitable recreation and using it as part of the explanation.

4 marks for four of the possible functions that experience might have :

❏ The recreation gives you freedom and opportunity to choose what to do in your free time.

❏ To gain physically and mentally from the activity you indulge in.

❏ To experience a range of fulfilling emotions.

❏ To experience a range of decision-making opportunities.

❏ To creatively learn more about yourself.

❏ And have the opportunity to socialize.

CONCEPTS and THEORIES of PLAY

2) a)

Explain the concept of play using Huizinga's definition and the characteristics drawn from it.

5 marks for five from :

❏ Play is an activity with immediate pleasure and no ulterior motive.

❏ Use of time and space is based on freedom / consensus.

❏ Only intrinsic values exist and so there are no material gains.

❏ The activity is spontaneous and has a minimal number of rules.

❏ It is presumed to be non-serious because there are no apparent outcomes in our society which is work orientated.

❏ The emotion of enjoyment is central to the activity in that play is fun.

2) b) i)

Play can be described as a number of different things:

Having observed a group of children at play, discuss freedom, reality, temporary significance, order and sharing.

5 marks for :

❏ Freedom exists in the use of time and space, in the choice of activities, and in who plays.

❏ Reality hardly exists in play because it is largely make-believe and there are few consequences.

❏ Temporary significance exists because when the play ends the value of play ends.

❏ Order is achieved because the play has objectives and limited rules.

❏ Sharing is normally involved because play involves mutual consent.

2) b) ii)

Select an example from children's play and adult play and explain the different function of play in these two cases.

2 marks for two from :

❏ In a skipping game children increase their mastery over reality by :
  ❏ Learning to perform successfully in a safe environment.
  ❏ Learning to play together.
  ❏ Experiencing various emotions and learning how to cope with them.
  ❏ Learning a lot about themselves.

CONCEPTS and THEORIES of PLAY - ANSWERS QUESTION 2 (continued)

2) b) ii) (continued)
Select an example from children's play and adult play and explain the different function of play in these two cases.

   2 marks for two from :
- ❑ In playing a game of squash adults escape from reality because :
  - ❑ They are releasing the tensions of their working and domestic life.
  - ❑ They are relaxing and enjoying themselves.
  - ❑ They are experiencing new creative moments of activity.

2) b) iii)
Use the picture of aboriginal children to explain play and display and explain this as an activity and an experience.

   4 marks for :
- ❑ Play elements reflect intrinsic values such as fun, friendship and healthy activity.
- ❑ While display is a reflection of extrinsic, normally visual elements of ritual, skill in performance and functional usefulness.
- ❑ The activity of play is what they are doing, the vehicle of purposeful movement.
- ❑ The experience of play is what they are learning from it which will change them as people.

2) c)
There are many theories offered to explain play. Select any two of these theories and use a play activity to explain them.
- ❑ One mark for selecting a feasible play activity and applying it, for example : 'Cowboys and Indians'.
     2 marks for two from :
- ❑ Civilisation preparation : they are playing a game which tests their loyalty to a cause.
- ❑ Role rehearsal : they are practising for future conflicts which question their identity.
- ❑ Instinctive practice : they are expressing their natural aggression.
- ❑ Surplus energy : using energy in an exciting vigorous way.
- ❑ Recapitulation : these rivalries are part of our heritage.
- ❑ Transmission of culture : play is a way of copying cultural characteristics in a non-serious way.
- ❑ Personality development : we learn a great deal in play which develops and changes our make-up.
- ❑ Cathartic function : it helps us to release inhibitions and heal mental wounds.
- ❑ Ego expansion : the imaginative nature and free expression of play helps individuals to learn more about themselves and express their needs.

2) d)
Discuss the function behind children playing hide and seek in Britain as against an Aboriginal community in the Australian bush.

   4 marks for any four pairings of:

British :	Aboriginal :
❑ Non-serious and playful :	❑ Serious in respect of finding anyone lost :
❑ A chase competition.	❑ A co-operative effort.
❑ A fun environment.	❑ A hostile environment.
❑ To win by getting 'home'.	❑ To survive by finding 'home'.
❑ Learning to compromise.	❑ Learning to hunt.

PHYSICAL RECREATION and SPORT

3) a) i)
Use Edward's definition and the Physical Recreation model to :
Explain the dimensions at which freedom operates in a physical recreation of your choice.
   Example : bathing in a community leisure pool.
   4 marks for four from :
- ❑ As we play, freedom is reflected in our use of time - we choose how long we play, but this may be influenced by cost and regulations.
- ❑ Our use of the space is not conditioned - except by the facility itself.
- ❑ You are free to choose your activity and the people you play with.
- ❑ These opportunities are available to you as a member of the community.
- ❑ You are free to satisfy your needs whether they are creative or 'relaxatory'.

PHYSICAL RECREATION and SPORT - ANSWERS QUESTION 3 (continued)

3) a) ii)
Describe Physical Recreation in the context of activity, experience and purposeful attitudes.
   3 marks for :
❑ Physical recreation consists of a number of activities which have a major physical component and as such they act as a vehicle for performance.
❑ Experience is the human element, where knowledge and values are gained through recreating in the activity.
❑ Purposeful attitudes arise as an anticipation of experiencing the activity, as an expression during the experience of it, and as a reflection of what it had felt like.

3) b)
Select four activities to explain Caillois' classification of sports.
   4 marks for :
❑ Competition in a social game of lawn tennis : it may involve an individual in personal challenges, sharing strategies with a partner, engagement in contests in rallies, and endeavouring to win the game.
❑ Pretence occurring in a football kick-about : in addition to imaginative moments of personal play, make-believe can occur when we adopt the identities and behaviourisms of our heroes, we even attempt to sell dummies and celebrate a goal as if it were in the F.A. Cup Final.
❑ Chance is present in all sport : going fishing with friends has the chance elements of favourable weather and water conditions, finding and catching the fish, and whether you or your friends catch them.
❑ Vertigo is common with mountain walking : the effort of climbing, particularly at altitude gives you a sense of 'headiness', you may actually become giddy when exposed on a high crag, and the climax of the climb when you reach the top is often a mixture of wonder and exultation.

3) c)
Coakley suggests that the definition of sport hinges on activity characteristics, organisational stringency and committed attitudes. Use this definition and the supporting model to discuss this theory.
   6 marks for six from :
❑ Certain activities have been traditionally identified as sports.
❑ When a recreation becomes a sport extrinsic values are added to the intrinsic values which exist at a recreative level.
❑ At an administrative level, a recreation becomes a sport when a well organised system of clubs and governing bodies exist.
❑ And when the activity is fully codified and regulated.
❑ A sportive experience involves committed attitudes and the expectation of a high standard of performance.
❑ With sport there is a need for sportsmanship at a highly developed level and where bad behaviour is punished.

3) d) i)
There can be no sport without sportsmanship. Explain the meaning of a functional - dysfunctional continuum.
   2 marks for :
❑ Functional is where the activity is seen to be a socially valuable experience; this can exist as a very positive influence or become progressively socially undesirable.
❑ Dysfunctional, where behaviour is antisocial and the activity can have a negative effect on social standards.

3) d) ii)
Use the model on functional and dysfunctional behaviour to suggest ways in which a game tests the ability of a player to play fair.
   6 marks for :
❑ At the highest functional level, a player makes personal ethical decisions, for example, 'walking' if out in cricket.
❑ Playing within the true spirit of the game, for example, only appealing in cricket if you are confident that you took a fair catch in cricket.
❑ Accepting the letter of the law, i.e. the umpire's decision.
❑ Playing to win with no moral intention, appeal for anything in cricket.
❑ Selfish disregard of the rules, for example, deliberately bowling wide.
❑ Disregard for others, for example, bowling beamers at weaker lower order batsmen.

| PHYSICAL EDUCATION and OUTDOOR EDUCATION

4) a) i)
Use the institutional pyramid to explain the three administrative sections to it.
   This is a triangle representing physical activity in a school or college. The three inner triangles have administrative associations with (3 marks for) :
❏ Education, which concerns PE as a compulsory curriculum subject.
❏ Sport, which refers to organised, optional extra-curricular sport activities.
❏ Recreation, which reflects activities freely engaged in by children in non-curriculum time.

4) a) ii)
Explain the three values, educative, sportive and recreative.
   3 marks for :
❏ Educative, identifies the knowledge and values which the teachers give the children as part of their necessary development.
❏ Sportive, identifies the desirable knowledge and values which sports can offer young people wishing to improve their performance and control their temperament through sport.
❏ Recreative, recognises the intrinsic values of opportunities to indulge in unstructured physical activities.

4) a) iii)
What is the significance of presenting this with the three triangles overlapping?
   2 marks for :
❏ The three motives should be identifiable at each administrative level, though one motive is likely to dominate.
❏ There should be an integrative and re-enforcing function to all levels of physical activity in school or college.

4) b)
Discuss the extent to which the two definitions contradict the pyramid theory.
   2 marks for :
❏ The definitions fail to identify sport and physical recreation as part of physical education in terms of their placement on the curriculum.
❏ Consequently, it suggests that extra-curricular sport and recreational activities do not / need not reflect the (manifest) values of PE, but can include less desirable values often found in sport and recreation in society. (The pyramid includes all three in a broader interpretation of school PE and is reflected in recent Australian projects.)

4) c)
Select one of the core activities you have been taught on the PE curriculum and explain how physical, personal preparation and qualitative values were likely to have been achieved.
   Individual activities like swimming and athletics being used as the example :
   2 marks for two from : (physical development values)
❏ Healthy exercise facilitating regular activity as a swimmer or athlete.
❏ Physical fitness involving endurance, strength and suppleness in increasing performance potential in swimming and / or athletics.
❏ Skilfulness to allow participation in bathing and athletic activity.
❏ Skills developed to a level of expertise to improve competitive performance.
   2 marks for two from : (personal development values)
❏ Testing oneself to increase one's self-knowledge and confidence.
❏ Performing with others to increase social awareness.
❏ Decision-making in social and competitive situations, increasing cognitive development.
❏ Opportunities to make sound ethical decisions.
❏ Emotional experiences leading to self-control and pleasurable occasions.
   2 marks for two from : (preparation for the future values)
❏ Preparation for active leisure in aquatics and athletics.
❏ Preparation for high level sporting achievement in swimming or athletics at club and / or representative level.
❏ Improve fitness and health for work.
❏ Preparation for a career in leisure and / or sport.
   2 marks for two from : (qualitative values)
❏ Enriching experiences which encourage creativity.
❏ Enriching experiences which encourage appreciation and sensitivity.
❏ Commitment leading to achievement.
❏ Commitment reflecting and re-enforcing vitality.

PHYSICAL EDUCATION and OUTDOOR EDUCATION - ANSWERS QUESTION (4 continued)

4) d) i)
Use the model on Outdoor Education to explain the ways in which perceived risk is encouraged and real risk avoided whenever possible.
   3 marks for :
❐ Perceived risk is an essential element of adventure.
❐ Adding excitement to experiencing the unexpected.
❐ Real risk has to be avoided wherever possible in OE by careful planning and by good leadership.

4) d) ii)
Take the example of a canoe trip or a mountain walk and explain levels of adventure which might occur.
   4 marks for :
❐ Confidence building procedures in new experiences, (canoe / mountain walk).
❐ Exciting tests of skill and confidence in difficult situations, (safe white-water rapids / scrambling on rocky crags).
❐ Perceived risk stretching individuals to new frontiers, (difficult manoeuvres in white-water / rock climbs in exposed situations).
❐ Misadventure - dangerously encouraging real risks to be taken, (ignoring safety procedures in dangerous water / allowing individuals to go beyond their capabilities).

SPORT and CULTURE

5) a)
Tribal cultures tend to retain a functional view of their sport. Explain why Western Samoan rugby is an adaptation of colonial rugby in a Polynesian style.
   6 marks for six from :
❐ The game of rugby was brought to Samoa by English colonialists and played by them.
❐ With ethnic sports and pastimes curtailed, they had little choice other than to adopt the game.
❐ Rugby involved aggressive physical contact and this reflected the pre-colonial lifestyle of the Samoans.
❐ As small communities with limited institutions they found small game versions, 7-a-side matches, more suited to their old tribal games.
❐ The desire to beat colonial countries at their own game was strong.
❐ In communities where the festival was central, the game took on a festival dimension.
❐ The ritual applied to ancient festivals was applied to rugby, as in the haka.

5) b) i)
Kenyan athletics started as an extreme version of elitist sport. Explain the levels at which this elitism existed.
   3 marks for three from :
❐ Athletics as a sport started as a colonial sport, not available to Africans.
❐ Only middle distance running was developed.
❐ Athletics was the only sport which was funded.
❐ The events only supported certain tribes in the hill-country.
❐ Only men were initially encouraged.
❐ The activity only suited a certain somatotype.
❐ It was the natural occupational activity of the high plains.

5) b) ii)
Link the subsequent development of this sport with the needs of an emergent nation.
   4 marks for four from :
❐ It gave the people in this part of Kenya an objective to attain.
❐ When champions existed they acted as role models.
❐ It reflected well on the government and national leaders.
❐ It brought the various tribes together under a national flag.
❐ It increased the health of the nation.
❐ With most of the runners members of the army or police, it had a law and order influence.
❐ The world stage of the Olympic Games gave the Kenyans exposure to the world's media and international respect for the government and the people.
❐ The athletes themselves brought money back to the country and became coaches in their own right.
❐ Success led to top women athletes and a transitional role for the female.

SPORT and CULTURE - ANSWERS QUESTION 5 (continued)

5) c)

Use the organisation of ice hockey in the USA and Russia to explain the differences between sport in each country.

  6 marks for six from :

USA :
- ❏ Top players are professional and earn huge sums of money.
- ❏ This money is paid for by results, but also by advertising.
- ❏ Top clubs are businesses and run to make money on a commercial basis.
- ❏ Spectators expect excitement, violence, spectacle and victory as part of their entertainment.

Russia :
- ❏ Top players received regular pay, but far less than the US professionals.
- ❏ They were not free to join any clubs, but represented a community.
- ❏ Focus was on skill because violence was not acceptable at a political level.
- ❏ Clubs were sponsored through trade unions rather than commercially and through spectators who were expected to behave well.

5) d)

Use the identified characteristics of high culture and low culture in the best behaviour to be found in rugby union and the worst behaviour to be found in professional soccer.

  6 marks for six from :

Rugby and high culture :
- ❏ A game played by gentlemen.
- ❏ Played according to the spirit of the game.
- ❏ Referee never questioned.
- ❏ Well behaved spectators who applaud good play.

Soccer and low culture :
- ❏ Players prepared to injure each other deliberately.
- ❏ And practise gamesmanship.
- ❏ Referees abused by players and fans.
- ❏ Violence in the crowd on the terraces and out of the ground.

CONTEMPORARY ISSUE of MASS PARTICIPATION in SPORT

6) a) i)

Use the diagram to explain the transition of motives from recreative to sportive in the concept of Sport for All.

  3 marks for three from :

- ❏ Sport for All is a wide concept which embraces recreative and sportive motives.
- ❏ It is up to the individual or the group he / she is playing with to decide when to switch from one to the other.
- ❏ Recreative motives are based on freedom to choose (what to do / who to play with / what attitudes to involve).
- ❏ Sportive motives tend to be more controlled and committed (how competitive to be / how organised the activity should be / how much effort and prowess is needed).

6) a) ii)

Use the diagram to explain the place of Sport for All in this pyramid and describe what should be happening at each level as far as mass participation in sport is concerned.

  4 marks for four from :

- ❏ Sport for All is a necessary ingredient of all sport and is a necessary factor in achieving individual excellence.
- ❏ Foundation involves the experience of wide ranging physical activity together with the development of positive attitudes.
- ❏ Participation involves the opportunity to choose what to do and who to play with and is influenced by the level of provision available and your level of personal esteem.
- ❏ Performance involves the desire and ability to achieve a high personal standard of endeavour, prowess and sporting attitudes.
- ❏ Excellence achieving the highest personal standards in specific activities in the public arena.

6 b) i)

Sport for All remains Sport for Some in the UK. Explain this statement in the context of opportunity.

  3 marks for three from :
  (not everyone has the opportunity to participate in sport because :)

- ❏ They are excluded from certain sports because of their class, race or gender.
- ❏ They are excluded because they lack the basic level of ability expected.
- ❏ They cannot afford to participate.
- ❏ People who are involved will not make them welcome or they lack contacts.

CONTEMPORARY ISSUE of MASS PARTICIPATION in SPORT - ANSWERS QUESTION (6 continued)

6 b) ii)
Discuss the principle of access in terms of provision.
    2 marks for two from :
- ❑ The building excludes you as with steps and wheelchair users.
- ❑ The rules of the organisation exclude you as in restricted membership or price.
- ❑ The facility is too far away, in other words distance excludes you.

6) b) iii)
Explain the problem that certain groups of people lack the self-esteem to take a full part in sport.
    3 marks for three from :
    (How you see yourself)
- ❑ You feel you are not good enough in ability terms.
- ❑ You are not confident enough to put yourself in a sport situation.
    (How you perceive sport and yourself)
- ❑ It may adversely affect your image and so you avoid it.
- ❑ It can harm you physically and so you exclude it from your intentions.
    (How you think others perceive you and sport)
- ❑ You feel you would not be welcomed; you feel you may be ridiculed.

6 c)
Describe some of the campaigns adopted by the Countryside Commission to encourage a wider involvement in outdoor recreation.
    4 marks for four from :
- ❑ Setting up the 10 National Parks by 1955 (anticipated the Countryside Commission being set up in 1968, but worth a mark).
- ❑ Establishment of picnic sites throughout the country.
- ❑ Maintenance of footpaths and setting up long distance pathways.
- ❑ Establishing country parks and wild life parks.
- ❑ Establishing the heritage coastline.

6) d)
Cultural factors may have determined the relative success of the Sport for All campaign. Link self-help, voluntarism and social ranking as factors which may have handicapped the development of mass participation in sport in this country.
    6 marks for six from : (maximum of 2 marks from each sub-group).
    Self help :
- ❑ Self-help was a 19th century policy where people without means should make the effort themselves to achieve things in life.
- ❑ It handicapped because it left the poor and the excluded to struggle rather than be helped to engage in sport.
- ❑ But it produced a route for improvement based on effort.
    Voluntarism :
- ❑ Is the notion that we should pay for our own sport rather than depend on the state (this is a natural extension of the self-help principle).
- ❑ A middle class ethic, it means that only those who are committed to sport and have the financial means, will carry this through into the next generation.
- ❑ It is necessary to encourage private (commercial sponsorship) and public (state aid) to encourage those not committed to sport to become interested.
    Social ranking :
- ❑ Historically sports have been socially exclusive, either excluding the lower classes or seen to be undesirable by the middle classes.
- ❑ This limits the notion of all sports for all people.
- ❑ Social ranking today is not just class ranking, but can mean ethnic, gender, age and ability. Ranking continues to exist in sport and is therefore a constraint on achieving Sport for All objectives.

SOCIETAL ISSUE : EXCELLENCE in SPORT

7) a)

Many nations in the world recognise the value of sport in terms of national prestige by producing Olympic gold medallists. Use the diagram to explain the existence of elitism in Ethiopia, Kenya and Britain.

6 marks for six from : (maximum of 2 marks from each sub-group) :

Ethiopia :

- ❑ Only sufficient money for one sport in such a poor country.
- ❑ Marathon running chosen because it is natural to the people.
- ❑ Men only trained initially.
- ❑ Non-technical event and so cheap to operate.
- ❑ Success brought world exposure and gave the people role models to follow.

Kenya :

- ❑ Success / world recognition has led to extending the elite activities to include games.
- ❑ Role models have produced a wider range of athletic events.
- ❑ Female champions are now emerging.
- ❑ Finalists in African Football Championships and success in World Cricket Championships.
- ❑ Wider involvement of people with different somatotypes.
- ❑ Resulting in integration of different tribal groups and regional groups.

Britain :

- ❑ As a wealthy country elitism should not exist.
- ❑ Opportunity, provision and esteem should exist.
- ❑ An administrative system should bring all potential top performers into a selection process and advanced programme.
- ❑ Traditional discrimination in our class system.
- ❑ Social discrimination against gender and ethnic groups.
- ❑ Problems with programmes for the young, bringing them through to excellence.

7) b) i)

Rugby Union has recently been professionalised. Identify the different types of participant in this process and explain the need for each to be professionalised.

4 marks for four from : (one mark for each sub-group) :

Players :   ❑ Amount of money negotiated at market value / standard of player and level of league.

Administrators :   ❑ Individuals who are knowledgeable about the game, but professionally qualified and paid to fulfil their specific role in the club or governing body.

Officials / Coaches :❑ Well paid and fully qualified referees and linesman, with paid time to establish high standards of performance and fitness / well qualified, professional coaches.

Spectators :   ❑ Opportunities to buy shares in the club.
   ❑ Influence on policy.
   ❑ High standards of behaviour maintained.
   ❑ Funding club through gate money and social activities.

7) b) ii)

Explain ways in which such values as endeavour, prowess, fair play and pleasure might be affected by the changes to professionalism.

5 marks for five from : (at least one mark from each sub-group) :

Endeavour :
- ❑ Contracted to be fit.
- ❑ Attend scheduled fitness programmes.
- ❑ Meet the expectations of the management in effort terms.

Prowess :
- ❑ A higher skill performance expected.
- ❑ Dependable standards maintained during games.
- ❑ Considerable effort to improve skills during practices.
- ❑ Co-operation and implementation of tactics.

Fair play :
- ❑ Pressure to win leading to gamesmanship.
- ❑ Possible prosecution for excessively violent play.
- ❑ Possible questioning of referee's decisions.

Pleasure :
- ❑ With salary at stake playing well is a major worry.
- ❑ Game is now work and so serious.
- ❑ Play is more physical and pain and injury more likely.

SOCIETAL ISSUE : EXCELLENCE in SPORT - ANSWERS QUESTION 7 (continued)

7) c)

Explain ways in which an agency like the National Coaching Foundation might influence recent initiatives.
4 marks for four from :

- ❑ The NCF might be given major operational responsibilities by the Sports Council.
- ❑ Coaching may be seen to be the way to improve our standards & that is the acknowledged role of the NCF.
- ❑ NCF is responsible for producing programmes of coaching at all levels and lottery money is available through them to sponsor coaches and coaching courses.
- ❑ NCF has money to sponsor teachers to attend coaching courses.
- ❑ NCF is responsible for promoting the use of lottery money to sponsor athletes as well as coaches.

7) d)

Discuss the need to change the balance of private, voluntary & public funding for high level sport in this country.
6 marks for six from : (two marks for each sub-section) :

Private :
- ❑ There is a tradition of sport being private in this country with private amateur clubs and limited liability professional clubs.
- ❑ This has reflected social class and gender stratification and limited opportunity and provision for some groups.
- ❑ Private funding / commercial sponsorship is in line with this country's market economy.
- ❑ But sponsors are attracted to the successful few as is the media.

Voluntary :
- ❑ This involves individuals paying for provision and / or giving their services for nothing.
- ❑ This amateur approach because of its inefficiency is increasingly outmoded.
- ❑ Subscriptions can usefully increase funds and give a sense of ownership.
- ❑ But can be exclusive if fees and expenses are high.
- ❑ No longer meets the financial needs of professional clubs and teams.

Public :
- ❑ Government aid given non-politically is likely to be more balanced and part of an overall plan.
- ❑ In Britain, sport has been politically low status and so Government funding has been inadequate to compare with other sporting nations.
- ❑ The lottery is a major financial aid which can be distributed fairly.
- ❑ It will enable innovations to be put in place and reduce the extent of voluntary contributions to achieve excellence.
- ❑ A mixed economy, one would require a balance of public money and private sponsorship.

8) a)

Sport England with its Active Sports programmes has energised school sport. Differentiate between the types of sports schools which have existed in the UK for a number of years, giving examples where possible.
6 marks for six from :

- ❑ Public schools specialising in sport.
- ❑ Such as Millfield School.
- ❑ These schools offer scholarships to promising young sportspeople.
- ❑ Centres of excellence.
- ❑ Such as Lilleshall.
- ❑ Where a football school has been run by the FA / a gymnastics school has been run by the AGA.
- ❑ Academies for football and rugby league.
- ❑ Such as Premier League soccer clubs.
- ❑ Sunday morning training for young local footballers.
- ❑ Junior clubs / sections in hockey, rugby and tennis.
- ❑ Colt teams in leading rugby union clubs.

8) b)

Describe the main features of the sports college in England.
8 marks for eight from :

- ❑ Specialist schools recognised by the D of E and E.
- ❑ Target of 200 sports colleges by the year 2002.
- ❑ Application open to schools with 11-16 year old pupils.
- ❑ Matching policy applies : private funding from the school matched by Government grant.
- ❑ Additional per capita funding of £100 per annum.
- ❑ Funding to increase staffing and resources.
- ❑ Must establish a major partnership with the community.
- ❑ College staff to visit and support primary feeder schools in the area.
- ❑ College to act as a beacon to other secondary / tertiary schools in the area giving advice and help.
- ❑ Required to introduce at least three new activities to the area.
- ❑ Meet stringent academic / examination targets and sports targets.

SOCIETAL ISSUE : EXCELLENCE in SPORT - ANSWERS QUESTION 8 (continued)

8) c)

Explain the Active Sport programme in the context of schools, community and sport.

6 marks for six from :

Schools :

❐ NCF controlled Coaching for Teachers courses.

❐ Sportsmark programme for secondary schools.

❐ Activemark programmes for primary / middle schools.

❐ TOPSPORT and TOPPLAY support programmes for primary children.

❐ Appointment of sports development officers / paid jointly by local authorities and Sport England.

Community :

❐ Focus on underprivileged areas.

❐ Community awards and competitions for young people.

Sports :

❐ Sports administration jointly by schools, governing bodies, clubs and local authorities.

❐ Five year development programme produced by Sport England.

❐ Nine priority sports for development, athletics, rugby union, basketball, cricket, girls football, netball, hockey, swimming, and tennis.

8) d)

Discuss the role of different agencies on the promotion of Active Sport.

5 marks for five from :

❐ Sport England is the leading authority and controls policy, documentation and funding.

❐ Much of the funding and planning is now in the hands of the local authority.

❐ Sport England and the Local Authority jointly employ Sports Development Officers to organise and operate the programmes.

❐ The National Coaching Foundation provides coaching courses in a wide range of sports.

❐ This is where the Coaching for Teachers programmes are highlighted.

❐ The Youth Sports Trust is responsible for major policy and planning decisions as well as funding scrutiny.

❐ Governing Bodies promote their own sport and supply coaching programmes and expertise.

❐ This is often dependent on interaction with local clubs.

SUB-CULTURAL ISSUES : SPORT and MINORITIES

9) a)

Suggest reasons why rugby football is still only played by a small proportion of women.

4 marks for four from : (ideally developed under following three headings) :

Opportunity :❐ Most girls do not learn the game at school.

❐ There are virtually no women-only rugby clubs.

❐ Still limited number of men's clubs running women's teams.

Provision : ❐ Facilities are not readily available for women.

❐ There are very few female coaches.

❐ The media fails to give the women's game any coverage.

❐ Sponsorship is limited.

Esteem : ❐ It is traditionally a man's game, organised by men.

❐ Women generally regard themselves to be too physically weak to play the game.

❐ They feel to play is to threaten their feminine image.

❐ Rejected as unsuitable by many men.

9) b) i)

Explain the popularity of track and field athletics to Afro-Caribbean (A-C) performers.

4 marks for four from :

❐ A-C role models make it attractive to young A-C performers.

❐ An inexpensive sport, basics are taught in all schools, top A-C performers and coaches give time and encouragement to help the next generation.

❐ A dream of making a break out, financially and socially.

❐ Natural athletic interest and potential.

❐ Popular for young males and females.

❐ Colourful and sponsored activity.

SUB-CULTURAL ISSUES : SPORT and MINORITIES - ANSWERS QUESTION 9 (continued)

9) b) ii)
Explain the term 'stacking' in professional soccer in Britain and explain the absence of black supporters on the terraces.

    1 mark to explain stacking :
- ❏ Society is still ranked socially in Britain and the same applies to some sports where white performers have an advantage over black.
- ❏ This applies less to football players, but does influence coaching, management ownership and spectator groupings.

    2 marks for two from :
- ❏ Professional football was traditionally dominated by white players.
- ❏ It was regarded as an Anglo-Saxon game, even with the emergence of black players.
- ❏ Certain positions in the centre of the field of play tended to be retained by white players.
- ❏ Adverse attitudes remained among managers and white players as a resistance to black players breaking through.
- ❏ Enthusiasm for the game and the potential wealth from success led to black professional players.
- ❏ Role models have now made the game attractive.

    2 marks for two from :
- ❏ The terraces have traditionally belonged to working class supporters.
- ❏ They have traditionally been violent and emotional, displaying hooligan tendencies against opposition teams.
- ❏ Any visual (black) feature is an excuse for verbal abuse.
- ❏ Racism is expressed on the terraces despite action by authorities.
- ❏ Fear for safety, particularly of families, any black groups would be outnumbered and 'set on' outside the ground.

9) c) i)
Discuss the problems which have arisen with young American tennis stars over the last decade.

    4 marks for four from :

Problems :   ❏ Too much localised explosive movement causes injury.
             ❏ Too much early years play wears out body, a high stress factor can psychologically burn them out.
             ❏ Focus on one sport excludes alternative activities, too serious, too early, excludes play attitudes and fun.

Needs :   ❏ Feeling that to reach the top, players must start young.
             ❏ Pressure from coaches who have girls at most 'focused' age.
             ❏ Pressure from parents to have winners in a win ethic society.
             ❏ Considerable potential financial rewards.

9) c) ii)
The lowest participant gender age-group is women over 47. Explain this problem and suggest ways of overcoming it.

    4 marks for four from :

Problem :   ❏ When young these women tended not to participate in sport.
                 ❏ Many were fully occupied rearing their families.
                 ❏ The gap in sporting activity after leaving school has eroded confidence to start again / limited self-esteem in this situation.
                 ❏ Access to provision limited.
                 ❏ Types of activities for that gender age-group limited.

Ways of overcoming : ❏ Increase marketing / advertising for this group.
                 ❏ Educate younger women into the need for lifetime sport.

9) d)
What are your views on able-bodied athletes playing wheelchair basketball?

    4 marks for four from :
- ❏ If wheelchair athletes agree to it then so be it.
- ❏ It is up to the Governing Bodies to decide.
- ❏ If it encourages wheelchair users to play.
- ❏ The advantage lies with genuine wheelchair users, given their strength and skills in the chairs, self-esteem will be increased.
- ❏ May lead to more facilities becoming available.
- ❏ May increase sponsorship and improve marketing.
- ❏ May increase understanding of special needs in sport.

    (Counter views arising from these should be taken into account / accepted, but no extra marks).

SPECIFIC ISSUES IN PE AND SPORT

10) a) i)

Select two types of drug used in sport and explain how they advantage performers who take them.

3 marks for each of two types with explanations :

❏ Stimulants.

Advantages : 2 marks for two from :

❏ Increased alertness. ❏ Reduced fatigue. ❏ Increased competitiveness. ❏ Increased hostility.

❏ Narcotics.

Advantages : 2 marks :

❏ Management of severe pain. ❏ Removal of mental stress.

❏ Steroids.

Advantages : 2 marks for two from :

❏ Increased muscle strength. ❏ Increased muscle bulk. ❏ Promote aggressiveness.

❏ Diuretics.

Advantages : 2 marks :

❏ Reduces weight quickly. ❏ Masking agent.

❏ Peptides etc.

Advantages : 2 marks :

❏ Growth hormones. ❏ Promotes growth of body tissues such as muscle and bones.

❏ Beta Blockers.

Advantages : 2 marks :

❏ Reduces heart rate. ❏ Calming effect.

10) a) ii)

Explain four reasons why drugs should not be allowed in sport.

4 marks for four from :

❏ Banning : can deny athletes the chance to perform.

❏ Cheating : unfair advantage is being taken of other performers.

❏ Role models : others may copy their heroes and endanger themselves.

❏ Risk : possibility of serious damage being done to the body / personality.

❏ Illegal : it is against the regulations of the sport / it may also be against the law.

10) b) i)

What are the advantages of having a sports school system?

4 marks for four from :

❏ Early selection of promising young performers.

❏ Opportunity to spend time with a group of enthusiastic young people.

❏ Opportunity to put the youngsters in ideal facilities.

❏ Use of expert coaches for specialist training programmes.

❏ Opportunity for more competitions.

10) b) ii)

Identify the types of sport school operating in this country and suggest their weaknesses.

4 marks for four from :

❏ Governing body centres of excellence : not available in all sports.

❏ Sports associations : only available after school / poor sponsorship.

❏ Specific public schools : tend to be elitist due to fees, even though bursaries are available.

❏ Individual clubs : (Manchester United) only functions for club members on a Sunday morning.

❏ Individual sports : rugby and tennis are well organised in clubs, but other sports not well organised / no opportunities if you aren't a club member.

10) c) i)

What are the benefits of advertising to the performer?

3 marks for :

❏ Can make a large income from it.

❏ Can get free equipment from the firm.

❏ Can get publicity through endorsements.

Answers

SPECIFIC ISSUES IN PE AND SPORT - ANSWERS QUESTION 10 (continued)

10) c) ii)

Explain the positive and negative associations between sport and a product like tobacco.

  2 marks for two from :

  Positive :

❑ Income of sponsorship to the sport.

❑ Allows them to pay performers more.

❑ Gives the product publicity / exposure.

❑ Gives the product tax relief.

  2 marks for two from :

  Negative :

❑ Healthy sport associated associated with unhealthy pastime like smoking.

❑ Role model association.

❑ Debate can give product bad publicity.

Bob Davis

SELECTED BIBLIOGRAPHY

Armstrong, N. (Ed)   1996   New Dimensions in Physical Education. Cassell.

Calhoun, D.W.   1987   Sport, Culture and Personality.   Human Kinetics.

Cashmore, E.   2000   Making Sense of Sport 3e.   Routledge.

Coakley, J.J.   2001   Sport in Society 7e. McGraw-Hill.

Coe, S. et.al.   1992   More than a Game.   BBC Publications.

Davis, R.J. et.al.   2000   Physical Education and the Study of Sport 4e.   Mosby.

Davis, R.J.   2000   Contemporary Issues, Teachers' Guides to Physical Education and the Study of Sport 4e.   R.J.Davis (102 High Street Pershore Worcs)

Davis, R.J. & Mace,   2000   CDROM Sport in Society - Leisure.   Sport in Mind.

Donnellan, C.   1999   Drugs in Sport. Independence Publishers.

Evans, J.   1986   Physical Education, Sport and Schooling.   Falmer.

Grisogono, V.   1991   Children and Sport.   John Murray.

Hargreaves, J.   1994   Sporting Females.   Routledge.

Hendry, L.   1978   School, Sport and Leisure.   Lepus Books.

Honeybourne, J. et.al. 2000   Advanced Physical Education and Sport 2e.   Nelson Thornes.
                       2000   Advanced Physical Education and Sport for AS level.   Nelson Thornes.

Houlihan, B.   1997   Sport, Policy and Politics. Routledge.

Jones, R.L.   2000   Sociology of Sport : Theory and Practice.   Pearson Education.

Lapchick, R.E.   1996   Sport in Society.   Sage.

Loy, J & Kenyon, G. 1969   Sport, Culture and Society.   Macmillan.

Lumpkin, A   1998   Physical Education and Sport.   McGraw-Hill.

Lumpkin, A   1994   Sports Ethics : Application for Fair Play.   McGraw-Hill.

Mason, T.   1993   Only a Game. Sport in the Modern World.   Cambridge University Press.

McIntosh, P.C.   1987   Sport in Society.   West London Press.

McPherson,B. et.al. 1989   The Social Significance of Sport.   Human Kinetics.

Mortlock, C.   1994   The Adventure Alternative.   Cicerone Press.

Polley, M.   1996   Moving the Goalposts.   Routledge.

Voy, R.   1991   Drugs, Sport, and Politics.   Human Kinetics.

Wesson, K. et.al.   2000   Sport and P.E. A Complete Guide to A Level Study 2e.   Hodder and Stoughton.

Williams, M.H.   1989   Beyond Training.   Human Kinetics.

POPULAR RECREATION - INDIVIDUAL ACTIVITIES   **HISTORICAL STUDIES**

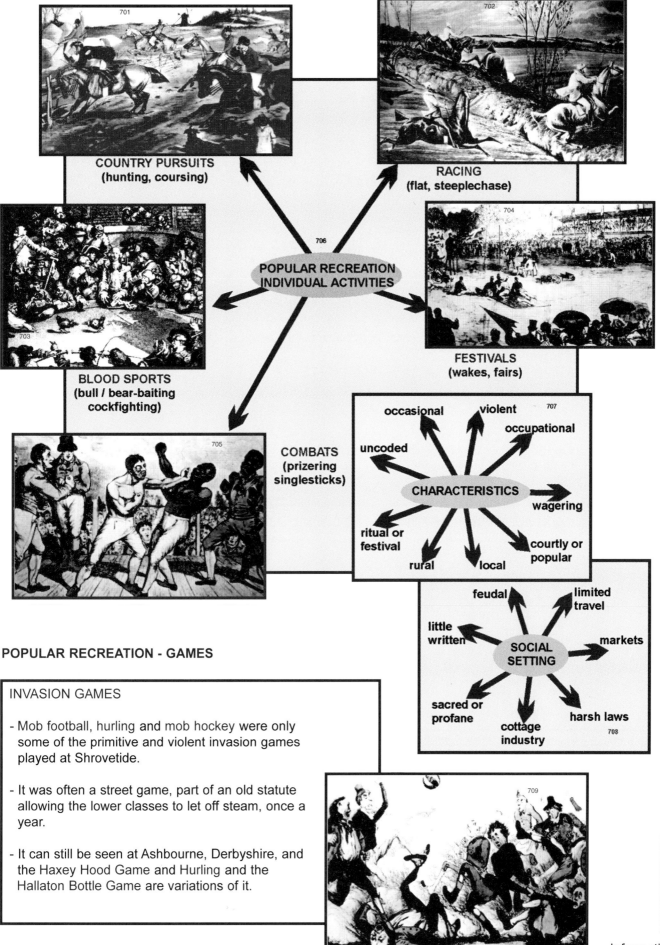

COUNTRY PURSUITS
(hunting, coursing)

RACING
(flat, steeplechase)

706

POPULAR RECREATION
INDIVIDUAL ACTIVITIES

FESTIVALS
(wakes, fairs)

BLOOD SPORTS
(bull / bear-baiting
cockfighting)

COMBATS
(prizering
singlesticks)

occasional   violent   707
uncoded   occupational
CHARACTERISTICS   wagering
ritual or
festival   courtly or
popular
rural   local

feudal   limited
travel
little
written   markets
SOCIAL
SETTING
sacred or
profane   harsh laws
cottage   708
industry

POPULAR RECREATION - GAMES

INVASION GAMES

- Mob football, hurling and mob hockey were only
  some of the primitive and violent invasion games
  played at Shrovetide.

- It was often a street game, part of an old statute
  allowing the lower classes to let off steam, once a
  year.

- It can still be seen at Ashbourne, Derbyshire, and
  the Haxey Hood Game and Hurling and the
  Hallaton Bottle Game are variations of it.

POPULAR RECREATION - GAMES (continued)

TARGET GAMES

- This group of games included primitive versions of cricket, rounders, bowls, skittles and quoits and the Scottish games of golf and curling.

- Cricket was the most popular English game because it allowed gentry and peasantry to play a team game in harmony.

- It first developed in the South Downs, where Kent was the first great county team and Hambledon the most famous village team in the 18th century.

- Developments led to the M.C.C. playing at Lords.

COURT GAMES

- The most famous court game was Real Tennis. Started in France, it came to England during the Tudor Dynasty and was restricted to the upper class for several hundred years.
- There are a number of features which reflect the exclusive group who play it.
- Special facilities and equipment, complex rules of play and etiquette, and laws limiting play to the nobility.
- The parallel game for the poor was rackets where any wall, but particularly the church or public house, allowed men to play a handball game or use rackets.
- We first find rackets in print in Pickwick Papers, where Pickwick finds himself in debtor's prison at Fleet and the game is played by the inmates.

PUBLIC SCHOOL ATHLETICISM - TECHNICAL AND SOCIAL DEVELOPMENT

Stage 1 - INITIAL BOYS DEVELOPMENTS
- Cricket started, but with established rules.
- Mob Football, differed in each school :
  - Eton, Field and Wall Game,
  - Rugby, handling game,
  - Harrow and Charterhouse, dribbling game.
- Local conditions determined structure.
- Rackets and Fives :
  - Started on walls of the Old School at Harrow,
  - Fives stared at Eton, Rugby and Winchester,
  - Courts different in each case.

Stage 2 - IMPACT OF LIBERAL HEADMASTERS
- Dr Thomas Arnold and others enacted reforms to produce responsible Christian Gentlemen.
- With concept of Godliness and Manliness (1820's - 1850's) :
  - Broader curriculum.
  - Reduced flogging.
  - Playground control by Sixth Form.
  - Exclusion of field sports and poaching.
- Games encouraged as a vehicle of social control :
  - Regular play.
  - Written rules.
  - Codes of honour and loyalty to school established.
- Expansion leading to House System and House competitions being established.

Information

PUBLIC SCHOOL ATHLETICISM - TECHNICAL AND SOCIAL DEVELOPMENT (continued)

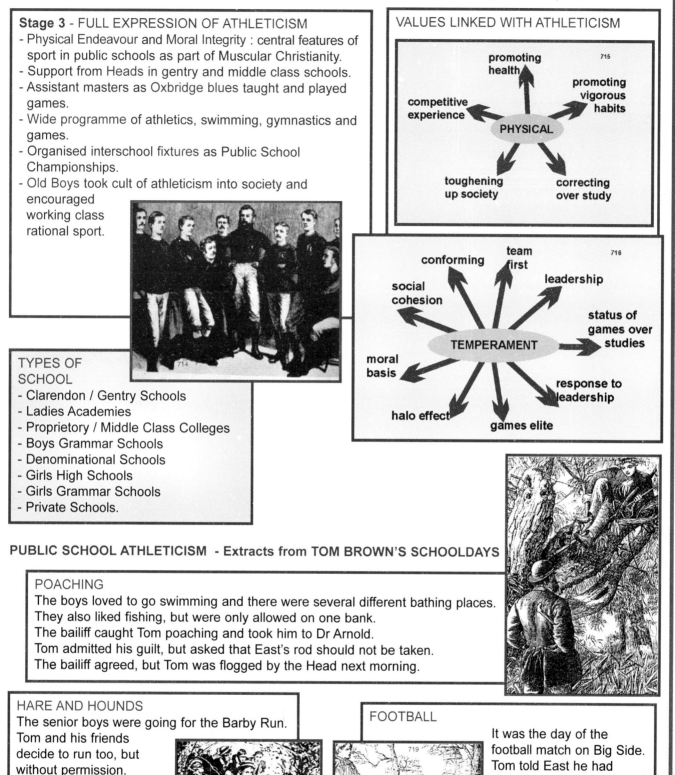

Stage 3 - FULL EXPRESSION OF ATHLETICISM
- Physical Endeavour and Moral Integrity : central features of sport in public schools as part of Muscular Christianity.
- Support from Heads in gentry and middle class schools.
- Assistant masters as Oxbridge blues taught and played games.
- Wide programme of athletics, swimming, gymnastics and games.
- Organised interschool fixtures as Public School Championships.
- Old Boys took cult of athleticism into society and encouraged working class rational sport.

VALUES LINKED WITH ATHLETICISM

715

PHYSICAL
- promoting health
- promoting vigorous habits
- competitive experience
- toughening up society
- correcting over study

716

TEMPERAMENT
- conforming
- team first
- leadership
- social cohesion
- status of games over studies
- moral basis
- response to leadership
- halo effect
- games elite

TYPES OF SCHOOL
- Clarendon / Gentry Schools
- Ladies Academies
- Proprietory / Middle Class Colleges
- Boys Grammar Schools
- Denominational Schools
- Girls High Schools
- Girls Grammar Schools
- Private Schools.

PUBLIC SCHOOL ATHLETICISM - Extracts from TOM BROWN'S SCHOOLDAYS

POACHING
The boys loved to go swimming and there were several different bathing places.
They also liked fishing, but were only allowed on one bank.
The bailiff caught Tom poaching and took him to Dr Arnold.
Tom admitted his guilt, but asked that East's rod should not be taken.
The bailiff agreed, but Tom was flogged by the Head next morning.

HARE AND HOUNDS
The senior boys were going for the Barby Run.
Tom and his friends decide to run too, but without permission.
The hares were set off and the pack followed with Tom and Co. behind.
Tom and friends got lost and returned very late, bedraggled.
The Head told them off for breaking the rules, but did not flog them because they had shown courage.

FOOTBALL
It was the day of the football match on Big Side. Tom told East he had played the game with village lads, but East said Rugby played real football. East was playing and was injured. When the ball came towards goal, Tom raced on and dived on it. Big Brook asked if he was hurt and then said that he was made of the right stuff.

PUBLIC SCHOOL ATHLETICISM - Extracts from TOM BROWN'S SCHOOLDAYS (continued)

Remember that this is fiction. It is what Thomas Hughes felt about his schooldays at Rugby under the headship of Dr Thomas Arnold.

It is thought that Tom Brown was in fact representing Thomas Hughes' adventures while at school. Hughes had a great respect for Dr. Arnold, but believed much more strongly in the value of sport as a character building experience as he belonged to a group of Muscular Christians.

THE FIGHT
Tom was asked to look after a little boy called Arthur. Arthur was a timid lad, but was bullied by Slogger a big boy.
Tom challenged Slogger to a fight and it was set up in the playground.
Big Brook supervised the fight, but Tom wanted to wrestle, but was not allowed. Dr Arnold came on the scene and stopped the fight and was angry with Brook for letting it take place.

THE CRICKET
Tom eventually reached the Sixth Form and was made Captain of Cricket. The final match was against the M.C.C. It was a good match, but Tom put Arthur in earlier than normally.
A young master suggested that Tom had risked the match by doing this, but Tom said that the result mattered little, but Arthur would remember this all his life. Tom also suggested that cricket was more than a game, that it was an institution. Arthur thought it was life itself.

RATIONAL RECREATION - INDIVIDUAL ACTIVITIES

HUNTING
- Has hardly changed except that fox hunting has taken over because of the scarcity of other quarry.

COURSING
- Is no longer in open fields, but in closed arenas.

BLOOD SPORTS
- Have been banned.

HORSERACING
- Has been effected by the railways.

THE REGATTA.
- Aquatics became very respectable.
- Rowing is controlled by the A.R.A. and is exclusive to the upper / middle classes.
- Swimming was now run by the A.S.A. and had its own amateur championships. It has developed from the Spa Movement and the Public Baths which were built to clean up the working classes.
- Sailing became very popular among the most wealthy members of Victorian society, headed by the Americas Cup.
- Canoeing, thanks to John MacGregor was popular on most rivers.

SPORTS FESTIVALS
- Sports Festivals became dominated by athletics with some equestrianism and some cycling.
- Athletics was run by the A.A.A. with amateur Championships and Athletic Sports in most towns at least once a year.
- The sports were mainly running to begin with, but later included jumps and throwing events.
- Cycling became a boom activity, with the C.T.C. controlling the touring side and the N.C.U. controlled track cycling.
- Tricycles were very popular while the Penny Farthings made bicycling a dangerous activity.

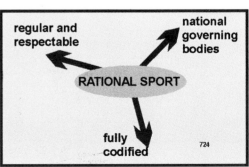

regular and respectable

national governing bodies

RATIONAL SPORT

fully codified

RATIONAL RECREATION - INDIVIDUAL ACTIVITIES (continued)

GYMNASTICS
- The first English Gymnasium was built by A. MacClaren and was a mixture of apparatus which you can see in the picture.
- Many of the ideas came from European developments, using Swedish beams and German bars, and the principle of systematised exercise became very popular in most towns.
- In addition to gymnastics there was fencing and boxing and the use of small apparatus like barbells and indian clubs.

BOXING
- From the corruption of the Prizering, boxing became a highly structured, respectable sport run by the National Sporting Club.
- Gloves were now used and three minute rounds according to the Queensbury Rules.
- Fencing almost disappeared, but then was copied from the Prussian Army and became an Olympic sport.
- It consisted of foil, epee and sabre competition.
- Wrestling, after years as a local festival sport or a music hall act, became an amateur Olympic sport.
- Existing archery associations expanded to form numerous clubs.

RATIONAL RECREATION - INVASION GAMES

RUGBY
- The R.F.U. was established in 1871 and separated from the association game.
- Strictly amateur, northern clubs split to establish a professional rugby league.

SOCCER
- The F.A. was established in 1863 and the F.A. Cup as a national competition.
- This was dominated by Old Boys teams, until professional northern clubs made it the Peoples' Game.

HOCKEY
- Mob hockey was re-organised by cricket clubs in the Thames valley who wanted a to play a winter game.
- Girls high schools played hockey, hence women playing.

RATIONAL RECREATION - TARGET GAMES

CRICKET
- Became the national game of England.
- Rules were revised by the M.C.C. and the County Championships established.
- Test matches were held regularly, with Australia and South Africa the main opponents.
- Amateurs improved to rival the professional players.

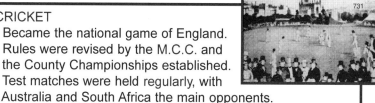

Rational Recreation: ritual, respectable, recreational, regionalised, referees, roles, regular, written rules, regulated, regulations

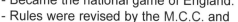
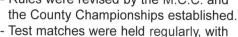
- Pub games became respectable with their own governing bodies.
- Bowls, skittles and quoits were played regularly in leagues.
- Lawn games also became popular among the middle classes, particularly croquet with a Championship at Wimbledon.
- Rounders was adopted by the USA and developed as baseball.

RATIONAL RECREATION - COURT GAMES

LAWN TENNIS
- Lawn tennis was developed by the middle classes as an alternative to real tennis.
- It was initially played in gardens, but where these were not large enough, private clubs were formed.
- It was played by women because of the privacy of not being seen in public.
- Wimbledon became the championship centre.

OTHER COURT GAMES
- Included the rational structuring of rackets and its off-shoot squash and the development of badminton from the old game of battledore.
- Golf was always the Scottish game, but it became very popular among the upper middle classes in England.
- From the USA we also had the development of basketball and volleyball.

SOCIAL SETTING OF RATIONAL SPORT

SOCIAL CLASS AND SPORT
- The gentry had already achieved a full sports programme with their preferred activities and plentiful leisure time.
- The emerging urban middle classes took these gentry sports and reorganised them according to amateur codes which excluded financial rewards.
- The industrial working classes had little time for sport, but when it was rationalised and seen to be a vehicle for social conditioning.
- Social Christians and industrialists encouraged the development of organised sport for the workers, who largely existed in urban poverty, see picture to right.
- There was considerable delay before women had the same opportunities.

WORK AND FREE-TIME

- The cottage industry had been a family affair where the timing of when to work was dictated by the amount to be done.
- Factory developments meant that the human element was controlled by machinery, as shutting off the machines meant loss of production.
- Factory work time started with a 72 hour week over six days, with Sunday a day of rest stipulated by sabbatharianism.

- This meant that the workers had no free time unless they were unemployed and then they had no money.
- The Saturday half day and the Early Closing Movement gave workers time for organised sport.

- Women were paid a quarter of what men got for the same work, and therefore did not have the union strength to obtain the Saturday half day.
- Benevolent employers built sports facilities for their workers.

URBANISATION AND LEISURE

- As towns grew, particularly the industrial towns, the countryside became farther away and so urban leisure facilities became a social necessity.
- Arboretums were initially built for the middle classes, but gradually public parks were also opened for walking in and later for sports.

- The centres of older cities were rebuilt removing the slums and building shopping and business centres.
- With back-to-back housing near the factories and mills, entrepreneurs realised that professional football clubs would bring in a lot of revenue from the gate money, these were built near the town centres.

- The pollution to the rivers running through the industrial towns, destroyed fishing opportunities for the working classes.

Information

SOCIAL SETTING OF RATIONAL SPORT (continued)

COMMUNICATIONS AND TRAVEL
- The use of the stagecoach opened up sport for the gentry, but meant that the lower classes were limited to local holidays and sports.
- With the coming of the railways, the middle classes gained access to the seaside and were able to travel to neighbouring towns for sport.

- The lower classes could not afford to go by rail regularly, nor did they have the time and so the excursion trip became the annual seaside visit for the lower classes.

- The roads deteriorated during the popularisation of the railways.
- But with the advent of middle class cycle touring, the roads were improved.
- And gradually, the gentry and the lower classes with their second-hand bikes, managed to travel to the countryside by cycle.

- Literacy was very limited until printing, the popular press and the pocket editions became available and compulsory education led to a literate working class.
- It was as a result of these changes that the sporting press was born.

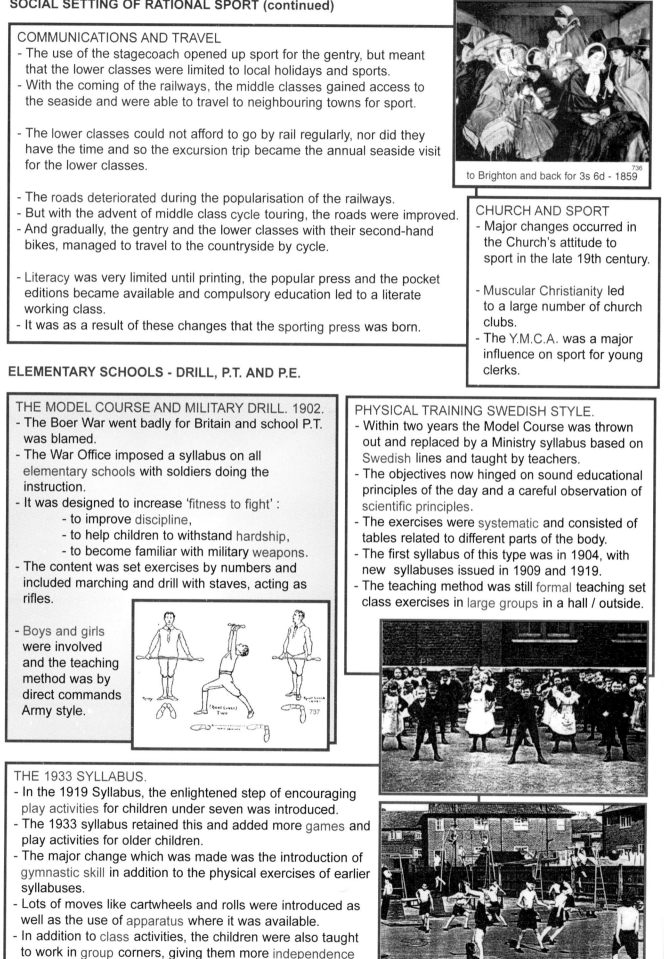

to Brighton and back for 3s 6d - 1859 [736]

CHURCH AND SPORT
- Major changes occurred in the Church's attitude to sport in the late 19th century.

- Muscular Christianity led to a large number of church clubs.
- The Y.M.C.A. was a major influence on sport for young clerks.

ELEMENTARY SCHOOLS - DRILL, P.T. AND P.E.

THE MODEL COURSE AND MILITARY DRILL. 1902.
- The Boer War went badly for Britain and school P.T. was blamed.
- The War Office imposed a syllabus on all elementary schools with soldiers doing the instruction.
- It was designed to increase 'fitness to fight' :
    - to improve discipline,
    - to help children to withstand hardship,
    - to become familiar with military weapons.
- The content was set exercises by numbers and included marching and drill with staves, acting as rifles.

- Boys and girls were involved and the teaching method was by direct commands Army style.

[737]

PHYSICAL TRAINING SWEDISH STYLE.
- Within two years the Model Course was thrown out and replaced by a Ministry syllabus based on Swedish lines and taught by teachers.
- The objectives now hinged on sound educational principles of the day and a careful observation of scientific principles.
- The exercises were systematic and consisted of tables related to different parts of the body.
- The first syllabus of this type was in 1904, with new syllabuses issued in 1909 and 1919.
- The teaching method was still formal teaching set class exercises in large groups in a hall / outside.

THE 1933 SYLLABUS.
- In the 1919 Syllabus, the enlightened step of encouraging play activities for children under seven was introduced.
- The 1933 syllabus retained this and added more games and play activities for older children.
- The major change which was made was the introduction of gymnastic skill in addition to the physical exercises of earlier syllabuses.
- Lots of moves like cartwheels and rolls were introduced as well as the use of apparatus where it was available.
- In addition to class activities, the children were also taught to work in group corners, giving them more independence and variety.

ELEMENTARY SCHOOLS - DRILL, P.T. AND P.E. (continued)

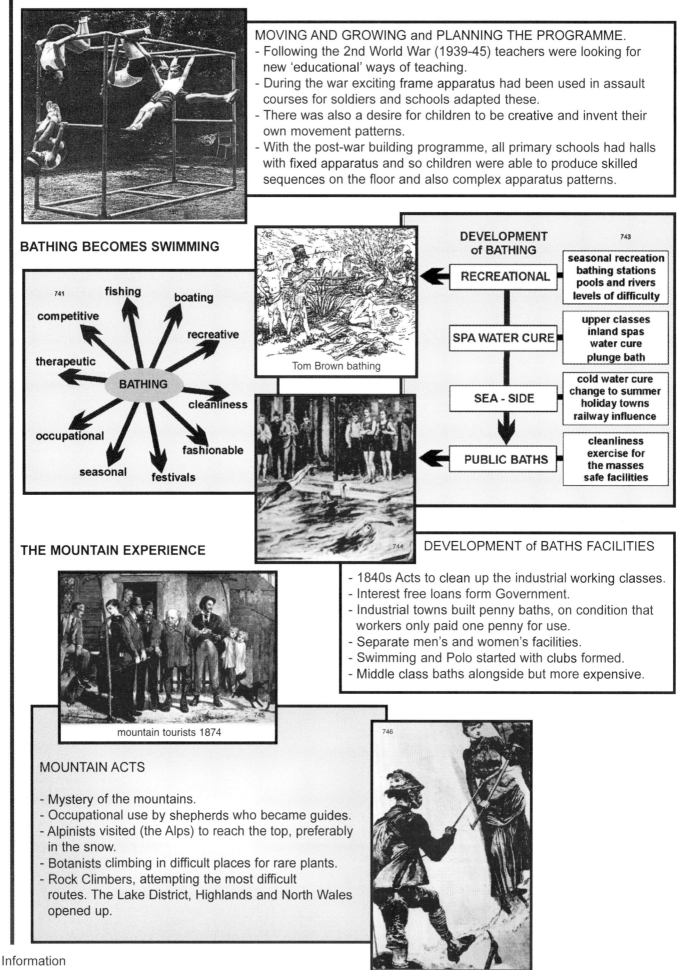

MOVING AND GROWING and PLANNING THE PROGRAMME.
- Following the 2nd World War (1939-45) teachers were looking for new 'educational' ways of teaching.
- During the war exciting frame apparatus had been used in assault courses for soldiers and schools adapted these.
- There was also a desire for children to be creative and invent their own movement patterns.
- With the post-war building programme, all primary schools had halls with fixed apparatus and so children were able to produce skilled sequences on the floor and also complex apparatus patterns.

BATHING BECOMES SWIMMING

fishing
boating
competitive
recreative
therapeutic
BATHING
cleanliness
occupational
fashionable
seasonal
festivals

Tom Brown bathing

DEVELOPMENT of BATHING

RECREATIONAL — seasonal recreation bathing stations pools and rivers levels of difficulty

SPA WATER CURE — upper classes inland spas water cure plunge bath

SEA - SIDE — cold water cure change to summer holiday towns railway influence

PUBLIC BATHS — cleanliness exercise for the masses safe facilities

THE MOUNTAIN EXPERIENCE

DEVELOPMENT of BATHS FACILITIES

- 1840s Acts to clean up the industrial working classes.
- Interest free loans form Government.
- Industrial towns built penny baths, on condition that workers only paid one penny for use.
- Separate men's and women's facilities.
- Swimming and Polo started with clubs formed.
- Middle class baths alongside but more expensive.

mountain tourists 1874

MOUNTAIN ACTS

- Mystery of the mountains.
- Occupational use by shepherds who became guides.
- Alpinists visited (the Alps) to reach the top, preferably in the snow.
- Botanists climbing in difficult places for rare plants.
- Rock Climbers, attempting the most difficult routes. The Lake District, Highlands and North Wales opened up.

WINTER EXCITEMENT

WINTER ACTS

- Ice Fairs : held on frozen rivers during winter as festival occasions.

- Speed Skating : very popular in Holland and on the Fens of England.
- Became professionalised.

- Figure Skating : started on the Serpentine in Hyde Park (London) once skates had edges.

- Skiing : Nordic skiing is very old, but the English started Alpine skiing.

CYCLING

BONE SHAKER
- A pretend horse.
- Young gentlemen showing off.
- A gimmick only.

DEVELOPMENTS
- Gentry preferred horses until Queen Victoria's daughters started a craze.

- Middle class men in towns formed clubs which excluded women initially.
- Too expensive for lower classes until second-hand trade started.

PENNY FARTHING
- Large wheel for speed.
- Too dangerous for women and old people.
- Tricycle was an alternative.
- Used for racing on the roads and on the track.

ROVER SAFETY
- Cog and chain ended need for large wheel.
- Safer for women and elderly.
- Not as fast until gears invented.

QUESTIONS

POPULAR RECREATIONS : INDIVIDUAL ACTIVITIES

1) a) Explain the similarities and differences between hunting and steeplechasing before the latter became professionalised. (5 marks)
b) Pedestrianism was far better than a normal occupation of the day. Discuss. (5 marks)
c) Explain the attractions of blood sports like cockfighting in pre-industrial England. (5 marks)
d) Describe five characteristics of popular recreation as they were evident in the Prizering and suggest the influences caused by the social setting. (10 marks)

POPULAR RECREATIONS : GAMES

2) a) Mob Games reflected the violence of the times.
    i) Describe one of the mob games which still exists today. (3 marks)
    ii) What part did the gentry play in the traditional mob games? (2 marks)
    iii) Why are most of the surviving mob football games held at Shrovetide? (3 marks)

POPULAR RECREATIONS : GAMES - QUESTION 2 (continued)

2) b) i) Why did cricket develop written rules before most other games?
(3 marks)

ii) Explain the main differences between old fashioned cricket and the way we play it today. (3 marks)

c) Picture 752 on the right shows Real Tennis being played in the 16th century. Use it to explain why this was a game which was limited to the nobility and justify the suggestion that rackets was its counterpart among ordinary people. (12 marks)

PUBLIC SCHOOL ATHLETICISM - TECHNICAL AND SOCIAL DEVELOPMENT

3) a) Explain how and why the game of mob football varied in different leading public schools in England in the early 19th century. (6 marks)
b) Use picture 753 on left of rugby at Rugby School to help explain the changes enacted by Dr Thomas Arnold while he was Headmaster.
(7 marks)

c) The development of the cult of athleticism in public schools produced an environment which resulted in rational sport spreading right through the United Kingdom. Discuss. (12 marks)

PUBLIC SCHOOL ATHLETICISM - EXTRACTS FROM TOM BROWN'S SCHOOLDAYS

4) a) Describe Tom's part in the Big Side football game. (5 marks)
b) Explain Tom's relationship with authority when he decided to do the Barby Run. (4 marks)

c) The fight exposed the differences between the boys code and that of Dr Arnold. Use picture 754 to help explain these differences. (6 marks)
d) Compare the main attitudes expressed by Tom when he was caught poaching with the episode in which he was the school cricket captain. (10 marks)

RATIONAL RECREATION - INDIVIDUAL ACTIVITIES

5) a) Use the boxing picture (755) to describe the changes which occurred when the National Sporting Club brought an end to Prizefighting. (5 marks)
b) Explain the development of amateurism in rational sport using athletics as your example. (5 marks)

c) Use picture 756 on left to describe the main features of the English Gymnasium, explaining the objectives underlying the major activities involved. (5 marks)

d) Discuss the two different administrative approaches taken by rowing as an elite sport and swimming as a universal sport in the 19th century. (10 marks)

RATIONAL SPORT - THE EMERGENCE OF RATIONALISED GAMES

6) a) Explain why lawn tennis was accepted by the middle classes as a favoured game. (6 marks)

b) **i)** Use picture 757 on right to describe some of the main changes which occurred to the game of cricket in the 19th century. (4 marks)

ii) Why was croquet one of the first games found acceptable for women in Victorian England? (3 marks)

c) Use the suggested characteristics of rational games to explain the changes which occurred in an invasion game of your choice. (12 marks)

THE SOCIAL SETTING OF RATIONAL SPORT

7) a) What was the impact of the railways on holiday patterns in Britain in the 2nd half of the 19th century? (5 marks)

b) Describe the development of parks in the context of urban expansion. (4 marks)

c) Explain the development and influence of the Saturday Half day. (6 marks)

d) Discuss the ways in which social class variables were reflected in 19th century rational sport. (10 marks)

ELEMENTARY SCHOOLS, MILITARY DRILL, P.T. AND P.E.

8) a) The 1904 Syllabus was the first attempt to produce an official syllabus with scientific and educational objectives. Explain this statement. (4 marks)

b) Describe the innovations to be found in the 1933 Syllabus. (6 marks)

c) What were the major changes in the book Moving and Growing (1952) which reflected post-Second World War attitudes? (5 marks)

d) Explain the purpose and format of the Model Course (1902) and discuss the reasons for its introduction and replacement. (10 marks)

DEVELOPMENT OF SWIMMING AND BATHING

9) a) Compare the sporting associations reflected in the two pictures (on the right 758 and 759) of a country town. (6 marks)

b) Use the figure below (760) to describe bathing at Rugby School in the 1830s. (4 marks)

c) Use the three pictures below to help you to describe the changes which occurred to bathing and swimming in the 19th century. (8 marks)

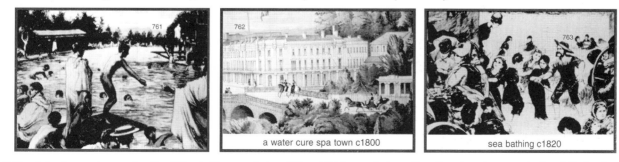

a water cure spa town c1800

sea bathing c1820

d) Explain the reasons for the Wash House Acts of the 1840s and describe the development of public baths in the larger towns. (7 marks)

THE DEVELOPMENT OF OUTDOOR PURSUITS

10) a) Explain the changing face of Mountain Activities during the 19th century.   (6 marks)
b) Explain why winter sports were so popular in the 19th century, but some were only available to the wealthy.   (4 marks)
c)   **i)** Describe the technical development of the cycle in the context of industrialisation and urbanisation.   (5 marks)
     ii) Use the design of the cycles shown in figure 764 on the right to discuss social class and gender involvement in cycling.   (6 marks)
d) Link the advent of the cycle with the development of travel facilities in the second half of the 19th century.   (4 marks)

ANSWERS

The answer for each mark awarded is notated by the ❒ symbol - where there are more ❒ symbols than there are marks available, marks would be given for any choice up to the maximum available. Usually, the precise wording specified in an answer would not be required - answers with the same meaning would be acceptable.

POPULAR RECREATION : INDIVIDUAL ACTIVITIES

1) a)
Explain similarities and differences between hunting and steeplechasing before the latter became professionalised.
     similarities :
     3 marks for :
❒   Similar social groups.
❒   Both equestrian.
❒   Both rural sports.
     differences :
     2 marks for two from :
❒   Steeplechasing tended to involve only men.
❒   A light hearted affair.
❒   Steeplechasing tended to include wagering.
❒   Hunting was a bloodsport.

1) b)
Pedestrianism was far better than a normal occupation of the day. Discuss.
     5 marks for five from :
❒   Normally pedestrians were drawn from the lower classes.
❒   Wages at the time were very low and much more could be earned in this sport.
❒   The life was much more exciting and rewarding.
❒   Money was to be won on wagers as well as prizes.
❒   It was a chance to travel the country, even the world.
❒   Patrons employed you and gave you a job which allowed you to race.

1) c)
Explain the attractions of blood sports like cockfighting in pre-industrial England.
     5 marks for five from :
❒   A violent and cruel activity when life was violent and cruel.
❒   A natural part of the rural scene.
❒   Peasantry could train their own game birds.
❒   Money to be made from prizes and wagering.
❒   Fitted in well with horse racing festivals.
❒   Plenty of blood and spectacle.
❒   Excitement of birds fighting to the death.

POPULAR RECREATION : INDIVIDUAL ACTIVITIES - ANSWERS QUESTION 1 (continued)

1) d)
Five characteristics of popular recreation using the Prizering, & the influences caused by the social setting are :
  Characteristics : 5 marks for five from:
❐ Big fights were only held occasionally and so they were special events.
❐ They were extremely violent and excited the crowd.
❐ Involved both the gentry as patrons and the peasantry as fighters.
❐ Were rituals where man fought man to the end.
❐ An occupation for the fighters that could bring high rewards.
❐ Involved considerable wagering.
❐ Was local and often fought out with local rules.
  Social setting : 5 marks for five from:
❐ Reflected the feudal partnership of gentry and peasantry.
❐ Was localised because of limited opportunities to travel great distances.
❐ Were often part of the festival atmosphere, linked with fairs.
❐ Harsh laws and lifestyle reflected in behaviour and sports.
❐ Cottage industry and large number of church festivals when sports were held.
❐ Rules were not written down, but a great following for big fights.

POPULAR RECREATIONS : GAMES

2) a) i)
Describe one of the mob games which still exists today.
❐ Name of one of these games, for example. Ashbourne, Haxey Hood, Hallaton Bottle Game.
  2 marks for two from : (common features included) :
❐ Violence.
❐ Involvement by the lower classes.
❐ Part of a festival occasion.
❐ Unlimited number of participants.
❐ Few rules, involving kicking fighting and handling.
❐ Competition between different sections of a community.
2) a) ii)
What part did the gentry play in the traditional mob game?
  2 marks for two from :
❐ Gave permission for it to take place.
❐ Attended as spectators.
❐ Often started the event and gave the award.
2) a) iii)
Why are most of the surviving mob football games played at Shrovetide?
❐ They were traditionally held on Shrove Tuesday.
❐ It was a holiday / Holy day period.
❐ It was a festival occasion marking the last day before Lent.
2) b) i)
Why did cricket develop written rules before most other games?
  3 marks for three from :
❐ It was the first game which involved the gentry and the peasantry.
❐ It was a game which could not operate without some basic rules.
❐ It was being played in public schools on a regular basis.
❐ It became a regular summer game which led to written rules.
❐ The gentry were literate and most of their games had written rules from early on.
2) b) ii)
Old fashioned cricket's main differences from the modern game are :
  3 marks for three from :
❐ Two wickets at each end.
❐ No special clothing.
❐ No safety equipment.
❐ Scorers notched on a stick.
❐ No boundary.
❐ Limited use of umpires.
❐ Underarm bowling.

POPULAR RECREATIONS : GAMES - ANSWERS QUESTION 2 (continued)

2) c)
The picture shows real tennis being played in the 16th century. Use it to explain why this was a game which was limited to the nobility and justify the suggestion that rackets was its counterpart among ordinary people.
    Real tennis :
    6 marks for six from :
❑ Brought over from France where it was a nobles' game.
❑ Very sophisticated written rules.
❑ Purpose-built facility.
❑ Special equipment used.
❑ Controlled by court with punishment if lesser people played.
❑ Etiquette designed for the nobility.
❑ Tradition of exclusive play by nobility.
    Rackets :
    6 marks for six from :
❑ Could be played against any wall.
❑ Very limited equipment used.
❑ Church wall or public house wall in every town.
❑ Tradition of being played informally.
❑ Known to have been played at Fleet Prison.
❑ Encouraged by public houses for business.
❑ Simple rules and structure allowing anyone to play.
❑ Inexpensive and no exclusivity statutes.

PUBLIC SCHOOL ATHLETICISM - TECHNICAL AND SOCIAL DEVELOPMENT

3) a)
Explain how and why the game of mob football varied in different leading public schools in England in the early 19th century.
    6 marks for six from :
❑ Some encouraged the dribbling game (Harrow and Charterhouse).
❑ Because they initially played the game in the Cloisters.
❑ Rugby played a running in and hacking game.
❑ Because they played on grass / Big Side / the Close.
❑ Because Webb Ellis pick up the ball and ran with it and this became a tradition.
❑ Eton played against a Wall, using a door at one end and a chalk mark at the other for goals.
❑ Because the wall was a prominent feature at the edge of the playing field.
❑ They also played a field game version.
❑ Because they had extensive playing fields.

3) b)
Use the picture of Rugby School to help explain the changes enacted by Dr Thomas Arnold while he was Headmaster.
    7 marks for seven from :
❑ The game looks well organised.
❑ The boys are in games kit.
❑ There are spectators / this includes Dr Arnold.
❑ He encouraged boys to organise their own games.
❑ He appointed a sixth form committee to run the school outside the classroom.
❑ He reduced the amount of flogging and suspended boys instead.
❑ He was looking for leadership skills.
❑ He was trying to make Christian gentlemen.

PUBLIC SCHOOL ATHLETICISM. TECHNICAL AND SOCIAL DEVELOPMENT

3) c)

The development of the cult of athleticism in public schools produced an environment which resulted in rational sport spreading right through the United Kingdom. Discuss.

12 marks for twelve from :
- ❐ Sports were played on a regular basis.
- ❐ Sports were being played by the sons of gentlemen.
- ❐ Sports became rule orientated and respectable.
- ❐ A wide range of sports and games were being played.
- ❐ Sports were felt to be character building.
- ❐ The boys themselves were responsible for their organisation.
- ❐ Headmasters encouraged sport to be played.
- ❐ Young assistant masters taught and played the games.
- ❐ Professionals were brought in to improve standards.
- ❐ The boys went to Oxbridge where the best won blues.
- ❐ Many returned to the schools as teachers.
- ❐ Others went into the army and spread sport at home and abroad.
- ❐ Some became factory owners and encouraged their workers to play.
- ❐ Some became vicars and encouraged sport in their parishes.
- ❐ Many formed old boys teams or formed private sports clubs.
- ❐ Others became local or national politicians and improved provision.
- ❐ Some took over their estates and encouraged rational sport among their workers.

PUBLIC SCHOOL ATHLETICISM. EXTRACTS FROM TOM BROWN'S SCHOOLDAYS.

4) a)

Describe Tom's part in the Big-Side football match.

5 marks for five from :
- ❐ He was not allowed to play initially.
- ❐ Although he claimed he had played the game with the village lads.
- ❐ East was injured trying to save a try.
- ❐ Tom rushed on and dived on the ball when the next attack occurred.
- ❐ He finished up under a scrum.
- ❐ Brook asked him if he was injured.
- ❐ Brook congratulated him saying he was made of the right stuff.

4) b)

Explain Tom's relationship with authority when he decided to do the Barby Run.

4 marks for four from :
- ❐ He was told that he was not old enough to run.
- ❐ Hiding behind a tree he ran anyway with some of his friends.
- ❐ They got lost and Tom took charge sending Tadpole home.
- ❐ On arriving back very late he was sent to Dr. Arnold who reprimanded him.
- ❐ For getting back late.
- ❐ And running when he should not have done.
- ❐ But did not flog him because of his obvious courage in tackling the difficult course.

4) c)

The fight exposed the differences between the boys code and that of Dr Arnold. Use the picture to help explain these differences.

6 marks for six from :
- ❐ Tom felt obliged to face Slogger as Arthur was in his charge.
- ❐ Slogger accepted the challenge.
- ❐ The boys in the playground crowded round to see the fight.
- ❐ Brook presided over the fight keeping it fair.
- ❐ Arnold would not accept fighting at any cost.
- ❐ Arnold claimed it reflected bullying.
- ❐ Brook defended his decision to let them fight to settle the matter.
- ❐ Brook claimed he would have stopped it if anyone was getting hurt.
- ❐ Arnold insisted on the fight being stopped, using his status as the highest authority in the school.

PUBLIC SCHOOL ATHLETICISM. EXTRACTS FROM TOM BROWN'S SCHOOLDAYS
- ANSWERS QUESTION 4 (continued)

4) d)

Compare the main attitudes expressed by Tom when he was caught poaching with the episode in which he was school cricket captain.

Poaching attitudes :

5 marks for five from :

❏ Willingness to go out of bounds.
❏ Willingness to poach fish.
❏ Prepared to be rude to the bailiff and attempt to bribe him.
❏ Willing to return with him and take his punishment.
❏ Admitted that he was wrong to the Head.
❏ Begged that it was unfair for East to lose his rod.
❏ Took his punishment like a man.

As cricket captain several years later :

5 marks for five from :

❏ As captain he was prepared to lead the team.
❏ He was prepared to make difficult decisions.
❏ He thought that this was the moment to 'blood' Arthur.
❏ Recognising the moment as more important for Arthur than for victory of the game.
❏ Recognised the significance of cricket as a character building experience.
❏ Greater than individual activities because of the importance of the team.
❏ Talked with great assurance to the assistant master.

RATIONAL RECREATION - INDIVIDUAL ACTIVITIES

5) a)

Use the boxing picture to describe the changes which occurred when the National Sporting Club brought an end to Prizefighting.

5 marks for five from :

❏ Gloves were now used.
❏ Three minute rounds.
❏ Fights were held according to the Queensbury Rules.
❏ The referee was in the ring.
❏ Boxing only, with no other techniques allowed.
❏ Boxing was now legal and respectable.
❏ With a governing body and championships.

5) b)

Explain the development of amateurism in rational sport using athletics as your example.

5 marks for five from :

❏ The term amateur means participation in sport for the love of it.
❏ The earliest amateurs were gentlemen amateurs where class determined admission.
❏ Wagering was involved at this time.
❏ Middle class involvement led to money becoming all important.
❏ Amateurs were not allowed to receive any money from the sport.
❏ Expenses were allowed in some sports.
❏ As the scope of sport increased so amateurism included payment for lost time.
❏ In some sports.

5) c)

Use the picture to describe the main features of the English gymnasium, explaining the objectives underlying the main activities involved.

5 marks for five from :

❏ Exercises involving indian clubs.
❏ To increase fitness and strength / teamwork.
❏ Vaulting and bar work.
❏ To improve gymnastic skills.
❏ Boxing / wrestling / fencing.
❏ To test toughness and as a military preparation.
❏ Climbing and swinging.
❏ Part of the naval tradition on sailing ships.

RATIONAL RECREATION - INDIVIDUAL ACTIVITIES - ANSWERS QUESTION 5 (continued)

5) d)
Discuss the two different administrative approaches taken by rowing as an elite sport as against swimming as a universal sport in the 19th century.
    10 marks for ten from :
- ❐ Rowing and swimming were sports for all at the beginning of the 19th century.
- ❐ Rowing on the Thames became elitist / particularly Henley Regatta.
- ❐ The A.R.A. banned all artisans from rowing in their regattas.
- ❐ Also anyone who had received money prizes or worked on boats.
- ❐ A regatta breaking this rule was banned from A.R.A. support.
- ❐ To qualify you had to have attended public or grammar school.
- ❐ To qualify you had to be a gentleman of private means.
- ❐ To qualify you had to be a university graduate.
- ❐ Swimming on the other hand allowed anyone to compete as an amateur.
- ❐ As long as they had not received money prizes.
- ❐ There was no exclusion clause / no limits on social class.
- ❐ No limits on female swimmers towards the end of the century.

RATIONAL SPORT - THE EMERGENCE OF RATIONALISED GAMES

6) a)
Explain why lawn tennis was accepted by the middle classes as a favoured game.
    6 marks for six from :
- ❐ It was a simplified copy of real tennis, the preserve of the nobility.
- ❐ It required ownership of a large garden which reflected status.
- ❐ It was a private facility which allowed one to entertain.
- ❐ It enabled ladies of the house to play a game privately.
- ❐ For those who had smaller gardens it was necessary for middle class people to form clubs.
- ❐ The middle classes joined together to form a private tennis club.
- ❐ Lawn tennis had been patented by Wingfield as a commercial proposition.
- ❐ The gentry had shown an interest playing the game on county cricket grounds.

6) b) i)
Use the picture to describe some of the main administrative changes which occurred to the game of cricket in the 19th century.
    4 marks for four from :
- ❐ The M.C.C. became a full Governing Body.
- ❐ Rules were finalised to be similar to today.
- ❐ Amateurs were not just gentlemen amateurs.
- ❐ Professional status was settled.
- ❐ The championship was established.
- ❐ International tests were regularised.
- ❐ Major grounds were built to take spectators.

6) b) ii)
Why was croquet one of the first games found acceptable for women in Victorian England?
    3 marks for three from :
- ❐ It was a social rather than competitive game.
- ❐ It did not involve the female in a display of her body.
- ❐ It did not involve sweating.
- ❐ It was in a private garden.

RATIONAL SPORT - THE EMERGENCE OF RATIONALISED GAMES - ANSWERS QUESTION 6 (continued)

6) c)
Use the suggested characteristics of rational games to explain the changes which occurred in an invasion game of your choice.
   (Six marks for identifying the characteristics and six marks for explaining them in a specific invasion game.)
   12 marks for six pairs from :
❐ Ritual :   ❐ High moments such as winning the cup.
❐ Respectable :   ❐ Played by all classes and morally based.
❐ Regulations :   ❐ On pitch size.
❐ Recreational :   ❐ Often played for the love of the game.
❐ Regulated :   ❐ Controlled by a governing body.
❐ Regionalised :   ❐ Friendlies, leagues and championships.
❐ Written rules :   ❐ Codes of play formalised.
❐ Referees :   ❐ Officials to control the games.
❐ Regular :   ❐ Played on a weekly basis at least.
❐ Roles :   ❐ Each player has a position to play in.

THE SOCIAL SETTING OF RATIONAL SPORT

7) a)
What was the impact of the railways on holiday patterns in Britain in the second half of the 19th century?
   5 marks for five from :
❐ They allowed people to travel farther in the same time.
❐ They were expensive and so not all people could afford to use them.
❐ It was some time before the tracks went to beauty spots.
❐ The gentry could use them nationally and internationally for long periods.
❐ This was because the gentry had free time and money.
❐ The middle classes tended to have a week's holiday.
❐ And went to the seaside by train.
❐ The lower classes could not afford the fares and so tended to go on an excursion train.
❐ For a day each year.
❐ Each class group preferred to go to different destinations.

7) b)
Describe the development of Parks in the context of urban expansion.
   4 marks for four from :
❐ Small towns had the countryside near by and so did not need parks.
❐ Older towns tended to have open spaces as commonland or river meadows.
❐ Industrial towns, built houses back-to-back, without open space.
❐ Initial parks were arboretums for the middle classes.
❐ Gradually each town built a park to walk in / often sponsored by a benefactor.
❐ Eventually parks were built by local councils to house working class games such as bowls.

7) c)
Explain the development and influence of the Saturday Half Day.
   6 marks for six from :
❐ Before (1870) industrial workers worked a 72 hour week.
❐ 6.00-6.00, six days a week.
❐ Sports were not allowed on Sundays / Sabbatharianism.
❐ Bank clerks won a half day in each week / Lubbock Act.
❐ Skilled workers won a 57 hour week (finishing at 2.00 p.m. on Saturday, (c.1870).
❐ Semi-skilled male workers won it over the next decade and then the unskilled.
❐ Much of this progress was due to strong union action.
❐ Many men then worked overtime and so abused the right.
❐ Women, largely because they lacked union strength, did not generally win these rights in the 19th century.
❐ This free time led to the development of the British week-end, with football or cricket on a Saturday afternoon.
❐ Most men were paid on Saturday so that they had money to spend at the week-end.

THE SOCIAL SETTING OF RATIONAL SPORT - ANSWERS QUESTION 7 (continued)

7) d)

Discuss the ways in which social class variables were reflected in 19th century rational sport.

    10 marks for ten from :

    Gentry :

❑ The oldest organised sports were developed by the nobility, for example, real tennis.

❑ This was followed by gentry organised sports like hunting, racing and cricket.

❑ They were able to do this because of their status / wealth / free-time.

❑ They retained exclusive rights to these where it suited them.

    Middle classes :

❑ Tried to copy the gentry.

❑ Could not afford the time to play and so had to rationalise the games.

❑ Preferred their sport to be well organised and not involve wagering.

❑ Preferred the lower classes not to have access to their sports, for example, lawn tennis.

❑ Had a very protective / closed attitude to women and sport.

❑ Excluded them from competition / public display / sweating.

❑ Tended to play sport at the week-ends, unless as amateurs they received expenses.

    Working classes :

❑ Old mob sports which tended to be violent / wagering.

❑ Limited free time meant that sports were occasional.

❑ Festivals / fairs and holy days / wakes were the main sporting occasions.

❑ Working class women had no organised sport.

❑ Shortage of facilities led to professional football.

❑ Patronage by industrialists led to factory sports facilities.

ELEMENTARY SCHOOLS, MILITARY DRILL, P.T. AND P.E.

8) a)

The 1904 Syllabus was the first attempt to produce an official syllabus with scientific and educational objectives. Explain this statement.

    4 marks for four from :

❑ To improve the health and physique of children.

❑ To use scientifically tested exercises.

❑ To develop qualities of alertness and decision-making.

❑ To establish control of mind over body.

❑ To improve respiration and circulation.

❑ To give children corrective exercises to improve posture.

❑ To give them control exercises to improve skill.

8) b)

Describe the innovations to be found in the 1933 Syllabus.

    6 marks for six from :

❑ Focus on the child's physical need for a good physique.

❑ Need for the acquisition of physical skills identified.

❑ Encouragement of wholesome outdoor recreation.

❑ Significance of character building through physical activities.

❑ Introduction of group work.

❑ Extension of the idea of short break, fun activities.

❑ Significance of enjoyment for children over seven.

❑ Notion of independent action by children arising from play motives.

❑ The upright child - postural and ethical.

ELEMENTARY SCHOOLS, MILITARY DRILL, P.T. AND P.E. - ANSWERS QUESTION 8 (continued)

8) c)

The major changes in the book Moving and Growing (1952) which reflected post-Second World War attitudes :

5 marks for five from the objectives linked with a war experience :

- ❏ Children made central :   Idealism of winning the war.
- ❏ Discovery method :   Desire to encourage independent thinking.
- ❏ Innovative apparatus :   Learned from commando tactics and training, or the result of rebuilding programme after the bomb destruction.
- ❏ No more formal tables :   Desire for individual freedom.
- ❏ Learning is fun / play :   Women and primary influence during the war.
- ❏ Skilfulness and skill central :   Desire to develop sporting links.
- ❏ Lots of child inspired games :   Result of a war which rated decision-making, and experiences in prisoner-of-war camps.
- ❏ Significance of fresh air :   Limited travel during the war, reflecting freedom / what we fought for / experiences by evacuees.
- ❏ Awareness of individual differences :   Learnt from rehabilitation of those injured during the war.
- ❏ Partner and group developments :   Lessons learnt about sharing and caring / expression of a new postwar world.
- ❏ Swimming & dance central experiences : Giving children lots of choices which the war years had not allowed.

8) d)

The purpose and format of the Model Course (1902), and the reasons for its introduction and replacement :

10 marks for ten from :

Purpose : (maximum of 3 marks)

- ❏ To increase fitness for military service.
- ❏ Experience military discipline.
- ❏ Learn to withstand the hardship of combat.
- ❏ Gain familiarity with weapons.

Format : (maximum of 3 marks)

- ❏ Appointed army instructors.
- ❏ Marching practice.
- ❏ Directed exercises.
- ❏ Weapon drill.

Reasons : (maximum of 3 marks)

- ❏ Setbacks during Boer War.
- ❏ Lack of fitness among recruits.
- ❏ Value of military discipline as a form of social control.

Replacement : (maximum of 3 marks)

- ❏ Unsuitable for young children.
- ❏ Particularly military exercises for girls.
- ❏ Teachers objected to military instructors.
- ❏ Military instructors lowered status of subject.
- ❏ Desire to separate P.T. from Cadet Corps.
- ❏ Swedish drill far more suitable.

DEVELOPMENT OF SWIMMING AND BATHING

9) a)

Compare the sporting associations reflected in the two pictures of a country town.

6 marks for six from :

River town :

- ❏ Bathing for recreative purposes.
- ❏ Learning to swim to save life.
- ❏ Swimming to win races.
- ❏ Impromptu races across and down the river.
- ❏ Cleanliness.
- ❏ Boating, Sailing, Rowing, Canoeing.
- ❏ Fishing and shooting.

Churchyard scene :

- ❏ Archery for military reasons.
- ❏ Archery as part of a village festival.

DEVELOPMENT OF SWIMMING AND BATHING - ANSWERS QUESTION 9 (continued)

9) b)
Use the figure to describe bathing at Rugby School in the 1830s.
> 4 marks for four from :
- ❏ The boys of Rugby School bathed in the river Avon.
- ❏ It was recreational.
- ❏ No masters were present.
- ❏ There were bathing places / stations where the depth of the water differed.
- ❏ The Wratislaw place had deep water for swimming.
- ❏ It was limited to older boys who could swim.
- ❏ Costumes were not worn because it was for boys only.

9) c)
Use the three pictures to help you to describe the changes which occurred to bathing and swimming in the 19th century.
> 8 marks for eight from :
> Recreational :
- ❏ Bathing for fun in the warm weather.
- ❏ Bathing in natural facilities, such as rivers and pools.
- ❏ Bathers learnt to swim to save themselves from drowning.
- ❏ Bathers also took this opportunity to wash.
> Water cure :
- ❏ The Regency Fashion of the Water Cure was developed around 1800.
- ❏ It was an upper class pursuit to improve health.
- ❏ The belief was that certain types of water had curative values.
- ❏ Special Spa towns attracted visitors for the cure (for example, Buxton or Bath).
- ❏ Special baths were built which included cold plunge baths.
> Sea bathing :
- ❏ Salt water became one of the water cures.
- ❏ People were attracted to the sea-side because it was free.
- ❏ Originally, people went in the winter months.
- ❏ Summer bathing made the custom more popular.
- ❏ The British sea-side holiday became the fashion, and sea-side towns developed.

9) d)
Explain the reasons for the Wash House Acts of the 1840s and describe the development of public baths in the larger towns.
> 7 marks for seven from :
> Wash house Acts :
- ❏ To clean up the industrial working classes (the smell, the dirt, the habits).
- ❏ To reduce the likelihood of epidemics (the health and disease problem).
> Developments of public baths :
- ❏ Government grants to build public baths in the larger towns.
- ❏ Particularly industrial towns with large working class numbers.
- ❏ Separate indoor heated baths for men and women.
- ❏ Maximum of one penny per visit, less for children.
- ❏ Included washing and cloth-washing facilities.
- ❏ A large plunge bath in which swimming took place.
- ❏ Competition swimming and water polo developed using the large pool.

THE DEVELOPMENT OF OUTDOOR PURSUITS

10) a)

Explain the changing face of Mountain Activities during the 19th century.

   6 marks for six from :

❑ Long distance walking was popular in England.

❑ The Lake District was very popular.

❑ Clubs were formed which visited beauty spots.

❑ This was extended to the Alps and formation of the Alpine Club.

❑ This was part of the 'Grand Tour' for the upper classes.

❑ The upper classes visited the Alps in winter.

❑ Mountaineering developed from the need to find the easiest route to the top for the view.

❑ Scientists, particularly botanists, learnt climbing skills to reach rare plants.

❑ Rock climbing developed from a competitive element, i.e. wanting to find the most difficult route to the top.

❑ The English Lake Distract, North Wales, and the Scottish Highlands became popular for rock climbing as well as distance walking.

10) b)

Explain why winter sports were so popular in the 19th century, but some were only available to the wealthy.

   4 marks for four from :

❑ The frozen land prevented agricultural work, therefore there was nothing to do but enjoy recreation.

❑ Severe winters led to fairs held on frozen rivers and their flooded meadows (the mini ice age of the mid to late 19th century led to severe winters in Britain for 40 to 50 years).

❑ East Anglia flat with abundant ice in cold winters became the centre of speed skating.

❑ Professionalised speed skating for championships, money and wagering.

❑ Figure skating was indulged in by the upper classes, since special skates were costly.

❑ Alpine skiing was started by British winter climbers, only the wealthy cold travel to the Alps.

10) c) i)

Describe the technical development of the cycle in the context of industrialisation and urbanisation.

   5 marks for five from :

❑ The bone shaker / hobby horse, was an invention for fashionable young men to use in the towns.

❑ Industrial revolution led to small factories well able to manufacture metal cycles.

❑ Horses were less easily stabled in large towns, leading to the cycle becoming the urban horse.

❑ The penny-farthing was an industrial invention to produce a fast cycle.

❑ The tricycle was invented for safety.

❑ The Rover Safety Bicycle was invented to make bicycling safer (not as high as the penny farthing).

❑ And as fast as the penny farthing (because of the chain and cog drive mechanism, which in effect geared the rear wheel).

❑ And so the Rover captured a bigger market.

10) c) ii)

Use the design of the cycles shown in the figure to discuss social class and gender involvement in cycling.

   6 marks for six from :

❑ The earliest hobby horses were ridden by upper class young men only.

❑ The invention of the penny-farthing also suited young men because they were fast but dangerous.

❑ However, upper class men preferred a real horse and middle class men used the cycles in towns.

❑ Women and children and elderly people found the penny farthing too dangerous (because of the height off the ground and the speed they were capable of).

❑ So the women, children, and elderly tended to buy tricycles.

❑ The safety bike allowed middle class women to ride and they joined clubs or went shopping (on the bikes).

❑ Cycles were too expensive for the lower classes until the second hand trade developed.

10) d)

Link the advent of the cycle with the development of travel facilities in the second half of the 19th century.

   4 marks for four from :

❑ With railways developing, the roads deteriorated.

❑ With the development of the penny-farthing came road touring clubs.

❑ Which then had problems with pot-holes in the roads.

❑ The middle class lobby led to Government intervention, and road improvements.

❑ Cycle clubs, through the CTC(Cycling Touring Club) established touring maps, repair shops, and cafes for cyclists on their routes.

❑ Railways used to take cycles long distances before starting a tour.

SELECTED BIBLIOGRAPHY

Armitage, J.	1977	Man at Play. Warne.
Birley, D.	1995	Land of Sport and Glory, Sport and British Society 1887 - 1910. MUP.
Birley, D.	1995	Playing the Game, Sport and British Society 1910 - 1945. MUP.
Birley, D.	1993	Sport and the Making of Britain. MUP.
Brailsford, D.	1998	British Sport, a Social History. Lutterworth Press.
Brailsford, D.	1988	Bareknuckles : a Social History of Prizefighting. Lutterworth Press.
Brailsford, D.	1999	A Taste for Diversions. Lutterworth Press.
Brasch, R.	1986	How did Sports Begin? A look at the origins of man at play. Gazelle Book Services.
DDvideo	1988	History of Sport Boxed Set. Classroom Resources.
Cox, R.	2000	Encylopaedia of British Sport. ABC Clio.
Davis, R.J. et. al.	2000	Physical Education and the Study of Sport 4e. Mosby.
Ford, J.	1971	Prizefighting. David and Charles.
Galligan, F.	2000	Advanced Level PE for Edexcel. Heinemann.
Gardner, B.	1973	The Public Schools.
Holt, R.	1989	Sport and the British. Oxford University Press.
Honeybourne, J.	2000	Advanced Physical Education and Sport 2e, Nelson Thornes.
H.M.S.O.	1952	Moving and Growing.
Hughes, T.	1852	Tom Brown's Schooldays.
Jewell, B.	1977	Sports and Games. Midas.
Lowerson, J.	1995	Sport and the English Middle Classes 1970-1914. MUP.
McIntosh, P.C.	1952	Physical Education in England since 1800. Bell.
McIntosh, P.C.	1987	Sport in Society. West London Press.
Mechikoff, R.A.	1998	A History and Philosophy of Sport and Physical Education 2e. McGraw-Hill.
Smith, W.D.	1974	Stretching Their Bodies. David and Charles.
Swanson, R.A.	1995	History of Sport and P.E. in the United States. Human Kinetics.
Viney, N.	1978	Ball Games. Book Club Associates.
Walvin, J.	1994	The People's Game : The History of Football Revisited. Mainstream Publishing.
Wesson, K. etal	2000	PE and Sport Studies, A Complete Guide to A Level Studies 2e. Hodder and Stoughton.
Wiggins, D.K.	1995	Sport in America. Human Kinetics.
Wigglesworth, N.	1992	The Social History of English Rowing. Frank Cass.
Williams, J.	1999	Cricket and England. Frank Cass.
Willis, R.	1982	Cricket's Biggest Mystery. Lutterworth Press.
Wymer, N.	1949	Sport in England. Harrap.

Pictorial evidence from slides by R.J.Davis, 102 High Street, Pershore, Worcestershire WR10 1EA.

THE COMPARATIVE PERSPECTIVE

COMPARATIVE STUDY

COMPARATIVE STUDY
involves the study of :
- Structures and mechanisms operating in a number of different social settings (i.e. countries).
- Comparing and accounting for similarities and contrasting differences in those social settings and the range of activities within those social settings.

You may have to :
- List or exemplify.
- Rationalise, justify, or account for such examples.
- Compare and account for similarities with other social and organisational frameworks.
- Contrast and account for differences in such frameworks.
- Consider the implications of such policies and relationships.

COMPARATIVE STUDIES

THE AREAS OF STUDY FOR EACH COUNTRY
- The nature of government and the level of its involvement in sport.
- The organisational and administrative features governing sport, physical recreation and physical education (both governmental and non-governmental).
- Issues arising out of the relationship between the above activities, their organisational structure and the social setting in which they operate.
- The social, historical, and geographical influences which have affected and still do affect the nature of the above activities in each of the countries or social settings given in the syllabus.

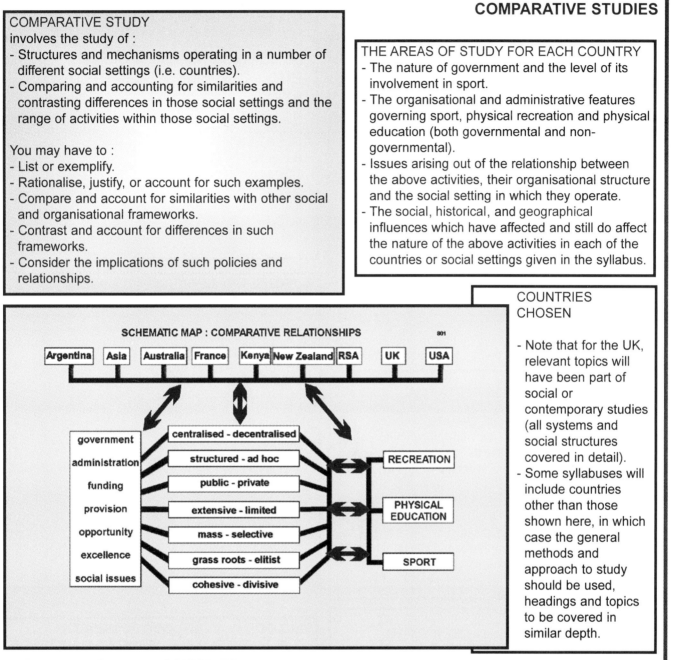

SCHEMATIC MAP : COMPARATIVE RELATIONSHIPS

| Argentina | Asia | Australia | France | Kenya | New Zealand | RSA | UK | USA |

government	centralised - decentralised	
administration	structured - ad hoc	RECREATION
funding	public - private	
provision	extensive - limited	PHYSICAL EDUCATION
opportunity	mass - selective	
excellence	grass roots - elitist	SPORT
social issues	cohesive - divisive	

COUNTRIES CHOSEN

- Note that for the UK, relevant topics will have been part of social or contemporary studies (all systems and social structures covered in detail).
- Some syllabuses will include countries other than those shown here, in which case the general methods and approach to study should be used, headings and topics to be covered in similar depth.

AUSTRALIA : GENERAL COMMENTS

SPORT and RECREATION as part of the AUSTRALIAN LIFESTYLE
- Most Australians live in urban areas and do not rely on the 'outback' for their recreation in the way that we often imagine to be the case.
- The diversity of terrain and climate ensures that opportunities exist for the most diverse range of activities.
- Outdoor Education and Recreation developments do not compare with the long established Summer Schools and 'Wilderness Trails' in the U.S., or the 'Classes Transplantée' and 'Centres de Vacance' in France.
- The Outward Bound Trust, well known in the UK, has been established in Australia since the 1960's, and in most Australian States outdoor education is now on the curriculum in schools.

CULTURAL ROOTS
- Common cultural roots with the UK by virtue of both its colonial origins & immigrants from the UK.
- Hence the growth of such institutions as 'Timbertops' (Geelong Grammar School), operating very similarly to Gordonstoun School in Scotland.
- More recently, a broader influence was introduced by more recent immigrants from both Europe, and most recently, Asia.
- Many Australian sports clubs were founded by immigrant groups.and games were often marred by ethnic rivalries.
- It is now illegal for clubs (example : 'Melbourne Croatia') to have names signifying ethnic origins.

AUSTRALIA : GENERAL COMMENTS - continued

CULTURAL LINKS
- The relationship between climate and coast is similar to parts of France and the West Coast of the USA and the lifestyle based on 'sun, sea and surf'.
- Colonial links with the UK are seen in team sports, particularly rugby and cricket.
- The heavy industrial base of the North of England has exported some of its recreational culture.
- This is seen most clearly in sports such as Rugby league (and to some extent soccer).
- The yearning for the country or the mountains as an escape from industrial grime has not been transplanted from the UK since much of Australia's early economy was pastorally based.
- The major sports were all spawned during the first wave of colonisation.
- A recent development has been the influence of professionalism and commercialism.
- Born of the 'pacific rim' influence of the USA and 'pay TV.'
- Both rugby codes have been particularly affected.

OUTDOOR RECREATION IN AUSTRALIA

CONTROL of OUTDOOR RECREATION
- The Department of the Arts, Sport, the Environment, Tourism and Territories (DASETT) has centralised administrative control over Australia's vast tracts of wilderness, desert, and scenic beauty.
- Each State has its own Departments of Environment / Tourism which oversee developments and policies within its boundaries and parks.
- Other areas of beauty are managed by the respective State Departments of Conservation, Forests and Land.

NATIONAL PARKS
- This term can be confusing as each State in Australia is in effect an individual country.
- National parks are therefore managed and controlled by the State in which they exist rather than by the Federal Government.
- An exception to the above is the Great Barrier Reef.
- This is managed by the Great Barrier Reef Marine Park Authority (GBRMPA) under the direct control of the Federal Government, rather than a State Department.
- There are well-established codes of behaviour for visitors to national parks and other areas of scenic and natural beauty.
- All agencies in Australia make much use of information technology and the 'Internet' in making such information available.

ABORIGINAL CULTURE
- Has not been allowed to contribute to the development of Australian sports and recreations.
- Aboriginal involvement in 'Australian Sports' is not unknown but opportunity is not universal.
- All State Governments now have departments whose purpose is to provide opportunity for participation and to develop programmes of integration for the aboriginal people.

ROLE-MODELS
- Are emerging from indigenous / ethnic groups and show greater opportunity and increased participation by such groups.

PARALLEL with the NATIVE NORTH AMERICAN
- Who, like his Aboriginal counterpart was almost wiped out by the colonising invader.
- The process of :
  - 'decimate'
    - 'isolate'
      - 'discriminate'
        - 'ignore'
          - 'pacify'
            - 'provide for'
              - 'include'
  is evident in both cultures, and cannot yet be said to be complete.
- Inclusion of native races and their cultures may be seen as the cleansing of conscience in regard to the genocide (as now perceived) during the respective periods of colonisation.

PHILOSOPHY of OUTDOOR RECREATION
- Both Australia and the USA are 'young societies'.
- Derived to some extent from colonial links with Britain.
- Both countries have since undergone large-scale immigration and are therefore multi-cultural societies to a greater degree than Britain.
- And to a much greater degree than France.
  - Most Australians are 'city dwellers' and have an affinity with recreations within the built environment.
  - The exception to this is their affinity for the beach and its associated recreations (most Australians live within an hour's drive of the coast).

AUSTRALIA - OUTDOOR EDUCATION

OUTDOOR EDUCATION
- Mirrors that in Britain and the USA, with provision made for programmes but no clear requirement to carry them out.
- Australian schools offer Outdoor Education programmes within a range of 'electives' which are often not compulsory.
- Compare the USA with wide provision (but no compulsion) for outdoor experience in its summer camps.
- However, Australia is beginning to make wider provision, and the Australian College of Education in Canberra now runs undergraduate programmes in this field.
- Implementation is up to individual schools.
- There is an increasing recognition to the affinity of the Aboriginal people for the outdoors.
- Special programmes are organised for Aboriginal students, and respect for their cultural heritage is being adopted within programmes of outdoor education.

DIVERSITY
- We tend to associate Australian outdoor sports and recreations with the sun and the sea.
- But the country is in fact a continent and encompasses a range of climatic conditions.
- Australian skiers and alpinists can train all-year-round without leaving Australia.
- The growth of such activities as 'triathlon' and other related sports gives examples of activities derived from the combination of good climate and technology.
- Together with the 'healthy outdoor' philosophy of the surfer.

ORIGINS
- Physical Education system is close to the UK.
- Colonial roots, Muscular Christianity, public and grammar schools led to similarities to UK up to the 1914-18 war.
- Current comprehensive system resembles the USA (and more lately the UK).
- Public school tendency towards religious foundations reflects France.
- Secularisation of the State system similar to France, and the USA.

PHYSICAL EDUCATION IN AUSTRALIA

STRUCTURE of DEVOLUTION of SPORT in AUSTRALIA   804

```
        FEDERAL MINISTER              ────►         ASC
     Youth, Sport, Recreation              Australian Sports Commission
              │       │                              │
              ▼       ▼                              ▼
  Education Minister      DEST                       AIS
                                          Australian Institute for Sport
       │                   │                         │
     ACHPER          State Sports Bodies  ◄───────────┘
       │                   │
  State Education    'Active Australia'
  and PE Bodies      Formerly 'Aussie Sport'
       │                   │
   teachers ── schools ── coaches
```

DEVELOPMENT
- Physical education is the responsibility of each individual State, with federal input through ACHPER.
- Involvement at National level is also shared by the Federal Minister of Education.
- Whose responsibility includes :
  - The inspection of schools on behalf of the Federal Government.
  - The Department of Environment, Sport and Territories (DEST) which works through the State Ministries of Sport and their institutes to develop initiatives such as 'Active Australia' and school sport programmes.
- SEPEP is a programme of sports awareness, including the concept of sportsmanship and 'fair play', training and officiating rather than simply a programme of sports participation.
- The federal Aussie system is different from the type of federal system in operation in the USA.
- The Australian Council for Health, Physical Education and Recreation (ACHPER) plays a central role in the development of physical education programmes for schools and the community Moneghetti report (Victoria 1993) initiated review of PE in schools.

FURTHER DEVELOPMENTS
- PASE (Physical and Sport Education), developed in Victoria.
- Contrast with developments in the UK.
- PE and Sport (in Aus) are being placed on the curriculum for all pupils within compulsory programmes.
- Sport is recognised as having value in its own right, rather than simply serving as a vehicle for 'education through the physical'.

- 'Aussie Sport' was designed as a programme for the development of junior sport whereas 'Active Australia' is a framework for all the population i.e. 6-60.
- 'Aussie Sport' was a targeted programme, and consisted of Sport to upper primary and lower secondary kids (only sport or modified sport).
- 'Active Australia' is a complete framework of participation for all ages.

PE EXAMS and CURRICULUM in AUSTRALIA

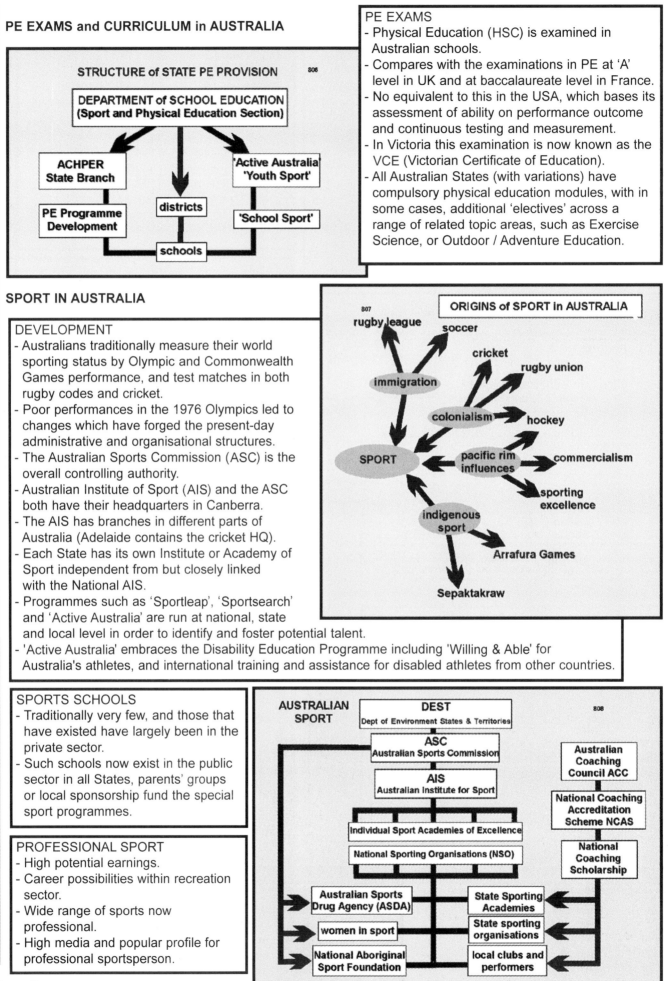

STRUCTURE of STATE PE PROVISION   806

DEPARTMENT of SCHOOL EDUCATION
(Sport and Physical Education Section)

ACHPER
State Branch

'Active Australia'
'Youth Sport'

PE Programme
Development

districts

'School Sport'

schools

PE EXAMS
- Physical Education (HSC) is examined in Australian schools.
- Compares with the examinations in PE at 'A' level in UK and at baccalaureate level in France.
- No equivalent to this in the USA, which bases its assessment of ability on performance outcome and continuous testing and measurement.
- In Victoria this examination is now known as the VCE (Victorian Certificate of Education).
- All Australian States (with variations) have compulsory physical education modules, with in some cases, additional 'electives' across a range of related topic areas, such as Exercise Science, or Outdoor / Adventure Education.

SPORT IN AUSTRALIA

DEVELOPMENT
- Australians traditionally measure their world sporting status by Olympic and Commonwealth Games performance, and test matches in both rugby codes and cricket.
- Poor performances in the 1976 Olympics led to changes which have forged the present-day administrative and organisational structures.
- The Australian Sports Commission (ASC) is the overall controlling authority.
- Australian Institute of Sport (AIS) and the ASC both have their headquarters in Canberra.
- The AIS has branches in different parts of Australia (Adelaide contains the cricket HQ).
- Each State has its own Institute or Academy of Sport independent from but closely linked with the National AIS.
- Programmes such as 'Sportleap', 'Sportsearch' and 'Active Australia' are run at national, state and local level in order to identify and foster potential talent.
- 'Active Australia' embraces the Disability Education Programme including 'Willing & Able' for Australia's athletes, and international training and assistance for disabled athletes from other countries.

ORIGINS of SPORT in AUSTRALIA   807

rugby league

soccer

cricket

rugby union

immigration

colonialism

hockey

SPORT

pacific rim influences

commercialism

sporting excellence

indigenous sport

Arrafura Games

Sepaktakraw

SPORTS SCHOOLS
- Traditionally very few, and those that have existed have largely been in the private sector.
- Such schools now exist in the public sector in all States, parents' groups or local sponsorship fund the special sport programmes.

PROFESSIONAL SPORT
- High potential earnings.
- Career possibilities within recreation sector.
- Wide range of sports now professional.
- High media and popular profile for professional sportsperson.

AUSTRALIAN SPORT   808

DEST
Dept of Environment States & Territories

ASC
Australian Sports Commission

AIS
Australian Institute for Sport

Individual Sport Academies of Excellence

National Sporting Organisations (NSO)

Australian Sports Drug Agency (ASDA)

women in sport

National Aboriginal Sport Foundation

Australian Coaching Council ACC

National Coaching Accreditation Scheme NCAS

National Coaching Scholarship

State Sporting Academies

State sporting organisations

local clubs and performers

Information

FRANCE : GENERAL COMMENTS

CULTURAL INFLUENCES
- 'Courtly' and aristocratic influences in sport and recreation meant that until the Revolution a pattern of recreation similar to England existed in France.
- Following the revolution, sport in France was influenced by militarism and nationalism (born during the Napoleonic period), and by the Olympianism of de Coubertin.
- Gymnastics had a strong influence, and the work of Clias at Joinville was similar to developments in England and (by others) in the former British colony of America.
- PE in French schools is still known as 'La Gym'.
- Both France and Britain have indigenous minorities striving to re-establish their own cultures (Bretons, Basques, Catalans - Cornish, Welsh and Scottish).
- Comparable with the indigenous populations of both Australia and the USA.
- Nationalism and sport are closely interwoven into the French culture (the influence of the Revolution, and reinforced by de Gaulle in the post-war period), this has never been so in England.
- Similarity exists with historical events in the USA.
- All three countries (France, UK, USA) have distinct 'regional separatisms' which come together under the national flag for major international sporting occasions.

STRUCTURE of ADMINISTRATION in FRANCE [809]

MINISTRY (issues policy and exerts central control)

Régions (22)

Départements (96)

Arrondissements (324)

Cantons (3549)

Communes (36385)

DEVELOPMENTS
- Although not as large as the United States or Australia, France is large enough to have climatic and topographical variety which supports a wide range of sports and recreations.
- The attraction of its winter sports facilities in both the Alps and the Pyrénées bring visitors from all over the world for both recreational and sporting purposes.
- A feature of French recreational patterns is the holi day month of August, producing an exodus to the coast on a large scale and 'Le Camping Francais' (compare Australia and the West Coast of USA).
- Failure in the Rome Olympics (1960) saw de Gaulle institute changes to the structure of sporting organisation hence the highly subsidised support of its national programmes and the 5-point plan (refer to page 8.7).

THE FRENCH POLITICAL (PRESIDENTIAL) SYSTEM
- Many political parties.
- Including extreme right-wing nationalism.
- Produced a centralised system of government reflected in the organisation of sport, recreation and physical education.
- Sport is heavily subsidised.
- The French system is heavily influenced by Paris to the disadvantage of the regions.
- This is changing with the development of commercial sponsorship alongside central funding.
- France participates internationally on an increasing scale, both rugby codes are well established in the South but become truly 'National' when 'le cockerel' appears on players' shirts.
- Soccer has a broadening appeal but France's oldest established 'international event' is the Tour de France cycle race.

OUTDOOR RECREATION IN FRANCE

SIZE
- France has approximately the same population as the UK but twice the land area.
- This encompasses a much broader climatic and topographical range.
- Winter sports and recreations are firmly established, as are the coastal resorts (particularly in the South – 'Le Midi') in the summer months.
- The widely spread nature of the society stretches communications.
- Many traditional recreations are strongly 'regionalised' because of this.
- Breton wrestling for example, takes place in the North, whilst Pélote (Provence) and bull fighting are established in the South.
- Numerous rivers and an extensive coastline mean that water-based activities have always had a place within the French recreational culture.

CONTROL
- France's 22 'Régions' take responsibility for what elsewhere might be described as 'National Parks'.
- This policy includes the preservation of the rural countryside and historic monuments and buildings.

PHILOSOPHY of OUTDOOR RECREATION
- The philosophy is of being at one with nature, the fresh air and the simplicity of a rural existence.
- This was shared with the naturalism movement of the English middle and upper classes of the second half of the 19th century.
- This philosophy was guided by the middle class ethic of spiritual and physical purity which also emerged in England at the same time.

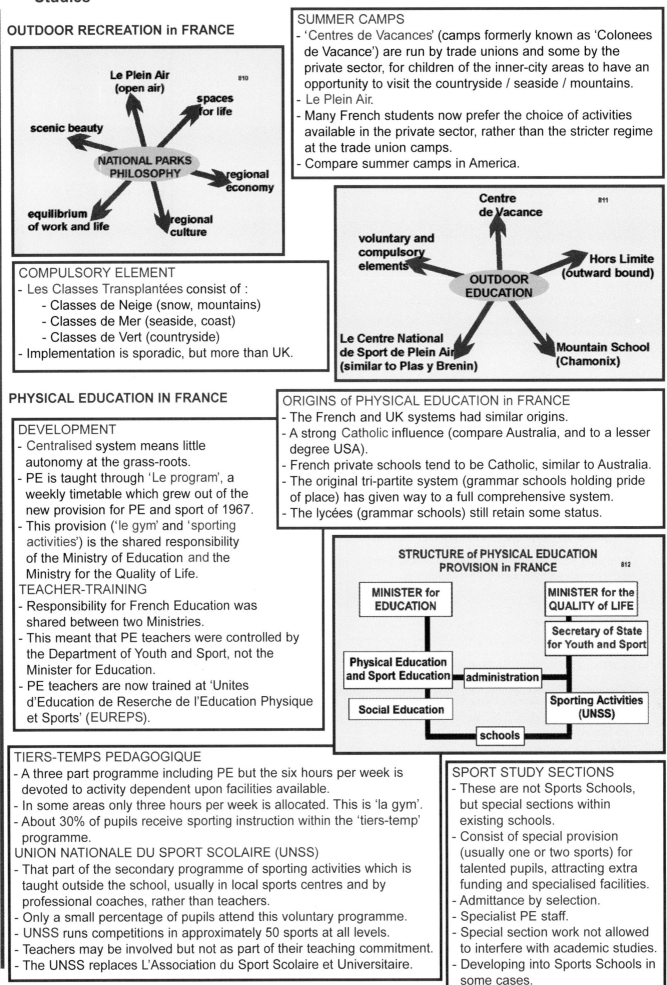

OUTDOOR RECREATION in FRANCE

Le Plein Air (open air)

spaces for life

scenic beauty

NATIONAL PARKS PHILOSOPHY

regional economy

equilibrium of work and life

regional culture

SUMMER CAMPS
- 'Centres de Vacances' (camps formerly known as 'Colonees de Vacance') are run by trade unions and some by the private sector, for children of the inner-city areas to have an opportunity to visit the countryside / seaside / mountains.
- Le Plein Air.
- Many French students now prefer the choice of activities available in the private sector, rather than the stricter regime at the trade union camps.
- Compare summer camps in America.

COMPULSORY ELEMENT
- Les Classes Transplantées consist of :
    - Classes de Neige (snow, mountains)
    - Classes de Mer (seaside, coast)
    - Classes de Vert (countryside)
- Implementation is sporadic, but more than UK.

Centre de Vacance

voluntary and compulsory elements

OUTDOOR EDUCATION

Hors Limite (outward bound)

Le Centre National de Sport de Plein Air (similar to Plas y Brenin)

Mountain School (Chamonix)

PHYSICAL EDUCATION IN FRANCE

DEVELOPMENT
- Centralised system means little autonomy at the grass-roots.
- PE is taught through 'Le program', a weekly timetable which grew out of the new provision for PE and sport of 1967.
- This provision ('le gym' and 'sporting activities') is the shared responsibility of the Ministry of Education and the Ministry for the Quality of Life.

TEACHER-TRAINING
- Responsibility for French Education was shared between two Ministries.
- This meant that PE teachers were controlled by the Department of Youth and Sport, not the Minister for Education.
- PE teachers are now trained at 'Unites d'Education de Reserche de l'Education Physique et Sports' (EUREPS).

ORIGINS of PHYSICAL EDUCATION in FRANCE
- The French and UK systems had similar origins.
- A strong Catholic influence (compare Australia, and to a lesser degree USA).
- French private schools tend to be Catholic, similar to Australia.
- The original tri-partite system (grammar schools holding pride of place) has given way to a full comprehensive system.
- The lycées (grammar schools) still retain some status.

STRUCTURE of PHYSICAL EDUCATION PROVISION in FRANCE

MINISTER for EDUCATION

MINISTER for the QUALITY of LIFE

Secretary of State for Youth and Sport

Physical Education and Sport Education — administration

Social Education

Sporting Activities (UNSS)

schools

TIERS-TEMPS PEDAGOGIQUE
- A three part programme including PE but the six hours per week is devoted to activity dependent upon facilities available.
- In some areas only three hours per week is allocated. This is 'la gym'.
- About 30% of pupils receive sporting instruction within the 'tiers-temp' programme.

UNION NATIONALE DU SPORT SCOLAIRE (UNSS)
- That part of the secondary programme of sporting activities which is taught outside the school, usually in local sports centres and by professional coaches, rather than teachers.
- Only a small percentage of pupils attend this voluntary programme.
- UNSS runs competitions in approximately 50 sports at all levels.
- Teachers may be involved but not as part of their teaching commitment.
- The UNSS replaces L'Association du Sport Scolaire et Universitaire.

SPORT STUDY SECTIONS
- These are not Sports Schools, but special sections within existing schools.
- Consist of special provision (usually one or two sports) for talented pupils, attracting extra funding and specialised facilities.
- Admittance by selection.
- Specialist PE staff.
- Special section work not allowed to interfere with academic studies.
- Developing into Sports Schools in some cases.

SPORT IN FRANCE

ORIGINS
- 'Olympianism'. De Coubertin (initiator of the modern Olympic movement) was a French aristocrat.
- Modern structure of Sport in France is based on whether sports are 'Olympic' or 'non-Olympic'.

YOUTH SPORT LINKS
- Maisons des Jeunes et Culture make provision for sport as part of central policy.
- Municipal groups (for example, the Fire Services) promote a range of recreational activities ('sapeurs-pompiers'), which includes inter-town competition and outdoor experiences.
- Tennis and golf have grown enormously in the last ten years.
- Easy access to facilities reflects a centralised policy which provides them on the basis of social need which reflects an acknowledgement of the value of the recreative process, as opposed to provision aimed purely at the production of excellence.

DEVELOPMENT
- All sport is funded through the National Olympic and Sports Committee.
- This is divided into two sections :
    - Top class (international) sport ('Olympic' and 'non-Olympic').
    - Sport for All (regional level and downward).
- Sport is controlled centrally by the Ministry of Youth and Sport through regional and departmental (district) directorates.
- The directorates have no autonomy and exist to carry out Ministry objectives.
- Sports organisations are divided into 'Olympic' and 'non-Olympic'.

- 'Multisport' federations and the federations of university and school sport make up the four major administrative threads of French sport.

- The success of France in international sport has now attracted commercial sponsorship to both individual sports and the central organisation that supports international and Olympic teams.

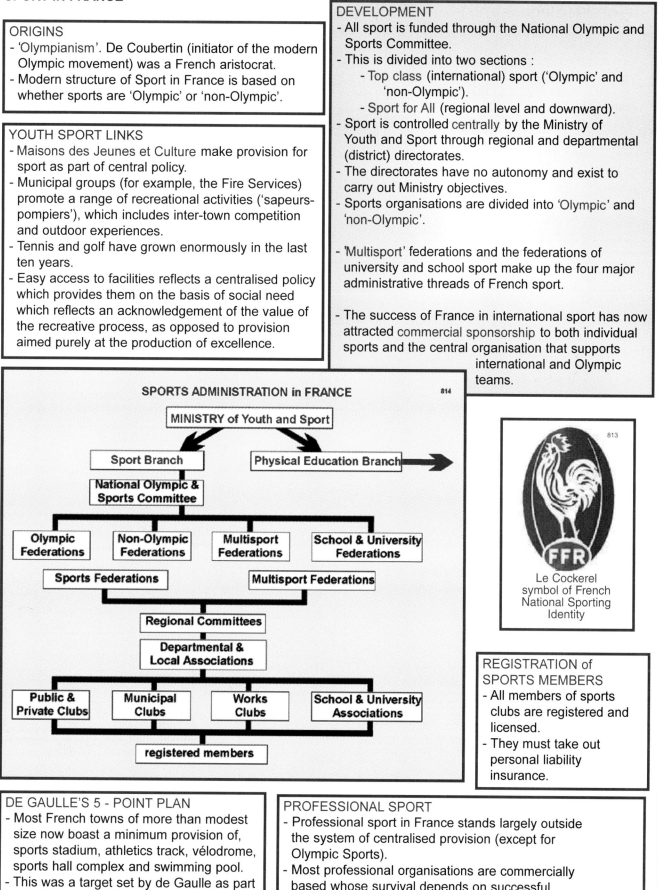

SPORTS ADMINISTRATION in FRANCE   814

MINISTRY of Youth and Sport

Sport Branch → Physical Education Branch →

National Olympic & Sports Committee

| Olympic Federations | Non-Olympic Federations | Multisport Federations | School & University Federations |

Sports Federations   Multisport Federations

Regional Committees

Departmental & Local Associations

| Public & Private Clubs | Municipal Clubs | Works Clubs | School & University Associations |

registered members

Le Cockerel symbol of French National Sporting Identity   813

REGISTRATION of SPORTS MEMBERS
- All members of sports clubs are registered and licensed.
- They must take out personal liability insurance.

DE GAULLE'S 5 - POINT PLAN
- Most French towns of more than modest size now boast a minimum provision of, sports stadium, athletics track, vélodrome, sports hall complex and swimming pool.
- This was a target set by de Gaulle as part of his plan for French sport, following the disappointing showing at the 1960 Olympiad.

PROFESSIONAL SPORT
- Professional sport in France stands largely outside the system of centralised provision (except for Olympic Sports).
- Most professional organisations are commercially based whose survival depends on successful performance.
- Sponsorship is increasing the greater profile of French Sport.

USA : GENERAL COMMENTS

CULTURAL INFLUENCES
- Comparable with Australia, both countries have suppressed the influence of an indigenous culture in sport and recreation (and across the social and political spectrum).
- Also influenced by British colonial presence.
- And (similar to Australia) by policies of mass immigration.
- The War of Independence, and the Civil War (compare with French and Russian revolutions).
- USA is a federal state (compare Australia).
- USA has wide topographical and climatic diversity (compare Australia and to a lesser degree France).

THE DECENTRALISED STATE
- The USA is the least centralised in terms of administration.
- The capitalist ethic has meant that independence of individual organisations is highly valued.
- Federality in the USA is expressed for international sporting events (the Olympics, the soccer World Cup and other World Championships).
- And for National legislation (for example, 'Title IX' - equal opportunities for women).
- Currently, federal funding is still substantial, but commercial sponsorship is increasing as the USOC and government accept that this is commonplace elsewhere.

STACKING
- Ensures the preservation of the White Anglo-Saxon Protestant (WASP) power base, with Vietnamese at the bottom of the pile on the 'last in' principle. This is also reflected in roles in sport, and only relatively recently have we seen black quarterbacks playing American football and black coaches on the sidelines.
- TV, professionalism and advertising have helped break down these barriers in the US as well as in Australia and elsewhere.
- But blacks and other ethnic groups are not allowed to rise to a level where they can exert control and generally do not become more than well-paid 'gladiators'.
- This is the 'glass ceiling' syndrome, which also applies to women.
- Blacks and ethnic minorities in the UK, and Aborigines in Australia are generally ascribed a more lowly status by society (in spite of legislation aimed at countering this), and although France has 'l'egalitarianism' written into its constitution, there are some groups, including Algerians, who would feel that they are still a political (and sporting) minority.

The image of women as cheer leaders contrasts with the philosphy of Title IX legislation

ISOLATIONISM
- All the major sports in the US (except for Track & Field) are 'contrived', indigenous sports.
- Their 'World Series' mentality is applied to sports that are not 'World Sports'.
- Hence US 'sports moguls' retain both control and the certainty of American success.
- The level of specialisation achieved within these sports is such that, as commercial interests orchestrate a projection of these sports onto the world stage, US teams are almost guaranteed to be ahead of their rivals.
- NBC have reported very low viewing figures for the 2000 Olympics. It seems that Americans also prefer major sport to occur in the USA - not elsewhere!

OUTDOOR RECREATION IN THE USA

CONTROL
- America's natural resources are centrally controlled by the Department of the Interior.
- The use of land and water space for recreational purposes is the responsibility of a whole range of Departments (Bureau).
- Influence of presidents Wilson and Roosevelt.

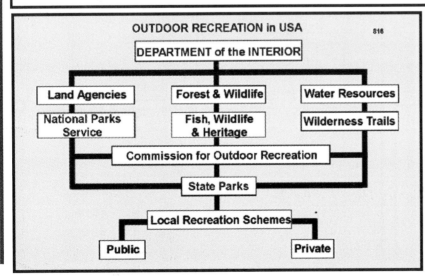

OUTDOOR RECREATION in USA

DEPARTMENT of the INTERIOR

Land Agencies | Forest & Wildlife | Water Resources

National Parks Service | Fish, Wildlife & Heritage | Wilderness Trails

Commission for Outdoor Recreation

State Parks

Local Recreation Schemes

Public | Private

SIZE
- USA has land area of 3.5 million sq. miles.
- Comparable with Australia but almost 15 times its population.
- Size and diversity helps recreation within a far superior communications infrastructure.

OUTDOOR RECREATION IN THE USA - continued

PHILOSOPHY
- USA is a 'young nation', created by adventurers and pioneers of the great outdoors (compare Australia).
- USA has wilderness areas (much less than Australia).
- Large proportion of population access these areas.
- Outdoor recreation embraces a much wider range of activity than the 'sea-shore' (as in Australia).
- Outdoor education is seen as very important but is delivered largely through the medium of 'summer camps' rather than school programmes.

NATIONAL PARKS
- Federal Law through the National Park Service controls America's great National Parks.
- These are distinct from State Parks, which are administered by the States in which they lie.
- The 'frontier spirit' which forged America is seen as an important ethic which should continue to be part of the cultural heritage of all Americans.
- Contrast with 'equilibrium of work and life' philosophy of French National Parks.

OUTDOOR EDUCATION
- Occurs more regularly outside schools.
- However, schools are often involved in placing students on State-run summer camp programmes.
- State authorities (aided by Federal funding) make provision for young people of limited means to attend State summer camps.
- Many camps are run privately and much kudos is derived from attendance at a 'prestige' venue.
- These camps are intended to introduce young Americans to nature and to each other.
- Some are founded on an educational basis, whilst others are purely for holidays / recreation.
- Socialisation is seen as an important part of the process as is a fostering of the competitive spirit.
- 'Fat camps' and 'puny camps' would seem to serve the purpose of isolation, rather than integration for the young people forced to attend them.
- Compare the French system for the 'outdoor experience'.
- Much greater statutory provision exists in USA and France than either the UK or Australia.

PHYSICAL EDUCATION IN THE USA

ORIGINS
- Western European influences.
- 'German' and Scandinavian (largely Swedish) systems of physical education.
- A mixture of public / private (education) provision
- Bi-polarisation between church and secular institutions (compare UK, France and Australia).

DEVELOPMENT
- Physical Education in the United States is run at local level by Local District School Boards.
- Who have the responsibility devolved down to them from the State Board of Education.
- And who, in turn, pass on day-to-day control to the Principal of each school.
- Policy is devolved down to the Local School Board only and NOT to the individual school.
- Therefore, unlike the PE teacher in the UK (who is responsible for his / her own teaching programme), the 'Phys Ed.' Teacher in the US is often responsible for teaching a programme devised by the Director / Superintendent of Physical Education in Schools at Local School Board level.
- However, some School boards (for example, those in Washington DC) allow considerable flexibility for teachers to devise their own programmes.
- Compares most closely with that in France, since teachers there have little or no flexibility to utilise their own professional judgement in determining the content of the programme they teach.
- French schools implement a National programme, but USA schools have a Local programme.

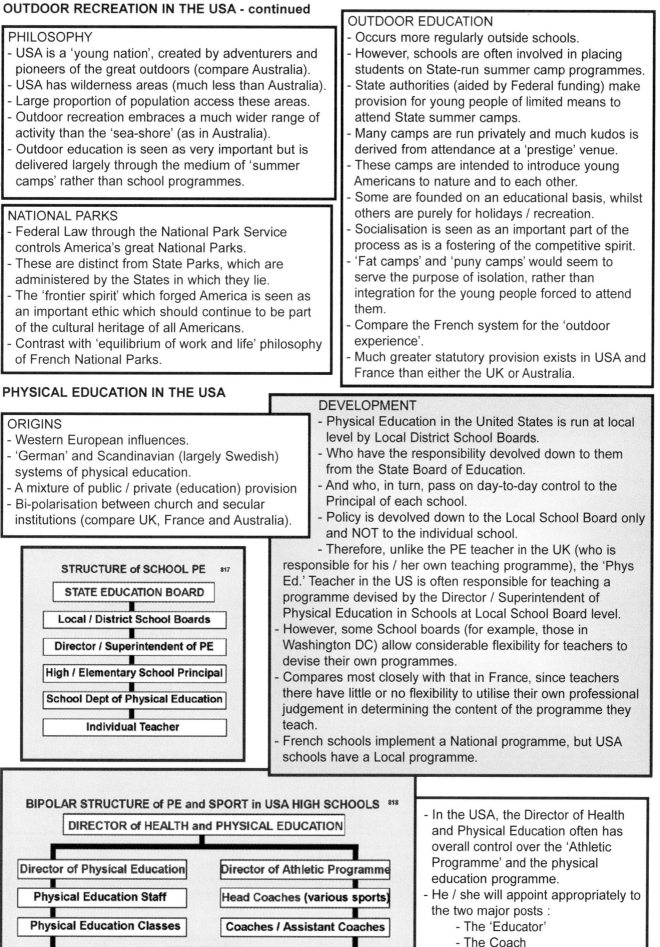

STRUCTURE of SCHOOL PE 817

STATE EDUCATION BOARD
Local / District School Boards
Director / Superintendent of PE
High / Elementary School Principal
School Dept of Physical Education
Individual Teacher

BIPOLAR STRUCTURE of PE and SPORT in USA HIGH SCHOOLS 818

DIRECTOR of HEALTH and PHYSICAL EDUCATION

Director of Physical Education
Physical Education Staff
Physical Education Classes

Director of Athletic Programme
Head Coaches (various sports)
Coaches / Assistant Coaches

Student Body — Student Teams

- In the USA, the Director of Health and Physical Education often has overall control over the 'Athletic Programme' and the physical education programme.
- He / she will appoint appropriately to the two major posts :
    - The 'Educator'
    - The Coach
- With distinct and separate roles.

Information

PHYSICAL EDUCATION IN THE USA - continued

BACKGROUND
- Some coaches may teach 'Phys Ed' to make up their time (or indeed an academic subject) but they are paid as coaches and 'job security' depends upon sporting and not academic success.
- Some 'Phys Ed' teachers may coach but this is more common in Junior High Schools than in their senior counterparts.
- This 'bi-polar' emphasis produces conflicts as to which aspect of a student's life should take precedence, with academic performance often losing out.
- In the USA, where High School and College sport reign supreme, professional clubs have to wait their turn for the recruitment of school age sportspeople.

SPORT IN THE USA

ORIGINS
- Colonial influence (compare Australia), note French colonial influence to the north.
- Mass immigration from Europe (late nineteenth and early 20th centuries).
- Emerging middle classes transplanted the sporting ethos of the English aristocracy / middle classes to the universities Cornell, Harvard, Princeton and Yale (Ivy League).
- This produced American (or 'grid-iron') football and compares to the 'Oxbridge' ethos in the UK.
- Innovators such as James Naismith presented basketball as a rationalised, acceptable recreation for the working classes, controlled by a middle-class, white élite.
- Institutions such as the Church / YMCA have had a major influence on the growth of US sport.
- The growth of Mass Education and the eventual influence of mass access to recreation.

DEVELOPMENT :
- Except for baseball and ice-hockey, sport in USA has developed through the collegiate system of sporting excellence.
- Here 'outcome' has largely ridden roughshod over 'process' (the end justifies the means).
- There are three co-existent cultures :
  - The Lombardian ethic : winning is all that counts. This is outcome led heightened by the needs of professionalism and a society that only acknowledges winners.
  - The Radical ethic : winning is important but not at all costs. The 'process' has intrinsic value, which outweighs the extrinsic outcome (for example, educational, personal enrichment, development of co-operative social skills).
  - The Counter-culture ethic : the process (or experience) is all that matters. This culture derides competition as pure selfish posturing.

COMPARISON of USA with other COUNTRIES
- Contrast with France where academic interests have always been given the higher priority.
- Similar to France where the majority of school sport under the UNSS system is supervised by paid coaches (working entirely outside the school system).
- In Australia, school sport is still run by teachers at school level but in conjunction with help from outside agencies, particularly in an administrative capacity.
- In the UK, school sport is run and organised by teachers with little outside help.
- Wilkinson Report (UK) removes promising schoolboy footballers from school sport altogether, basing them at Premier League centres of excellence. The FA now runs the national schools under 15 side, not teachers. This would never happen in the USA, where school and college sport reign supreme, and professional clubs have to wait their turn.

ETHNIC ISSUES
- Baseball, without the same 'college roots' as other sports, gave opportunities to a range of ethnic sportsmen long before it was feasible in football and basketball.
- Black influence in sport has grown since the 'civil rights' successes of the sixties and seventies.
- Hispanic influences are strongest in baseball but the influence of the Vietnamese, has still to be felt.
- The White Anglo-Saxon Protestant (WASP) group remains the source of power and influence, utilising wealth and social status to prevent other groups from climbing the ladder (the glass ceiling).

STRUCTURE
- Collegiate Sport has two 'divisions': the National Collegiate Athletic Association (NCAA) and the National Association of Inter-Collegiate Athletics (NAIA).
- The former powerful Amateur Athletic Union (AAU) was replaced by individual sports governing bodies in 1977/8 and the former Association of Inter-Collegiate Athletics for Women (AIAW) was absorbed into the NCAA in 1981.

NATIONAL OLYMPIC COMMITTEE	
NCAA	NAIA
Regional Conferences	
High School Sport	Collegiate Sport

PROFESSIONAL SPORT IN THE USA

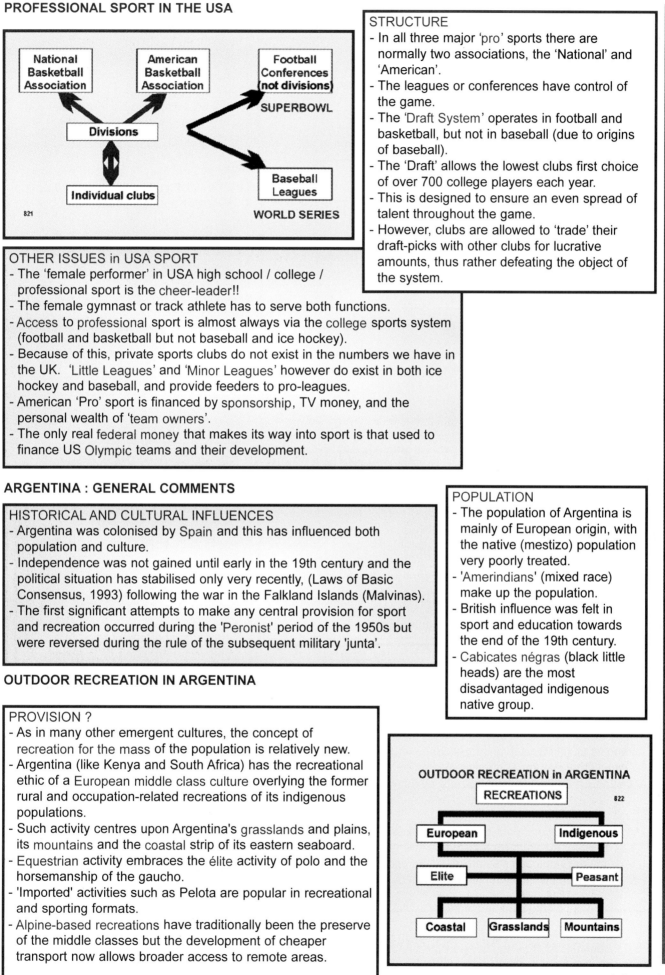

National Basketball Association	American Basketball Association	Football Conferences (not divisions)

Divisions

SUPERBOWL

Individual clubs

Baseball Leagues

821

WORLD SERIES

STRUCTURE
- In all three major 'pro' sports there are normally two associations, the 'National' and 'American'.
- The leagues or conferences have control of the game.
- The 'Draft System' operates in football and basketball, but not in baseball (due to origins of baseball).
- The 'Draft' allows the lowest clubs first choice of over 700 college players each year.
- This is designed to ensure an even spread of talent throughout the game.
- However, clubs are allowed to 'trade' their draft-picks with other clubs for lucrative amounts, thus rather defeating the object of the system.

OTHER ISSUES in USA SPORT
- The 'female performer' in USA high school / college / professional sport is the cheer-leader!!
- The female gymnast or track athlete has to serve both functions.
- Access to professional sport is almost always via the college sports system (football and basketball but not baseball and ice hockey).
- Because of this, private sports clubs do not exist in the numbers we have in the UK. 'Little Leagues' and 'Minor Leagues' however do exist in both ice hockey and baseball, and provide feeders to pro-leagues.
- American 'Pro' sport is financed by sponsorship, TV money, and the personal wealth of 'team owners'.
- The only real federal money that makes its way into sport is that used to finance US Olympic teams and their development.

ARGENTINA : GENERAL COMMENTS

HISTORICAL AND CULTURAL INFLUENCES
- Argentina was colonised by Spain and this has influenced both population and culture.
- Independence was not gained until early in the 19th century and the political situation has stabilised only very recently, (Laws of Basic Consensus, 1993) following the war in the Falkland Islands (Malvinas).
- The first significant attempts to make any central provision for sport and recreation occurred during the 'Peronist' period of the 1950s but were reversed during the rule of the subsequent military 'junta'.

OUTDOOR RECREATION IN ARGENTINA

PROVISION ?
- As in many other emergent cultures, the concept of recreation for the mass of the population is relatively new.
- Argentina (like Kenya and South Africa) has the recreational ethic of a European middle class culture overlying the former rural and occupation-related recreations of its indigenous populations.
- Such activity centres upon Argentina's grasslands and plains, its mountains and the coastal strip of its eastern seaboard.
- Equestrian activity embraces the élite activity of polo and the horsemanship of the gaucho.
- 'Imported' activities such as Pelota are popular in recreational and sporting formats.
- Alpine-based recreations have traditionally been the preserve of the middle classes but the development of cheaper transport now allows broader access to remote areas.

POPULATION
- The population of Argentina is mainly of European origin, with the native (mestizo) population very poorly treated.
- 'Amerindians' (mixed race) make up the population.
- British influence was felt in sport and education towards the end of the 19th century.
- Cabicates négras (black little heads) are the most disadvantaged indigenous native group.

OUTDOOR RECREATION in ARGENTINA

RECREATIONS   822

European	Indigenous

Elite	Peasant

Coastal	Grasslands	Mountains

PHYSICAL EDUCATION IN ARGENTINA

BACKGROUND
- Early developments in PE occurred in the private schools and in and around the city of Buenos Aires.
- Prior to the 'Laws of Basic Consensus' there was no 'nationally effective' programme of physical education in Argentina's schools.
- The National Institute of Physical Education was created in 1985.

SPORT IN ARGENTINA

STRUCTURE OF SPORT
- The Asociación Deportiva Estudjantil (ADE) organises sport in private schools' but state school sport centres largely in the province of Buenos Aires.
- In all other provinces sport is provided by sports clubs not schools.
- Elite sport was organised by the Confederacion Atletica de Deportes (CAD) but in 1989 this became the Secretaria de Deportes de la Nacion (National Secretariat of Sport) and is responsible directly to the national president.
- In theory its aim is to co-ordinate community, educational, high performance (including professional) and Olympic sport.
- In practice, it awards scholarships to gifted athletes and organises Olympic preparation and selection in conjunction with the Comite Olimpico Argentino.

CONTENT
- The contents of the PE programme are part of the General Basic Education (EGB) and consist of four learning blocks:

- Block 1: The body & movement with gymnastics as the main medium of learning.

- Block 2: Bodily health and well-being in the world around us: the acquisition of simple and complex skills.

- Block 3: Motor games and 'play' to integrate personality, expression and develop motor skills.
- Move towards playing and understanding adult games with appropriate rules.

- Block 4: The application of knowledge of the body, abilities and motor skills to spontaneous and regulated games.
- Hygiene and consideration for the body and those of others.
- Conservation of the surroundings.

KENYA - GENERAL COMMENTS

SOCIAL AND CULTURAL INFLUENCES
- Similar to other former colonies with sport, recreation & physical education developed by largely Christian and 'Empire' influences, which overlaid ancient tribal cultures.
- Independence (1963) has seen development in 'selected' sports and activity largely centred in a few urban centres.
- Infrastructure development is very poor and recreational provision is made largely for the wealthy and tourist classes.

THE ECONOMY
- A very poor economy based on agriculture and 'foreign' interests own much of its production (e.g. coffee).
- Such exploitation means that profit goes elsewhere and this has serious implications for a government, which:
  - Is very much affected by 'tribal conflicts'.
  - Is struggling to make any real provision for much of its population due to lack of revenue.
- There are areas affected by drought and malnutrition with very poor school attendance in some regions.

OUTDOOR RECREATION IN KENYA
(including outdoor education)

RECREATIONS
- Historically, recreations tend to reflect life-styles and preparation for life as a warrior influenced the fighting and weapon-orientated activities for boys.
- Girls tended to mimic their elders also but dance was (and still is) an important cultural aspect of recreation for both sexes.
- Modern recreational patterns influence only those in the (minority) urban areas who can afford them but most of the population still largely rural in situation and lifestyle.

CONSERVATION - NATIONAL PARKS
- The former 'colonial lifestyle' that made the hunting of game and safaris popular is still catered for and this now embraces issues of both conservation and élitism.
- The national parks (e.g. The Massai Mara) are utilised by the few rich Kenyans who can afford the expensive lifestyle along with wealthy tourists who (ironically) bring in a large proportion of the country's foreign currency earnings.
- Lack of revenue means that little provision for recreation is made outside of the major centres such as Nairobi and Mombassa.

PHYSICAL EDUCATION IN KENYA

PROVISION OF PE
- The development is typical of former colonial countries with PE being developed within the private sector in (largely) religious foundations.
- Provision outside the private sector was (and still is) poor and current programmes are poorly implemented outside the major urban areas.
- Poor attendance contributes to this but lack of finance means that in practice the nature of (facility) provision in many schools relies on the tradition of Harambee (collection) amongst parents.
- The state provides the initial buildings and pays the staff but little else.

SCHOOL SPORT
- Reasonably well supported and is administered through the country's fifty-five regions.
- This structure is reflected in the nature of sporting competition in which there are district, regional and national championships.
- This is largely in 'European sports' such as soccer, cricket and netball.
- There is little provision for indoor sport outside of the private sector.
- There is considerable strength in track and field athletics and soccer is highly popular.

SPORT IN KENYA

STRUCTURE and PARTICIPATION
- Sport in Kenya today is run from the office of the Vice President and Ministry of Home Affairs, Heritage and Sports, which also has a huge brief encompassing many other areas.
- Basketball and cricket both have a strong following but athletics is the most successful and soccer the most popular sport.
- All these sports have strong professional links.
- Golf is played largely by 'well to do' Kenyans and visiting tourists.

OLYMPIC SPORT
- The Kenyan National Olympic Committee (NOCK) is an independent organisation, free from government control.
- It is privately funded and controls all amateur as well as Olympic sport.
- The Kenya National Olympic Association and the Kenya Amateur Athletic Association were both founded in 1952 in the days when the country was still a British colony.

SOUTH AFRICA (RSA) - GENERAL COMMENTS

CULTURAL INFLUENCES
- The cultural roots of sport are set the days of the British Empire and colonialism, with the muscular Christian ethic being a prime influence.
- A major difference between South Africa and Kenya is that South Africa has considerable mineral wealth.
- Also, (until very recently) independence left a white 'European' culture in power.
- Sporting cultures have been firmly set in the 'European' context and native populations were so completely marginalised that only the recent overthrow of 'apartheid' has begun to change things.
- One outcome of this is that soccer is now the 'game of the masses' whilst rugby remains the province of the former white groups.

OUTDOOR RECREATION IN SOUTH AFRICA

STRUCTURES
- SANREC develops community recreational programmes with a network of nine Provincial Committees (PRORECS) which administer its programmes within each province.
- The SANGALA project consists of :
  - Community Sangala - the whole community
  - Training Sangala - training community leaders.
  - Corporate Sangala - middle and senior management in both private and public sectors.
  - Senior Sangala - encourages physical activity among senior citizens.
  - Street Sangala - life-skills project for homeless children.
- RSA has fifty-three national parks or protected areas including the world famous Kruger National Park.
- These areas have been the preserve of the privileged whites but also attract foreign tourists and currency.

ACCESS AND PROVISION
- Programmes sponsored by SANGALA (South African National Games and Leisure Association) are the beginning of a long process of empowerment of ordinary people in access to and provision for recreation that will take some time to develop fully.

- The SANGALA programmes are the result of co-operation between SANREC and the Department of Sport and Recreation and were launched in 1996 with the aim of involving all South Africans in healthy recreational activities as part of the nation-building process.

PHYSICAL EDUCATION IN SOUTH AFRICA

HISTORY AND STRUCTURE
- National Advisory Council on Physical Education compiled the first 'Syllabus for South African Schools' in 1940, based initially on the 'British system' and later the Danish gymnastics of Neils Bukh.
- Currently, only some of the private 'white' schools' have good facilities and PE programmes in the newly developing 'State-system' are poorly funded.
- School sport is run under the auspices of the United School Sports Association of South Africa (USSASA) which was formed in 1994 out of the South African Primary Schools Sports Association and several other schools sport bodies.

SPORT IN SOUTH AFRICA

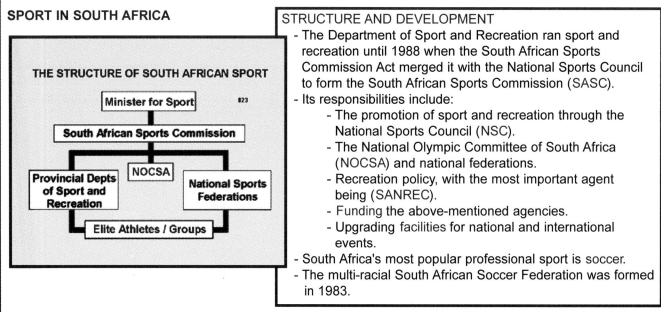

THE STRUCTURE OF SOUTH AFRICAN SPORT

STRUCTURE AND DEVELOPMENT
- The Department of Sport and Recreation ran sport and recreation until 1988 when the South African Sports Commission Act merged it with the National Sports Council to form the South African Sports Commission (SASC).
- Its responsibilities include:
    - The promotion of sport and recreation through the National Sports Council (NSC).
    - The National Olympic Committee of South Africa (NOCSA) and national federations.
    - Recreation policy, with the most important agent being (SANREC).
    - Funding the above-mentioned agencies.
    - Upgrading facilities for national and international events.
- South Africa's most popular professional sport is soccer.
- The multi-racial South African Soccer Federation was formed in 1983.

NEW ZEALAND : GENERAL COMMENTS

HISTORY AND CULTURE
- Treaty of Waitangi (Te Tiriti O Waitangi) (1840) ensured that Maori rights were respected by white settlers.
- Maori women obtained the vote in 1893, whereas Aborigines were not granted full voting rights until 1967.
- A healthy agricultural economy has influenced both an outdoor lifestyle and a well funded social infrastructure.
- As in many cultures, the Empire & colonial values of the 19th century has influenced current sporting practices.

POPULATION

	Land Area (million sq km)	Population (million)
Australia	7.6	18.3
New Zealand	0.3	3.8
South Africa	1.2	43.3

New Zealand is small but very successful at sport!

OUTDOOR RECREATION IN NEW ZEALAND

NATIONAL PARKS AND CONSERVATION

- NZ has fourteen national parks under the control and management of the Department of Conservation.
- The policy of including Moari rights and culture ensures that likely impact upon sensitive areas is negotiated and written into updates of the Treaty of Waitangi.

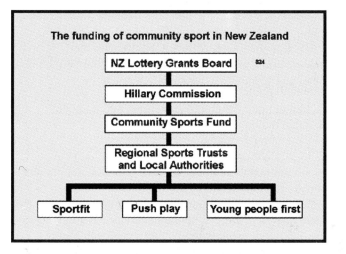

The funding of community sport in New Zealand

PHYSICAL EDUCATION IN NEW ZEALAND

HEALTH AND PE
- This area of the NZ curriculum is compulsory for all students up to Year 10.
- The programme is centred upon the Maori word 'hauora' (a sense of well-being).
- This reflects the inclusion of the country's native culture.
- Many of the key terms are expressed in the Maori language as well as in English.
- There are eight stages of learning within seven 'key areas', which are:
  - Mental health.
  - Sexuality education.
  - Food and nutrition.
  - Body care and physical safety.
  - Physical activity.
  - Sport studies.
  - Outdoor education.

THE NZ SECONDARY SCHOOLS SPORTS COUNCIL
- Set up in 1992.
- Its regional structure helps promote a wide range of sporting activities in the country's schools.
- The council's regional directors also act as administrators of the 'Sportfit' programme.
- This is one of the initiatives sponsored by the Hillary Commission.
- Which encourages the young people of New Zealand to become actively involved in sport and recreation.

SPORT IN NEW ZEALAND

THE NZ SPORTS FOUNDATION (NZSF)
- Set up in 1972.
- Principal provider of funding and services to New Zealand sport.
- A private organisation although its funding comes from government via the Hillary Commission.
- Hillary Commission established by Act of Parliament in 1987.
- Its role looks at all aspects of sport and recreation, including the funding of programmes of excellence.
- The NZSF and the Hillary Commission collectively perform a similar role to that of the ASC and AIS in Australia.
- The country's rugby teams are legendary but there has also been success on the athletics track, the cricket field and in cycling in a country that values sport very highly.

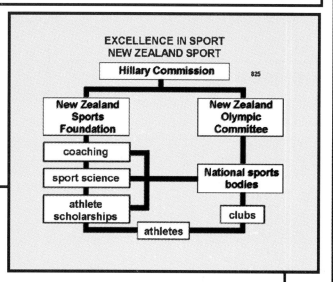

EXCELLENCE IN SPORT
NEW ZEALAND SPORT

ASIA - GENERAL COMMENTS

CULTURE
- Many parts of South and East Asia were influenced by British colonialism or the influence of British trading communities.
- This included the sub-continent of India, and of course, China, which was never colonised but became a centre of trading activity from 1840 until early in the 20th century.
- Japan and Korea retained their own cultures.
- China re-established its own cultural heritage with the formation of the 'People's Republic' in 1949.

DEVELOPMENTS
- Developments in sport and recreation have come as a result of the globalising influence of international sport.
- Due to growth of modern communications technology and international markets for western goods and lifestyles.
- Many commercial concerns now utilise south east Asia as both part of an expanding global market and a source of cheap labour.

OUTDOOR RECREATION IN ASIA

RECREATION
- Chinese and Japanese culture have both traditionally valued recreation.
- Recently, both India and Pakistan have made considerable efforts to develop a centralised infrastructure.
- Examples :   - India - Sports Authority of India.
  - Pakistan - Pakistan Sports Board.
- In both cases government funding is provided despite poor economies & huge social problems.

MASS SPORT
- Mass sport in Japan has a definite 'Olympic' flavour. - The Japanese Olympic Committee and the Japanese Amateur Sports Association organise activities for the whole community, including the Junior Sports Club (founded in 1962).
- There are nine branches throughout Japan with sports meetings organised at local and regional level for the 1.5 million members.
- In N. Korea, the Children's Games and National Games reflect the political overtones found in China with its 'workplace sport' & mass exercise programmes.

PHYSICAL EDUCATION IN ASIA

PE PROGRAMMES
- Vary across this region and reflect differing cultures and / or political persuasions.
- China and N. Korea have centralised systems which are highly structured.
- India and Pakistan have embryonic state systems which are poorly funded.
- Elsewhere there is a mixture of 'British schools' (examples : Hong Kong & Singapore) teaching PE as it occurs in the UK.
    - Local systems still very much based on 'the games ethic' - little or no formalised teaching.

STRUCTURES
- Japan - Ministry of Education, Science & Culture: ('Monbusho') Physical Education Bureau: Boards of Education. Great emphasis of sport for life.
- China - the State Physical Education & Sports Commission: Provincial Physical Education Commissions. Very highly structured.
- India - Dept. of Education: Central Board of Secondary Education.
    - Specific syllabus - but not fully implemented.
- North Korea - Education Committee: Physical Culture & Sports Guidance Committee.

SPORT IN ASIA

CULTURE AND POLICY
- Sport in Asia consists of a mixture of ancient activities that have in some cases been overlaid by colonial influence and by more recent global sporting trends in others.

- Most cultures now have policies of excellence but their focus is often upon globally popular sports rather than those reflecting indigenous activities.

- There are some exceptions to this generalisation.
- China particularly promotes its own culture in addition to that of the global sporting arena.

ECONOMICS
- Most Asian economies now centrally fund and support programmes of excellence.
- Not always based on effective mass participation programmes.
- The clear aim here is to gain short-term success without the infrastructure and cost associated with programmes of excellence based on full participation.
- Highly organised sporting structures also exist in schools - sometimes at the expense of effective programmes of physical education.

- In India, Pakistan, China and N. Korea there is strong military influence in both sports participation and facility / programme provision.

BRIEF NOTES

The brief notes above are examples of a way of annotating information into brief 'chunks'. You may wish to expand or modify them and add additional 'themes' or 'topics'. You should examine the 'Comparative Relationships' model on page 8.1 above and add any areas you think are missing.
    You should be able to :
    a) Recall and list facts about each of the countries.
    b) Make comparisons between facts and situations in each country, and account for these situations.
    c) Make analytical and objective comment in connection with comparative relationships, both within a given country and between different countries.

QUESTIONS

RECREATION / OUTDOOR EDUCATION

1) a) Compare the statutory provisions for outdoor education / recreation in the United Kingdom, with that of another culture you have studied, on the basis of :-
    i) The nature and extent of statutory provision.
    ii) Centralised organisation.
    iii) Centralised funding.
    iv) Equality of opportunity / access.   (4 marks)
b) Give three reasons why the 'outdoor experience' seems to be a much more highly valued process in the United States than it appears to be in the UK. Bear in mind the fact that one culture has a much greater diversity of climate and topography than the other.   (3 marks)
c) The French approach to recreation & outdoor education centres on the philosophy of 'La Plein Air'.
    i) Can you briefly explain just what is meant by this term?
    ii) Give a brief account of two programmes it helped to bring about.   (4 marks)

RECREATION / OUTDOOR EDUCATION - QUESTIONS (continued)

2) a) Many sports and recreations in France tend to be very 'regionalised'. For example, rugby (both codes) tends to be based in the south. Can you account for this 'regionalisation', with regard for :-
  i) Governmental influences.
  ii) Topographical influences.
  iii) Climatic influences.
  iv) Cultural influences?   (8 marks)
b) Give two examples of sports / recreations in the UK which are 'regionalised. Suggest a possible reason for this in each case.   (3 marks)

3) a) The 'frontier spirit' and 'wilderness experience' are two phrases often used in connection with America's 'great outdoors' philosophy.
  i) To what extent is this philosophy reflected in the outdoors movement here in the United Kingdom?
  ii) How do 'national parks' in the US compare to those in this country?   (4 marks)
b) Why is it that Australians seem to spurn the outdoor experience so sought after by Americans and Europeans?
                                                                                              (2 marks)
c) In Australia, its many national parks (with the exception of the Great Barrier Reef) are maintained by the State within which they lie. How does this administration, as well as scale and diversity, compare with the 'national parks' in the UK?   (3 marks)

PHYSICAL EDUCATION

4) PE and Sport in French schools has traditionally been held in rather low esteem but this is now changing.as evidenced by sport facilities built all over France.
a) Identify any two developments which may have contributed to this change.   (2 marks)
b) The organisation of sport for French secondary school students differs from the way in which school sport is run here in the UK. Give brief details of these differences, and account for these differences in terms of government policy and how this influences the structure of all sport in France.   (6 marks)
c) Compare the role of the PE teacher in the UK with that of his / her counterpart in the USA. Make your comparison in the following areas, supporting your comments with explanatory statements :
  i) Control or input into the teaching programme.   (2 marks)
  ii) Extension of role into extra-mural sports and activities.   (2 marks)

5) a) Schools in France are in the process of progressing from 'Sports Study Sections' in some schools, catering for one or two sports at higher level, to 'Sports Schools' offering a much wider range of expertise. Why is this policy much easier to implement in France than it would be in the UK, and give two reasons why are there no state-sponsored sports schools in the USA?   (4 marks)
b) Examinations in physical education are now in place in France, Australia and in the UK. Why do you think this is not the case in the United States?   (3 marks)
c) Individual schools fund their own sports programme in the United States. This is also very largely the case in the UK. If these approaches are so similar, why is the end-product so different? Give three possible reasons, with a short supporting statement in each case.   (6 marks)

6) a) There is clear division between sport and physical education in high schools in the United States. Explain why this is the case, and compare the situation in the USA with the situation in the UK, France and Australia.
                                                                                              (4 marks)
b) Sport in Australian schools is still largely run by teachers at 'grass roots' level in a similar way to UK. Give two examples of differences in the administration and support given to school sport in each country.   (2 marks)
c) The programme of physical education taught to French students is dictated by government policy and allows little room for local flexibility or 'interpretation' on the part of teachers. Compare this with the UK.   (2 marks)

7) a) Physical Education programmes in the US would appear to be largely 'outcome-orientated' and rely heavily on student scores (i.e. a testing stand measurement approach). How does this approach compare with PE within the National Curriculum here in the U.K.? Phrase your answer with reference to the value of the educative process, and the value of 'outcome-led' testing procedures.   (4 marks)
b) The inclusion of team and individual sports in PE programmes has been a thorny subject for many years. How would you justify the inclusion of such activities on the basis of their educational worth, as opposed to merely providing 'extra coaching' for the best performers? Give three reasons with an argument for each.   (6 marks)

SPORT

8) a) Following disappointing results in the 1976 Olympic Games in Montreal, the Australian Government decided to take a hand in improving that nation's sporting performances. Briefly outline what these steps were at 'National' level, and at 'State' level. (3 marks)

b) How does the structure / organisation of sport in the US differ from that in Australia in terms of Government control of sport, funding of developmental and excellence programmes, and provision for particular groups such as disabled sportspersons or ethnic minorities? (6 marks)

c) The Australian Aboriginal has been badly treated by a succession of governments and cultural invasions. What steps have been taken to 'include' these native populations into the mainstream of Australian sporting life, and what impact, if any, are people of the aboriginal race currently making in the sporting sphere? (6 marks)

9) a) Soccer is fast becoming the 'global sport'. However, this does not appear to be the case in either Australia of the United States. Why is this? Frame your answer in a short paragraph rather than notes, and make specific reference to both Australia and the United States. (4 marks)

b) Write a short account comparing the development of 'Aussie Rules' football and the American 'grid-iron' game. Organise your answer to show what parallel influences there have been in respect of both games in terms of origin, establishment of cultural identity, ethnic groups involved, rule structure, and 'National spread' in terms of popularity. You must support any comments you make in a way that shows an understanding of how and why such similarities and differences occurred. (10 marks)

10) Cultural philosophy often dictates the values controlling the 'ethics' in sport and sportsmanship.

a) What, until relatively recently, have been the two traditional sets of values under which sport has been played and name one major influence which has caused a 'blurring' of these sets of values? (3 marks)

b) In the United States there are three main groups of 'sub-cultural ethics' influencing attitudes to sporting competition. Name these ethics, and briefly explain the essence of each one. What, other than 'outcome', contributes to the development of such 'ethics' or sets of values? (5 marks)

11) a) Account for the wider provision of public access facilities in France compared to the more traditional model of private provision in the UK, in which there has been only relatively recent growth in fairly limited public provision. (2 marks)

b) What implications are there in provision in the UK for opportunities for mass participation, and the pursuit of excellence? (4 marks)

12) Careful analysis shows that in the case of both Australia and France, a particularly low point in the level of international sporting performances 'sparked off' a drastic re-assessment of sports development programmes.

a) Identify these 'low points' in respect of each country, and identify a similar 'low point' in respect of British sport. (3 marks)

b) In the case of sport in Britain what changes have been made in order to address this problem? Explain why such low points do not appear to have been experienced in the USA. (4 marks)

13) a) Why is it that provision for excellence has long been in place in France but has only recently begun to be implemented in the UK? (2 marks)

b) How does the provision for sporting excellence in the USA compare with that in place in France? Make particular reference to the concepts of centralisation, the 'win-ethic' and programmes of mass participation. (6 marks)

OTHER CULTURES: (Edexcel)

14) a). Neither Argentina nor China were ever British colonies but nevertheless, the sporting development in both countries in the last half of the nineteenth century showed distinct British influence.

   i) How do you account for this in respect of one of these cultures?

   ii) To what degree in respect of either one of the above cultures, have subsequent political developments changed this, if at all? (6 marks)

b) How do you account for the fact that Kenya has developed an international presence in only a limited number of sports? (3 marks)

c) Why is it that the Maori population of New Zealand were never marginalised in terms of both sporting and broader opportunities in the same way that occurred in either Australia or South Africa? (2 marks)

OTHER CULTURES: (Edexcel) - QUESTIONS (continued)

15) a) In the case of either India or Pakistan, explain why :
    i) the emergence of that country into the international arena of sport sees emphasis on sports of 'European origin' rather than of its own culture. (3 marks)
    ii) investment in sporting infrastructures centres very much on programmes of excellence rather than broad participation. (3 marks)
b) In the case of either China or Japan, explain the value and reason for the place of worker sport and exercise programmes and explain why such activities are not part of the UK culture. (4 marks)

16) a) Explain why, in the context of one of South Africa, New Zealand or Australia, the concept of a Test Match against the former 'mother country' assumes greater proportions than sporting contests against other international teams? (4 marks)
b) In Kenya, 85% of the population live in rural areas. Explain why this might have a detrimental effect upon programmes of mass participation. (2 marks)

17) a) Selecting a culture you have studied in depth, identify and explain clear differences or similarities with the UK in the following areas :
    i) The nature and timing of programmes of excellence.
    ii) Resistance to commercial involvement in sport.
    iii) Cultural / historical influences on sport.
    iv) The nature and timing of government involvement in sport. (8 marks)
b) In some cultures there is distinct military influence in control, provision and participation in sport. Identifying a specific culture of your choice, explain why this might be the case, and outline the evidence that things might (or might not) change. (6 marks)
c) Name, describe the role of, and give two initiatives supported by the organisation responsible for mass recreation programmes in either South Africa, New Zealand or Australia. (4 marks)

ANSWERS

The answer for each mark awarded is notated by the ❐ symbol - where there are more ❐ symbols than there are marks available, marks would be given for any choice up to the maximum available. Usually, the precise wording specified in an answer would not be required - answers with the same meaning would be acceptable.

RECREATION / OUTDOOR EDUCATION

1) a)
i) *Statutory provision :*
    1 mark for :
❐ Provision in the UK within the national curriculum but this is not mandatory.
ii) *Centralised organisation in the UK :*
    1 mark for one from :
❐ Absence of centralised control allows dilution of policy intent.
❐ Individual schools can override policy intent if circumstances dictate.
❐ Lack of local funding.
❐ Lack of suitable facility provision.
iii) *Centralised funding in the UK :*
    1 mark for one from :
❐ Funding is diluted by devolution (for example, LMS).
❐ Allocation of funding resources is at discretion of individual schools.
❐ No central control of funding.
iv) *Equality of opportunity / access in the UK :*
    1 mark for one from :
❐ Opportunities in UK limited to those who can pay.
❐ Access determined by policy of individual schools.
❐ Lack of centralised control limits enforcement.

RECREATION / OUTDOOR EDUCATION - ANSWERS QUESTION 1 (continued)

1) b)
Valued outdoor experience in the USA :
   3 marks for three from :
❐ Settlement in USA reflects the 'pioneer spirit'.
❐ Settlement in UK is largely industrial.
❐ Natural environment in the UK is far more limited.
❐ Attitude in USA reflects that of the 'frontiersman'.
❐ UK is far smaller than the USA.
❐ The pioneer ethic in the USA reflects the quest for riches, and such experiences are reflected in attitudes to outdoor life.

1) c)
The French approach to outdoor recreation and education :
i) 'La Plein Air' :
   2 marks for :
❐ Explanation including 'love of fresh air'.
❐ 'Appreciation of the outdoors'.
ii) *Two programmes within the French approach to outdoor education and recreation :*
   2 marks for two from :
❐ 'Les Classes Transplantées'.
❐ 'Classe de vert'.
❐ 'Class de neige'.
❐ 'Class de vert'.
❐ 'Centres de Vacance'.

2) a)
The reasons for 'Regionalised' sport in France :
i)   Governmental :
   2 marks for two from :
❐ Paris is a beaurocratic centre.
❐ Lack of communication.
❐ Localised interests.
ii)   Topographical :
   2 marks for two from :
❐ Great variety of topography.
❐ This develops a wide range of activities.
❐ For example mountain activities / water sports.
iii)   Climatic :
   2 marks for two from :
❐ Climatic variation.
❐ Which gives rise to diverse activities
❐ For example, snow sports / track and field.
iv)   Cultural influences :
   2 marks for :
❐ Varied cultural influences give rise to differing activities.
❐ For example, Breton wrestling / bull fighting.

2) b)
'Regionalised' recreations / sports in the UK :
   2 marks for two examples :
❐ Rugby League in Lancs / Yorks.
❐ Curling in Scotland.
   2 marks for good 'reason' in each case :
❐ Rugby League - working class origins, breakaway from the Rugby Union because of the need for 'broken time' payments for players - hence sport becoming professional.
❐ Curling - presence of ice conditions for practice and competition.

RECREATION / OUTDOOR EDUCATION - ANSWERS (continued)

3) a)

i) *'Frontier spirit' is not reflected in the outdoors movement in the UK because :*

2 marks for :
- ❏ Limited scope for wilderness experience in the UK.
- ❏ UK not on same scale as US.

ii) *National parks in the USA compared to the UK :*

2 marks for two from :
- ❏ Major difference between USA and UK is in sheer size / scale and variety.
- ❏ Also controlled directly by federal authorities in U.S. (National Parks).
- ❏ Indirectly in UK. For example, the National Parks are mostly privately owned and farmed / forested, with private charitable organisations like the National Trust owning some land. Access is therefore not guaranteed (possible access legislation being enacted).

3) b)

Outdoor experience in Australia :
- ❏ Americans had much more choice than Australians in whether or not they faced the 'wild outdoors'.
- ❏ Historically and culturally they (frontier Americans) had to cross barren land to get to the West Coast.
- ❏ The Australian 'outback' was not a barrier in the same way, therefore they could choose to ignore it.
- ❏ Australian population centres on the narrow coastal plain.

3) c)

Compare the state maintained National Parks of Australia with what happens in the UK?
- ❏ Administration : England's National Parks are the responsibility of the Countryside Agency and in Wales of the Countryside Council for Wales. Scotland does not at the moment have designated 'National Parks'.
- ❏ Scale : Britain's parks are much smaller than those in Australia. Many of them lie within very easy reach of visitors, whereas this is not always the case in Australia. Population levels are very different, and overcrowding occurs in many of Britain's parks.
- ❏ Diversity : Australia's parks embrace a much wider range of terrain and climatic variation, stretching from tropical regions in the north, to temperate conditions in the south.

PHYSICAL EDUCATION

4) a)

PE and Sport in French schools were of low status which is now increasing because of :

2 marks for two from :
- ❏ High academic emphasis (basic subjects) was traditional.
- ❏ Lowly status of PE teachers in the past.
- ❏ PE teachers only recently trained at Universities.
- ❏ Poor facilities / funding for PE in the past, much improved facilities now available.

4) b)

The differences in organisation of school sport in UK and France :

2 marks for two from :
- ❏ In France, sport is largely taught outside schools.
- ❏ Taught through UNSS.
- ❏ Whereas teachers are fully involved in the UK.
- ❏ No central policy in UK.
- ❏ French teachers are not involved in organising sport.

In France, Government policy influences sport in the following way in comparison with the UK :

4 marks for :
- ❏ Government policy controls all sport in France.
- ❏ School sport is part of the overall policy in France.
- ❏ School sport in UK is voluntary and there is no central control or funding.
- ❏ School sport in UK is controlled by teachers, not by bureaucrats.

4) c) i)

The role of the PE teacher in respect of control or input to the teaching programme :
- ❏ USA : teacher delivers the programme but has no power to change it.
- ❏ UK : teacher has input into syllabus, and has local autonomy.

4) c) ii)

Role extension into extra mural sports and activities :
- ❏ USA : teacher is paid to teach, not to coach.
- ❏ UK : teacher fully involved in sports programmes / extra-mural activities on a voluntary basis.

PHYSICAL EDUCATION - ANSWERS (continued)

5) a)
Schools in France are progressing from 'Sports Study Sections' to 'Sports Schools', this is easier to implement than it would be in the UK because :
  2 marks for two from :
❐ France already has a centralised system.
❐ Any central policy must be implemented.
❐ 'Sports Study Section' already in place, and therefore it would be easy to extend this into sports schools.
❐ An infrastructure for coaching already exists.
The reasons there are no state sponsored sports schools in the USA are :
  2 marks for two from :
❐ In the USA, federal authority devolves power to local level.
❐ No federal mandate for state sponsored sports schools.
❐ 'Sports schools' already exist in that the school sports programme is geared to excellence.
❐ The US system is based on private enterprise rather than federal intervention.

5) b)
The reason that there are no exams in PE in the USA :
  3 marks for three from :
❐ US system is geared to excellence.
❐ Results, not 'process' are demanded by USA system.
❐ Value is ascribed to sports performance rather than 'valued experiences'.
❐ 'Phys. Ed.' is seen as an 'active programme' and is not academic.
❐ No value is attached to academic performance in this area (PE).
❐ There is no kudos to be gained from examination success in PE in the USA in schools.

5) c)
Sports programme funding UK / USA :
  6 marks for six from (answer and statement linked in pairs) :
❐ Levels of funding are very different.
❐ American system much more geared to results.
❐ Sponsorship and private funding are much more a part of US system than in UK.
❐ Funding depends on results in the US.
❐ 'Win ethic' part of USA motivation.
❐ Educational value is more important in UK.
❐ Social expectancy is different in the two countries.
❐ 'Laissez-faire' approach is more prevalent in UK.

6) a)
Explain the division between Sport / PE in the US, and compare this with UK, Australia and France :
❐ In the USA, outcome is important in sport but not in PE (Lombardian ethic).
❐ UK : there is no clear division, Sport and PE are all part of the educative process.
❐ France : sport is ascribed low academic esteem, and so operates outside the school system.
❐ Australia : sport is given high value, both in its own right and as part of the educative process.

6) b)
Two examples of differences in administration and support given to sport in Australian and UK schools :
  2 marks for two from :
❐ In Australia, there is much closer support / relationship between teachers and programmes such as 'Active Australia'.
❐ There is also public funding for administration / organisation of sport at State level.
❐ And paid officers in Departments of Education support and finance sporting ventures.
❐ School sport has much higher profile than in the UK.
❐ No state funding for UK school sport, national organisations rely on individual sponsorship deals.

6) c)
PE in France is dictated by government policy with little room for flexibility, compare this with the UK :
  2 marks for two from :
❐ UK has the National Curriculum but this offers 'flexible guidelines' rather than a 'dictat' (as in France).
❐ UK teachers have the flexibility to adapt / evolve their own programmes within this framework.
❐ French teachers have their responsibilities much more clearly defined.
❐ UK teachers are encouraged to become involved in the development of localised teaching programmes.

PHYSICAL EDUCATION - ANSWERS (continued)

7) a)

Compare PE programmes in the US (with its a testing and measurement approach) with PE within the National Curriculum here in the UK?

2 marks for two from :

❏ The value of the educative process outweighs the short-term validity of 'trials'.

❏ 'Testing' belongs with the coach.

❏ Learning processes have intrinsic value.

2 marks for two from :

❏ The value of 'outcome-led' testing procedures are that regular tests provide the child with a barometer of his / her progress.

❏ Testing provides a yardstick by which progress can be measured.

❏ The emphasis of the end result being more important than the way in which it is achieved.

7) b)

Justify the inclusion of team and individual sports in PE programmes on the basis of their educational worth.

6 marks for :

❏ The social and co-operative aspects of team games.

❏ And the character-building qualities associated with individual sports justify their inclusion.

❏ Physiological development is promoted.

❏ Within a meaningful competitive / co-operative context.

❏ The social prominence of such activities.

❏ The arduous physical nature of activities justifies their inclusion on the grounds of physiological development.

SPORT

8) a)

In Australia, a poor performance in '76 Olympics caused the Government to takes steps to improve National Sport :

3 marks for :

❏ Nationally, setting up the Australian Institute of Sport.

❏ And setting up the Australian Sports Commission.

❏ At State level, setting up of State sporting academies / institutes.

8) b)

The structure / organisation of sport in USA / Australia :

6 marks for :

❏ The difference between centralised federal model in Australia.

❏ As opposed to de-centralised federal model in USA.

❏ Funding in Australia, mixture of central / private sponsorship.

❏ Funding in USA entirely private apart from federal investment in Olympic programmes.

❏ Federal provision for disabled or ethnic minorities is nominal in US but private fund-raising very necessary.

❏ Massive government support in Australia for disabled and ethnic minorities, plus excellent state-sponsored coaching programmes.

8) c)

The steps being taken to include Australian Aborigines in sporting life, and the impact being made by this group :

6 marks for six from :

❏ All States now have a Department of Aboriginal Affairs.

❏ Schools are including indigenous cultural topics on their syllabuses.

❏ Aborigines have their own recreational sporting programmes.

❏ Aborigines are being integrated into 'mainstream' policies.

❏ 'Role-models' (for example, Evonne Goolagong, Cathy Freeman) are beginning to emerge.

❏ 'Aussie Rules' football was an early avenue of success for aborigine males.

❏ Sporting festivals are now beginning to include 'ethnic' activities.

❏ Legislation prohibits sectarian policies / programmes.

SPORT - ANSWERS (continued)

9) a)

Soccer in the US, and comparison with Australia :

    4 marks for four points within a paragraph, not annotated points :

❒ Loss of 'control by US sporting 'moguls', used in controlling their 'own sports'.

❒ (In USA), other sports are firmly established as leading sports.

❒ (In USA), high school / college / 'pro-sport' dictate the nature and range of activities.

❒ Soccer seen as 'European', not 'American' by USA citizens.

❒ Australia has 'Aussie Rules' as 'the peoples' game'.

❒ (In Australia), soccer is only popular with ethnic minorities.

❒ Awareness in both countries that they (National soccer teams) cannot be 'winners' for some considerable time.

❒ May be some anti-English feeling involved particularly in Australia.

❒ Soccer has never been accepted by the respective 'power-groups' in either country.

9) b)

Development of 'Aussie rules' / 'Grid-iron' :

    10 marks - two from each section - for :

    Origins :

❒ US : 'grid iron' developed from rugby.

❒ AUS : 'Aussie rules' developed from rugby but only in Victoria.

    Cultural identity :

❒ US : 'grid iron' is embedded in the WASP culture.

❒ AUS : 'Aussie rules' was popularised against establishment.

    Minority / ethnic :

❒ US : 'grid iron' has little or no involvement of ethnic minorities.

❒ AUS : 'Aussie rules' was a limited early vehicle for the advancement of ethnic groups.

    Rule structure :

❒ US : 'grid iron' is highly technical with many set plays and teams for different situations.

❒ AUS : 'Aussie rules' is apparently lacking sophistication with continuous flexible movement.

    'National spread' :

❒ US : 'grid iron'is a 'national game'.

❒ AUS : 'Aussie rules' exists mainly in Victoria but is now spreading.

10) a)

What two sets of values have until recently controlled sport, and what factor has blurred these:

    3 marks for :

❒ Amateur values and :

❒ Professional values.

❒ Sponsorship / commercialism / TV have blurred the distinctions between these two sets of values.

10) b)

In USA, there are three main groups of subcultural ethics influencing attitudes to sport :

    3 marks for :

❒ Lombardian : 'win at all costs' ethic, developed for professional games.

❒ Radical : 'winning is important but not at all costs', the process has intrinsic value which could include personal enrichment, development of cooperative social skills.

❒ Counter-culture : 'the process is all that matters', this ethic derides competition, and looks for intrinsic satisfaction only.

Contribution to values are developed via :

    2 marks for two from :

❒ 'The educative process' - the lifelong socialization and learning process.

❒ Development of attitudes via peer groups and family - example, 'winning is not all important'.

❒ Or 'Winning is not important at all', just the intrinsic enjoyment of participation.

11) a)

Public access facilities in France compared to private provision in UK :

    2 marks for two from :

❒ In France, the centralist model provides what is needed.

❒ The centralist model is supported by a culture which believes in the vaue of the 'recreative' process.

❒ Central control means that implementation is much more straight forward than in the UK.

❒ Where provision (in UK) is dictated by budget and not by need.

SPORT - ANSWERS QUESTION 11 (continued)

11) b)
Implications for mass participation of provision in UK :
   1 mark for one from :
❏ Participation is limited to those who can afford.
❏ Participation is limited to those who can gain access.
And the implications of UK provision for the pursuit of excellence :
   3 marks for :
❏ The pursuit of excellence is affected by mass participation levels (the base of the pyramid is reduced therefore fewer people of relevant talent are developed to excellence levels).
❏ And policies for excellence within limited resources (little time / facilities made available for elite training).
❏ Selection process not always fully accessible (selection of talent may depend on availability of facilities near at hand or on whether the talented individual can afford to pay for them).

12) a)
Identify the 'low points' in respect of the performance of France and Australia in major games, and identify a similar 'low point' in respect of British sport.
   3 marks for :
❏ 1960 Olympics – in respect of France.
❏ 1976 Olympics – Australia.
❏ 1996 Olympics – in respect of Britain.

12) b)
In the case of sport in Britain what changes have been made in order to address this problem?
   2 marks for two from :
❏ Establishing of a system of regional high performance centres linked to Universities.
❏ Sport England / Scotland / Wales / Northern Ireland as regional funding agencies for potential talent.
❏ Provision of lottery funding for sportspeople.
Explain why such low points do not appear to have been experienced in the USA?
   2 marks for two from :
❏ USA has the high school / collegiate sports programmes which regularly feed through high quality performers.
❏ The population base is very large, therefore a number of elite athletes would usually be produced.
❏ Scholarships are provided for sportsmen at USA colleges which enable full time training for this elite.
❏ The competitive element is very high in the USA system, the win ethic.
❏ The colleges represent a more dedicated structure for excellence.
❏ Usually providing excellent facilities which can be used freely and exclusively for the elite.

13) a)
Provision of excellence in France / UK :
   3 marks for three from :
   Centralisation:
❏ Political philosophy in France more amenable to this concept.
❏ America very much for 'individualism' and free enterprise.
   'Win ethic':
❏ Not naturally a part of the French 'psyche' - background in Olympism and 'fair play.'
   Mass participation:
❏ Population base and sport-driven culture provide opportunity without centralised provision in US.
❏ French attitude much less driven by the need to win and recognised that true provision should start with provision for 'ALL' - not just potential winners.

13 b)
Provision of excellence in USA / France :
   6 marks for six from :
❏ In France, excellence is produced out of a structure that also embraced a provision for mass participation.
❏ In USA, excellence drives a non-centralised élite programme in high schools and colleges.
❏ Because winning in the USA also has been traditionally tied to financial rewards.
❏ This is only a recent development in France.
❏ The French philosophy values 'process' just as much as 'outcome'.
❏ The US philosophy of élitism works because of a huge population base.
❏ The USA has its 'winning philosophy' supported by its culture and its media.
❏ The tradition in France has until recently been of 'Olympic' amateur sport.

OTHER CULTURES

14) a) i)

British influence on the development of sport in Argentina / China :

3 marks for continuous prose answer for :

❑ British trade / industry was exported all over the world, including China / Argentina.

❑ Business communities built their churches and opened schools and other institutions such as the YMCA.

❑ British sport was transferred to these cultures almost as effectively as if they had been colonies.

14) a) ii)

To what degree have subsequent political developments changed this, if at all?

3 marks In respect of one culture only for :

Argentina

❑ European influences still predominate.

❑ Embracing the European concept of sporting activity.

China

❑ Subsequent centralised politics.

❑ Communism.

❑ Re-asserted ancient cultural values so that European influence was minimised.

14) b)

Kenya has developed only a narrow range of sports :

3 marks for three from :

❑ Sport developed in a few urban centres.

❑ Kenya has a poor agricultural economy and can't afford cash for development of facilities.

❑ Tribal conflicts limit opportunity.

❑ Rural environment with poor infrastructure led to the need for youngsters to run to school - hence talent development in track running.

❑ Soccer playing skills have been developed outside formal facilities.

14) c)

Why has the Maori population of New Zealand been able to develop sporting excellence?

1 mark for :

❑ The Treaty of Waitangi ensured that minority rights were respected.

1 mark for one of :

❑ The Maoris were fierce opposition / warlike tribes / difficult to defeat in battle.

❑ Whereas in South Africa / Australia, early white settlers / immigrants subdued the native populations.

15) a) i)

India / Pakistan - emergence into the international sports arena emphasises sports of European origin because :

3 marks for three from :

❑ Most international sports are now professional.

❑ Televised sport brings in revenue and funding.

❑ Participation has to be in 'recognised sports'.

❑ In which British / European influence has historical significance.

❑ Globalisation dictates the sporting market.

15) a) ii)

Investment in sporting infrastructures centres on programmes of excellence rather than broad participation :

3 marks for three from :

❑ Looking for 'quick return' on limited investment.

❑ Poor economy limits levels of funding.

❑ Mistaken belief that excellence can be identified quickly through élitist policies.

❑ Divisive social (for example the 'caste') system excludes some groups.

15) b)

China / Japan : the place of worker sport and exercise programmes.

2 marks for :

❑ Both have maintained links with ancient cultures which value such activity highly.

❑ 'Collectivism' in China or Industrialisation in Japan have both found the 'cohesive values' in such activities serve the needs of their respective cultures well.

The reason why worker sport and exercise programmes are not part of UK sport.

2 marks for two from :

❑ Cultural heritage / influences have changed over centuries.

❑ Much culture destroyed by industrialisation rather than preserved.

❑ Resistance to centralised ethos by UK people.

❑ Class system ensured that sub-cultural values for each class were different.

Answers

OTHER CULTURES - ANSWERS (continued)

16) a)
Test matches (for RSA, NZL and AUS) assume great significance against UK rather than other countries:
    4 marks for four from (in respect of one country) :
- ❐ Maintaining links with 'home'.
- ❐ Establishment of own identity.
- ❐ Need to match up to the standard of the mother country.
- ❐ Reinforcements of colonial values.
- ❐ To beat their former 'masters'.

16) b)
Explain how the fact that 85% of Kenya's population live in rural areas affects mass participation in sport:
    2 marks for two from :
- ❐ Population are spread over a wide areas making facility provision difficult and expensive.
- ❐ Establishment of administration is difficult due to great distances.
- ❐ More expensive than in areas of dense population.
- ❐ Poor economy limits levels of provision anyway.

17) a) i)
From a culture you have studied in depth:
The nature and timing of programmes of excellence.
    2 marks for guidelines as follows :
- ❐ Centralised or de-centralised.
- ❐ Triggered off by failure or success in Olympic or major international sport.

17) a) ii)
Resistance to commercial involvement in sport.
    2 marks for :
- ❐ Tradition of amateur ethos prevents this.
- ❐ Cultural / political resistance - for example, communism.

17) a) iii)
Cultural / historical influences on sport.
    2 marks for two from :
- ❐ Again a tradition of amateur ethos would be a hstorical influence.
- ❐ Or the influence of ancient cultures / traditions: e.g. China, N. Korea or Japan.
- ❐ Also accept that Pakistan / India do not have the same 'active recreational culture' as other countries.

17) a) iv)
The extent of government involvement in sport.
    2 marks for two from :
- ❐ Indirect funding from the state (via Sport council / government in the UK pre 1996).
- ❐ Through the national lottery from 1997 in the UK.
- ❐ Full government funding - as in China - N. Korea - France.
- ❐ Partial government funding as in Australia, N.Z., India, Pakistan.

17) b)
Within a culture of your choice outline the effects of military influence on provision / participation in sport, and how this might change :
    1 mark for one from :
- ❐ Correct identification of military control of sporting provision and participation in a culture.
- ❐ For example, provision of facilities via army clubs in Russia (was more so in USSR).
    3 marks for three reasons for control from :
- ❐ Control of individuals (which sport / competitions should be done in the interests of the state rather than the individual) as athletes.
- ❐ Control of income derived from competition.
- ❐ Control of shop window effect for the state.
- ❐ Maintenance of National teams as opposed to individual's profit.
- ❐ Reduce the influence of commercial interests and enhance the importance of the state in the mind of their public.
- ❐ Provide an ideal environment (facilities / time to train) for the participants in elite sport.
- ❐ Control the bulk of the population who may or may not use the facilities (it would be a great perk to be able to use the military sports clubs).

OTHER CULTURES - ANSWERS QUESTION 17) b) (continued)

2 marks for two from :
- ❏ Evidence or reasons for likely change, such as the end of the cold war and reduction in military spending.
- ❏ Presence of a military government or centralised political influence which embraces the military (as in China).
- ❏ Move from totalitarian (military) state to democratic state where the influence of the military / state is reduced on every day matters (like sport).
- ❏ Reduction in size of military machine for economic reasons.
- ❏ Reduction in size of state as an entity (with the break up of Soviet Union for example) and hence the economic viabililty of military control of sport activity.

17) c)
Name and describe the role of organisations of mass recreation within RSA, NZL, or AUS :

1 mark for correct identification :
- ❏ South African National Recreation Council.
- ❏ New Zealand - Hillary Commission.
- ❏ Active Australia (AA).

1mark for role description :
- ❏ SANREC develops community recreational programmes with a network of nine Provincial Committees.
- ❏ Hillary Commission suggests structures for every aspect of physical activity - other sports organisations report to it.
- ❏ Active Australia is a framework for all the populatation aged 6 - 60, and encourages participation in physical activity for all.

2 marks for initiatives from :
- ❏ South Africa - SANGALA programmes.
- ❏ Community Sangala (or other Sangala initiatives), 'recrehab' and 'street programmes'.
- ❏ NZL - Hillary Commission programmes.
- ❏ NZL - 'Push play', or 'thirty minutes'.
- ❏ Australian Sports Cimmission - 'Active Australia'.
- ❏ AA - 'Willing and Able' for disabled athletes.
- ❏ AA - Community provision for 6 - 60.

Frank Galligan

SELECTED BIBLIOGRAPHY

Adair, D. Vamplew, W.	1997	Sport in Australian History.	Oxford University Press.
Booth, D.	1999	The Race Game.	Frank Cass.
Cashman, R.	1995	Paradise of Sport.	Oxford University Press.
Beashel, P.	1996	Physical Education at Advanced Level.	Thomas Nelson.
Davis, R.J. et. al.	2000	Physical Education and the Study of Sport 4e.	Mosby.
Davis, Kimmet, Auty.	1986	Physical Education Theory and Practice.	MacMillan.
Galligan, F & Hill, M	1997	'Ozfax'.	
Galligan, F et al	2000	Advanced PE for Edexcel.	Heinemann.
Holt, R.	1981	Sport and Society in Modern France.	MacMillan.
Honeybourne, J. et. al.	2000	Advanced Physical Education and Sport 2e.	Nelson Thornes.
Mackintosh, P.	1997	America's National Parks. (Unpublished paper : courtesey of T.C. Whitmore, Eastbourne.)	
Nixon	1988	Sport and the American Dream.	Human Kinetics.
PASE	1996	Physical Education and Sport PASE Education Section, Melbourne, Victoria.	
Sage, G.H.	1999	Power and Ideology in American Sport 2e.	Human Kinetics.
Senn, A.E.	1999	Power, Politics and the Olympic Games.	Human Kinetics.
Swanson, R.A.	1995	History of Sport and PE in the United States.	WCB McGraw-Hill.
Vamplew, W. et. al.	1994	Sport in Australia.	Oxford University Press.
Wesson, K. et. al.	2000	Sport and PE, A Complete Guide to A Level Study 2e.	Hodder & Stoughton.
Wiggins, D.K.	1995	Sport in America.	Human Kinetics.

THE OLYMPIC GAMES - A CASE STUDY IN GLOBAL SPORT

HISTORY OF THE ANCIENT GAMES
- The Games of the ancient world (known collectively as Panhellenic Games) are the earliest well-recorded civilised athletic festivals.
- The Games of Olympia the best known of these.
- Others were :
    - The Pythian Games (Delphi)
    - The Isthmian Games (Isthmia)
    - The Nemean Games (Nemea)
- These were known as 'Crown Games' as victors received a laurel or other crown rather than money.
- The first recorded victor, in the Stade of 776BC was Koroibus of Elis, who was (unusually) a baker.
- Other events included :
    The Diaulos.
        The Dolichos.
            Wrestling.
                Pankration.
                    Boxing.
                        The Pentathlon.
                            The Race in armour (Hoplite or Hippolite)
- Boys events were sometimes held but never girls.

HISTORY PRE 20TH CENTURY
- The Cotswold 'Olympik' Games, were begun by Robert Dover in 1612.
- The Wenlock Olympian Games held at Much Wenlock by William Penny Brooks in 1850.
- The Gog MaGog Olympik Games (1620) are the earliest recorded 'Olympic' resurgence.
- Other events included the Olympian Festivals of the National Olympian Association in the 1860s. 70s and 80s and the Liverpool Olympic Festivals held for a short time in the 1860s and 70s.
- De Coubertin visited English public schools (including Rugby) and was impressed with English games and Thomas Arnold.
- He believed that it was the character developed by exercise and games that was the key to the re-building of France after the Franco-Prussian War.
- De Coubertin's Olympic dream came into being on Easter Sunday 1896 when 311 athletes from 13 countries contested nine sports.

AMATEURISM AND SOCIAL CLASS
- The issue of professionalism was contentious in Olympic sport.
- It revolved not just around whether sportsmen were paid but whether they were gentlemen.
- Early Olympians would have been white, middle or upper class and wealthy.

A case study of global sport

amateurism · history · 901 · paralympics · race and ethnicity · THE OLYMPIC GAMES · deviance · commercialism · gender · politics

THE IOC
- Avery Brundage :
- President of the IOC from 1952 to 1972.
- Staunch supporter amateurism but also was racist.
- Coincided with the problems of Germany, Korea and China; the Hungarian uprising, the Middle East and Vietnam.
- Associated with the 'Black Power' salute of Mexico 1968 and his statement 'the Games must go on' after the massacre of the Israeli athletes at Munich in 1972.
- Attempted to persuade the free world not to boycott the Berlin Games of 1936 (was criticised for this).
- Juan Antonio Samaranch :
- Current [2000] IOC President, his term of office beginning in 1980.
- Has had to deal with political boycotts and the growth of professionalism in sport.
- Integrity of the IOC and its commissioners has been challenged and his own conduct as President scrutinised.
- Has presided over the return of South Africa to the Olympics and the holding of Olympics in Seoul.

RACE AND ETHNICITY IN THE OLYMPICS

THE OLYMPIC CREED

- States that athletes should be free to participate irrespective of race, colour or creed.
- Mass access to sport requires that constraints upon cultural and sub-cultural groups should be removed.
- In order for minority groups to have equality they must also have access and provision.

- Access can be denied by :-
    - A numerically superior culture.
    - Self-imposed cultural constraint.
    - Economic / topographical limitations.
- The major issue therefore is the exclusion of racial minorities from existing opportunity, or the failure to extend provision to all.

- Olympic Solidarity programmes and the various IOC commissions are responsible for education and provision in areas of need.
- Funded by income from television rights.

STACKING AND CENTRALITY

- These concepts reflect the cultural values within nation groups.
- The WASP culture of Britain, the USA and Europe was initially reflected in the Olympic movement.
- But the IOC is a now more cosmopolitan body with over 100 delegates from all over the World.

- The IOC is also a 'self-perpetuating club' without democratic accountability, but this is about to change.

- The concepts of stacking and centrality exist in nearly all cultures and is caused by the inclination of the most powerful group to perpetuate its own well being and values.

- One result of this is the 'glass ceiling', which refers to the invisible bar to advancement for ethnic and gender groups.

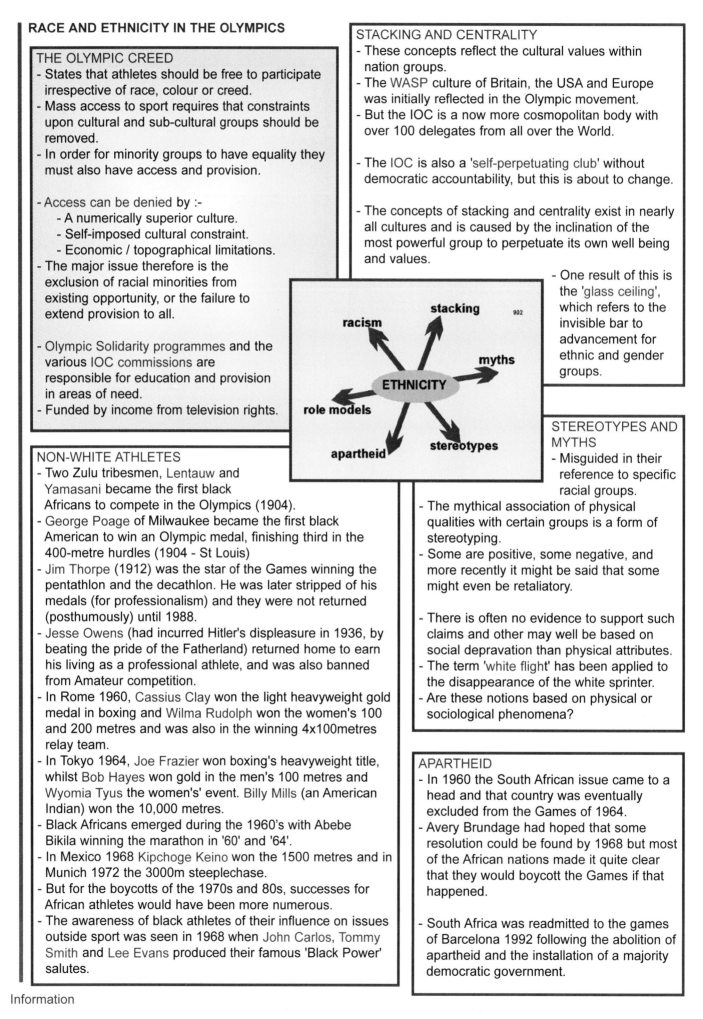

NON-WHITE ATHLETES

- Two Zulu tribesmen, Lentauw and Yamasani became the first black Africans to compete in the Olympics (1904).
- George Poage of Milwaukee became the first black American to win an Olympic medal, finishing third in the 400-metre hurdles (1904 - St Louis)
- Jim Thorpe (1912) was the star of the Games winning the pentathlon and the decathlon. He was later stripped of his medals (for professionalism) and they were not returned (posthumously) until 1988.
- Jesse Owens (had incurred Hitler's displeasure in 1936, by beating the pride of the Fatherland) returned home to earn his living as a professional athlete, and was also banned from Amateur competition.
- In Rome 1960, Cassius Clay won the light heavyweight gold medal in boxing and Wilma Rudolph won the women's 100 and 200 metres and was also in the winning 4x100metres relay team.
- In Tokyo 1964, Joe Frazier won boxing's heavyweight title, whilst Bob Hayes won gold in the men's 100 metres and Wyomia Tyus the women's' event. Billy Mills (an American Indian) won the 10,000 metres.
- Black Africans emerged during the 1960's with Abebe Bikila winning the marathon in '60' and '64'.
- In Mexico 1968 Kipchoge Keino won the 1500 metres and in Munich 1972 the 3000m steeplechase.
- But for the boycotts of the 1970s and 80s, successes for African athletes would have been more numerous.
- The awareness of black athletes of their influence on issues outside sport was seen in 1968 when John Carlos, Tommy Smith and Lee Evans produced their famous 'Black Power' salutes.

STEREOTYPES AND MYTHS

- Misguided in their reference to specific racial groups.
- The mythical association of physical qualities with certain groups is a form of stereotyping.
- Some are positive, some negative, and more recently it might be said that some might even be retaliatory.

- There is often no evidence to support such claims and other may well be based on social depravation than physical attributes.
- The term 'white flight' has been applied to the disappearance of the white sprinter.
- Are these notions based on physical or sociological phenomena?

APARTHEID

- In 1960 the South African issue came to a head and that country was eventually excluded from the Games of 1964.
- Avery Brundage had hoped that some resolution could be found by 1968 but most of the African nations made it quite clear that they would boycott the Games if that happened.

- South Africa was readmitted to the games of Barcelona 1992 following the abolition of apartheid and the installation of a majority democratic government.

COMMERCIALISM AND THE IOC

FINANCING THE GAMES
- The financial difficulties experienced by Montreal following the '76' Games made it clear that the funding of the Games had to change its marketing strategy.
- It was the Games' own success that had made it so expensive to stage.
- Criticism of the college scholarships in the USA and massive central funding in the Eastern bloc left many countries with no alternative but to seek similar funding or assistance from commercial interests.
- The Moscow Games (1980) were centrally funded.

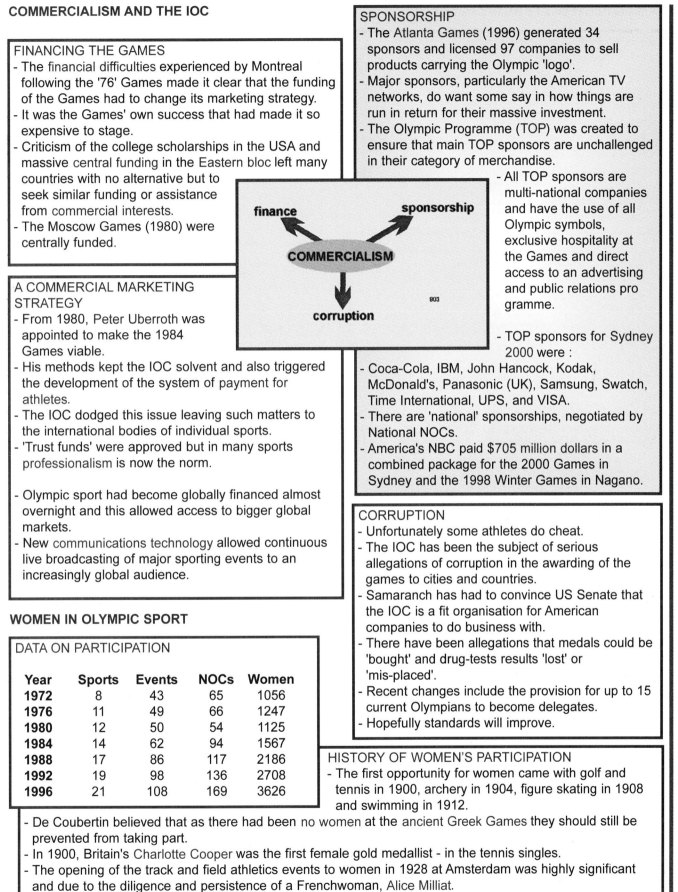

A COMMERCIAL MARKETING STRATEGY
- From 1980, Peter Uberroth was appointed to make the 1984 Games viable.
- His methods kept the IOC solvent and also triggered the development of the system of payment for athletes.
- The IOC dodged this issue leaving such matters to the international bodies of individual sports.
- 'Trust funds' were approved but in many sports professionalism is now the norm.

- Olympic sport had become globally financed almost overnight and this allowed access to bigger global markets.
- New communications technology allowed continuous live broadcasting of major sporting events to an increasingly global audience.

SPONSORSHIP
- The Atlanta Games (1996) generated 34 sponsors and licensed 97 companies to sell products carrying the Olympic 'logo'.
- Major sponsors, particularly the American TV networks, do want some say in how things are run in return for their massive investment.
- The Olympic Programme (TOP) was created to ensure that main TOP sponsors are unchallenged in their category of merchandise.
- All TOP sponsors are multi-national companies and have the use of all Olympic symbols, exclusive hospitality at the Games and direct access to an advertising and public relations pro gramme.
- TOP sponsors for Sydney 2000 were :
- Coca-Cola, IBM, John Hancock, Kodak, McDonald's, Panasonic (UK), Samsung, Swatch, Time International, UPS, and VISA.
- There are 'national' sponsorships, negotiated by National NOCs.
- America's NBC paid $705 million dollars in a combined package for the 2000 Games in Sydney and the 1998 Winter Games in Nagano.

CORRUPTION
- Unfortunately some athletes do cheat.
- The IOC has been the subject of serious allegations of corruption in the awarding of the games to cities and countries.
- Samaranch has had to convince US Senate that the IOC is a fit organisation for American companies to do business with.
- There have been allegations that medals could be 'bought' and drug-tests results 'lost' or 'mis-placed'.
- Recent changes include the provision for up to 15 current Olympians to become delegates.
- Hopefully standards will improve.

WOMEN IN OLYMPIC SPORT

DATA ON PARTICIPATION

Year	Sports	Events	NOCs	Women
1972	8	43	65	1056
1976	11	49	66	1247
1980	12	50	54	1125
1984	14	62	94	1567
1988	17	86	117	2186
1992	19	98	136	2708
1996	21	108	169	3626

HISTORY OF WOMEN'S PARTICIPATION
- The first opportunity for women came with golf and tennis in 1900, archery in 1904, figure skating in 1908 and swimming in 1912.
- De Coubertin believed that as there had been no women at the ancient Greek Games they should still be prevented from taking part.
- In 1900, Britain's Charlotte Cooper was the first female gold medallist - in the tennis singles.
- The opening of the track and field athletics events to women in 1928 at Amsterdam was highly significant and due to the diligence and persistence of a Frenchwoman, Alice Milliat.
- Mildred 'Babe' Didrickson won two gold medals and a silver in the 1932 Los Angeles Games.
- At these Games there were 1,300 male competitors - but only 120 women!
- Fanny Blankers-Koen won four gold medals in the 1948 Games in London, still unsurpassed at a Games.
- Since then, the women of eastern Europe have made the biggest impact, not always for the best of reasons.

WOMEN IN OLYMPIC SPORT (continued)

FURTHER DEVELOPMENTS
- Even though women were included in athletics in 1928, the 1936 Games saw only four sports providing women's events.
- There was a significant increase in the number of women in London in 1948.
- Twenty years later in Mexico there were still only eight women's sports.
- Numbers increased again following the 1976 Games in Montreal but even at the Games of 1996 there were 97 events open to women in 24 sports, whereas the total events open to men was 163.

DENIAL OF ACCESS
- Women have traditionally been denied access to Olympic sport on four levels :
  Global.
  Institutional.
  Cultural.
  Domestic.

WOMEN IN THE IOC
- Pirjo Haggman of Finland was appointed in 1981 and Britain's Dame Mary Glen-Haig in 1982.
- HRH The Princess Royal was appointed in 1984.
- A number of women have been appointed since.
- But men still outnumber women heavily.

THE MODERN SPORTING FEMALE
- The overwhelming constraints placed upon early sporting women were those of modesty, propriety and restraint.
- A young Olga Korbut, called into the Soviet team in Munich in 1972, changed all that with a daring and flirtatious floor sequence.
- Others: Nelli Kim, Vera Cáslavská and Nadia Comaneci, plus a host of others from the eastern bloc moved gymnastics - and women's sport - out of the age of the 'gymslip'.

THE POWER OF THE SPORTING FEMALE
- Marketability means power.
- Although much resistance has been overcome, some women athletes also have to break down more localised resistance before they can enjoy the same freedoms.
- The women of Morocco, led by Nawal El Moutawakel (400m hurdles winner 1988) have begun to overcome the resistance of a religious culture which discourages women from engaging in public display.
- Generally, the image and power of female athletes is growing but the failure of some women stars to attract equal sponsorship to men remains an issue.

POLITICAL USES OF THE OLYMPICS

POLITICAL AND OLYMPIC IDEALS
- The Olympic Charter opposes any political abuse of sport but such events are not new.
- The 1916 Games were cancelled due to World War 1 and invitations to the Games of 1920 were withdrawn from Austria, Bulgaria, Germany, Hungary and Turkey.
- The 1940 Games were cancelled and invitations not sent to Germany or Japan for the Games in 1948.
- The development of the 'East German machine' grew out of the use of sport by the former GDR as a tool of display / propaganda.
- The Soviet system was also politically motivated.
- The latest arrivals are the gymnasts, swimmers and distance-runners of the People's Republic of China.

THE OLYMPICS AS A POLITICAL TOOL

black power · reconciliation · 904 · recognition · apartheid · global protest · shop window · propaganda · corruption · devolution

PROTEST
- 1968 saw the first participation of the GDR and the protest of the 'Black Power' salute.
- Terrorism at the 1972 Games and the need for greater security removed the freedom and openness for which the Games had stood.
- There was political opposition to Britain's participation in Moscow in 1980 and the US government directed the withdrawal of its team from the same Games.
- This led to the withdrawal of USSR and other Soviet bloc countries from the Los Angeles Games of 1984.

OTHER POLITICAL USES
- Expulsion of South Africa over the apartheid issue, and the boycott of games by black Africa protesting at sporting links with South Africa.
- The Berlin Games was used as a political shop window for Hitler's Germany.
- Ping Pong diplomacy, the reinstatement of relations between USA and China.
- The shop window policy for countries to display the talent of their athletes as an advert for the political system - the advent of Eastern Bloc supremacy in many sports.

OLYMPIC BIDS AND POLITICS - HOW THE GAMES ARE AWARDED

BIDDING PROCEDURE
- This is concluded six years before a Games takes place but bids must be lodged at least two years earlier.
- Any number of cities may bid but the IOC will only accept one bid from any member country, a decision made by its own NOC.
- The members of the IOC take a vote, and the city with a clear majority is successful but if there is no clear majority, the least popular city is eliminated.
- Further rounds of voting then take place, with one city being eliminated each time.
- There are now more bids for any Games than was the case up to Montreal in '76' and British bids for '92' and '96' had 20 and 25 opponents respectively.
- The Winter Games of 2002 had ten bids and this forced the IOC to change the process so that cities were first of all reduced to four by selection prior to any voting.
- It is the bidding process that has attracted criticism, with accusations of IOC delegates allegedly acquiring gifts, cash and other 'favours' in return for their votes.
- Four Commissioners have been removed from office and a further six have resigned.

DEVIANCE AND THE OLYMPICS

CHEATING
- Difficult to define as differing cultures view such things in different ways.
- The 'win-at-all-costs' ethic, born of American football coach Vince Lombardi, is often cited as the point at which cheating became 'OK'.
- However, early British ventures into European soccer saw many British footballers astounded at the antics of their European counterparts.
  In cricket, 'sledging' is considered by many Australians to be 'fair game'.
- Eastern bloc countries had a political ideology which sanctioned any action that would bring success.
- The globalisation of sport has made definition of the term 'sporting' increasingly difficult.

DEVIANCE
- The reasons why rules are framed are not uniform and agreed.
- Deviant behaviour refers to those who will find a way around the rules however they are framed.

- Deviant behaviour falls into one or more of the following categories :
  Institutional.
     Group specific.
        Individual.
- And is either :
  Voluntary.
     Co-operative.
        Enforced.
- Sports bodies develop strategies to limit deviance - anti-doping, drug control, red carding, yellow carding, penalties - backed up by specific and detailed rules.

WHY DO CITIES BID?
- Following the intervention of Uberroth in 1984, popularity has grown largely in line with technological advances.
- Television companies are (increasingly) prepared to pay considerable sums for broadcasting rights.
- Without these additional revenues the Games could not pay its way.
- There are now high stakes to be played for, in terms of potential benefits to host cities and to business, commercial and media interests.
- Potential host cities are prepared to gamble millions for a chance to reap unprecedented financial returns.

RECENT BIDS
- The Manchester bids (1992 and 1996).
- People now believe that the well prepared and presented Manchester Olympic bids for the Games of 1992 and 1996 were doomed to failure.
- There were clear shortcomings in the way the IOC made its deliberations.

- Athens bid (1996).
- The awarding of the '96' Games to Atlanta rather than Athens.
- Samaranch had declared publicly that Athens was the clear favourite - but remarkably the Games was awarded to Atlanta, which just happened to be the home of the Coca-Cola company.

SPORTSMANSHIP
- An intention to compete within the rules and the intended spirit of the rules.
- In the past, the gentleman sportsman subscribed to the view that it was better to lose honourably than win by cheating.

GAMESMANSHIP
- The intention to compete to the limit of the rules - and beyond if possible.
- The current view seems to be, 'you get away with whatever you can'.
- The potential rewards often outweigh moral considerations.
- But is this right?

DEVIANCE AND THE OLYMPICS (continued)

ANTI-DOPING
- The IOC's anti-doping campaign is based upon three principles :
  - The protection of the health of athletes.
  - Respect for medical and sports ethics.
  - Ensuring an equal chance for everyone during competition.

- Since 1994 testing procedures have included blood as well as urine samples and all international bodies are now under pressure to adopt the IOC's medical code for international competitions.

- This includes 'random' testing, so that top athletes can now be tested at any time during the year.
- Some fifteen per cent of tests are taken out of season.
- The latest challenge centres on the use of erythropoietin (rEPO), which increases blood oxygenation by forming additional red blood cells and hence improves stamina.
- The first testing for this drug was in Lillehammer in 1994.

THE IOC AND DRUG CONTROL
- The first drug-related death (the Danish cyclist Knud Jensen) occurred in the 1960 Games in Rome.
- The IOC's current interpretation includes the deliberate and inadvertent use of performance-enhancing substances.
- The establishment of a medical control, responsible for drug testing, has been operative since the 1968 Games.

- IOC Medical Commission involves establishing all routines and practical aspects of collecting urine samples and ensuring that they are securely transported to the accredited laboratory for that Games.
- The Commission works closely with the International Sporting Federations as well as the accredited laboratory.
- IOC rules do not prevent further sanctions against guilty parties by the international federations of individual sports.

PARALYMPICS

HISTORY
- In 1944 Dr. Ludwig Guttmann opened, a spinal injuries centre at Stoke Mandeville Hospital.
- He pioneered a new approach to rehabilitation centred on sport.
- The Paralympics movement began life as an organised sports competition for war veterans with spinal cord injury in 1948.
- Within a short time competitors from Holland were also taking part.
- In 1960 a Games on the Olympic pattern was organised and in 1976 in Toronto competition was expanded to include other disability groups.
- The Games were initially an independent event but have shared the main Olympic venue since Seoul in 1988 and Albertville in France for the Winter Games.
- It was not until 1988 that a commitment was made by the IOC to assist the IPC with the organisation of the Games.

IMPAIRMENT CLASSIFICATIONS
- Cerebral Palsy (CP-ISRA).
- Spinal Cord Lesion, Spina Bifida and Polio (ISMWSF).
- Athletes with Blindness (IBSA).
- Les Autres or Amputations (ISOD).

MARKETING AND IMPAIRMENT
- The first 'Olympic Games for the Disabled' took place in Sweden in 1980, and the first use of the term 'Paralympics' was at the Games in Seoul in 1988.

- Samaranch supported the disabled movement, but he felt that too close an association with disabled sport might harm the market potential of the Games.
- There were apparently three allegations :
  - He did not want the title 'The Olympic Games for the Disabled' used, for marketing reasons.
  - He would not allow the Olympic flag or symbols to be used.
  - The IPC were not to ask for inclusion of disability events in the main Olympic programme.

- The Paralympics now has its own symbol (three teardrops).
- Wheelchair events were held (on a demonstration basis) in the track and field programme in Sydney 2000.

LINKS WITH THE OLYMPIC MOVEMENT
- The number of athletes involved has increased from 400 in 1960 to just over 3000 in Atlanta in 1996.
- The numbers in the Sydney Games were even higher and the general opinion is that the Sydney organisers gave disability sport the stage it deserves.
- Clearly, venues are now shared with the 'big brother' Games of much longer standing and since 1988 the IOC has, at least officially, acknowledged and embraced the Paralympics.

QUESTIONS

THE OLYMPIC GAMES

1) a) What is meant by the term 'Crown Games' and how did they differ from others?   (2 marks)
b) Who were:-
    i) Robert Dover?
    ii) William Penny Brooks?
    iii) What part did each play in the re-emergence of 'Olympianism'?   (4 marks)
c) The 1936 Olympic Games in Berlin saw performances by Jesse Owens which outshone those of German athletes.
    i) Why did this displease Hitler?
    ii) Why was it felt in some quarters that the IOC should have moved the Games?
    iii) Which section of American society was most against the Games taking place, and why?   (6 marks)

2) a) Avery Brundage was known to be stubborn, hold set views on the topic of amateur sport and was considered by many also to have racist views. Give three examples which exemplify each of the above points.
                                                                  (6 marks)
b) It is a matter of record that SANOC, the National Olympic Committee of South Africa was not a racist organisation. That being the case can you explain why :
    i) It was unable to select teams from across the social spectrum.
    ii) If SANOC was a non-racial body, were South Africa excluded from the Olympic movement prior
    to the Games of 1964?   (4 marks)
c) The 'WASP' culture predominated in Olympic sport during the early years of its life. Give three examples of how and why this influence has gradually diminished.   (6 marks)

3) a) The Montreal Games of 1976 represented a 'watershed' in the way that Games were financed. State why this was the case and what was the outcome in terms of :
    i) The provision of facilities.
    ii) Advertising at Games venues.
    iii) The nature of amateur status.   (10 marks)
b)   **i)** Frame an argument in favour of the withdrawal of Olympic medals from athletes from former eastern
    bloc countries.   (4 marks)
    ii) State possible oppositions to this view, saying why the status quo should be maintained.   (4 marks)

4) a) 'Traditional sporting values have no part to play in modern Olympic sport'. How would you justify this viewpoint?   (4 marks)
b) Disability sport seems at last to be receiving the recognition it deserves. In you opinion, should the Paralympic movement be fully embraced by the IOC under the banner of the five rings, or should it continue under the 'Three Teardrops' and develop as an independent organisation?   (10 marks)

SUMMARY OF GLOBAL FACTORS

The following four pages chart the factors and issues which affect global sport, and form a summary for the nine countries / areas chosen for study in this text.

Answers

Themes	Australia	France	USA	UK
Topography and Climate	Huge land area. Varied physical features. Varied climate.	Large land area. Varied physical features. Varied climate.	Huge land area. Varied physical features. Varied climate.	Lack of size and defined climate reduces range of available sports.
Historical Influences	British colony. British, European, Asian immigrants.	Colonial power. Colonial, North African immigrants.	British colony. Negro, European, Hispanic immigrants.	Colonial-industrial empire. Reformist influences.
Political Systems	British then Federal Government.	Revolution to social democracy.	British, then capitalist Federal Government.	Democratic bicameral parliamentary system.
Cultural Influences	Suppression of Aboriginal culture and subsequent Asian cultures (stacking).	Embracing of former colonial cultures : (l'egalitarianism).	Suppression of native, black, hispanic and east European cultures.	Diminution of class divide has reduced middle class dominance of sport.
Philosophical Approach	Mixed capitalist / socialist ethic.	Intellectualised socialism.	Capitalist ethic : WASP syndrome.	Blurring of capitalist socialist ethics. Minority inclusion.
Economic System	Agriculture based but embracing new technologies and its position on Pacific Rim.	Mixed economy drained by heavy social programme and subsidies.	Profit motive rules. Produces some 'winners' but many 'losers'.	Move from heavy to technological economy creating leisure and unemployment.
Education	State education within federal system. Some private schools mainly R.C. Devolved to State level.	National Education very centralised. Private system mainly RC schools. Little devolution of power.	State education within federal system. Small private system. Decentralised.	State education system but significant and influential private sector.
PE Teachers	No specialists in primary sector. Teachers also coach but with good support structure.	Specialists only in the secondary sector. Limited involvement in school sports. This is done through UNSS.	PE teachers rarely involved in coaching. Specialist staff coach sport.	'Laissez faire ' approach has required 'all purpose' roles of PE teachers.
Sports Schools	Growing number of these schools. Largely self-funded. Traditionally in the private sector.	Formerly only 'sports study sections' but 'sports schools' now being introduced. Funded centrally / privately.	Few sports schools as such but 'win ethic' ensures that all schools aim for sports excellence.	A few private (for example, Millfield, Kelly College). Some state schools have 'designated status' as sport schools.
Power Base	Generally, still the white Western groups.	Paris retains its central role but growing regional influence - sponsorship of sport is bringing some change.	The WASP males hold power. Based on wealth and social status.	Diminishing aristocracy replaced by ascendant middle class meritocracy.
Centralisation	Two levels of centralised control : federal, state.	Most centralised via Ministry of Youth & Sport (no devolution).	Least centralised. Complete devolution to grass roots.	Some centralised control via QANGOs. No centralised policy.
Stacking	In evidence, with East Europeans, Asians, Aboriginals in that order.	In practice, North Africans (especially Algerians) at the bottom of the pile.	Very much in evidence, Vietnamese now last in line.	Some deprivation on ethnic or poverty grounds has this effect.

Information

Argentina	Kenya	South Africa	Asia	New Zealand
Huge land area Varied physical Features Varied climate.	Large land area: varied physical features : varied climate inc. drought.	Large land area Varied physical features: good but varied climate.	Huge variation in the physical geography/ features: huge landmass to small islands.	Land area and climate roughly equal to that of Britain: varied topography.
Former Spanish colony, much British influence in industry & education.	Former British colony: Independent since 1963.	Former British colony White colonial influences, Ethnic dispossessions.	Some British colonies: others (e.g. China) 'colonised' by British trade and commerce.	Former British colony / cultural heritage. Maori people & culture included within its democracy.
Spanish - then various 'national' & military governments until free elections following the Falklands war.	Independence : to social democracy. Conflict between European and older tribal cultures.	British, then nationalist (Apartheid) gov't. Recent adoption of democratic principles.	Ancient / dynastic cultures overlaid (varying degrees) by British trade / colonial expansion. Diverse political models.	Constitutional democracy. Treaty of Waitangi (1864) established the equal rights and ancient customs of Maori.
85% 'European' population and culture. 'Amerindians' and 'mephistos' make up the rest.	European colonialism overlaying ancient tribalism: factionalism based on ancient tribal differences.	Suppression of native, black, and Asian cultures.	Suppression of ancient cultures. Assimilation of 'global sporting cultures driven by economic reward.	Full inclusion of ancient (Maori) culture within political and social frameworks.
Militarist influences still present but on the decline.	Democracy but ridden with inter-tribal conflict.	Capitalist ethic overlain by recent adoption of social demcracy.	Ancient 'spiritual' values often govern attitudes to sport in the modern world.	British colonial values have been adapted to accommodate aggressive competitive tendencies.
Agriculture based but embracing new technologies slowly.	Very poor agricultural economy with many farmers exploited by 'western interests'.	Huge reserves of natural resources but re-distribution and ownership an issue.	Varies from centralist (China & N. Korea) to capitalist (Japan) and from agricultural to industrial / technological.	Largely agricultural economy with reliance upon both British and Pacific rim markets.
State education within federal system : some private schools : mainly R.C. Devolved to provincial level.	National education system but poorly funded : also private system - many church schools.	State system devolved to nine 'provinces' but poorly funded in contrast to established private system.	State education exists in all cultures but with much variation: for example : heavily 'politicised' in China, N. Korea.	National education system - centralised with control devolved to nine regional authorities: private system largely religious bodies.
Newly established in both primary & sec. sectors. Teachers do some coaching but most sport taught at 'junior' club level.	Some specialists in the secondary schools but largely in the private sector. Involved in sport but limited facilities.	High level of teaching in private schools but not in State system: very poor facilities, even in some private 'white' state schools.	Specialists in all sectors in China, North Korea and Japan but not elsewhere. Poor provision elsewhere.	Specialists in primary & secondary sectors: heavy emphasis on school sport: Highly structured PE programmes.
No: see comments above.	No, but some private schools are strong.	Not as yet but new infrastructure still developing.	Highly significant in China but developing in India and in N. Korea.	No significant developmentt but high level of school sport is the norm.
Generally, those of Spanish / Western. European origins.	Many European business interests and small native group.	Currently changing: whites still have much influence economically.	Central political control in China, Pakistan and N. Korea with significant military influence.	Former 'Colonial' influences predominate but indigenous groups have significantly more input than elsewhere.
Centralised structure is being developed.	Little centralisation.	Slowly developing a centralised structure.	Yes in China & N Korea. Yes for elite sport in India and Pakistan.	Yes, established fully from 1976 onwards:
Still in evidence, with 'Mestizos' and 'Cabicates Négras' at the bottom of the pile.	White Europeans with indigenous tribal cultures 'stacked' below them.	Officially this no longer exists but will take some time to be effective in practice.	Most evident in India and Pakistan.	Some isolated incidents of racial prejudice

Themes	Australia	France	USA	UK
Government Funding	Federal Government devolves power and funding to each State. Growing private sector funding.	Heavy government involvement in sport. Centralised funding and control, but now some input from commercial interests.	Little involvement at government level. State bodies pass power to grass roots level. Much private funding.	UK Sport controls lottery funding - for capital projects and athlete income. No direct government control over policy.
National Initiatives	Poor performance at 1976 Olympics caused Government intervention - set up AIS and ASC.	Poor performance at 1960 Olympics caused De Gaulle's 5 point plan, and setting up of Sports academies.	No outstanding failures, but highly motivated by Soviet success 60's to 80's. None specific.	Failure at 1996 Olympics heightens debate on National Sporting Academy.
Mass Participation	Federally sponsored programmes run at State and local level., for example, 'Active Australia'. 'Aussie Able' caters for disabled people. 'Women sport' urges women into sport.	'Sport pour Tous' aims to encourage a multi-sport approach through the family means 'within everyone's reach'. Growth of 'pro' sport also means more junior club sections as talent bases.	No 'federal' plans. 'Little league' sport caters for kids. Adult programmes run by men's and women's organisations and as part of school or college programmes.	Major initiatives 'Sport for All', 'Top Sport'. Thought to be insufficient. NGBs run schemes (for example, athletics, swimming, gymnastics).
Elite Sport	ASC and AIS control national programmes and élite development. State academies foster talent within a State and work with the AIS on programmes. Such as 'Sportsleap' and 'Sportsearch'.	National centres of excellence (INSEP). Regional sports and PE centres have developed programmes and there is a centre for Research and Technology. Some undergraduates can use sporting achievements as part of their degree.	The 'Lombardian' ethic (win at all costs) sits at the heart of sport in the US. Élitism is at the heart of most sporting activity, and is, in effect, a programme for excellence.	Amateur (participation) ethic being replaced by money led outcome or professional approach.
Poverty	Officially not a bar to access. Funding allows scholarships to academies of sport. Some groups still feel excluded.	Heavily funded programmes for talent identification allow access to all. Funding spreads down to local levels of provision.	The sports scholarship is the only access to sports programmes. In effect the only programmes for excellence.	Insufficient centralised funding and 'diversionist' allocation policies produce insufficient provision in most needy areas.
Women's Issues	Currently very much an issue. 'Womensport Australia' is a loud political voice. Women have greater % of medals than men at major Games.	Equality exists by right. However, not always so in practice. Social / family pressures have restricted participation but recent role-models have broken new ground.	'Title IX' a major boost for women. But the 'matriarchal' society is not too keen to 'divert' women from their 'real purpose'.	Policies for 'equality' exist, but lack of centralised system inhibits implementation.
Athletes with Disabilities	Australia has a superb programme of development for disabled sportspersons via 'Active Australia' and 'Willing and Able'.	The notion of equality exists in legislation but sadly not always in practice.	Active assimilation policies exist. The 'Atlanta experience' upset many disabled athletes, provision allegedly very poor.	Growing awareness and participation levels but much left to voluntary associations. Lack of a clear centralist approach.

Argentina	Kenya	South Africa	Asia	New Zealand
Central Gov't devolves (limited) power and funding to provinces.	Central provision in theory but poor economy limits support.	Much broader provision under new gov't. but massive task ahead.	Full Gov't funding in China / N Korea. Partial funding in Japan. Elite sport only in India and Pakistan.	Government funding in all areas.
Yes in Physical Education and Olympic Sport. Other areas developing slowly.	Largely in Athletics. Little development in other areas.	SANREC funding of SANGALA programme.	China - full range of Gov't funded programmes. Japan - National Children's Games. India - Boys Sports Companies (Army).	'Sportfit' 'Pushplay' 'Thirty minutes'.
Developing provision by the Secretaria de Deportes de la Nacion but this is developing very slowly with most growth in the province of Buenos Aires. (see below)	Growth of professional sport has stimulated interest in athletics, soccer and basketball but little in the way of effectively funded mass participation programmes.	No 'federal' plans : 'little league' sport caters for kids : adult programmes run by 'men's' & 'women's' org's. and as part of school & college programmes.	Long established programmes in China and Japan - also North Korea but now developing in India, Pakistan and elsewhere in Asia. Problems with Islamic women.	The NZSF and the Hillary Commission sponsor programmes such as 'Sportfit', 'Thirty Minutes' and 'Push-play': all designed to encourage mass participation and an active lifestyle.
The Secretaria de Deportes de la Nacion and the Argentine Olympic Association make provision for the funding of élite sport. The 'Secretaria' is also responsible for mass sport but its work is very ineffective thus far.	Nation-building ethic and limited central funding dictate that a limited range of sports is catered for. The Kenyan Olympic committee is funded voluntarily - not by government.	The 'Lombardian' ethic (win at all costs) sits at the heart of sport in the US : élitism is at the heart of most sporting activity - and is, in effect, a programme for excellence.	Élite sport in China long established as part of political model: India (SAI) and Pakistan (PSB) much more recent: Structures in place in Japan and N. Korea but in rather differing political scenarios.	Well-funded and developed by the NZSF in conjunction with the NZOC where appropriate. New Zealand has a small population base and achieves very highly despite this drawback.
High unemployment (20%) and presence of disadvantaged groups (see stacking) means that poverty is an issue in Argentina.	High levels of poverty, particularly in rural areas. Drought and resultant famine create major problems for government.	The sports scholarship is the only access to sports programmes : in effect the only programmes for excellence.	Not an issue in China, or N. Korea, nor in Japan, but India and Pakistan have economic problems with access and funding, and some groups are excluded on the basis of culture or religion.	Poverty is not a major issue in new Zealand. Indigenous cultures have traditionally not been excluded: in stark contrast to the situation in Australia.
Not (yet) a major issue. Provision in women's sport is made for those who are already 'advantaged' and others do not yet have a powerful enough voice.	Cultural resistance to change. Many Kenyan women find family objections - which only subside when prize money is seen to be an alternative to poverty.	'Title 1X' a major boost for women : but the 'matriarchal' society not too keen to 'divert' women from their 'real purpose'.	Japan and China have policies of equality in the case of women athletes. This however is not yet the case in India and Pakistan, particularly in the case of those of the Islamic faith.	New Zealand women, including Maori women are equal in terms of legislation, general practices and opportunity.
Provision was made in the 'Peronist' period but subsequently declined. The 'Laws of Basic Consensus' have yet to really address this issue.	No apparent policy in sport. Some funding from IOC initiatives and some participation from the few who ma have independent means.	'Active assimilation policies exist : the 'Atlanta experience upset many disabled athletes - provision allegedly very poor but increased in the run-up to the Sydney Olympics.	Again, the centrally funded programmes of China provide for disability sport but the ethic (nor the funding for it) has not yet spread to some parts of Asia.	Disability sport is centrally funded in the same way as able-bodied sport.

ANSWERS

1) a)
What is meant by the term 'Crown Games' and how did they differ from others?
❏   'Prizes of crowns' of laurel, fig, or wild celery leaves were given to winners in 'Crown Games'.
❏   Other Games had 'money' prizes.

1) b) i)
Robert Dover :
      1 mark for one from :
❏   Was a lawyer.
❏   17th century gentleman.
❏   Started Robert Dover's Games.

1) b) ii)
William Penny Brooks :
      1 mark for one from :
❏   Was a local doctor.
❏   Magistrate / JP.
❏   Started local reading groups.
❏   Developed Much Wenlock Olympian Sport.
❏   Co-founded the National Olympian Association.
❏   Was visited by de Coubertin.

1) b) iii)
What part did each play in the re-emergence of Olympianism?
      2 marks for :
❏   They resurrected the ancient traditions of Olympia.
❏   They were connected with Coubertin.

1) c) i)
The 1936 Olympic Games in Berlin saw performances by Jesse Owens which outshone those of German athletes. 'Hitler's displeasure' :
      2 marks for :
❏   Owens destroyed his theory of Ayrian supremacy.
❏   He could not stand the sight of 'a black man' destroying his wonderful white athletes.

1) c) ii)
Why was it felt in some quarters that the IOC should have moved the Games?
      2 marks for any two from :
❏   There were clear concerns about Hitler's political manipulation of the Games.
❏   He was known to have strong racial views.
❏   People in Germany were being persecuted because of their racial origins.

1) c) iii)
Which section of American society was most against the Games taking place - and why?:
      2 marks for any two from :
❏   The Jewish community because of Hitler's known treatment of their own kind in Germany.
❏   The black community because they knew Hitler was a racist.
❏   The black community because they did not want other Blacks to be used as tools by a white administration that supported Hitler's racist policies.

2) a)
Avery Brundage was known to be stubborn, hold set views on the topic of amateur sport and was considered by many also to have racist views. Give three examples which exemplify each of the above points. :
      6 marks for :
❏   Brundage was known to declare that if the blacks boycotted Mexico they would not be missed.
❏   He refused to sanction the posthumous return of Jim Thorpe's medals because he insisted he was not an amateur.
❏   He declared that if a sportsman was paid, that was work.
❏   And work could not be sport.
❏   He supported America's participation in Berlin in 1936.
❏   He declared that sport was more important than any dispute the Jewish people might have with Hitler's regime.

ANSWERS - QUESTION 2 (continued)

2) b) i)
It is a matter of record that SANOC, the National Olympic Committee of South Africa was not a racist organisation. That being the case can you explain why It was unable to select teams from across the social spectrum :

2 marks for :
- ❏ SANOC was not able to override social divisions.
- ❏ Which meant that multi-racial selection was impossible under Apartheid.

2) b) ii)
If SANOC was a non-racial body, were South Africa excluded from the Olympic movement prior to the Games of 1964?

2 marks for :
- ❏ Although SANOC was expelled, its own policies were not in question.
- ❏ It was the policies of its government (of South Africa) that was under scrutiny.

2) c)
The 'WASP' culture predominated in Olympic sport during the early years of its life. Can you give three examples of how and why this influence has gradually diminished.

6 marks for six from :
- ❏ Independence was granted to former colonies.
- ❏ This broadened power structures into indigenous cultures.
- ❏ Success was achieved by certain individuals from ethnic groups.
- ❏ This paved the way for others.
- ❏ There was a realisation by many governments / power groups that such exclusion was wrong.
- ❏ There was a growing influence of the 'British Commonwealth of nations'.
- ❏ This had an influence on Olympic issues.

3) a) i)
The Montreal Games of 1976 represented a 'watershed' in the way that Games were financed. State why this was the case and what was the outcome in terms of :
The provision of facilities.

3 marks for three from :
- ❏ Facilities not a burden on local resources.
- ❏ Facilities funded by private enterprise.
- ❏ Facilities donated to and of benefit to local community after the Games.
- ❏ First time an outside entrepreneur (Ubberoth) had been brought in to oversee the overall building programme.

3) a) ii)
Advertising at Games venues.

3 marks for three from :
- ❏ First time advertising allowed in stadium.
- ❏ First time advertising allowed on athletes' numbers.
- ❏ Considerable increase in revenue from television.
- ❏ Adoption of notion of 'approved' advertisers or sponsors.

3) a) iii)
The nature of amateur status.

4 marks for four from :
- ❏ First acceptance by IOC that money could be paid to athletes.
- ❏ This was forced because of IOCs own acceptance of 'planned financial income'.
- ❏ Instrumental in 'trust funds' being set up.
- ❏ Paved the way for individual sponsorship / advertising contracts for individual athletes rather than their associations.
- ❏ 1 additional mark for an answer presented in prose, in a clear, logical format.

3) b) i)
Frame an argument in favour of the withdrawal of Olympic medals from athletes from former eastern bloc countries.

4 marks for four from :
- ❏ Most performances are now considered to be 'suspect'.
- ❏ Some former eastern bloc athletes have admitted cheating.
- ❏ Any records created are obviously not sound.
- ❏ It would be a fair conclusion for those athletes deprived of medals by cheats.
- ❏ It would show that the Olympic movement does not condone cheating.

ANSWERS - QUESTION 3) b) (continued)

3) b) ii)
State possible oppositions to this view, saying why the status quo should be maintained.
    4 marks for :
❏   Not all 'alleged cases' of cheating have been clearly proven.
❏   The IOC might be seen to be taking a 'political' stance.
❏   It would be impossible to administer such a radical move fairly and impartially.
❏   Some medal-winners who did not cheat may lose medals 'by association' with those who did.

4) a)
Traditional sporting values have no part to play in modern Olympic sport'. How would you justify this viewpoint?
    4 marks for :
❏   We cannot be expected to subscribe to values that are outdated.
❏   Each generation / period in history must be allowed to make its own values.
❏   Interpretation of philosophical and / or moral values must be made by the current generation.
❏   The financial context of modern sport makes such amateurish morality redundant.

4) b)
Should the Paralympic movement be fully embraced by the IOC under the banner of the five rings?
    10 marks for :
❏   Extended answer required.
❏   The Paralympics involves human beings and all should be embraced under the five rings.
❏   The IOC should not be allowed to discriminate against disabled people.
❏   The disability sport community should be allowed to decide for themselves under which banner they wish to operate.
❏   Disability sport will make greater progress if it is identified in its own right.
❏   Not as a benevolent off-shoot of the IOC.
❏   The marketing implications of disability sport are that the commercial value of the sport (for sponsorship / advertising) may be enhanced.
❏   Or may be reduced.
❏   The large number of competitors now competing in disabled sport widen the target group for marketing.
❏   The image of the disabled athlete - striving against adversity - might be worth bringing under the Olympic banner.

                                                                Frank Galligan

SELECTED BIBLIOGRAPHY :

Bale, J.	1996	Kenyan Running.	Frank Cass.
Booth, D.	1998	The Race Game.	Frank Cass.
British Olympic Association	1999	Education Pack for Schools.	BOA.
DDVideos	1981	History of Sport - Boxed Set.	Classroom Resources.
Chronicle	2000	Chronicle of the Olympic Games 2e.	Dorling Kindersley.
Daniels, S.	1999	'A Proper Spectacle' - Women's Olympic Participation.	
			ZeNaNA and Walla Walla Press.
Hill, C.R.	1996	Olympic Politics : Athens to Atlanta.	MUP.
Lucas, J.	1992	The Future of the Olympic Games.	Human Kinetics.
Senn, A.E.	1999	Power, Politics and the Olympic Games.	Human Kinetics.
Swanson, R.A.	1995	History of Sport & PE in the United States.	WCB, McGraw-Hill.
Terry, D.	2000	'Early English Olympism', in, Sports History for 'A' Level,	
			British Society of Sports History.
Wenlock Olympian Society	1996	William Penny Brookes and the Olympic Connection.	WOS.
Whitfield, C.	1962	Robert Dover and the Cotswold Games.	Henry Sotheran, London.

SYNOPTIC QUESTION & ANALYSIS FRAMEWORK

ASSESSMENT PROCEDURE

THE QUESTIONS
- Each of the Examining Boards have been required to include synoptic questions in their A2 examination.

- There are a number of different potential formats to be considered and candidates should check the specification and revision material of their particular board.

- All questions must link AS module(s) with A2 module(s) and include reference to applied performance.

- Due recognition must be given to compulsory and optional modular content.

MARK ALLOCATION
- The allocation of marks vary with each Board.
- There is a requirement that the synoptic assessment will be 15% of the overall assessment total.

- Boards may allocate synoptic marks from one or two final units which may include a performance unit or an assignment.

- Boards have the right to mark the synoptic question using content marks, banded criteria or a combination of the two.

THE APPROACH
- Thematic approaches may be :
A. General questions involving full range of compulsory modules with choice of options.
B. Subject based, such as the Olympic Games, amateurism,etc. with multi-disciplinary analysis.
C. Science based and may include physiological / biomechanical / psychological content.
D. Socio-cultural basis involving contemporary studies with historical / comparative content.

- Questions may be essay type or structured.

QUESTIONS

A. Essay, General Question.

1) To achieve sporting excellence it is necessary to have scientific support and the social opportunity. Discuss this in the context of a specific physical activity.

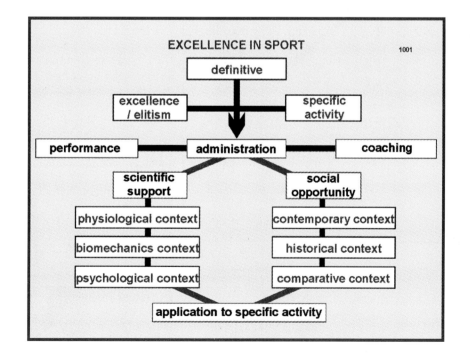

B. **Subject** thematic: semi-structured.

2) Specific Olympic Games have always fairly accurately reflected the concept of amateurism at that time.

i. Trace the interpretation of amateurism by looking at a number of different Olympic Games.
ii. How has the scope of the Olympics expanded amateurism globally?
iii. Explain the changing role of the modern coach given the present interpretation of amateurism.

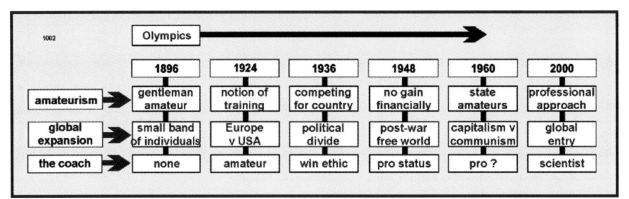

C. **Scientific theme linking** compulsory modules such as applied anatomy and physiology and skill acquisition with options such as biomechanics and sport psychology.

3) a) It is suggested that there are a number of values in school physical education that can be influenced by scientific knowledge.

i) Pursuing your particular physical activity has required you to know something about the control of blood supply during exercise.

Briefly identify the pulmonary and systemic circulatory networks and the factors linked with venous return.

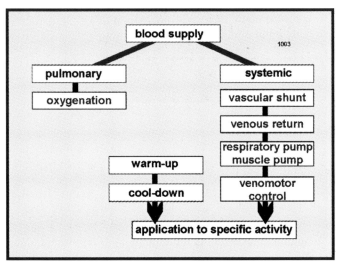

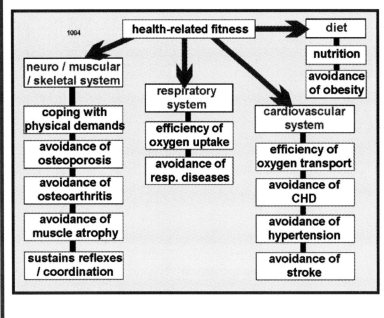

ii) How might you justify fitness in you own performance activity with the importance of health-related fitness for life?

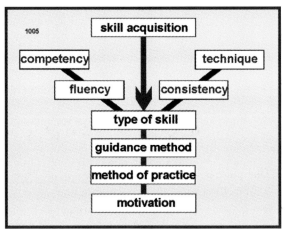

iii) Explain the importance of skill acquisition in the context of an activity of your choice with reference to competency, fluency, consistency and the successful application of technique.

QUESTION 3 (continued)

EITHER

3) b) Explain the factors that may either enhance or hinder the effective performance of a group or team training in a physical activity of your choice.

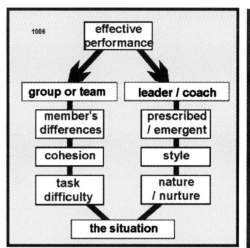

OR

3) c) Explain the ways in which forces are applied to yourself or your surroundings in a sports skill of your choice using pin and force diagrams where relevant.

D. Socio-cultural theme linking Contemporary Studies with either Historical or Comparative Studies, in a structured form.

4) a) The structure and function of sport is largely determined by its social setting.

i) Describe the qualities of the performance pyramid shown in Figure 1008. Illustrate your answer using your own preferred sport.

EMERGENT COUNTRIES
- Nation building.
  Integration.
    Health.
      Social control.
DISPROPORTIONATE FUNDING
  Elitism.
    Selectivity.
      Occupational.
        Excellence.
INTERNAL APPEASEMENT / EXTERNAL EXPOSURE
  Role models.   World recognition.
    Opportunity.   Funding attraction
      Provision.   Talent feedback.

ii) Explain why emergent nations tend to disproportionately fund one particular sport.

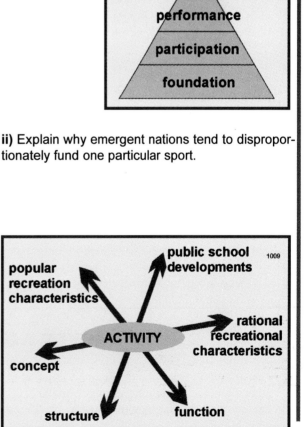

EITHER

4) b) Sport has changed in its organisation and values since the industrial revolution.

i) Using an activity of your choice, explain how it has changed over the last 150 years.

QUESTION 4 (continued)

4) b) ii) Analyse the social factors which might have influenced these changes.

	FACTORS	
industrialisation		**urbanisation**
media	**communications**	**travel**
class	**social**	**gender**
religious	**associations**	**secular**

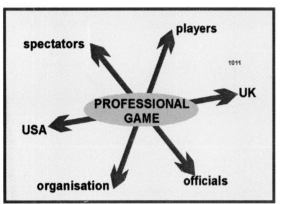

OR

c) Studying another country helps us to better understand our own.

i) Describe the similarities and differences between a professional team game played in the USA and the UK.

ii) Discuss the cultural factors which might have influenced these variables.

	FACTORS	
ideological	**geographical**	**historical**
political	**economic**	**social**

ANSWERS

The answer for each mark awarded is notated by the ❒ symbol - where there are more ❒ symbols than there are marks available, marks would be given for any choice up to the maximum available. Usually, the precise wording specified in an answer would not be required - answers with the same meaning would be acceptable.

A. ESSAY, GENERAL ANSWER

1)
To achieve sporting excellence it is necessary to have scientific support and social opportunity. Discuss this in the context of a specific physical activity.

Definitive statement on excellence in sport.
❒ Can be elitist or optimum personal achievement.
❒ Influenced by opportunity, provision and self-esteem for the performer.
❒ Influenced by the quality of administration, funding and coaching.
❒ Illustration applying a specific physical activity.

Scientific support.
   Anatomical and Physiological context.
❒ Suitability of physique for specific activities.
❒ Hereditary factors (fibre type composition).
❒ Ability to apply training principles to the chosen activity.
❒ Knowledge associated with warm-up and the recovery process.
❒ Ability to evaluate and monitor performance.
❒ Awareness of legitimate and illegal methods of performance enhancement.

   Acquisition of Skill context.
❒ Suitable age for the development of fundamental motor skills related to the specific activity.
❒ Alternative ways of learning these skills depending on the activity.
❒ Understanding how the information process operates.
❒ Ability to interpret reinforcement, transfer variables and motivation.
❒ Aware of alternative teaching styles in your particular activity.

ANSWERS - QUESTION 1 (continued)

Biomechanical content as an optional context.
- ❏ Significance of length of levers in joint structure in your sport.
- ❏ Types of motion you set out to achieve in your activity.
- ❏ Understanding the need for conservation of momentum.
- ❏ Ability to explain the forces acting on you when performing a skill in your activity.
- ❏ Understanding the most effective arrangement of forces.

Sports Psychology content as an optional context.
- ❏ The importance of coaches and effective practice conditions.
- ❏ Adequate mental preparation and application of commitment.
- ❏ Awareness of the significance of personality and positive attitudes.
- ❏ Goal setting and other methods of stimulating performance.
- ❏ Influence of social facilitation on you and the development of self-efficacy.

Social Opportunity.
Contemporary Sports Scene in the UK.
- ❏ Advantage of being an advanced, wealthy society in a densely populated country.
- ❏ Understanding the policies and administrative structures which enable opportunity and provision in your sport.
- ❏ Aware of the relative status of sport in the UK reflected in media coverage and funding.
- ❏ Appreciating the continued existence of disadvantaged minority groups.
- ❏ Place of sport in schools as a foundation for excellence in your chosen sport.

Historical dimension as an optional context.
- ❏ Impact of social class and gender discrimination in sport in the past.
- ❏ Sporting excellence in the context of popular recreations.
- ❏ Aware of the impact of 19th century public schools on excellence in sport.
- ❏ Understanding the cultural changes which brought about rational sport in the context of your particular sport.
- ❏ Aware of the changing face and scope of amateurism and professionalism over the last 150 years.

Comparative / global dimensions as an optional context.
- ❏ Demographic variables affecting the development of excellence in another country in your chosen sport.
- ❏ Ideological variables in another country which may have caused similarities and differences to exist.
- ❏ Understanding the extent to which discrimination exists in another country compared to the UK.
- ❏ Administrative variables in another country which has influenced the achievement of excellence in your sport.
- ❏ What reformative strategies might we usefully adopt with more global knowledge and understanding?

N.B. The expectation is that the marks will be drawn equally from the compulsory modules in the respective specifications, with the inclusion of at least one optional context where available.

B. SUBJECT THEMATIC : SEMI-STRUCTURED

2)
Specific Olympic Games have always fairly accurately reflected the concept of amateurism at that time.
2) i)
Trace the interpretation of amateurism by looking at a number of different Olympic Games.
- ❏ 1896, as the first modern Olympic meeting, marked the ending of the gentleman amateur as an exclusive, mobile, male-dominated society, involving only those wealthy enough to travel to Athens.
- ❏ 1924 Olympics, subject of Chariots of Fire, displayed the pure notion of amateurism among the Europeans who participated for its own sake with no financial gain and reflecting the dominance of the upper and middle classes on amateurism at the time. The American athletes on the other hand were already committed to training schedules which were barely accepted by the Europeans.
- ❏ 1936 Olympics reflected the extreme nationalism of Germany, but also the acceptance of the win ethic coming into the games together with national rather than individual identity.
- ❏ 1948 London Games were identified as the Victory Games and reflected the end of extreme nationalism and the emergence of a new world of common fellowship for both men and women of all social and racial groups. It reflected a time when most sports acknowledged that to allow all worthy competitors to participate there must be funding available to cover expenses.
- ❏ 1960 (and 64 / 68) Olympic Games showed the marked impact of state sponsored amateurism from the USSR and Eastern Europe. Full time training, enhanced lifestyle, the preffessional training of coaches.
- ❏ 2000 Sydney Olympics marked the professionalisation of all activities by the richer nations, reflected in full-time performers, professional coaches and outstanding facilities. Emergent nations, on the other hand focused on specific sports where they could compete on equal terms, recognising that Olympic sport was not only big business but a nation building exercise.

ANSWERS - QUESTION 2 (continued)

2) ii)
How has the scope of the Olympics expanded amateurism globally?
❒ 1896 brought a small band of individual gentlemen together to celebrate their privileged lifestyle. An extension of the Grand Tour it brought occasional Americans and members of the Dominions into European high culture. It was very much the product of colonialism and particularly the export of sport through British colonial schools.
❒ 1924 marked the arrival of the New World on the sports scene, where the notion of the gentleman was replaced by the athlete.
❒ 1936 marked a massive increase in the number of nations taking part and with it the conflict between the white European and the black American as identified in Jessie Owens. Though demonstrating an increased scope in terms of activities, involvement by females and additional countries, it also reflected the differences between nations, as sport became a vehicle for the promotion of nationalism.
❒ 1948, probably the last truly amateur games was a celebration by the whole world with even the smaller nations struggling to send representatives and where effort was valued more than achievement.
❒ 1960 brought in communist countries which had hitherto boycotted the Olympics. This countered the American process of athletic scholarships at university.
❒ 2000 reflect a global entry, but with major focus on excellence, standards of performance was placed first, if only to keep the number of competitors to a manageable size. More countries than ever before participated in more activities and the number of European countries achieving medals reflected a determination by Europe not to be dominated by dynamic countries like the USA and Australia.

2) iii)
Explain the changing role of the modern coach given the present interpretation of amateurism.
❒ in 1896 coaches were either honorary, ex-gentlemen amateurs or very low status professional coaches drawn from the professional ranks. Majority of gentlemen performers did not accept the principle of training or coaching.
❒ 1924 training acceptable by middle classes, but majority of coaches continued to be unpaid gentlemen enthusiasts. Chariots of Fire suggests that the Americans were employing professional coaches and Harold Abrahams broke the British tradition with the professional coach Sabartini, but the latter was not allowed into the Games.
❒ 1936 and the win ethic had become central for some countries. Those with strong nationalist / political intentions like Nazi Germany and Italy, but also the Americans with the emergence of high status professionalised games in the States, and the win ethic justified professional coaching. The initial notion of competing as an individual was retained France and the UK and the Commonwealth countries, but even here individuals did have help from a small number of professional coaches.
❒ 1948, arguably the last 'amateur' Games, was supported by professional coaches, but the number of them and their qualifications tended to be limited to their experience as competitors.
❒ 1960, coaches were not only professional but politically active and supporting the use of performance enhancing drugs.
❒ From 1956 and the entry of communist East European teams, changed the picture of coaching to a well paid highly qualified set of professional coaches who dominated the development of career athletes. The 'free world', with the exception of the USA, delayed this process and failed to keep pace. First France, then Italy, Spain and Australia took the step to fully professionalise their coaching system, with the UK finally recognising the importance of a highly qualified scientific approach to coaching, supported by high funding and advanced selection procedures.

N.B. The four sections chosen would normally be given equal mark value with answers written using a good prose format.
The allocation of content marks as against banded criteria would be at the discretion of individual Boards.

C. SCIENTIFIC THEME: STRUCTURED FORMAT

3) a) i)
Control of blood supply: Briefly identify the pulmonary and systemic circulatory networks and the factors linked with venous return.

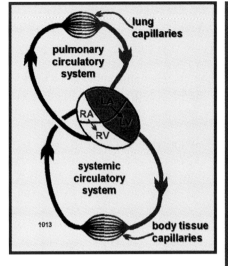

- ❐ The pulmonary circulatory network takes deoxygenated blood from the right ventricle of the heart via the pulmonary arteries.
- ❐ To the capillary network in the lungs (surrounding the alveoli).
- ❐ Where blood receives oxygen from inspired air.
- ❐ During a process called gaseous exchange.
- ❐ And then this oxygenated blood returns to the left atrium of the heart via the pulmonary veins.

- ❐ The systemic circulatory network carries oxygenated blood from the left ventricle of the heart via the aorta and the major arteries and arterioles.
- ❐ To the capillary networks in the muscular (and all other parts of the body) system.
- ❐ Blood flows freely (vasodilation) and in large quantities to muscle tissue where the demand for oxygen and energy is high during exercise.
- ❐ Blood flow to less active tissue (organs - liver and gut) is reduced (vasoconstriction).
- ❐ This is the vascular shunt.
- ❐ At muscle tissue sites, the blood gives up its oxygen to working tissue.
- ❐ The deoxygenated blood returns to the right atrium of the heart, via venules veins and vena cavae.
- ❐ The venous return mechanism involves the respiratory and muscle pumps.
- ❐ The respiratory pump mechanism assists venous return via changes in intrathoracic pressures.
- ❐ A decrease in thoracic pressure and an increase in abdominal pressure during exercise squeezes the veins (and vena cavae) which lie within the thoracic cavity, and forces blood past the venous pocket valves and hence towards the heart.
- ❐ The muscle pump involves the action of skeletal muscle (during exercise) pressing on the veins and forcing the blood up against gravity if necessary) past the pocket valves within the veins back towards the heart.
- ❐ As does venomotor control (limited venoconstriction of veins) which reduces the capacity of veins to store blood. This means that more blood is moved back towards the heart.
- ❐ Therefore warm-up in which muscles are worked prior to activity acts to increase venous return, cardiac output and stroke volume and hence make greater amounts of blood available to working muscle.
- ❐ Similarly, during cool-down muscle action keeps the blood flow going (venous return) hence maintaining cardiac output thus enabling more oxygenated blood to flow to oxygen-starved working muscle.
- ❐ To complete the metabolic process after hard exercise has stopped, and remove metabolites such as lactic acid which would otherwise cause muscle soreness.

3) a) ii)
How might you justify fitness in your own performance activity with the importance of health-related fitness for life?
- ❐ The long-term effect of fitness training on the muscular system is to increase strength and muscle endurance.
- ❐ Muscle flexibility and neural recruitment of muscle fibres improves thereby improving coordination.
- ❐ And response time also improves.
- ❐ The effect on the skeleton is to keep its strength and integrity.
- ❐ This reduces the long-term risk of osteoporosis and osteoarthritis.
- ❐ The effect on the cardiovascular system is to increase the blood pumping capacity of the heart by bradycardia.
- ❐ And to keep the blood transport system efficient (pliable and reactive arterial muscle walls).
- ❐ And to keep the venous return mechanism functioning properly.
- ❐ And to keep the availability of oxygenated blood (via functioning capillaries) to muscle and vital organs.
- ❐ This reduces the risk of CHD and thrombosis / stroke, hypertension and atherosclerosis.
- ❐ The effect on the respiratory system is to increase the efficiency of the breathing system.
- ❐ And avoid respiratory diseases (asthma, bronchitis, pneumonia).
- ❐ This lessens the decline (with age) of $\dot{V}O_{2max}$ and lung volumes / capacities.
- ❐ And hence the availability of oxygen.
- ❐ This improves the availability of energy for living.
- ❐ Fitness training will also reduce obesity by burning off excess fat during and after exercise.
- ❐ Combine with a balanced diet - which will contribute to the avoidance of obesity and related conditions.
- ❐ This enables you to cope better with the physical demands of life.

Answers

C. SCIENTIFIC THEME: STRUCTURED FORMAT - ANSWERS QUESTION 3 (continued)

3) a) iii)

Explain the importance of skill acquisition in the context of a physical activity of your choice with reference to competency, fluency, consistency and the successful application of technique.

- ❏ This most effective way of learning a skill and making it consistent depends on the type of skill.
- ❏ Closed or open, gross or fine, self or externally-paced, discrete, serial or continuous (possibly other types).
- ❏ You must analyse your chosen activity in terms of these variables.
- ❏ This affects the method of guidance.
- ❏ Whether to use verbal, visual or manual guidance in the first instance.
- ❏ Also affects the method of practice.
- ❏ The 'whole' method - suitable for highly organised skills which are difficult to split up into subroutines?
- ❏ Or is the method the 'part' method - suitable when the skill can be split up into subroutines?
- ❏ There are various other methods 'whole-part-whole' for example.
- ❏ Practice at the skill with due guidance to assure competency and fluency of technique.
- ❏ Plenty of correct practice will assure consistency.
- ❏ You would need to be motivated to continue the learning process (particularly if difficulties occur).

3) b)

Explain the factors that may either enhance or hinder the effective performance of a group or team training in a physical activity of your choice.

   Group or team members' factors :
- ❏ Cohesion - do the members of the team work well together?
- ❏ Member characteristics - are the team members able to compete at the level required?
- ❏ Faults and losses - do the team fail because of lack of tactics or ability?
- ❏ Social loafing (the Ringlemann effect) - do team members not pull their weight at all times?
- ❏ Motivational losses - do all members of the team have the same motivation to win? Some may just play for enjoyment or to keep fit, and this may affect team performance.

   Leader / coach factors :
- ❏ Is the leader an emergent leader - elected by the team members - this may be suitable for individual sports?
- ❏ Or is the leader a prescribed leader - appointed by management - more suitable for team sports?
- ❏ Has the leader got qualtities of communication, enthusiasm, ability, charisma?
- ❏ Does the leader respect the team members, and effectively influence their behaviour?
- ❏ Has the leader got the respect of the team members (due to his qualities)?
- ❏ What leadership style is used?
- ❏ Authoritarian - task-oriented and best for large groups.
- ❏ Democratic - people-oriented and best for individiuals or those who are highly skilled.
- ❏ Laissez faire - no real leader, but best for highly motivated and skilled performers.

3) c)

Explain the ways in which forces are applied to yourself or your surroundings in a sports skill of your choice using pin and force diagrams where relevant.

- ❏ This depends on the activity, and whether the motion of the performer is static or motion at constant speed, or accelerating or decelerating.
- ❏ Newton's laws of motion apply.
- ❏ Newton's First law applies to static situations of balance.
- ❏ Or to movement at constant speed.
- ❏ Then all forces acting on the performer must cancel out exactly.
- ❏ Newton's Second law applies to situations of acceleration or deceleration.
- ❏ Then the formula $F = m \times a$ can be applied to link the mass of the performer to the force and the acceleration.
- ❏ This would apply to the case where a jumper is taking off, and a **net** upward force will cause a **net** upward acceleration, and cause take-off.
- ❏ Newton's Third law applies when one body applied a force to another.
- ❏ Reaction forces are produced on a performer when he / she pushes on the surroundings in some way.
- ❏ See figure 1014 reproduced here.
- ❏ The nature of the force will affect its direction and size.
- ❏ Weight, air resistance, friction, and reaction forces will be the main forces acting on the body.
- ❏ See figure 1015 reproduced here for an example of a pin man diagram showing forces acting on a runner. The black arrow represents the **net / resultant** force acting on the runner.

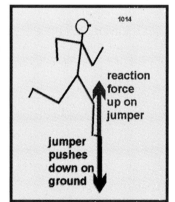

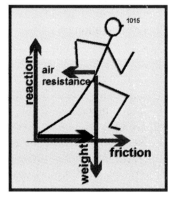

ANSWERS - QUESTION 3 (continued)

N.B. The four sections chosen by the candidate would normally be given equal mark value with answers written in good prose format.

The allocation of content marks as against banded criteria would be at the discretion of individual Boards.

D. SOCIO-CULTURAL THEME LINKING CONTEMPORARY STUDIES WITH EITHER HISTORICAL OR COMPARATIVE STUDIES, IN A STRUCTURED FORM.

4) a)
The structure and function of sport is largely determined by its social setting.
4) a) i)
Describe the qualities of the performance pyramid shown in Figure 1008. Illustrate your answer using your own preferred sport.
❏ Performance pyramid: represents a selective progression from mass participation to excellence (answer must show an example from your chosen sport).
❏ Foundation necessary with particular effort to engage young people / increase the number of target group performers.
❏ Participation implies regular serious involvement, with coaching support.
❏ Performance demands selection and commitment to considerable time and effort and reflects ability and desire.
❏ Excellence at personal and interpersonal level demands total commitment in your most talented activity taking you to an optimal level of achievement.
❏ Examples from your chosen sport should be given as part of each of these answers.

4) a) ii)
Explain why emergent nations tend to disproportionately fund one particular sport.
❏ Limited financial and technical resources make disproportionate focus necessary.
❏ Achieving a high level in any one major sport gives the country world recognition.
❏ Sporting achievement gives citizens of that country pride, hope and role models.
❏ Success in sport is seen as a nation building exercise.
❏ In emergent multi-racial societies, sport can integrate tribal and racial groups.

4) b)
Sport has changed in its organisation and values since the industrial revolution.
4) b) i)
Using an activity of your choice, explain how it has changed over the last 150 years.
   Guidelines for an answer :
❏ Describe the origins of a particular sport, preferably one with a well documented history.
❏ Explain popular recreational characteristics which apply to your chosen activity in a pre-industrial society.
❏ Explain the contribution made by public school athleticism, identifying the main changes which apply to changes in your activity.
❏ Pinpoint the organisational changes which occurred as rational recreation spread in our industrialised society.
❏ Explain the changes in scope of your sport in the 20th century with its increasing globalisation and professionalisation.

4) b) ii)
Analyse the social factors which might have influenced these changes?
❏ Industrialisation: changes in work time and conditions with the beginning of the factory system. 72 hour week reducing to 57 hours with Saturday half day. Patronage from factory owners with sports facilities.
❏ Urbanisation: changes from rural scene. Initial problem with facilities, improved as councils developed swimming baths and parks. Pollution of rivers and distance from the countryside. Formation of town clubs and team games with larger population.
❏ Communications: particularly travelling with the railways increasing speed and distance, but still with a cost constraint. Roads improved with political pressure coming firstly from the bicycle and later the motor car.
❏ Communication: in terms of media the impact of improved literacy and the printing press followed by the telephone and radio added to the popularity, knowledge, and speedier reporting.
❏ Religion: had positive and negative influences. The negative impact of Puritanism and the Protestant Work Ethic on popular recreation, followed by the rise of muscular Christianity and the positive impact of groups like the YMCA in the development of religious sports clubs.

Information

ANSWERS - QUESTION 4) b) ii) (continued)

- ❐ Secular: the spread of private sports clubs facilitated a major expansion of many sports and associations like the friendly societies sponsored sports festivals.
- ❐ Educational Institutions: though possibly mentioned in the previous section, schools, particularly private and public schools in the 19th century, had a major impact on the rationalisation of sport and led to it becoming part of working class life, at a professional level in cricket and football and as part of the amateur scene in most other sports.
- ❐ Gender: the introduction of sport for women durin the Victorian / Edwarding period (lawn tennis / cycling).
- ❐ Female role models (Olga Korbut, Cathy Freeman) encouraging female mass participation in sport.
- ❐ Billy Jean King campaigned for equal commercial rights for women professional tennis players.
- ❐ Equal opportunity legislation in sport (USA 'Title XII' legislation).

4) c)
Studying another country helps us to better understand our own.
4) c) i)
Describe the similarities and differences between a professional team game played in the USA and the UK.
- ❐ Team Games: in most cases the US versions tend to be high scoring, influenced by the media and strictly controlled in terms of time. Conversely, UK games like soccer are low scoring, still have only limited interference from the media and in the case of cricket go on for a longer time.
- ❐ Players: until recently US professionals received much more money, but in the case of soccer, the UK is catching up. In both countries the professional ranks represent opportunities for members of discriminated social groups. In both cases major professional team games are dominated by male players. There is a well organised draft system in the US which differs from the transfer system in the UK.
- ❐ Coaches and referees: the hire and fire tradition for US games coaches and managers and coaches in British soccer and cricket is similar, but until recently, American officials have received much more money than their British counterparts.
- ❐ Administration: the principle of franchising American professional clubs is not done in the UK where clubs have a traditional local identity. Many US clubs are privately owned, whereas British soccer clubs in particular tend to be limited liability companies. The facilities associated with American clubs are normally well ahead of UK counterparts many of which go back to the 19th century. This is particularly the case of parking facilities.
- ❐ Spectators: differ greatly in the behaviour expectation, where the hooligan element does not appear to exist in the USA, with the possible exception of baseball. This may be because in Britain there is a young, working class male dominance as against a family tradition in the States. The size of the USA means that there is very little tradition of spectators travelling to away grounds as in the UK and this might account for the absence of hooliganism. Provision for spectators and alternative entertainment is considerably better in the US grounds than in the UK

4) c) ii)
Discuss the cultural factors which might have influenced these variables.
- ❐ Ideological: the dominance of the 'win-at-all-costs' (Lombardian) ethic is much stronger than in the UK.
- ❐ Geographical: the size of the USA prevents spectator travel; size of population increases the overall player and spectator group which influences funding; climate variations in the US has led to seasonal factors and the growth of professional ice hockey.
- ❐ Historical: team games came from Europe to the US in a primitive form and has since changed to match the emergent new world culture, whereas professional games in the UK have largely retained their traditions.
- ❐ Political: the autonomy of each American State has led to rivalries which have tended to be on a urban community basis in the UK and even country cricket has a loyalty which is not politically based.
- ❐ Economical: the capitalist focus on commercialism has been more influential in the States as has the impact of the media, but the UK is becoming part of the same market-run industry.
- ❐ Social: the pluralist approach to a massive emigrant population has led the US professional scene to be a potential expression of emergent racial groups, whereas the stability of the social class system has made class the battlefield in the UK. In recent years representation by Afro-Caribbean players in the UK has brought soccer in the UK into this social mobility arena.

N.B. The four sections chosen by the candidate would normally be given equal mark value with answers written in good prose format.

The allocation of content marks as against banded criteria would be at the discretion of individual Boards.

Bob Davis

Index